PERSONAL
ADJUSTMENT IN THE
AMERICAN CULTURE

Under the Editorship of
GARDNER MURPHY

Personal
Adjustment in the
American Culture

Franklin J. Shaw
PURDUE UNIVERSITY

Robert S. Ort
FORMERLY WABASH COLLEGE

*Ft. Wayne
Center*

Harper & Brothers   Publishers   New York

PERSONAL ADJUSTMENT IN THE
AMERICAN CULTURE

Copyright, 1953, by Harper & Brothers

Printed in the United States of America

K-C

Library of Congress catalog card number: 53-11324

Contents

Contents

Preface

An attempt is made in the present volume to organize psychological subject matter around the concept of interaction in environments that can be characterized largely as social, cultural, or interpersonal. The general theme can be discerned from the chapter headings of the book, which rely heavily upon the adjective *interactive* and its corresponding noun.

It has been the authors' feeling that personal adjustment has all too often been considered more or less apart from the cultural settings in which the individual participates and develops. Although no one has denied, of course, that interaction does occur in social contexts, psychologists have been somewhat prone to see the individual as an entity unto himself. A great deal may be gained in comprehension of personal adjustment through seeing him against the background of his culture and subculture. The authors are indebted in no small measure to the influence of their colleagues in sociology and cultural anthropology for whatever success they have achieved in comprehending the individual against the background of his culture. This influence is apparent in the title selected for the book.

Strong as our indebtedness is to sociology and cultural anthropology, the authors have been guided consistently in their thinking by the concepts of learning environment and learning experience. Our indebtedness on this latter score, of course, lies within our own field. Personal adjustment has been thought of by the authors as a function of the individual's learning history, and readjustment has been conceptualized in terms of altered conditions of learning. Learning is pervasive, as the late Professor McGeoch was fond of observing. The authors have been concerned with demonstrating its pervasiveness in relation to personality development and functioning.

In addition to the theme of interaction in social learning environments, the authors have also been preoccupied with the theme of adaptability or integration. The whole problem of "adequate adjustment" does not lend itself to glibness. The authors are not content with a "fitting in" or conformity criterion, but it is also their feeling that ability to act in accordance with cultural standards cannot be entirely ignored as an aspect of realistic interaction. The attempt to resolve this problem can be summarized by the statement that behavior can be "normal" and at the same time be adaptive or integrative, but that "normality" or conformity to cultural patterns is not necessarily evidence of adaptability or integration. Adaptability and integration are defined in terms of the individual's effectiveness in maintaining himself in his environment, and behavior disorders are thought of as departures from interactive integration. A given adjustment may or may not contribute to such effectiveness. The authors' further reasoning is that adjustive patterns prescribed by one's culture may be, and often are, in accord with interactive integration, but neither blind reliance upon nor blind rejection of such patterns is likely to prove highly effective in maintaining oneself in his environment.

A final thought which seems worthy of inclusion in this preface has to do with the authors' concern with the role of principles or generalizations as statements of knowledge. Although it is elementary to observe that principles are the stuff of which science is made, there is some doubt as to whether students always realize this and learn to organize their thinking around principles. The book accordingly opens with a discussion of the organizing function of generalizations and the whole problem of explanation and theory and the allied problem of creative thinking are explored more fully in the last chapter.

The authors collaborated in the planning and "thinking through" of the book while the senior author carried out the writing. Unless otherwise specified, case materials are drawn from the authors' experience; identity of individuals has been carefully obscured, of course. We are indebted to Purdue University and Wabash College for stimulation provided by students and col-

leagues as well as for provision of clerical help in the preparation
of the book. Mrs. Gertrude Clary rendered able assistance in
preparing revised copy.

Our deepest gratitude, of course, goes to our wives and children who stood by with great patience, encouragement, and reassurance as we struggled with completion of a manuscript that
at times seemed to defy completion. It is to our wives and children
that we would like to dedicate whatever parts of our efforts have
resulted in some increment of enlightenment about human behavior, since they represent our best efforts and best signify our
affection.

F. J. S.
R. S. O.

September, 1953

PERSONAL ADJUSTMENT IN THE AMERICAN CULTURE

Overview

The purpose of this book is to present concepts and principles that will help the reader to understand the process of personal adjustment. We shall be particularly interested in the efforts of the individual living in the United States to cope with his environment and his own feelings. Hence, the title, *Personal Adjustment in the American Culture*. Whether a person lives in the United States or elsewhere his ways of thinking and acting will be strongly influenced by, and will at the same time influence, the ways of thinking and acting that prevail in the society in which he lives and in his relationships with others. In the first chapter attention is directed, accordingly, to man's social relationships. In subsequent chapters various aspects of the individual's interaction with his social environment in his attempts to adjust or to preserve his feeling of well-being in the American culture will be discussed. The individual will be viewed as a flexible organism whose modes of adjustment are learned and "unlearned" and whose development goes on throughout life—whether in a direction considered desirable or undesirable—as he interacts with his environment. The adjustive process may aid or hinder the individual's adaptability, which is the ability to maintain oneself or to "get along" effectively in the environment, and a recurrent theme will revolve around the concept of adaptability.

Each chapter will conclude with a summary of principles or generalizations. The reason for this kind of summary is to stimulate the reader to think in terms of explaining human behavior. "Generalization," as Reichenbach (*1951*) puts it, ". . . is the very nature of explanation." His further explanation is worth noting:

What we mean by explaining an observed fact is incorporating that fact into a general law. We observe that as the day progresses a wind begins to blow from the sea to the land; we explain this fact by incorporating it into the general law that heated bodies expand and thus become lighter with respect to equal volumes. We then see how this law applies in the example considered: the sun heats the land more strongly than the water so that the air over the land becomes warm and rises, thus leaving its place to an air current from the sea. We observe that living organisms need food in order to exist; we explain this fact by incorporating it into the general law of the conservation of energy. The energy which the organisms spend in their activities must be replaced from the calories of the food. We observe that bodies fall down when not supported; we explain this fact by incorporating it into the general law that masses attract each other. The great mass of the earth pulls the small masses toward its surface.

If the reader learns to incorporate facts about human behavior into generalizations or principles, facts take on meaning rather than existing simply as facts just as the wind blowing from the sea to the land as the day progresses takes on meaning when understood in the light of the principle that heated bodies expand and thus become lighter with respect to equal volumes. The summaries of principles at the conclusion of each chapter will give the reader experience with generalizations about human behavior. The whole problem of developing such generalizations will be treated in detail in the last chapter.

CHAPTER 1

Social Interaction

Introductory Summary

⌊The process of personal adjustment cannot be understood in the United States or in any other culture apart from the social setting in which it occurs⌋ Attention is directed, accordingly, in the first chapter to man's social environment and social relationships.

⌊The individual and his surroundings are in constant process of influencing each other.⌋The surroundings are a stage on which the individual plays his life role and the acting out of this role affects the stage itself. The life role is played directly or indirectly in relationships with other people. These relationships are of many kinds, and include person-to-person relationships, such as that between a man and his wife or a parent and his child, and person-to-group relationships, such as that between a teacher and his class or a minister and his congregation. These relationships also include the individual's interaction with his culture, the general modes of life that are characteristic of his society. These modes of living envelop the individual and tie him to his total social environment. The individual in turn exerts his influence on the social environment. Through analyzing the various social relationships covered by the general categories of person-to-person interactions, person-to-group interactions, and person-to-culture interactions, a better understanding of man's behavior can be achieved.

MAN'S ENVIRONMENT

↯ *Man's behavior is a process of interaction with his environment.* The individual in his environment not only reacts to other individ-

3

uals, situations, and objects but he also influences his surroundings. A man may react to a stone by kicking it but at the same time acts upon the stone by moving it if he has had the good judgment to select a stone that will move when he kicks it. One may not only retort with an angry reply but at the same time arouse anger in the person he is reacting to. Even the man who sits in the corner staring into space is reacting to his surroundings with retreat, indifference, or withdrawal and also influencing his surroundings by ignoring them rather than acting more positively toward them. *Interaction, then, is a twofold process of reaction to and influence upon the environment.* However, the environment is not only reacted to and influenced but also provides a setting or context for interaction.

This setting must be known in order to understand man's behavior. The physical environment must be known because it forces certain kinds of behavior upon people. If food is scarce or hard to get, for example, considerable activity, time, and energy will have to be devoted to ways and means of laying hands on this basic necessity of life. Numerous additional examples of the activities, outlooks, and adaptations that the physical environment requires or fosters come to mind. A hot climate will force a more leisurely tempo than a cold climate. People living in geographically isolated communities will ordinarily be more suspicious of strangers than people living in regions more easily reached by outsiders. People are more likely to earn their living by raising corn in Iowa than by mining silver. The leisureliness of a hot climate, the suspicion of outsiders growing out of geographical isolation, or the interest in agriculture resulting from growing up on an Iowa farm may very well become prominent characteristics of personality that persist even after a person moves to a different kind of physical environment later in life.

As important as the physical environment is to man's behavior, it must be recognized that the meaning it has for him depends largely upon the way he learns to evaluate it in his relationships with other people. Grandpa's chair, a physical object, for example, is not just a chair but arouses some of the same feelings that Grandpa arouses. Pictures, bracelets, watches, handkerchiefs,

and lockets of hair have a romantic significance that is not inspired by their physical attributes. A mother may teach her child
a fear of darkness, a physical aspect of the environment, by
threatening him with the "bogyman" or simply by displaying her
own fears of darkness to the child. In one instance a woman
taught her daughter-in-law to have an intense distaste for the
very streets and buildings of a certain town by the domineering
attitude she held toward the younger woman when they lived
under the same roof in this town. Shaffer (1936) cites the case of
a girl who had a fear of the open spaces of her physical environment that sprang from an underlying fear of death; the latter
was associated with heaven which the girl thought of as a big
open place. The association between death, heaven, and open
spaces obviously had to be learned through the direct or indirect
influence of other people. Reactions to practically any physical
setting one can think of are determined by such influence.

The direct or indirect influence of other people makes up the
social environment of the individual. Each individual is a member
of the social environment of other individuals and, as such, he
plays the role of one who influences others as well as of one who
is influenced by others. Influence can take many forms. Influence
is present when people confront each other face to face as in
ordinary conversation. The conversation might affect one so
thoroughly as to change his whole philosophy of life or only to
the extent of not listening very closely to what the other person
is saying. One might also be affected in a face-to-face contact by
the mode of dress or facial characteristics of another person. Over
and beyond such obvious sources of influence in face-to-face
contacts, there are forms of stimulation from others of which we
are not as clearly aware that, nevertheless, produce effects upon
us. A person may be outwardly relaxed, for example, but in-
wardly tense and we sense that he is not entirely comfortable
with us or we with him but cannot understand why this is the
case. Similarly, a slight twist of a person's gestures or posture
may please or antagonize without our knowing what it was that
produced our reaction. Indirect influences exist in the form of
objects and situations that in some way represent other people.

An artist can be absent but, nevertheless, influence people through his paintings which represent him. Petty's drawings of beautiful girls, for example, are said to have changed or contributed to a changed conception of feminine beauty. The Gibson girl of a previous era had broad hips whereas Petty's girls were more slender. An author indirectly influences others by his books and an architect by buildings which he has designed. Tom Paine's pamphlets united the people in a common cause during the American Revolution and Frank Lloyd Wright's designs have established trends in American construction. The impact of their ideas was and is transmitted to others indirectly. Influence, then, can be direct or indirect, written or printed, spoken or unspoken. It can be found in many contexts, and social relationships can take many forms.

SOCIAL RELATIONSHIPS

The social relationship is one in which the individual is in contact with the direct or indirect influence of another individual, of a group of individuals, or of a culture. Important phases of social relationships can be discussed in terms of these person-to-person, person-to-group, and person-to-culture interactions.

Person-to-Person Interactions

A husband and his wife, an employer and an employee, a teacher and a pupil, a playmate and his friend all interact in person-to-person relationships. Each of these relationships is worthy of considerable attention in and of itself in the study of the individual's social behavior. His modes of response to and effect upon others are determined to a very large degree by the nature of the relationships he has had with his parents, or those who have taken the role of parents, and siblings (brothers and sisters in the same family), in childhood. In an excellent example of this, Fisher and Hanna (1931) tell about a barber who had been intimidated throughout childhood by his father and an older brother and became so agitated when anyone with an authoritative manner requested his services that he was unable to wield his clippers. Since parent-child and sibling-sibling relationships are so basic to all other interpersonal relationships, we shall confine our discussion of person-to-person relationships to these two significant types of social interaction.

PARENT-CHILD RELATIONSHIPS

1. *Indulgent Overprotection.* The overprotective situation is one in which the parents act as a screen or filter between the child and his environment.[1] One form of such screening is indulgence. Indulgent overprotection provides an influence in the social environment, in this case the parent, that enables the child to avoid penalties for socially disapproved behavior and to expect fulfillment of his desires without interference. Individuals with this type of background have little or no concern for the consequences of their behavior presumably because they have been allowed "to get away with anything" in childhood. This disregard for consequences carries over into situations outside the home and also persists into later life. For example, they may go into debt with a minimum of concern about paying back what they have borrowed. This lack of concern about the consequences of their behavior leads to uninhibited behavior that others react to as "rushing in where angels fear to tread." Driving recklessly, attempting to become familiar with others without an invitation to do so, telling obscene stories without regard for how they will be received are examples of the kind of uninhibited behavior under discussion. In spite of the insensitivity to feelings of others that is indicated by this lack of inhibition, these individuals are frequently very engaging and possessed of a considerable amount of personal charm until they are blocked whereupon they react with surliness or lack of comprehension of why anyone should be disturbed about their actions. Their personal charm as well as the baffled reaction to being blocked would both seem to stem from the absence of expectation of disapproval. Luella Cole (1936) furnishes the following interesting example of the kind of behavior we have been discussing:

Dr. Franklin is a woman professor nearly forty years old. During her undergraduate days she seemed in general a normal person, al-

[1] The concept of overprotection is treated at length by Levy (1943) in *Maternal over-protection.*

though she showed even then a tendency (a) to become irresponsible if the work were uninteresting or too difficult and (b) to impose on her friends. She had two or three serious arguments with her teachers and on one occasion had to be moved from one section to another because she and the teacher had become so profoundly antagonistic. She participated freely in nonacademic activities but, while efficient, she did not command much confidence from her associates because they sensed her irresponsibility. She was a member of several class athletic teams. On some days she would play well and on other days poorly, but she always resented being taken out of a game even though she knew she was playing badly. She knew she was supposed to retire early the night before any class game but she would often stay up late, either because she became interested in something or from sheer negative suggestibility, and then would play poorly the next day. In spite of several such experiences she never learned to go to bed on time or to submit to any other training rule.

After leaving college she took graduate work and became a professor of history in a small college. This position she held for two years but was then asked to resign. Three reasons were given: First, she was irregular about meeting her classes; if she were interested in doing something else she would simply cut class. Second, her teaching was often careless; her presentation was sure to be badly prepared if she happened not to feel like teaching. Finally, she had developed several intense feuds with members of the faculty and administrative officers. Anyone who criticized her at once became her enemy. She constantly justified her absences from class and her poor teaching by complaining about the "inferior students"; actually, the students were above average in ability and preparation. At other times she would complain of overwork, absence of academic freedom, or lack of sympathetic understanding.

After losing her first job she obtained a position as assistant in a research project being carried on by a national foundation. Here she had the same difficulties. She accused her superiors of prejudice against her, of unnecessary criticism, and of overworking her. She had been so generally unsatisfactory that when she handed in a careless and inaccurate report of certain funds she had had charge of expending, this matter was made an excuse for eliminating her.

For over a year Miss Franklin had no job. Eventually, however, she was offered a chance to take over the contract of a former friend for the duration of the academic year, with the understanding her appointment would be renewed in case she was satisfactory. In spite of knowing she was on probation, Miss Franklin again neglected her classes and antagonized people. This particular position paid a much larger salary than she had ever had, but instead of saving the money, she spent it on excursions to various large cities where she remained for several days and naturally failed to meet her classes. By the end of the year she realized she would not be reappointed, became very indignant, and left without ever turning in the grades for her courses. In spite of urgent requests she flatly refused to turn in any report. Finally, the college sent a personal messenger, who discussed the students' work with her and succeeded in getting from her some verbal statement of each student's standing. But even this information was difficult to obtain because of her constant complaints about the poorness of the material, the inadequacy of the library, and the lack of academic freedom.

There next intervened four or five years during which her only employment was writing book reviews, typing theses, tutoring, doing minor research jobs or library work for other people. During this time she became permanently embittered and turned to communism and other forms of propaganda as outlets for her emotional attitudes. One of her more objectionable traits became emphasized during this period; she "sponged" constantly on every acquaintance for meals, transportation, cigarettes, books, shows, or anything else. There were several people who would willingly have supplied her with such things if she had not tried so obviously to get them for nothing. In spite of her serious characterological defects, she was an intelligent and stimulating conversationalist. For an evening's entertainment one could hardly have a more charming guest. For short periods of time and in a congenial atmosphere none of her outstanding defects appeared at all. But she always defeated her own ends by her grasping attitude.

Through the combined efforts of several friends, Miss Franklin finally obtained a summer school position in a normal school. Here she repeated the identical tactics which had led to her dismissal from three previous positions. At the end of the appointment, she was again out of a job. During the following years she succeeded in supporting herself, rather precariously to be sure, with odd jobs, but with the beginning of the depression she became completely destitute. For the last four years she has been on the relief rolls and is regarded as a totally unemployable individual, in spite of her high level of education and very real intellectual capacity.

Although we are not given information about the possible childhood origins of Dr. Franklin's behavior, a psychologist might readily form the hypothesis that indulgent overprotection played a significant part in determining the behavior she exhibits. Her classmates in college sensed her irresponsibility which also showed up later in her carelessness in teaching and other kinds of employment. Lack of inhibition in her behavior is suggested, among other things, by her simply cutting class when she was a teacher if she felt like doing something other than meeting the class. Her feuds with other teachers and administrators were also quite possibly the result of uninhibited behavior, the consequences of which she could not anticipate because of lack of experience with penalties for socially disapproved behavior in her earlier experience. Furthermore, the strained relations with associates, it seems likely, were baffling and difficult to comprehend because from her point of view she had not misbehaved or done anything wrong. The very thing she had not learned was any conception of misbehavior on her part that might be considered by others as a misdemeanor or as wrong. The absence of this kind of learning or the conditions making for it is the crux of indulgent overprotection. It might be thought that such learning might occur later as a result of experience with penalties for socially disapproved behavior if it had not occurred earlier. Whether it occurs or not probably depends upon the extent to which the individual has been overindulged and the amount of later experience necessary to offset the earlier experience. A strong hindrance to later learning of a different kind, however, is that when the individual has not learned to expect penalties for his behavior he at the same time learns to consider his environment as unreasonable when he is penalized. He, therefore, does not relate the penalties to anything that he might have been responsible for, and his behavior goes unchanged because it had nothing to do with the penalties so far as he is concerned. A final observation to be made about Dr. Franklin is that "for an evening's entertainment one could hardly have a more charming guest." It was noted above that personal charm could also stem from an absence of expectation of disapproval inasmuch as not expecting disapproval lends itself to being at ease with people.

While Dr. Franklin shows the consequences of what was quite possibly an overindulged childhood, there are everyday instances which are less striking. The clubwoman who wants things done her way or apparently not at all may very well have been her mother's "darling daughter" but probably not to the extent of the individual described above. While attention-getting behavior may have its origin in other conditions, it is not unlikely that the perennial "show-off" whom associates tire of having to pay attention to has also been subjected to overindulgence during the course of his development.

2. *Restrictive Overprotection.* Another form of overprotection is restriction. Restrictive overprotection prevents the child from acting on his own initiative. It differs from indulgent overprotection in that the latter permits the child to act and shelters him from penalties whereas restrictive overprotection does not permit him to act or, at least, seriously inhibits his acting on his own. Restrictive overprotection provides the kind of influence in the child's environment making for dependence and submissiveness. Its chief effect is to block the child's independent development. The father who never gives his children any experience in making decisions for themselves because he always makes the decisions for them and the mother who constantly hovers over Johnny or Mary to make sure that her offspring doesn't get hurt are both engaging in restrictive overprotection. Restrictive overprotection may stem from the satisfactions the parent derives from keeping a child closely attached to himself or herself. An unhappy mother can easily convert her child into an overdevoted companion. A father can bolster his sense of importance by overdirection of his child's affairs. These examples demonstrate ways in which parents influence their children with little awareness of the exact nature of their influence; the father who gives too much direction to his child, for example, is not likely to be aware that his influence on the child is in the nature of restrictive overprotection. Dependence develops, nevertheless, and becomes a part of the

child's personality through his interaction in an environment in which restrictive overprotection looms large. As an adult he all too frequently has to seek instructions from superiors or associates before going ahead on his own or relies excessively on his marriage partner for sympathy, guidance, or support. The presence of restrictive overprotection and its implications for the individual's future social behavior are brought out clearly by the following account:

John was an only child, the son of Mr. and Mrs. C. of Great City. He was born the year his father started his own business. Financially it was a hard struggle for Mr. C., and Mrs. C., who craved money and social position, was impatient with the slow development of the business. As time passed, the business did prosper. Mr. C. was able to have an office in the main business district, and the family moved to one of the best residential districts of the city. In the meantime, Mrs. C. dreamed of Johnny's future and was determined that he would be no "ordinary child." The family's income was now sufficient to aid Mrs. C. considerably in this determination. She saw to it, for example, that his Christmas gift to his first-grade teacher was the most outstanding and expensive in spite of the fact that Johnny had a different idea about what the teacher might like and sensed, although he couldn't put the feeling into words, that the teacher and the other children would be more pleased if he had chosen the gift himself. At yearly birthday parties for her son, Mrs. C. also planned the entertainment which unquestionably had the effect of impressing the children and parents who came to the party, but the planning was Mrs. C.'s, not John's. He was not directly coerced into acquiescing to Mrs. C.'s ideas in such matters, but a suggestion was always made first as to what "would be nice" rather than first consulting John to see what ideas he might have in the matter. The result was that John agreed with his mother without any question arising as to whether there were other ways of thinking or acting on such occasions. When he did think of something for himself, however, the idea was vetoed when it did not correspond to Mrs. C.'s way of thinking. At one time he wanted to do as some of the other boys in the neighborhood were doing, for example, and have a paper route of his own, but his mother persuaded him that such a project was really unnecessary since she could give him money when he needed it. She approved, on the other hand, of his taking music lessons and he did become an accomplished musician because he could gain some sense of achievement in learning to play the piano which he was not able to gain in such activities as having a paper route.

By the time John was in high school he was a well-mannered, well-dressed young man with whom his mother was proud to be seen. His mother continued to "help" him by becoming friendly with the teachers and taking an active part in the high school parents' organization. John was not inclined to be too active socially but his musical ability made it possible for him to be in the school orchestra which played for all of the big school dances. Mrs. C. came to these dances and John felt that he would not be showing her the proper sense of consideration if he did not dance with her when he could be relieved by another orchestra member.

By the time John graduated from high school and decided to attend the state university his father's business had grown to the point of requiring Mr. C. to travel and be away from home a large share of the time. This afforded a pretext for Mrs. C. to take up residence in the town where the university was located. John by this time had grown so dependent upon his mother that he did not protest this plan.

After enrolling in the university, John found that courses in writing and literature appealed to him strongly, and that this interest could be shared with Mary, one of his fellow students. He gradually became more fond of her but at the same time experienced a vague feeling of disloyalty to his mother. This feeling of disloyalty was not relieved in any way by his mother's intimating that Mary was really not the girl for him, since her family had no social position to speak of. His interest in Mary persisted, nevertheless, and when it was evident in his senior year that he hoped to marry her, Mrs. C. skillfully managed to secure a position for John in Great City in his father's business.

Shortly after John and his mother returned to Great City, Mr. C. died leaving the responsibility for the business largely with John. None of his previous experience had prepared him for this kind of responsibility, but it had developed a strong attachment to his mother and he insisted that she come to live with him and Mary. His sense of inadequacy in the business and the conflict of loyalties he felt to his mother and wife resulted in irritability that was accompanied by continual headaches and indigestion. Although he blamed Mary for not being a more sympathetic wife, he also resented his mother's hints that he would be a happier man if he did not have such a wife. The situation finally became sufficiently unbearable to make it impossible for them to live together any longer. Mary left and was granted a divorce. After this happened John turned on his mother and accused her of ruining his life, but she was at a loss to understand why her son should feel this way inasmuch as she felt that she had never had anything but his best interest at heart. Following this outburst John lived alone for a short period, but all of his previous learning predisposed him to feel helpless without his mother and he finally renewed the bond with her that she had welded so strongly throughout his life.

The dependence fostered by restrictive overprotection is clearly demonstrated in this story of the relationship between John and his mother. He was not permitted to select the gift that he thought would be appropriate for his first-grade teacher, to have a paper route, or to plan his own birthday parties. These restrictions were imposed by his mother in her determination to keep John from being an "ordinary child" and illustrate the satisfactions a parent can derive from controlling a child's life. It is also evident that his mother was gratified by his devotion to her as he grew older. Her lack of awareness of the nature of her influence upon her son is shown by the surprise with which she reacted on the occasion when he did voice his resentment. His lack of preparation for marriage, business responsibility, or living alone represents the kind of psychological crippling that emerges from restrictive overprotection. If different conditions had prevailed when John was growing up, the above story would in all probability have had a different ending. If his father had spent more time with him, for example, and encouraged him in such independent activities as having a paper route it is probable that the attachment to his mother would not have been as strong. Mrs. C., being the person she was, might have blocked any such efforts on the part of the father, however, and in so doing set up an interaction between John and his father making for less and less interest in one another, unless Mr. C. had persisted in his efforts.

Restrictive overprotection does not, of course, prepare a person for an assertive role. Since a man is expected to be more or less assertive in our society, the effects of such overprotection are especially damaging to a boy's development. The conflict between dependence and self-assertion may show up in stuttering, for example, since speech can be regarded as a form of self-assertion. Many less striking results of restrictive overprotection such as shyness, excessive caution, and overresponding to praise as well as criticism show up in the personalities of men as well as women. Shyness and caution would, of course, be expected to accompany the lack of a sense of self-reliance that emerges from blocking an individual's independent development. It is not as apparent that overresponding to praise and criticism would be produced by barriers to experience in acting on one's own, but the lack of confidence engendered by these barriers establishes a tendency to look to others for guidance. Reassurance is, accordingly, gained when others offer their approval, and the individual's inability to guide himself also makes him especially sensitive to criticism. This sensitivity is not helpful, needless to say, to interaction in a world in which the individual will not be spared criticism.

3. *Rejection.* Rejection is the kind of influence in the social environment that results in making the individual feel that he is not wanted or accepted. It may take obvious forms such as harsh treatment or intimidation. Parents may also reject their children by giving them everything they want in a material way but finding no time to spend with them. It might be pointed out that there is no hard and fast distinction between overprotection and rejection. A parent who in reality did not want a child may engage in indulgent overprotection to relieve his sense of guilt over not wanting the child; the underlying lack of affection exists, nevertheless, and can be transmitted to the child. The disregard that the adult who has been an overindulged child has for others may very well have its origin not only in his having failed to learn what others are sensitive to as a result of having been able "to get away with anything" but also in his lack of experience with affection and really being wanted by his parents. Lack of affection from others does not predispose one to be affectionate toward others. Restrictive overprotection, which does not permit the child an opportunity to "try his own wings" by making his own decisions or acting independently in other ways, implies a dis-

respect for the child's capacity to grow up psychologically as well as greater interest in keeping the child dependent than in permitting him to develop his own resources. This disrespect and failure to let the child develop on his own, insofar as possible, demonstrates a refusal to accept the child as an individual, and, therefore, might be considered a form of rejection.

Some of the effects of rejection can be discerned from autobiographical reports such as the following:

It seems to me that my father failed as a parent in his inability to understand or to show understanding even though he might not have approved of what I did. There was the time, for example, when I broke my arm playing football. When I got home, his first remark was, "You so and so kids shouldn't be raising hell all of the time out there in that vacant lot anyway. I guess this will teach you." My father was right about the lot, since the owner had told us to keep off, but it seemed to me at the time, and still does, that my father might have tried to do something about my arm first and bawl me out afterwards. I think I would have felt that he at least understood then. On another occasion he told me that if I would cover our driveway with gravel he would see to it that I got the parts for an old motor that I was trying to rebuild. What he didn't understand was that it was more important for him to work on the motor with me or to show some interest in what I was doing then getting me the parts for the motor. That is, it was more important to me. As it was, I had the feeling that he thought my interest in motors was silly or perhaps childish but that he had resolved to put up with it, rather than understand.

When I married, the old man, as usual, disapproved. He thought I was too young, and that my wife was intent upon ruining "my career." As I look back on it, it probably wouldn't have done any harm for us to wait a few years. But dear old father apparently didn't remember that people have been getting married for a long time and that his son wasn't necessarily a freak for wanting to follow the old custom. He has never accepted Betty even though she has done more than anyone else to encourage me to go ahead with my education. I sometimes feel like dropping out of school because I am a good enough student to get by, but not much more. The strange part of the whole thing is that I would probably like more than anything else for my father to accept Betty, although this is the first time I have really admitted it. And that brings to mind other times when I have wanted my father's acceptance probably without knowing it. I had to give a speech one time in high school to a group of teachers. I managed to get through it but I still don't know quite how. I think that if my father had in some way shown that he was "plugging for me," I would have felt a lot more sure of myself. I still get the same feeling of uneasiness today when I talk with a superior that I have and had when I was around the old man. I wonder if it would be there if my father and I had been closer to one another.

Perhaps the effects of rejection can be summarized best by saying that it deprives the child, a comparatively helpless human being, of someone's being behind him which is essential to the growth of a feeling of self-confidence. Standing behind a child with affectionate interest differs from overdirection or over-guidance of his activities. An adult can be ready, for example, to catch an eighteen-month-old child when he climbs up on a chair in case he should fall, but let the child go ahead in his own effort to get on the chair, rather than lift him on to it or prevent his getting on it. Through going ahead on his own the child acquires a sense of being able to contend with his environment. Since he is comparatively helpless, however, he also requires the reassurance that comes from affection and the certainty that help will be forthcoming when difficulties arise that are beyond his under-standing. The toddler gains confidence through moving about precariously without an adult's supporting hand but is glad to have the hand proffered when he comes to a stairway that he cannot climb alone. Similarly, a youngster learns to read through exploring the printed page on his own initiative, but gains assur-ance in his ability to go ahead independently when given occa-sional help with material that is beyond his comprehension. This kind of constructive help is also furnished when a parent gives children a chance to straighten out their own squabbles but now and then offers a suggestion of a fair solution of differences. No rule of thumb can be given as to how every parent can proceed on every occasion to strike the balance between giving too much or too little assistance to a child, but a general intent on the part of the parent to avoid the extremes can develop an underlying conviction in the child that he is accepted as an individual.

Rejection of a child frequently works in vicious circles. For example, a parent may reject a child in the first place by ignoring his desires to play with other children, and then reject him further by exhibiting disgust at a later time when the child is afraid to play with others. In the autobiographical account given above, the father apparently rejected his son by not showing that he was "plugging for him" when he had to give a speech. The son may have given a poor speech because of this rejection, but it can also be imagined that the father was scornful of the poor performance and again rejected the son. The vicious circle of rejection provided by these examples involves behavior on the part of the child that is produced by rejection but that also leads to further rejection. Such behavior can serve the purpose of revenge. The poor speech of the above example could have the effect of embarrassing the father which could serve as revenge from the boy's point of view. It is not unreasonable to assume that rejection sets up desires to "get even" with those responsible for it. While no specific plan to get even may be present in the first place, as when the boy gave the poor speech, once having engaged in behavior that has the effect of getting even, such behavior may be perpetuated. The boy might tend to give poor performances of a similar kind in the future, for example, as a way of embarrassing his father even though other factors would also influence him in another direction. This tendency could exist without the boy's being aware of it just as a younger child might wet the bed as a way of getting even with rejecting parents without knowing the purpose the bed-wetting was serving. In the process of interaction with his environment the rejected child not only reacts with conscious or unconscious feelings of not being wanted, accepted, or respected, but also frequently influences his environment inadvertently in ways that bring about further rejection.

4. *Acceptance.* Acceptance of a child implies affection and respect for him. As has already been pointed out in the preceding discussion of rejection, acceptance combines a willingness to help the child with a willingness to let him alone. It also involves a reliability in parents' behavior that creates a feeling in the child

that he is living in a reasonable and stable environment. Thus, if a parent follows through with his promises when he has told a child that he can go on a picnic or have an ice-cream cone, the child feels that he can trust his parents. Similarly, there is a reliability in the parent's behavior when a penalty that has been promised for doing or not doing something is actually administered rather than forgotten about. Thus, if a child is told that he cannot have an ice-cream cone if he writes on the wall and the parent carries through by not letting him have the cone, the child may not like what happens in this instance but he does learn that the parent's word can be counted upon. The penalty need not be severe or harsh in order for it to be reliable. The accepting parent will also take the trouble to relate it to the child's behavior rather than administer it in such a way that the child does not know what he is being penalized for. A very young child has difficulty in relating a delayed penalty to an act that has occurred some hours before, and an older child is also confused when a parent expresses disapproval in one way or another without indicating what he is displeased about. The necessity for penalties tends to be minimized in a relationship between parents and children that is characterized by acceptance, in any case, because a spirit of coöperation exists that tends to reduce or eliminate "misbehavior" on the part of either the parent or child. This coöperation is developed through companionship and working together that exists when mother and daughter plan a meal together and father and son make the repairing of a machine a mutual enterprise.

It was said earlier that no rule of thumb can be given as to how every parent can proceed on every occasion to strike the balance between giving too much or too little assistance to a child, but that a general intent on the part of the parent to avoid the extremes can develop an underlying conviction in the child that he is accepted as an individual. The same observation can be made about reliability in the parent's behavior that creates a feeling in the child that he is living in a stable and reasonable environment. A parent cannot always be consistent, for example. A child might be allowed to jump up and down on a certain piece of furniture on one occasion but not on another; the parent can make the effort to explain why it is permissible in one instance and not in another, however. No standard rules can be given that guarantee companionship and a spirit of coöperation either, but a general interest in these objectives on the part of the parent will tend to bring about their realization. It is also in order to point out that there is greater likelihood of the child's being accepted if the parents accept each other. A parent cannot easily escape seeing traits of his mate in his child. If he has strong distaste for these traits, it will be difficult for him to accept the child. If the mother has a manner of speaking that the father barely tolerates and the child acquires this same manner of speaking, the father will tend to be irritated by the child as he is by his wife. A final consideration concerning acceptance is that the parent's ability to like people, in spite of not always approving of what they do, will tend to insure affection for the child. A man can like his wife even though he may not like some of her speech mannerisms, and one can like a friend even though he sometimes exhibits an unpleasant characteristic such as stinginess. A parent, similarly, can like and understand a child without always approving of what the child does.

Acceptance in a parent-child relationship is illustrated nicely by means of the following case:

Dick's arrival as a newborn baby was looked forward to eagerly by both of his parents. While they exhibited some of the concern over the child's welfare that is not unusual in new parents, they tended in general to look upon Dick as someone to be enjoyed and who they hoped would enjoy them in turn. They could easily adopt the point of view expressed by the doctor before Dick was born that while parenthood was not necessarily an unmixed joy it also provided opportunity for experiences in humor and companionship that could not be found elsewhere.

When Dick started to school, his parents were interested in how well he would get along away from home and were pleased because he was not frightened or disturbed by the new experience. They had tried to prepare him for school by encouraging him and making it possible for him to play with other children before he was old enough to go to school. Although he did not prove to be an outstanding student as he advanced in school, he was well accepted by most of his classmates and seemed capable of "standing up for himself" when he was not liked. On one occasion a group of boys started to "gang up" on him and some of his friends after school, and although his parents were tempted to interfere because Dick came home with a bloody nose for several afternoons running, they encouraged him to fight back (after determining that the odds were fairly even) and tried to give him pointers in organizing his group to take the offensive.

As Dick expresses interest in various vocations during the course of growing up his parents exhibit a corresponding interest but do not try to guide him by comments to the effect that he would like a certain occupation or would not like another. He often makes business trips with his father and sometimes thinks he would like to go into the same business. His father has responded by giving Dick information about the business that is meaningful to a boy of his age, but has not tried either to "sell" him on the business or to discourage his interest.

Dick now has two sisters and the family plan frequent trips, outings, and parties together. Dick and his father join together in such things as washing the car or "keeping out of the way" of his sisters and mother when preparations are underway for these occasions. Dick's and his sisters' friends frequent the home. Dick's parents sometimes "clamp down" when the children seem intent upon "wrecking the place" and insist that they take their share of the responsibility in looking after the house. In general, though, one has the impression that the children's friends are always welcome and that Dick's mother and father like them and are genuinely interested in them just as they are in their own children.

Acceptance is illustrated in many ways in the preceding description of the relationship between Dick and his parents. He is encouraged to become independent as shown by the parents' pleasure in his getting along satisfactorily "on his own" when he started to school. A general spirit of companionship seems to be present in the family and the relationship between Dick and his father appears to afford opportunity for him to learn masculine forms of behavior that a boy prizes. His parents are by no means indifferent to his vocational interests but there is no effort on their part, either, to plan his future for him. In general, they seem to be interested in his developing in such a way that he will be able to handle his own life. They "clamp down" on occason and make certain demands upon the children, but their firmnes itself can be interpreted as providing security. It can be so interpreted because it is administered in such a way as to furnish the children with a sense of responsibility of their own. Moreover, the general affection for the children and their concrete demonstrations of it that can be inferred allow for little possibility of the parents' firmness being reacted to as "meanness." Dick is genuinely liked, and, by virtue of being treated with affection, will in all probability be genuinely capable of liking others himself. His parents have at the same time tried to prepare him for "carrying on" when he might be disliked without being "crushed" by people's rejection of him when it does occur.

SIBLING-SIBLING RELATIONSHIPS

At the beginning of the discussion on person-to-person interactions it was pointed out that parent-child and sibling-sibling relationships have a significant effect upon other interpersonal relationships. We tend to react to other persons in much the same way that we have reacted to parents and to siblings (brothers and sisters in the same family). A brother and sister who have had a companionable relationship will probably have less difficulty, other things being equal, in making adolescent adjustments to the opposite sex than brothers and sisters who have not had such a relationship. This furnishes an example of the way in which a sibling-sibling relationship can be basic to other interpersonal relationships. Another illustration is that of two subordinates competing for the favor of the boss in much the same way that they may have competed with brothers and sisters for parental approval when they were children.

A certain amount of rivalry between siblings is probably inescapable in any family, and a certain amount of it also provides the child with experience in contending with a reality that is not always altogether pleasant. If Johnny is not permitted to do something he wants to do because he has not mowed the lawn but his brother, who has attended to his assignment to rake the lawn, is permitted to do it, John may feel that his brother is being favored. The experience is unpleasant for John but it may have the effect of lessening his surprise when he has similar experiences in which he is not favored later in life. In this instance John would probably not have too much trouble in seeing why his brother was favored. In other instances deep-seated antagonisms are set up between siblings. When a younger child is usually given better toys or clothes and the older child is expected to make concessions to this procedure on the grounds that the younger child is younger, it is not to be expected that the older child's feeling toward the younger will be devoid of resentment. Neither is one sibling's affection for another sibling promoted by playing them off against one another in competition for grades in school or other kinds of achievement. Rivalry between siblings is reduced, on the other hand, when parents attempt to be fair by treating them equally and praising coöperation between them. When parents also make an effort to include the other children in the family in their activities when they have to give a good deal of attention to a particular child, rivalry and resentment between the children is lessened. If one child is sick, for instance, the parent can still talk to the children who are not sick or perhaps enlist their aid in looking after the sick member of the family. No completely equal distribution of attention and interest to all of the children in the family is necessary to promote a good feeling between them if the child senses interest, affection, and willingness to help (when help is needed) on the part of the parent.

Behavior having ramifications for the individual's whole adjustment that had its origin in sibling rivalry is discussed by Dollard (1942) in the following case:

The pet aversions and oddities which many people have are . . . often based upon foolish fear. If a well-meaning friend blunders on to one of these subjects he gets a short, and sometimes a sharp, answer. This was the case with a woman whose name was Mary. To further identify her, her friends would add "the one who always wears blue." This was appropriate because three-quarters of Mary's wardrobe was blue. Her taste was a mystery to her friends, especially her women friends, because she had brown eyes and hair, and blue was unbecoming to her. Her men friends knew that something was wrong with her appearance but, in the stupid way of men, did not know quite what it was. I ventured to joke with Mary one day about her fondness for this color but found that she could see no humor in the situation whatever, and I was forced to conclude that behind this personal oddity were forces of great importance in her personality. She did not wish to learn about these forces herself and did not want them noticed by anyone else.

Mary had another problem which seemed, to the outward eye, not related in any way to her taste in clothes. She was on very bad terms with her younger sister and the relationship had reached the point where an open breach seemed inevitable. Her own conscience as well as her family urged on her the duty of being friendly with her sister. But her own wish was to see as little of the sister as possible, and expressed the feeling that "never again would be soon enough." She avoided family reunions where the sister was present and even took a trip to escape being bridesmaid at her sister's wedding. The discussion of this topic, like the matter of the blue clothes, was very unwelcome. It was apparently ringed around with painful fears for her.

It was my opinion that Mary might well seek specialized help on this problem, but this was, unfortunately, impossible. There was no psychoanalyst, psychiatrist or other mental hygiene consultant within reach of her home or her purse. She had either to bear the conflict or try to do for herself what others could not aid her to do. She had the greatest reluctance to begin self-study, but with some long-distance aid she did begin and was able to make a real advance in overcoming fear.

Her current problems seemed to wind their way back into the events of childhood, as do so many adult difficulties. Mary's sister was about two years younger than she. The sister had been a lovely child, with blue eyes and blond hair, and she was adored by the mother and father. The parents, though attempting to be impartial in expressing love for their children, unreasonably favored the younger sister. The older child concluded that she was not loved or wanted and that it was her pestilential sister who was responsible. Her jealousy was focused particularly on her father who seemed never to tire of petting and admiring the pretty, blue-eyed sister. As the head of the house, his affection was particularly craved by the older girl and the denial of it was felt as an unbearable rejection. She dared not blame her parents for this unjust treatment but she harbored the strongest feelings of resentment against her little sister.

When she attempted to express these feelings she was punished by her parents. Fighting with her sister, bullying her, or stealing her

toys always brought down parental wrath. On one occasion her be-
loved father spanked her severely for pushing baby sister off the porch.
Mary was deprived of parental love and at the same time powerless to
make her resentment felt against the sister who seemed to be the cause
of her unhappiness. Slowly she forgot the whole tragic conflict, but
the wishes and repulsions engendered by the conflict survived. She
could not learn to like the sister who had been the source of so much
pain.

But what was the relationship between wearing blue clothes and
her resentment of her younger sister? This problem was finally solved
by a significant recollection. Little sister was always dressed in the
blue clothes which were so very becoming with her light complexion
and fair hair. In trying to gain the love of her father Mary unwittingly
adopted the blue garments which had seemed to be so successful when
worn by her sister. Her preference for blue was a vain appeal for the
love which had been denied to her, and it had survived all the years
since her bitter disappointment in childhood.

The way in which favoring one child in preference to another
brings about sibling rivalry and antagonism is abundantly evident
in the foregoing description of Mary's childhood experience. One
of the outstanding results of this experience in Mary's behavior in
later relationships with people was, in all probability, an underlying feeling that people would probably dislike her. It is also
quite possible that she would tend to dislike attractive women
who readily gained atention from men in much the same way
that she had resented her sister. If her father had had some awareness of what was happening to Mary when he held her younger
sister on his lap and gave exclusive attention to her, Mary probably would have grown up with different attitudes and feelings
toward people. The father's exclusive interest in the younger
sister is an example of the failure to include all of the children
in the activities and interest of the parent. This inclusion, or the
absence of it, is probably the most central factor in fostering or
minimizing sibling rivalry.

Parent-child and sibling-sibling relationships are only two of a
vast number of interpersonal relationships in which an individual
takes part in his life experience. Principal attention has been
focused on them in this discussion of person-to-person interac-

tions because of the profound effect they have upon other relationships. The child who has been rejected by his parents tends to anticipate rejection from others. The overindulged child is bewildered by the lack of indulgence in relationships outside the family and home. Sibling rivalry or sibling coöperation can have an important bearing on a person's later relationships with fellow workers. Knowledge of parent-child and sibling-sibling relationships supplies significant clues to the individual's chief modes of dealing with people and to his interaction in groups.

Person-to-Group Interactions

The individual's interaction takes place in a social setting, context, or environment, and this setting is made up in large part of the groups of which the individual is a member. These groups consist of large social organizations such as political parties, veterans' organizations, and national or international labor unions as well as smaller groups such as the family or play-group. The individual occupies a place or position in each of the groups to which he belongs. In the family a man is a father; in the business world he may be a clerk, salesman, or executive; in the religious group he may be a deacon, member of the congregation, or interested visitor to the church. Each of these groups has attitudes concerning what his behavior in the position he occupies should be. The family may hold the attitude that the father should furnish it with financial support and leadership; the members of a business firm tend to hold the attitude that a clerk should keep good records, a salesman should be cordial in meeting people, and an executive should be able to make decisions; and the religious group holds the attitude that a deacon should be dignified, a member of the congregation loyal, and a visitor to the church respectful. These attitudes are an important environmental influence of the group upon the individual inasmuch as attitudes reflect expectations as to what his behavior should be. Although the individual's behavior does not always conform to what is expected of him, these attitudes serve as a framework for his behavior.

If the individual is to function comfortably and more or less efficiently in his social environment he must know what group expectations are. In the absence of such knowledge he is thrown into confusion and conflict, because he does not know the acceptable mode of social conduct. The boy who moves into a new neighborhood, for example, may be puzzled for a short time at least because he does not know the expectations of the neighborhood group of boys as to how a boy in that neighborhood is supposed to behave. The group might expect a new boy in the neighborhood to pick a fight before being accepted into the group. Even if the new boy knew how to fight well enough, he could still be confused because of lack of knowledge of what the group expected of him. The immigrant to a new country is in a very similar position to that of the boy in a new neighborhood, although he may be even more lacking in knowledge of group expectations. Similarly, the individual drafted into the Army from civilian life is often at a loss because of the limited knowledge he has as to what is expected of him now that he is in the Army.

The group transmits its expectations to the individual in many ways. Parents are expected to transmit group standards to their children, for example, so that the children will become "law-abiding citizens." Individuals in influential positions are expected to set examples in their behavior and by so doing transmit group codes. The President of the United States was criticized severely on one occasion for using profanity in a press conference because it was out of keeping with standards of the groups that criticized him. As an influential person he was not setting the kind of example that transmitted the expectations of these groups. Channels of communication such as the radio and newspaper also serve the purpose of transmitting group expectations. Thus, the loudspeaker and the printed page exhort us to drive safely, to fulfill our patriotic obligations by buying government bonds or joining the armed services, to be honest in financial transactions, and so on.

Group expectations are not always transmitted consistently. A particular group, for example, might expect a young woman to prepare for a business or professional career and at the same time expect her to act as though she were not interested in such a career, but only wanted a future as a wife and mother. An immigrant to America is sometimes expected to believe that all men are equal but at the same time expected to believe that Americans born in the United States are superior to immigrants or foreigners. Group expectations are not only sometimes inconsistent but they also shift from one period of time to another. A well-known example is the frequent change in women's styles of dress. A hat with feathers is in keeping with group expectations one year whereas a hat that fits tightly over the head is "the thing" the following year. Similarly, there was no general acceptance of women's smoking fifty years ago but such acceptance is more widespread today.

The extent to which the individual is subjected to inconsistencies and changes from one period of time to another in group expectations and the necessity for moving into new groups where expectations differ from those of previous groups vary from one society to another. The individual who is born and spends his life in a rural mountain community is probably confronted with less of such inconsistency, change, and movement than the individual born in a town in Michigan or New Jersey who subsequently moves from one part of the state or country to another. In either case, the individual will not be able to escape a certain amount of such inconsistency, change, and movement. Accordingly, getting along comfortably in a group requires a certain amount of flexibility on the part of the individual in his interaction with his environment. Strong emotional adherence to particular attitudes may make it difficult for an individual to adapt himself to expectations based on different attitudes. One who has been strongly impressed with the virtues of thrift, for example, may find it hard to spend money freely when he has earned enough to make this possible, and is expected by new associates to do so because it is a practice of the group. Inflexibility based on emotional adherence to previous attitudes also sometimes occurs when the same group changes its standards. A political party may change its policies, for example, in such a way that measures are supported that were not favored by the party previously; emotional attachment to the old policies may be the chief factor preventing some members of the party from being sufficiently flexible to make concessions to the new policies. Automatically adopting the new policies without appraising the issues for one-self might also be considered inflexibility, however, in that it is suggestive of overdependence upon group attitudes. Such over-dependence makes it particularly difficult for an individual to contend with inconsistencies in group expectations. The immi-grant, spoken of previously, who is expected to believe that all men in America are equal, on the one hand, but who is also some-times treated as though he was inferior because of his accent, will be much more troubled by what seems to be a malicious environment if he is overinclined to look to the group for guid-ance than if he can appraise the situation for himself with the realization that group standards are not always to be taken too seriously.

A final observation to be made about person-to-group interac-tions is that the individual is not only influenced by group stand-ards, practices, and attitudes but that he also can and does in-fluence such standards, practices, and attitudes. Two significant conditions under which the individual can bring about group change are being in a powerful position or satisfying a latent group need. A group that is fearful of the loss of an important member will conform to his wishes. The boy who owns the bat, ball, and catcher's mitt can name the time and place of the game as well as the members of his team. The best batter in a neighbor-hood gang can also demand similar concessions to his wishes. A powerful position through which the individual can influence the group, then, may depend upon possession of either material goods or services essential to the group welfare.

In addition to influencing a group by means of a powerful position, the individual can also affect the group by supplying innovations for which the group has a need. Henry Ford changed the habits of a nation by satisfying a need for cheaper automotive transportation, and Thomas Edison in satisfying the need for illumination extended the waking hours of the world. The group need not be consciously aware of the need that is satisfied by the individual who introduces the innovation, but once the possibility of change is demonstrated, abandonment of old standards, practices, or modes of living often begins to take place. People were probably relatively content with existing devices for illumination before the invention of the electric light bulb, for example, but once it was invented an awareness of the possibility of and a demand for improved illumination came into being. It is evident, then, that the effects of the individual's interaction with the group are not necessarily anticipated even though group expectations do profoundly influence the individual's social behavior.

Although two of the significant conditions under which the individual can bring about group change are being in a powerful position or satisfying a latent group need, a group is composed of individuals, each of whom is influencing some or many others constantly. It is not merely the powerful or inventive members who influence the group. Even quiet conforming is a way of demonstrating what conformity is and not participating in a group itself often has the effect of making other members of the group feel rejected by the individual, just as the individual who does not participate often feels rejected by the group.

Person-to-Culture Interactions

"Culture" is a broad term which is used to designate general habits, customs, and modes of thought, action, and interpersonal relationships that prevail in a society. These general modes of interaction envelop the individual, and it is not too far from correct to say that his culture is his environment. The simple act of eating is culturally determined. Knives and forks are appropriate in one culture, fingers are appropriate in another. Knives and forks, moreover, will be as much subject to disapproval in another culture as fingers are in our culture. The individual's whole point of view or outlook on life depends upon his culture. Loyalty to the group is overstressed in Japan from an American's point of view. Individual accomplishment and initiative is overstressed in America from a Japanese point of view. Gorer (1948) brings out another interesting contrast between American and Japanese culture in pointing out that "respect and awe are the usual emotional responses to personified authority, and are therefore among the most painful emotions that the Americans recognize, and are as carefully avoided by them as the feeling of shame-facedness is by the Japanese." Values, attitudes, and modes of life in the American culture and their effects upon the individual can be discerned from the following rather comprehensive description.

A basic assumption in the American culture is that each individual, through his own efforts, has an opportunity for distinction and economic success. If an individual attains such distinction and success, he is accorded a prestige position which is roughly associated with his personal achievement. Feelings of personal worth tend to be associated with the prestige position attained. The cultural belief in the possibilities of attainment frequently results in the individual's setting a goal far above realistic expectation of achievement. Business cycles, opportunities for education, illness, etc., often occur in such a way that the individual cannot achieve in accordance with his desires. The anxiety and the confusion resulting from the differences between expectation and realization have produced demands for social legislation which would serve to reduce uncertainty. Social legislation pointed specifically at increasing the individual's security such as old age pensions, aid to dependent children, health insurance plans, etc., might be thought of as cultural attempts to increase the feeling of security provided in an earlier era by the frontier and the opportunities it symbolized.

Another aspect of the culture which makes for confusion and a sense of guilt as well is childhood training in relation to expression of love and affection. During adolescent training, the child is often made to feel guilty if he expresses feelings of love overtly. Yet, at the time that an individual is married, he is expected to behave in ways quite contrary to his adolescent training. Inability to express feelings of love and affection freely in the marital situation often results. The romantic themes of motion pictures and popular fiction might be interpreted as a kind of compensation for thwarted expressions of love. Still another source of conflict which is prevalent in the American culture is that which results from the teaching of humanitarian sentiments in the one instance and in the other the sanctioning of competitive striving between individuals and groups. The individual is taught to behave toward his fellow man on the basis of the Golden Rule, love of his fellow man, love of humanity, and so forth, yet he may be forced to behave in terms of personal ambition and business practices which do not always take into account the feelings of his fellows. The guilt which arises from this situation can be relieved through charity activities and other forms of "social service" which can be understood in part as institutionalized techniques for reducing guilt.

However, the American culture does not only offer conflict for the individual but also presents him with a fairly flexible social structure which affords opportunity for individual expression and creativeness. Rigid definitions of superior-subordinate relationships are resisted; although concepts of "social betters" or "inferiors" and "knowing one's place" are not foreign to the culture, neither have they settled comfortably upon it. Abstract concepts of freedom, moreover, have their counterparts in everyday insistence upon freedom from being "bossed around." Substantial pressures, therefore, not only support the rights of the individual but also create opportunity for the expression of individual ingenuity. This ingenuity has probably been reflected most clearly in the country's economic development, but evidences of the "frontier spirit" appear in other areas as well. "Fads" in education, for example, although sometimes disconcerting to the populace, can also be seen as forms of experimentation in a culture which permits experimentation and allows people's "screwy ideas" to be tried. The idea of giving children freedom, similarly, even though sometimes applied without consideration for giving them a sense of responsibility, has been countenanced in the American culture without undue deference to traditional ideas. The appearance of this idea in the culture, incidentally, would appear to be a further evidence of the culture's orientation toward developing a "free way of life" for the individual.

An overall view of the American culture, then, reveals it as one in which individualistic ambition and striving generate many conflicts. On the other hand, individual expression, freedom, and ingenuity are furnished with strong support. The individual, accordingly, is not expected to be a passive victim of frustration, and is given considerable freedom in molding his world. Individualistic striving probably cuts the individual off to some degree from a sense of unity with others and is not altogether consistent with humanitarian ideals held in the culture. The reconciliation of these ideals with the exercising of individual ingenuity would appear to be the most challenging problem faced by this culture.

The psychological make-up of the individual and his corresponding interaction in his environment cannot be considered apart from his culture. Americans, for example, are not born with the drives toward individual success or "getting ahead in the world" that are discussed in the passage above, but develop this kind of motivation as a result of living in a particular kind of culture. Hopi Indians, in contrast, are embarrassed by individual competitiveness as shown by the resistance of Hopi children to playing classroom games requiring a child at the blackboard to turn around as soon as he has finished a problem and thereby distinguish himself from the rest of the group if he has finished first (see Klineberg, 1940). A Hopi child growing up in the American culture or an American child growing up in the Hopi culture would be quite different psychological specimens from what they are when reared in their own cultures.

To gain a clearer idea of the effects of the culture upon the individual and his interactions, it is helpful to consider the fact that a society may have subcultures. An individual's subculture, as well as his culture as a whole, must be taken into account in order to understand him and his interactions with his environment. The subcultures in American society can be classified into three categories: social classes, ethnic groups, and color castes.

Social anthropologists and sociologists who have lived in certain American communities and studied them carefully have found that the people of these communities can be rated and rate each other according to their social prestige. This prestige ranking can be divided into three categories; upper, middle, and lower, with subdivisions of upper and lower within each of these categories.[2] These prestige-ranked groups may be thought of as

[2] These subdivisions and methods of determining them are discussed by Warner, Meeker, and Eells (1949), in Social class in America.

social classes. The attitudes and modes of life of individuals of upper, middle, and lower classes vary considerably from one class to another. An upper class person, for example, will have a consciousness of "family line" and an interest in ancestors that is not as likely to characterize a middle class or lower class person. Although individual success-striving and attainment are more distinctive of American culture as a whole than of many other societies, middle class individuals will tend to be more preoccupied with success than lower-lower or upper-upper class people.

Ethnic groups are subcultures that are more or less set apart from and not completely assimilated into the larger culture. Nationality groups of various kinds are examples of ethnic groups in the American culture. French-Canadians in Maine, Chinese in New York or San Francisco, Mexicans in the Southwestern states, and Polish or Italian people in any of a number of American communities make up ethnic groups. The practices, attitudes, and ways of life of these groups differ noticeably from those of the larger culture. In a particular ethnic group, for example, the practice of the parents' choosing a husband for a young woman may be accepted. Such a practice, needless to say, might be a source of conflict for the young woman who is not only a member of her ethnic group but who also lives in the larger American culture in which parental choice of a mate is scorned. In spite of this conflict, we can see how this same young woman might in the future expect to place her "stamp of approval" on her own daughter's choice of a husband, since the attitudes of the subculture in which she had grown up could easily have become a part of her own set of attitudes. Total aspects of husband-wife and parent-child relationships as well as food preferences and the value placed upon education or certain kinds of education can be appreciably determined for the individual by his ethnic group. The individual can also influence his ethnic group. The aforesaid young woman, for instance, might contribute to a change in the group's attitudes toward marriage by not getting married in the traditional group fashion. In her interaction with her environment she might also contribute to a modification of the larger culture by bringing customs of her ethnic group into the larger culture. The type of humor relished by her own ethnic group, for instance, might "catch on" in the larger culture through her storytelling as well as that of other members of her subculture.

In addition to social classes and ethnic groups, color castes comprise still a third type of subculture in American society. Caste, like class, is a prestige system. It differs from class in that moving from one class level to another is permissible, but if one is born white, he remains in the white caste and if born colored, he remains (with a limited number of exceptions) in the colored caste. This restriction of one's social environment in itself is a clear influence upon the individual's life experience; it means that whites will tend to associate most intimately with other white people and colored people with other colored people. Furthermore, a greater sense of being able to participate fully in the culture as a whole is more likely to be present among members of the white caste. The range of occupational choice, in general, is broader for white people, for example, than for colored people. The interaction of white and colored people has tended to modify even this aspect of the total culture to some extent, nevertheless. Colored individuals, for instance, are now able to play on major league baseball teams. This example, in itself, may not appear to represent any major alteration in the American culture. However, baseball figures large in the American cultural pattern, and it is often said to be *the* American game. The appearance of face-to-face interpersonal relationships between Negroes and whites in the playing of this game at the professional level may, accordingly, be a significant result of earlier social interactions between whites and Negroes as well as a significant form of social interaction in itself.

SUMMARY OF PRINCIPLES

Since a knowledge of principles contributes so greatly to insight into personal adjustment, interpersonal relationships, and social interaction, a summary of these principles will be presented at the end of each chapter. No principle, it might be noted, is final. Because the sun has always risen in the morning does not furnish a guarantee that it will always continue to rise in the morning. Furthermore, the theory, which may have been accepted as indisputable, that explains its rise may prove to be quite inadequate in the light of future evidence. In attempting to formulate principles, nevertheless, the individual is able to bring order into events that would otherwise be meaningless to him. Some of the principles contained in the present chapter that may contribute to a better understanding of interpersonal relationships and social interaction are these:

1. The environment provides a setting or context for interaction, a process in which the individual not only reacts to other individuals, situations, and objects but also influences his surroundings. Closely related to this principle is the further principle: Each individual is a member of the social environment of other individuals and, as such, he plays the role of one who influences others as well as of one who is influenced by others.

2. The individual's modes of response to and influence upon others are determined to a considerable degree by the nature of the relationships he has had with his parents, or those who have taken the role of parents, and siblings (brothers and sisters in the same family) during childhood. Principles which can be included under this general principle are the following:

a. Individuals with backgrounds of indulgent overprotection tend to have a disregard for the consequences of their behavior.

b. Restrictive overprotection tends to foster dependence.

c. Rejection tends to result in making the individual feel that he is not wanted or accepted.

d. Acceptance of the individual predisposes him to accept others.

e. Sibling rivalry or sibling coöperation can have an important bearing upon a person's later relationships with fellow workers, associates, and friends.

3. The psychological make-up of the individual and his corresponding interaction in his environment cannot be considered apart from his culture. Specific aspects of this general principle are the following:

a. The individual is not only influenced by group standards, practices, and attitudes but also can and does influence such standards, practices, and attitudes.

b. Knowledge of group expectations contributes to comfortable and efficient functioning in the social environment.

CHAPTER 2

Interactive Development

Introductory Summary

The individual's interaction in his environment can be considered from the point of view of what is necessary to preserving his sense of well-being. In seeking a sense of well-being he demands from himself and his environment a sense of safety in his environment, control over his environment, and belonging in his environment. Associated with these demands are certain needs and drives, such as hunger, thirst, sex, affection, etc. These drives, needs, and demands provide the impetus to interaction, and their arousal and expression are modified by the interactions that take place throughout the individual's life. These modifications are the result of interactive development which is that aspect of interaction of the individual in his environment that makes him, or contributes to making him, the kind of person he is with his particular interests, attitudes, values, skills, likes and dislikes, and so on.

INTERACTIVE DEMANDS

The individual's present interaction is governed not only by the immediate situation but also by the development that has taken place as a result of his earlier interaction. To state this point differently, one acts and reacts not only in relation to the present set of circumstances but also as a product of his past experiences. The reader, for example, not only looks at the words on this page, but as a product of his past interaction with his environment, he also brings meaning to these words, meaning which has been acquired through previous interactions. A man's reaction to and

38

action upon his employer are not merely determined by his present employment situation but also by the attitudes toward authority which have emerged from his previous relationships. Attitudes toward authority furnish an example of results of development that is likely to have taken place primarily in childhood. The attitudes that correspond to a child's fear or feeling of mutual respect, as the case may be, in relationships with his parents are likely to transfer to figures of authority, such as the boss, later in life.

The early years of interaction with the environment shape the individual to no small extent. This is not to say, of course, that development stops when the individual reaches adulthood or that no changes can be brought about of tendencies that have been established during the early formative years. These tendencies are strong and furnish numerous elements in what might be called a basic orientation toward living, but interactive development continues throughout life. Appreciable understanding of a person can be gained by examination of his early as well as his later interactive development in his environment. *Interactive development is that aspect of interaction of the individual in his environment that makes him, or contributes to making him, the kind of person he is with his particular interests, attitudes, values, skills, likes and dislikes, and so on.*

The individual possesses certain needs and drives that provide the impetus to interaction in the environment. The manner in which these needs and drives develop will depend upon the nature of the environment in which the individual interacts. The hunger drive will develop into a liking for a particular kind of food in one environment and distaste for this same food in another environment. Grasshoppers, for example, are considered a delicacy in certain Oriental cultures whereas they are looked upon with less favor as a food in the American culture. The thirst drive develops into an acceptance of wine as a regular part of meals in Italy whereas a craving for milk is more common in America. A drive may not only be modified in respect to the way in which it is satisfied, as shown by the foregoing examples, but also in respect to the way in which it is aroused. Slender women arouse men's sexual drives in one culture whereas stout women arouse these drives in another culture. From these examples it can be understood that the modification of drives is the result of the interactive development of the individual in a particular environment.

It seems reasonable to infer that the individual strives toward a general sense of well-being as he interacts in his environment. To preserve this sense of well-being the individual must make certain demands upon himself and his environment. He must secure food and water from his environment and must exert himself to gain these necessities. He must also exert himself to secure other kinds of goals such as sexual stimulation, or to avoid such stimulation if his past experience has developed attitudes of revulsion in relation to sexual matters. Similar observations can be made about goals having to do with oral demands, excretory demands, and many other demands which might be enumerated at greater or lesser length to include demands for oxygen, demands for heat when the temperature is too low, less heat when the temperature is too high, and so on, The term "demand" is a broad one covering drives—or inner tensions such as hunger and thirst; needs which refer to the seeking of certain kinds of stimulation such as recognition, affection, food, approval, etc.; and more general pressures and requirements associated with the preserving of a sense of well-being.

To preserve a sense of well-being the individual must make three general types of demands upon himself and his environment.[1] First, he must demand safety from his environment and exert himself to become or remain safe. Correlated with the demand for safety is the need to avoid threats, injury, and other fear- or pain-provoking conditions. Interference with securing food, water and other goals can threaten the individual's feeling of safety and it is, therefore, evident that such goals and the drives associated with them have safety significance. In addition

---

[1] The demands for safety, control, and belonging were suggested by Maslow (1943), who speaks of safety needs, esteem needs, and love needs as well as other needs. Our concepts of safety, control, and belonging correspond only roughly to Maslow's concepts.

to demanding safety in order to preserve a sense of well-being, the individual also requires a certain amount of control over his environment. Control and safety are, of course, closely related in that safety cannot exist without a certain degree of control. This control over the environment may involve assertion and mastery. It is also related to drives such as hunger, thirst, and sex inasmuch as control is jeopardized when the individual is not able to secure food, water, sexual stimulation, and other goals. A third general type of demand the individual makes in order to preserve a sense of well-being is that he be able to fit in or belong in his environment. He must fit in in the way that a fish belongs in water. That is, his environment must be suited to his resources for living and self-expression in the way that water is suited to a fish's resources for living. What might be called self-expression drives, then, are associated with belonging in the environment. Drives to seek acceptance by and membership in the group are also important in this connection. Furthermore, the extent to which the environment makes it possible for the individual to satisfy his other needs will also affect the individual's assurance about belonging in his environment. Sexual drives are perhaps of particular significance in relation to belonging inasmuch as they can lead to intimacy and closeness, which are aspects of belonging goals, in interpersonal relationships.

In summary, then, the individual's motivation or striving to preserve his sense of well-being can be considered from the points of view of safety, control, and belonging. All of the drives that are involved in preserving a general sense of well-being are modified as the individual interacts in his environment.

SOME ASPECTS OF THE SOCIAL MODIFICATION OF SAFETY MOTIVATION

The interrelatedness of safety, control, and belonging is shown by the fact that the individual must have a sense of control over and belonging in his environment in order to preserve his sense of safety. Being unable to do anything about a false and damaging rumor about oneself, for example, undermines one's sense of control as well as any assurance one might have about acceptance in the social group and threatens one's sense of safety at the same time. Fear arises under such conditions and motivates the individual to restore the sense of safety. Since fear drives arise as a result of a threat to the sense of safety, they deserve primary consideration in a discussion of the social modification of safety motivation. Because fear and apprehension can become associated with numerous drives such as hunger, thirst, sexual, and excretory drives, attention must also be given to their relationship to fear drives.

Fear Drives

The social modification of fear that takes place in the individual's interaction in his environment is clearly demonstrated by the differences in the circumstances that arouse fear in different cultures. Expressions of disrespect for ancestors are not particularly productive of fear among Americans, for example, but they are more likely to create apprehension in a culture in which ancestor worship is practiced. On the other hand, death or the prospect of death is apparently a more fear-laden event for Americans than for people of cultures in which life is not as highly revered. An American soldier, who had a part in training soldiers from another land, related an incident about the foreign soldiers' pushing one of their fellows from an airplane without a parachute and then laughing hilariously as he hurtled toward the earth. The bewilderment with which Americans react to such a story illustrates a sensitivity and awe about life and death that seems to be more highly developed in the American culture than in some other cultures. Many other illustrations can be cited of differences between cultures in the conditions that arouse fear. Practices that go unnoticed in America and evoke little or no feeling stimulate dread in certain primitive societies. Interpersonal relationships may be regulated in such a way, for example, that speaking to a sister-in-law is forbidden and taken as a serious violation of tribal custom. An instance in which it occurred, then, would be an occasion for panic. No such violent reaction takes place on such an occasion in the American culture. Members of subcultures also react fearfully to events that do not arouse fear among individuals of the total culture not belonging to the subculture. Members of a minority group will tend to react with fear and anger as well when their group is slandered whereas such slander does not as readily bring about such reactions among individuals of the larger culture outside of the minority group.

Fear is not only modified in the course of the individual's social interaction in respect to the conditions that arouse it but also in respect to its expression. There are occasions in some cultures when an individual risks rejection by the group if he cries out in pain when burning coals are applied to the flesh or when subjected to similar excruciating experiences. It is hard to think of times when any person is expected to go to such extremes in suppressing expressions of pain and fear in the American culture. Within the American culture, there are differing expectations relating to men's and women's expression of fear, however. It is generally more permissible for women to express fear openly than for men to do so. A boy learns that it is "unmanly" to cry, for example; a girl does not learn that it is necessarily "unwomanly" to do so. A girl, in fact, can quite easily learn that it is not only acceptable for her to cry but that crying can sometimes be quite useful. The significance of the cultural influence in America upon crying as an expression of fear by men is shown by the fact that American soldiers who have demonstrated bravery in battle beyond any doubt have been deeply humiliated by experiences in which they cried under stress. Another significant social influence upon the expression of fear in America is the valuing of individual strength and fortitude. Turning to others for help is, of course, acceptable but fighting one's battles alone and acting as though one were "captain of his fate" is highly prized. Showing that one can "take it" rather than yielding to any expression of fear is, therefore, often striven for.

The arousal and the expression of fear are both closely related to the conformity which every society attempts to exact from its members. Anticipation of disapproval arouses fear and the behavior that is motivated by such fear tends toward conformity. An individual might anticipate disapproval for using obscene language, for example, and "tone down" his language accordingly. The penalties that a society imposes for moral and legal transgressions provide reason for the individual members of the society to be afraid of committing such transgressions. Conformity on the basis of fear presents the individual with a certain amount of conflict in the American culture, because fear is not compatible with being "captain of one's fate" or "master of one's soul."[2] Americans hold to the conviction that the individual can control and shape his own life by his own efforts. Fear is not easy to tolerate, then, because it damages this conviction; one cannot "believe in himself" and be afraid at the same time. Conforming on the basis of fear, therefore, is inconsistent with the desire to believe that one acts on his own initiative rather than because of external compulsion. Resistance to external compulsion is shown by the resentment Americans display when they believe they are being "shoved around." It is interesting in this connection to observe that breaking laws or regulations is in many instances not regarded as a moral offense by Americans. College students, for example, sometimes expend considerable energy in working out ingenious methods of cheating on exams without experiencing pangs of conscience. There, in fact, is a certain glee that frequently accompanies such practices that can be interpreted as defiance of the external compulsion that authority represents. Similarly, breaking speed laws and violating income tax regulations do not always occur because of necessities for driving faster or saving money but often seem to be expressions of defiance of external compulsions that are incorporated into law.

The fact that fear is not easy to tolerate, because it damages the conviction that the individual is not a puppet of fate but an independent agent who is the potential master of all that he surveys, sometimes makes it difficult for Americans to admit their fears to themselves. This reluctance to admit that one is afraid is a significant aspect of the modification of expressions of fear that comes about in the course of interactive development in the American culture. Such reluctance to admit fear can be an

[2] Dollard *et al.* (1939) point out that "Americans advertise themselves as 'masters of their fate,'" in their discussion of the direction of aggression in American democracy.

especially acute problem because it may result in avoidance of the situations that arouse fear. This avoidance in turn prevents overcoming the fear through experiences in meeting the feared situation. An individual who is afraid and timorous when he attends parties, for example, but cannot admit this fear because it makes him feel inadequate may avoid parties and invitations to parties. The avoidance does not permit him to overcome his fears by attending parties and discovering that they are not necessarily threatening.

A readiness to avoid situations that are feared might be expected to be particularly strong in an individual who has been taught to feel that he is worthless if he does not achieve high goals but who has also been kept from learning to achieve by means of his own efforts. Being kept from learning to achieve by means of his own efforts undermines his confidence and predisposes him to be afraid, but being afraid is intolerable because it makes him feel worthless and unable to achieve high goals. Because of the intolerable quality of fear he readily resorts to withdrawal and avoidance of feared situations. Neither the urging toward high goals nor the interference with a child's achieving on his own are too uncommon in the American culture. A prominent aspect of the "American scene" is the hope of parents that their children will earn more money and have more prestige than they have had. This hope may result in nothing more than the parents' taking pleasure when their children are successful. In many cases, however, parents are so concerned about their children's making what they regard as satisfactory progress and becoming outstanding that the children's lives are taken over and planned for them. The planning may range all the way from selection of clothes to selection of a vocation, as was pointed out in the discussion of restrictive overprotection in Chapter 1. The child learns to feel that it is necessary to become outstanding if he is to have his self-respect but the inability to develop self-reliance when his life is planned for him deprives him of the assurance that is essential to independent achievement.

Self-reliance is not only undermined by parents' taking over a child's life and planning it for him, but also by the kind of interaction between parent and child that makes the child feel that he is a "bother." A father who is himself so preoccupied with achieving high goals in his business or professional career that he relegates children to the outer circle of his life can easily develop the feeling in his children that they are essentially "nuisances" even though he never tells them as much in so many words. Feeling that one is a nuisance can in itself damage confidence and a corresponding sense of self-reliance. The father who relegates his children to the outer circle of his life may do the same thing to his wife who can then easily turn to the children for emotional gratification and further damage the development of self-reliance by making the children too dependent upon her. Cameron (1947) points out that "the literature of behavior pathology cites well-authenticated cases of small boys who have been trained, or encouraged, to develop overt reactions toward their mothers that are typical of adult courting behavior." Such reactions might easily be fostered when the mother does not feel that she is a part of her husband's life.

Interactions within the family involving the valuing of high goals, the blocking of the development of self-reliance in the child, and the emergence of withdrawal and avoidance modes of behavior in the course of interactive development are illustrated in the following case:

Mrs. Brown was a woman who valued her neighbor's good opinion and was eager to make the "right impression." Mr. Brown was relatively successful in his business, but had always wanted to be a lawyer and regretted that he had never attained the necessary education. He also was interested in economics and world affairs, but found his wife relatively unresponsive when he tried to discuss these matters with her. They both agreed, however, that it would be very nice if Tom, their son, became a lawyer. Because he had relatively little in common with his wife, Mr. Brown spent a large number of evenings at his office, although he also felt that this was necessary to the success of his business. Mrs. Brown frequently commented that it was certainly nice to have Tommy around the house with her when his dad had to be away from home so much of the time. Her friends observed that she and Mr. Brown did not seem too happy together and that the attachment between her and the boy was unusually strong. Mr. Brown, they observed, on the other hand, was impatient with Tommy and seemed to frighten him. The more discerning friends said that it was not surprising that Tommy was a shy child when one considered that he was loved too much by his mother and intimidated by his father. When Tommy entered school he didn't seem to mix well with the other children. Both Mr. and Mrs. Brown were anxious for him to do well in school, however, which he sensed and which contributed to his fears since being in school with the other children was already somewhat frightening. Tommy preferred to come right home after school and play around the house rather than get out with the other children. When he was in the first grade he came home on one occasion without his cap and related to his mother how he had been chased by some of the boys who had taken his cap from him. When his father heard about this he was disgusted, and it didn't occur to him to spend some time teaching Tommy how to defend himself because he was thinking about his business. When he was in the second grade his teacher selected him to take part in a children's play that the parents were invited to come and see. Mr. and Mrs. Brown were very pleased, but Tommy was only frightened by the rehearsals which didn't permit his coming home as soon as school was out. He was more frightened the night the play was put on for the parents and forgot his lines. Mr. and Mrs. Brown were not able to conceal their disappointment, because Tommy's forgetting his lines was hard to explain to the neighbors and neither did it bolster their hopes of Tommy's becoming a lawyer. Tommy simply became a little shyer. In the succeeding years he didn't do very well in school, although tests indicated that he had the ability to do much better. In high school, on the other hand, his grades improved, but his teachers and classmates noted that he tended to stick pretty much by himself, and, in fact, preferred studying and reading apparently to taking part in any of the school activities. He also seemed to become rattled sometimes when called upon to recite in class. He would like to have asked one or two girls to go out with him, but couldn't seem to work up the courage to actually invite them, and thought they wouldn't be interested, anyway, although several of the girls said among themselves that he was good-looking. Tom did go to college, but didn't study law as his parents hoped he would. He was a good student and his instructors encouraged him to do graduate work. After getting an advanced degree, he took a research job and seemed to be happy in it. He disliked having to present the results of his research to his superiors, however, and seemed to be more troubled by indigestion and headaches when this was necessary than he was ordinarily. As the years went on, he continued to be recognized as a good research man, but never became the director of the laboratory because he was always more comfortable working by himself than giving others instructions.

The high aspirations that parents can have for a child's success as well as the existence of conditions that thwart the growth of self-reliance in the child are shown clearly in the foregoing case. Mrs. Brown's eagerness to impress the neighbors and Mr. Brown's disappointment with his own educational and professional attainment combined in the setting of high goals for their son. Their married life was not congenial, on the other hand, and afforded reason for Mrs. Brown to encourage a strong attachment between herself and Tommy. He was, thus, rendered overdependent upon his mother, but his father, who was apparently more interested in his business than his family, was impatient with him. The interaction between Mr. and Mrs. Brown and Tommy, then, was more productive of fear than self-reliance in Tommy's personality. Since he had been taught to seek high goals and act as though fear had no place in his life, it might be expected that he would have difficulty in admitting he was afraid when he had to take part in the school play as a youngster and later when he had to present the results of his research to superiors. The withdrawal that can serve the purpose of preventing fear's becoming too strong, and the acknowledgment of fear when it does arise, was characteristic of Tommy's interaction in his environment.

Early interactive development that predisposes an individual to be afraid can, of course, be counteracted by later interactive development. Tommy of the above case, for example, acquired at least some confidence so far as his occupation was concerned even though fear continued to plague him in many ways. The confidence that he did have resulted quite possibly from later interactions with people who encouraged his work as well as from his continuing to endeavor in spite of his fears to find some way in which he could control his environment rather than be dominated by it. His research skills and ability were apparently his chief means of gaining some sense of control over his environment. They may have been selected because he could engage in research without having too much contact with people, whom he seemed to fear most. It is possible that being able to accept and admit these fears and endeavoring to learn to meet and deal with people as he dealt with research problems might also have added to his confidence considerably in his interaction in his environment during adulthood.

Hunger, Thirst, and Safety

Previously it was pointed out that fear can become associated with numerous drives. Since food and water are necessities of life, it is evident that apprehension can become strong when the organism is exposed to long periods of deprivation of these necessities. When such experiences have been persistent, starvation fears develop and often remain and continue to influence interaction long after the danger of starvation has passed. Hunt (*1941*) found that animals that had been deprived of food during infancy later hoarded significantly more food than animals that had had free access to food during infancy. Many examples of what appear to be counterparts of this behavior in humans can be found. Scarlett O'Hara in *Gone with the wind* resolved that she would never be hungry again after coming close to starvation. The development that took place during this experience affected her later interaction by impelling her to be successful in business. A highly successful businessman, who was often forced to rummage through garbage to get something to eat during childhood, stated that he felt that he never could make enough money even though his income was adequate, ten times over, to provide himself and his family with food, clothing, shelter, and plenty of leisure. While isolated examples of this kind do not prove anything, they do strongly suggest a relationship between threats to the satisfaction of hunger and thirst and later fears over material security.

Feeding infants according to a schedule means that they can only eat at fixed periods and may, accordingly, be hungry a certain part of the time. It has been suggested by several writers that this infantile hunger may produce fears over material security of the kind discussed above. Gorer (1948) has said in this connection that although the American people are unusually generous, they have fears about sending shipments of food abroad. He attributes these fears to the widespread practice in America of schedule-feeding of infants. Whether one believes the American people have such fears or accepts such an explanation of whatever caution Americans may have about sending food out of their country, it can be seen that intense hunger experiences during infancy could have a profound effect which could be manifested later in apprehension lest one be without food and possibly shelter and possessions in general. Such an effect would be an example of how early interaction contributes to making the individual the kind of person he is. At the same time, an effect of this kind is not necessarily fixed nor does the individual necessarily remain exactly the same kind of person; as noted earlier in the chapter, interactive development continues throughout life and the changes resulting from later interaction can counteract the effects of earlier interaction.

Sexual Drives and Safety

Attitudes toward sex vary greatly from one culture to another. Margaret Mead (1928) has described the culture of Samoa in detail and presents what seems to be a picture of complete and uninhibited sexual indulgence from the point of view of the American culture. However, it is not likely that the people of Samoa regard their sexual customs as "indulgence" any more than Americans evaluate any of the day-by-day practices that are generally accepted in their culture as "indulgence." The very fact that such a term comes to mind in discussions of sexual motivation in America probably reflects what have often been called puritanical values in the American culture. These values, carried to the extreme, would forbid any thought or expression of sexual impulses, since such thought would be considered indecent in the light of such values. While it would be inaccurate to hold that the forbidding of sexual desires generally reaches such an extreme in American culture, it is true that fear frequently becomes associated with sexual drives. The threat to the

individual's sense of safety that is entailed can be understood as
a conflict between fear drives and sexual drives. One of the most
common manifestations of this conflict in the American culture
is the distress and feeling of worthlessness that accompanies
masturbation or the temptation to masturbate. There is a tendency to regard it as a degenerate and harmful practice even
though there is no evidence to support the popular belief that in
itself it seriously damages physical structure and functioning.
The damage to the individual's sense of safety, security, and
well-being, because of the attitudes that are held toward it, can
be very great. These attitudes become a part of the individual in
the course of interactive development in his culture. The spectacle
of the individual's being torn between these sexually fearful attitudes on the one hand and his sexual desires on the other hand
is more than clear in a case that Cole (1948) relates:

Frank was a really critical and extreme case of adolescent fear and
bewilderment. Between the ages of thirteen and fifteen he had
changed from a pleasant-mannered boy who did good, though not
brilliant, schoolwork to a disagreeable adolescent with a secretive manner and a fund of smutty stories. On one occasion a teacher had found
him sitting in the boys' dressing room after school hours crying bitterly,
but when she tried to talk to him he had simply cursed her and left.
Things came to a head one evening when he stole an auto, drove it out
into the country, connected a pipe from the exhaust into the car, closed
the windows, and started the engine. A state policeman happened by,
started to tag him for parking on the road, and then went into immediate action to save the boy's life. Upon investigation it appeared that
Frank was in a panic because he had been masturbating and had been
told that (1) he would die of tuberculosis; (2) he would go insane;
(3) he would never be able to marry; (4) he would become infected;
(5) he might die in convulsions at any moment. His constant pandering of smutty talk was merely an effort on his part to pick up information. . . .

It is worth noting that the stories that the boy of the above
case had been told about the effects of masturbation are a cultural
phenomenon. They circulate in a culture in which there is a
forbidding attitude toward sex. The attitude may not reach the

point of complete prohibition of sexual interests, and it certainly does not reach this point in present-day American culture as a whole, but it can, nevertheless, become sufficiently strong to create the kind of conflict that is described in the above case.

Forbidding attitudes toward sex not only create conflicts having to do with masturbation in the American culture but they are also related to impotence and frigidity. Impotence refers to a man's inability to gain sexual satisfaction or difficulty in gaining it and frigidity to such inability or difficulty in a woman. Since fear interferes with sexual excitement and gratification, it would be expected that an individual who has learned attitudes of fear in relation to sex would become impotent or frigid to some extent. These attitudes are easily learned in the American culture. While pictures of girls with few or no clothes can be found in abundance on billboards and calendars, instances of punishing children for masturbating, putting off children's questions about sexual matters, and avoidance of direct and open discussion of sex, except under special circumstances when "off-color" stories are permissible, can also be found in abundance. The nude and seminude pictures of women and "off-color" stories can, in fact, be taken as manifestations of preoccupation with sex stemming from the absence of direct and open expression of sexual interest. The kind of behavior resulting from the cultural prohibition of direct and open discussion of sex is illustrated by the statement in the above case concerning the boy who was distraught over masturbation: "His constant pandering of smutty talk was merely an effort on his part to pick up information." The secretive and fearful attitudes toward sex that are shown by this illustration can be acquired fairly readily in the American culture and afford bases for the individual's developing impotence or frigidity as he interacts in this culture.

Excretory Drives and Safety

Excretory functions are surrounded with regulations and taboos varying from one culture to another. In the American culture parents tend to disapprove of the interest that children exhibit in the products of excretion and there is a corresponding tendency to try to complete toilet training at a relatively early age. This age varies somewhat from one socioeconomic level to another. When strong pressure is brought to bear upon the child to achieve anal and bladder control, fear tensions may arise that affect his sense of safety in his environment. The irritation and impatience of the parent stimulates this fear and it will not be reduced in any way if the pressure is imposed before the child is capable of anal and bladder control. The social modification of excretory drives and functions is illustrated quite clearly by the fact that in some cultures little or no stress is placed upon the child's toilet training; remarkably enough, from the point of view of the American culture, children in these cultures learn toilet habits without much specific instruction or guidance. This learning is informal and apparently comparable to the "picking up" of such things as manners of speech and language habits that are often acquired without any formal guidance; children sometimes, for example, learn swearing from their parents, and to the distress of their parents, without having been given any formally arranged lesson in swearing or the techniques of swearing.

Toilet training and stress on cleanliness tend to go hand in hand, and fear in connection with dirt in general can develop just as it can be acquired in connection with the products of excretion. Children whose parents have a minimum of tolerance for dirt become disturbed over such things as their hands becoming muddy when they are playing with other children. They may also give their clothes unusual care as in the case of a youngster who can be observed brushing off his overalls repeatedly even when given assurance that it is all right to let them get dirty. Interaction in the environment during childhood can establish a trend toward preoccupation with cleanliness that may run through a person's life, although the trend can also be altered by later interaction. The manner in which a strong trend can be "put into motion" and maintained can be illustrated by means of a hypothetical life history. Let's say that Mary's mother was a very spick-and-span housewife. Even when she was an infant, Mary's mother tried to keep her in clean clothes continuously although this necessitated a staggering number of changes of clothes each day. Toilet training was exacting, and soiling and spilling food were discouraged to say the least. As in the case of the youngster previously mentioned, Mary did not like to get mud on her clothes or hands and anticipated scolding and disapproval when she and mud did come into actual contact. When Mary entered school, her mother praised neat drawings and papers and sometimes asked why they couldn't be neater. In grade school her teacher commented on how neatly she kept her books and how careful she was about her papers. Mary's mother similarly commended her for keeping her room so nicely. In high school she complained about sharing a locker with another student who was less neat and was supported in this complaint by the teacher who had supervision of the locker room. In college Mary felt that it was necessary to change roommates because she couldn't tolerate a roommate who didn't empty her ash trays often enough. When Mary graduated from college she got a position as a first-grade teacher and couldn't understand how mothers let their children be so slovenly. After two years of teaching, Mary married a man who came as close as one could to her ideals of neatness. They subsequently had a child and Mary's neighbors never ceased to be amazed at the number of times she changed the baby's clothes.

In the foregoing life history the trend that runs through Mary's life may appear to be almost too consistent and not in keeping with actual life experiences. If one has been quite regularly praised for neatness and cleanliness and censured for the lack thereof, however, it can be seen how a tendency might readily develop to influence one's social environment in such a way as to achieve approval for cleanliness. This approval would, of course, reinforce cleanliness behavior. Mary might seek out teachers and playmates, for example, who were impressed by neatness and then make it a point (although without her necessarily being aware of what she was doing) to display her neatness and cleanliness in some way to them. She might also make it a point to avoid people who were not overly impressed with neatness as she did with a college roommate. The roommate apparently disturbed Mary's sense of safety and security in her environment by not keeping the room as neat as Mary desired. Her changing roommates, then, illustrates a way in which safety motivation can influence interpersonal relationships. It might also be thought of as a way in which Mary attempted to gain greater control over her environment.

SOME ASPECTS OF THE SOCIAL MODIFICATION OF CONTROL MOTIVATION

Safety and control are intimately related in that control over the environment can insure one's safety. Crying as a means of bringing attention and relief from distress, or a lack of safety, is learned by a baby as a way of controlling his environment. Adults have a greater number of skills and techniques available to them as means of controlling their environments and achieving their goals, although their methods are sometimes evaluated as infantile. In America there is a certain amount of cultural sanction given, in fact, to some seemingly infantile or childlike methods of controlling others as when girls use baby talk to "wind men around their fingers." The baby's crying, a girl's using baby talk, a farmer's plowing his field, a politician's planning how to win an election are all ways of controlling the environment. One form of control or another is necessary to bring safety and satisfy needs. When the individual is left without resources or feels that he is without resources for controlling his environment his helplessness leads to "breakdowns," panic, and the development of disorders such as acute withdrawal or wild attacks upon or ventures into his environment that are designed, however poorly, to restore his sense of well-being.

Although the individual must have some means of controlling his environment in order to achieve safety and the gratification of his needs, mastery over the environment will take different forms in different cultures. Passive resistance, for example, is more likely to be found in India than in the United States where active resistance or fighting to achieve one's ends is more readily found. It is also interesting to observe that control through mastery over the physical environment is more highly valued in the American culture than in other cultures. Americans are noted for their industrial prowess and pride is taken by Americans in their manufacturing "know-how." Since the American culture is competitive, individual initiative, struggling against odds, and self-assertion in the face of challenge are esteemed in much the same way that the resourcefulness that is called "know-how" is esteemed. Assertive impulses and drives can be considered from the point of view of control motivation.

Assertion and Control

The necessity for controlling the social environment by outdoing others seems to be more highly developed in the American culture than in many other cultures. It was pointed out in Chapter 1 that personal competitiveness is foreign to the culture of the Hopi Indians and that the children of this culture are only confused and embarrassed by competitive procedures used in American classrooms. While personal competitiveness is not as foreign to the British culture, it also seems to differ from the American culture in respect to rivalry between individuals. Many observers report, for example, that Englishmen wait patiently in lines for theatre tickets, railroad tickets, taxis, and so on. Americans wait in line for similar purposes, but one would hesitate to call their waiting patient and it is not unusual for them to attempt to best one another by breaking into a line or pushing ahead restlessly. Similarly, athletic contests in England do not appear to inspire the same kind of competitive zeal that such contests stimulate in the United States.

The necessity for outdoing others in personal competition can manifest itself in many ways. The "social climber" is generally recognized as an individual who feels this necessity strongly and who goes to extremes in his efforts to exceed others. The desire to "climb" or "get ahead" is not confined by any means to the individual who is known as a social climber. Personal ambition is widespread in the American culture and sometimes conflicts with other values. One may think it wrong to try to be "better" than others, for example, but his ambition at the same time drives him toward trying to best them. Similarly, his needs for affection and approval may conflict with his desires to "get ahead." Thus, one may fear that he will be disliked by others if he "goes up in the world" or beats others out in competition. On the other hand, fears of failure or of not "going up in the world" can be highly developed. The tension and nervousness that students sometimes have over examinations is a fear of failure that more often than not has its roots in personal ambition and the sense of worthlessness the individual anticipates if he does not succeed. This fear of failure also manifests itself with pilots in training who have shown every promise of becoming good pilots but "freeze at the stick" during "check hops." Fear of failure is not restricted to people who have not realized their ambitions but is also found among individuals who have apparently been highly successful. Business executives, for example, frequently have high blood pressure or heart attacks that sometimes appear to result not simply from the pressure of work but more from the necessity they have of driving themselves relentlessly to make sure that they won't fail.

Ambition and needs for personal assertion and triumph can produce fears when the individual has learned to check anger and assertion to the point of not letting himself feel angry when circumstances would justify it. Horney (1937) cites the example of a man's saying nothing in the face of another's taking credit for important ideas that had originated with him. In such a case the person may not only fail to say anything but actually fail to feel anger, although some other feeling such as that of a headache may arise. Such inability to experience anger can be traced to conditions that have existed in the childhood background that have on the one hand provoked hostility but on the other hand have made its expression dangerous. A child may resent restrictive overprotection, for example, but at the same time fear to express his resentment because of the helplessness that restrictive overprotection fosters. He may also resent intimidation but fear expressing the resentment against a person who has been powerful enough in his eyes to intimidate him in the first place. Horney (1937) points out that making a child dependent, intimidating him, emphasizing the sacrifices that have been made for him, or controlling him by shame, all tend to make him feel helpless, afraid, or guilty and are conditions that produce an underlying conviction that expression of his hostility would be dangerous. It can be inferred from Tom Brown's life history that is presented on pages 46 to 48 that he did not have the capacity for feeling and expressing anger when it would have been to his advantage to do so. He ran away when his cap was stolen, for example, rather than getting angry and fighting back. The reasons for his inability to be appropriately motivated by anger are clear enough when we consider the whole nature of his interaction with his environment during childhood. He didn't dare to exhibit anger because of the helplessness his mother had fostered through making him overdependent. He was also afraid of his father and this fear was an additional reason for not daring to be angry lest he oppose too powerful a foe. It can be imagined that the fear he exhibited toward his father might have been reacted to by the father as a lack of confidence on the part of his son which irritated the father and resulted in further intimidation of the boy. Future interaction might, of course, offset fears of expressing hostility of the kind that were present in Tom Brown's case. A timid person, for example, sometimes stands up to a bully and finds that he can take care of himself after all.

The expression of hostility, self-assertion, and anger varies from one American subculture to another. Davis (1944) makes this point clear by his description of aggression in the middle and lower classes of the American culture. Concerning middle-class aggression he says:

With regard to overt aggression, the middle-class boy must learn, for example, (1) to fight when attacked by another boy, (2) not to attack a boy unless he has been struck, (3) not to attack girls or supervisory adults under any circumstances, but also (4) not to withdraw when in a normal, approved competitive situation.

Davis comments on lower-class aggression as follows:

The important consideration with regard to aggression in lower-class adolescents is that it is learned as an *approved and socially rewarded* form of behavior in their culture. An interviewer recently observed two nursery-school boys from lower-class families; they were boasting about the length of their father's clasp-knives! The parents themselves have taught their children to fight not only children of either sex, but also adults who "make trouble" for them. If the child or adolescent cannot whip a grown opponent, the mother or father will join the fight. In such lower-class groups, an adolescent who does not try to be a good fighter will not receive the approval of the father, nor will he be acceptable to his play group or gang. The result of these cultural sanctions is that he learns to fight and to admire fighters. The conception that aggression and "hostility" are neurotic or maladaptive symptoms of a chronically frustrated adolescent is an ethnocentric view of middle-class individuals. In lower-class families in many areas, physical aggression is as much a normal, socially approved and inculcated type of behavior, as it is in frontier communities and in war.

The foregoing observations make it clear that aggression is expressed less directly in the middle class than in the lower class. In spite of these differences between subcultures, there is justification for concluding that personal assertiveness as a means of controlling the environment is taken seriously in the American culture as a whole. As was pointed out earlier in this chapter, there is a tendency in the American culture for the individual to believe that he is potentially master of all that he surveys. Stagner (1950) brings out a practical significance of this tendency in a discussion of industrial conflict by pointing out that such conflict cannot be resolved until adequate recognition is given to the personal assertion needs of both management and labor. His remarks furnish what might be regarded as a general summary of the relationship between assertion and control in the American culture:

Ours is a competitive, ego-centered culture. Our philosophy and our advertising alike stress achievement, prestige and power. "Superman" is no accidental hero; his adventures canalize the desires of American youngsters in a pattern that fits our society. We cannot expect executives to be the only persons craving free self-expression, enhanced status, a sense of planning and doing worthwhile things. Workers imbibe these influences and crave these goals—less intensely, less unanimously, but regularly.

The problem of industrial conflict is the problem of democratic self-assertion versus self-assertion without democratic controls. Executives want ego-satisfaction; so do workers. The problem of industrial harmony will not be solved until we develop techniques for sharing these ego-goals.

Perhaps as good a way as any to sum up this idea is to quote a union organizer on the subject of a recent strike in a small Illinois factory. Asked what the real issue was, he replied: "The real issue wasn't the 15¢ an hour we asked for or the 5¢ we got. The real cause of the strike was that we had to convince that guy he couldn't be a little dictator any longer."

SOME ASPECTS OF THE SOCIAL MODIFICATION OF BELONGING MOTIVATION

An important component of a sense of well-being is the feeling that one belongs in his environment. The popular expression "like a fish out of water" is used to describe individuals who are thrown into situations in which their accustomed modes of inter-action are not appropriate or in which their interests cannot find expression. Although a general feeling of "warmth" in inter-personal relationships may be striven for to a greater extent in some cultures than in others, it can also be seen as an aspect of belonging goals. Sexual and oral gratifications are elements of this "warmth." Whether such "warmth" in interpersonal relation-ships is achieved to any high degree or not, it is clear that the individual must have some sense of membership in his culture if he is to maintain himself with any degree of comfort. Lack of this sense of membership arouses fear, threatens safety, and impels the individual to restore a sense of belonging in one fashion or another even if by nothing more than creating his own world, in which he is accepted, by means of fantasy.

Self-Expression and Belonging

Interests vary considerably from one culture to another and from one group to another within the same culture. Americans are more interested in baseball than are Chinese; farmers are more interested in crops than are city dwellers. When a person cannot devote time and energy to strongly developed interests, his environment seems foreign to him and self-expression and a sense of belonging in the environment are thwarted at the same time. In response to such thwarting he attempts to alter his environment in such a way as to make possible the expression of his interests. This alteration may be accomplished by changing the present environment, as when a man who likes chess teaches his wife to play chess, or by seeking out a new environment, as when the retired farmer living in the city returns to the farm.

Interests can be pursued with great intensity. Although being able to pursue them enhances an individual's feeling of belonging in his environment, it is also true that their intense pursuit is apparently sometimes motivated by insecurity and uncertainty that is suggestive of a sense of lack of belonging. Many outstanding writers, artists, musicians, and scientists have been known to be unhappy individuals whose satisfactions in living were primarily limited to their work. These satisfactions in many such cases served partially to counteract underlying doubts and fears about living. From these cases it cannot necessarily be concluded that creative achievement has to be motivated by insecurity. Although there is good reason for believing that it often is so motivated, it is also possible that the individual possesses creative drives which can be expressed most fully when a person is free from the distraction of insecurity. People with similar interests sometimes "lose themselves" in a discussion, for example, and develop new ideas during the course of the discussion that can be considered creative outcomes of the energy they have been expending. A group of students in such a discussion might figure out new ways of studying a subject so as to grasp the basic principles or concepts of the subject more readily. When people are "lost" in such discussions, they are often apparently more or less free from any feeling of threat for the time being at least and if the discussion has to do with their work, the work becomes play. Examples of this kind make it plausible to believe that an individual may be more ready to "lose himself" in creative activity when he is secure and feels that he belongs in his environment just as he has greater readiness to play at such times. It is to be recognized at the same time that such "losing oneself" can and does occur when one is not secure as in the cases discussed above of highly creative individuals who have been known to be torn by doubts and fears and fundamentally lacking in many ways in a sense of belonging in their worlds.

The sense of belonging in the environment that comes with self-expression taking the form of creative achievement, as it is known in the American culture, is probably more essential to individuals of some cultures than others. Concerning the people of the Balinese culture, Bateson (1941a) says, "They seem to take a very definite pleasure in mere activity in the present—in the very instant—either enjoying their own busyness or else ignoring what they are doing, letting their muscles run on automatically with the activity while their attention is given to some unreal world, singing the songs from the last opera which was performed in the village." In American and European culture, on the other hand, activity is much more definitely directed toward certain ends or goals. Interruption of goal-seeking activity gives rise to dissatisfaction and annoyance, and a sense of achievement seems to be essential to morale and well-being. Freeman (1936) tells of a carpenter who was paid very well for constructing targets. The products of his labor were shot to pieces after he completed them, a circumstance that proved so frustrating to him that he took another job which paid less but made possible a sense of achievement that he couldn't get from his previous work.

In the American culture which directs self-expression toward achievement, the individual's confidence and sense of well-being will be determined to a fairly considerable extent by the success he has had in his efforts toward accomplishment. Feelings of inferiority are to be expected when the individual has been persistently blocked in such efforts. This is particularly true when failure has occurred in connection with an activity which is generally evaluated as important, such as male participation in athletics. A famous scholar, for example, confided to an intimate that he would be willing to give up the reputation he had earned in his field if he could have been the quarterback on his high school football team. This illustration makes clear that outstanding achievement is often motivated by underlying feelings of inferiority. In any event, the individual's sense of personal worth in the American culture is closely related to his accomplishment. The child who has not been rewarded either in athletic or scholastic participation is more likely to grow up into a disgruntled citizen than the child who has had some measure of success in such activities, other things being equal. Other things are often not equal, however; a child coming from a home which stresses excelling in all activities will feel failure more keenly than a child coming from a home which tends more toward emphasis on satisfaction derived from different activities for their own sake rather than as ways of excelling. Two contrasting cases can be used to illustrate this point:

Sally's mother had been a schoolteacher and was anxious for her children to do outstanding work in school. Three of her children lived up to her expectations very satisfactorily. Sally's name was never to be found on the honor roll, however. She not only sensed her mother's disappointment, but knew that her teachers, who had also had her sister and two brothers in their classes, compared her unfavorably with the other children in the family. Sally's freckles didn't contribute to her attractiveness when she reached adolescence. She also tended to be sullen because of the favoritism with which she felt her sister and brothers were treated by her parents and teachers. She was not readily selected by the boys in her class as a favorite object of attention because she reacted to them with sullenness and in so doing influenced them to dislike her. Her sister was popular, however, and could be considered accomplished not only as a student but also as a young lady who could have as many dates as she wanted. Sally finally married a young man who himself had met with relatively little success scholastically or socially. Their friends and respective families, however, noticed that they tended to be retiring and seemed to prefer the company of each other to that of other people. The part that the blocking of achievement had played in Sally's interactive development in her environment is clear.

Betty, on the other hand, was no better as a student than Sally, and while she didn't have freckles she was quite a bit heavier than her male classmates considered desirable in a girl. She was a likable person, however, and got her share of invitations to go out with the boys even though no one ever expected her to compete with Hedy Lamarr in evoking gazes of admiration from her male contemporaries. Her parents had made it a point to refrain from comparing her grades with those of children who did better in school. They recognized that Betty had some feelings of inferiority about her weight, but tried to get her to see that it wasn't necessarily a problem unless she made one of it by her own self-consciousness. This gave her a perspective which diminished the tendency to feel that she always had to try to excel in competing with other girls as a model of physical attractiveness.

The two cases presented above bring out important differences in the development of self-expression. In the one case the individual learned to express her interests, abilities, and resources in terms of personal achievement that exceeded that of others, and suffered from a feeling of inferiority and lack of a sense of belonging when such achievement was not forthcoming. In the other case the individual did not learn achievement through personal competition as a mode of self-expression to the same extent and a sense of belonging in the environment was, therefore, not as dependent upon such achievement.

Acceptance Needs and Belonging

The extent to which the individual feels accepted by others has a bearing, of course, upon his sense of belonging in his environment. While the necessity for manifestations of "warmth," affection, and friendliness is felt to different degrees by individuals of different cultures, some indication of acceptance by the group is probably necessary to a sense of well-being in any culture. Even in a culture which is so thoroughly competitive that interpersonal relationships appear to be shot through with suspicion and hostility, there is not likely to be complete indifference to the support and approval of the group. Seeking approval might be particularly apparent in such a culture in the seeking of recognition for skill in beating out fellow members of the group in one way or another. Furthermore, there is reason to believe that when this skill is developed to too high a degree even in a competitive culture, it may lead to frustration of a sense of well-being resulting from the individual's competitively cutting himself off from the group to the extent of feeling alone and abandoned. In any case, a certain amount of dependence upon the group is a part of living in any society, and abandonment by the group is likely to arouse needs for acceptance and support.

The very fact that the human being begins life in a state of complete dependence furnishes a basis for seeking and continuing to seek support from others in order to preserve a sense of belonging in his environment. The extent to which this support is sought and the way in which it is sought depend upon the kinds of interpersonal relationships that prevail in the individual's culture. If direct manifestations of personal affection are common, the individual comes to feel that something is wrong if he does not receive demonstrations of such affection. If such manifestations are not particularly common, the individual does not have as much reason for feeling rejected in the absence of such demonstrations. In the American culture, personal affection is prized and its absence gives rise to what Levy has called "affect hunger." The following case, reported by Levy (1937), provides an illustration of this condition:

A patient was referred to the Institute for Child Guidance at the age of nine years, with a complaint of enuresis and temper tantrums. A visitor to the foster home wrote a letter to the Institute from which the following excerpt is taken: "He is starved for affection. His mother rarely visits him, although she is urged to do so frequently. When she is there, he acts very infantile, climbing up on her lap, always wishing to be with her, and showing off. Then as time elapses after her visit, he becomes more unmanageable and disagreeable." The history of the case is featured by the child's affectionate response to grown-ups, his making up to any stranger, the explosive and dangerous temper tantrums, and marked jealousy of the other children in the foster home. The "hunger" element in the difficulty is seen in the response to grown-ups and to the mother, with whom he acts in complete disregard of what is usually a strong inhibiting influence—the presence of other boys. When his mother is about he is always sitting in her lap, he holds his face up to be kissed and puts his arms around her neck. According to the foster mother, he acts in these situations quite like an infant. Though affectionate to the foster mother, he makes no such display with her. The severity of the temper tantrums must be mentioned. On one occasion he tried to break up a game in which the other boys were playing. The foster mother sent him to his room, whereupon he tore up the bedding and pulled all the pictures off the walls. On another occasion he attempted to hit a boy with an axe. On another, he chased the teacher and the children out of school.

The patient lived with his father and mother in the first year of life. After the death of the father he was placed in an institution for a year, then for two years in a boarding home from which he was removed by his mother. He was placed again with the previous boarding mother. He was moved again to a foster home in which he had been living for a year and four months at the time of referral. There are certain elements in the history that indicate a certain modicum of affection from the mother and in the homes in which he was placed. In one boarding home there was an affectionate mother. The foster mother also was affectionate with him. Furthermore, his own mother, though very spasmodic and infrequent in her visits, was affectionate while with him.

In this case, treatment consisted in getting placement with a foster mother who could give him a great deal of affection. There were only four interviews with the psychiatrist. They consisted largely of chats about the foster home. Marked improvement in behavior occurred and continued for two years. A follow-up study made when the patient was twelve years six months old, showed complete cessation of the temper tantrums, good school adjustment, growth in responsibility, though no improvement in the enuresis.

The deprivation of affection that led to the problems described in the above case occurred in a cultural setting in which personal affection and demonstrations of "love" are widespread. It was pointed out that the absence of such demonstrations might be particularly disturbing when they are common in the culture. When they are not common the individual does not expect them and the basis for feeling "unloved" in the absence of personal affection is not established or not established to the same degree at least. In another culture, then, in which relationships are more impersonal—or impersonal from the point of view of the American culture—the kinds of behavior that the boy of the above case exhibited would either not be as likely to occur or would have a different basis if they did occur. The different basis for the behavior in another culture is of particular interest in view of the fact that the treatment, which consisted of giving the boy a great deal of affection, would not necessarily have produced similar changes in behavior. It can be seen at the same time that such treatment would be particularly important and appropriate with children deprived of personal affection in the American culture.

The seeking of personal affection in the American culture is directed toward the development of heterosexual relationships culminating in marriage. The demonstration of such affection in man-woman and boy-girl relationships and the yearning for it when it is not demonstrated are represented in popular songs having to do with love and romance. Many writers have pointed out that marriage problems in the American culture often seem to arise because romantic expectations that have been acquired before marriage are not fulfilled in the actual marriage relationship itself. A girl may expect her newly acquired husband, for example, to continue to exhibit personal attentiveness and assertions of love for her after marriage whereas he may not be inclined to maintain the highly romantic aspects of their relationship to the same extent after marriage. A husband may also, of course, expect similar attentiveness and make insufficient allowance for his wife's inability to maintain romantic manifestations toward him; she may not always feel like getting his breakfast and bidding him good-by in the morning with an animated wifely kiss, for example. Such marriage problems furnish another illustration of the disturbance to a sense of belonging that can come about when demonstrations of personal affection are not present in a culture in which they are considered important and are interpreted as indications of the individual's being accepted. It does not necessarily follow, it might be added, that a culture in which personal affection is not as highly valued would be lacking in problems having to do with acceptance by the group; the problems would be of a different kind in such a culture, however.

The culmination of the seeking of personal affection in marriage in the American culture may be and often is blocked by affectional ties to parents. In the case of John C., pages 12–14, attachment to the mother prevented the continuation of the marriage relationship. While the bond between the mother and son was unusually strong in this case, everyday observation makes clear that men and women in the American culture frequently have difficulty in transferring their affection to their wives or husbands even when the marriage does not break up. A wife may not want to move to a town where her husband's work requires him to be, for example, because she would have to be away from her parents. A husband may also fail to understand why his wife gets irritated with his desire to visit his parents as often as possible.

In addition to strong parental ties, attachments to individuals of the same sex may also block the seeking of personal affection in marriage and heterosexual relationships. In the American culture, boys tend to associate with boys and girls with girls prior to adolescence. If a boy plays with girls too much, he runs the risk of being labeled a "sissy" and if a girl plays with boys a great deal she is likely to be called a "tomboy." While it is probably more permissible for a girl to be a "tomboy" than for a boy to be a "sissy," the avoidance of these tags in either case can reduce companionship between boys and girls. Transition to an interest in individuals of the opposite sex during adolescence, then, is not always easy. While boys begin to show such interest during adolescence by combing their hair more often, to take one example, and girls by giggling over matters that have not previously evoked the same amount of giggling, embarrassment in relationships between boys and girls is also well known at this age. This embarrassment may be especially strong in a boy who has not developed the confidence to make overtures toward girls or in a girl who lacks confidence in her ability to attract attention from boys. In such cases the tendency may very well be to maintain relationships with members of one's own sex. The tendency will not be diminished if circumstances have combined to make the individual distrustful of the opposite sex. If the parent of the opposite sex, for example, has been harsh, dominating, or prone to exercise excessive control, the individual may become inclined to be leery of the opposite sex in general. Neither will friendliness toward the opposite sex be fostered if a girl has been repeatedly told that men are "beasts" or a boy has been overimpressed with the idea of "losing his freedom" to a girl who will someday make him wash behind his ears or harass him in other ways. "Getting out with the boys" during adulthood by means of such recreation as poker and hunting or "being with the girls" by absorption in bridge clubs may become ways of avoiding the opposite sex and finding expression of preference for one's own sex when negative attitudes have developed toward the opposite sex. Such activities might also be expected, of course, as forms of maintaining relationships with one's own sex even when attitudes toward the opposite sex are not particularly negative.

What has been called self-love or narcissism as well as parental ties and attachments to individuals of the same sex may play a part in interfering with the culmination of the seeking of personal affection in marriage. Some writers hold that there is a basic and presumably inherent self-love that is characteristic of all human beings. Whether this assumption is true or not, it can be seen how an individual might become self-centered when he has not received personal affection from others, particularly in a culture in which personal affection from others is highly valued. That is, his own vanity could function as a substitute for affection from others. It can also be seen that an excess of attention and fondling could produce self-centeredness and vanity. In either case the vanity might function in such a way as to make the individual intent upon attention and admiration from others to the exclusion of offering affection to others.

Self-love or narcissism has sometimes been analyzed as fixation at or regression to early levels of development. The oral gratifications obtained by kissing, chewing, "hitting the bottle" in the consumption of alcohol, etc., have been related to early oral gratifications secured from sucking the breast or bottle. Self-centered seeking of affection has also been seen as a manifestation of an earlier stage of development including the so-called oral stage presumably. It so happens that the mouth looms large in the individual's early relationship to his environment when he is highly self-centered. Self-centered seeking of affection from others is, nevertheless, more readily understood as a matter of developing a sense of belonging in the environment than as a yearning for oral gratification as such. The alcoholic, who is often preoccupied with conflicts having to do with dependence upon and affection from others, may gain oral gratifications from hitting the bottle, but his problems in living give a stronger impression of his trying to bolster his sense of belonging than they do of "orality."

In spite of the fact that oral gratifications as such may not be too important in relation to the individual's sense of belonging, it is true that the individual's earliest mode of relating himself to his environment is "via the mouth" to a very considerable extent. Furthermore, there is evidence that needs for oral stimulation exist independently of hunger and thirst and it can be inferred that the gratification of these needs contributes to a sense of well-being. The significance of this point becomes clear when it is understood that the persistence of thumb-sucking into later childhood is related to emotional difficulties and problems of adjustment, problems which are not solved by forcibly restraining the child from sucking his thumb. As with so many other problems of personal adjustment arising in the course of the individual's interaction, the solution lies in finding and altering the conditions making for a lack of a sense of belonging and well-being.

SUMMARY OF PRINCIPLES

The purpose of this chapter has been to examine the individual's development as he interacts in his environment and strives to preserve a sense of well-being. The sense of well-being has been analyzed in terms of safety, control, and belonging, and various motivations have been considered from these three points of view. Although this procedure has served the purpose of organizing the discussion, the objective has not been to present any rigid classification of drives nor to offer a complete list of drives. The fundamental principle that has been assumed is that development (of one kind or another which may be "positive" or "negative") takes place as the individual interacts in his environment and strives to preserve a sense of well-being. Such principles are, of course, more fundamental to an understanding of personal adjustment, interpersonal relationships, and social interaction than lists or classifications of motivations. Some of the chief principles suggested in this chapter are as follows:

1. The individual strives to preserve a sense of well-being as he interacts in his environment.

2. The individual's present interaction is governed not only by the immediate situation but also by the development that has taken place as a result of his earlier interaction. Principle 3 must be taken into account as well as principle 2, however. It is as follows:

3. Early interactive development can be counteracted by later interactive development.

4. Fear is modified in respect to the conditions that arouse it as well as in respect to its expression. Some principles having a bearing upon the modified arousal or expression of fear are as follows:

   a. Every society attemps to exact conformity from its members.

   b. Reluctance to admit fear may result in avoidance of the situations that arouse fear and remind the individual of his fear.

5. Fear can become associated with various drives. Subsidiary to this general principle are the following:

   a. Persistent or intense threats to the satisfaction of hunger and thirst drives tend to be associated with later fears over material security.

   b. Forbidding attitudes toward sex are related to the development of impotence and frigidity.

   c. When strong pressure is brought to bear upon the young child to achieve anal and bladder control, fear tensions may arise that affect his sense of safety in his environment.

6. When the individual is left without resources or feels that he is without resources for controlling his environment, his helplessness leads to breakdowns, panic, and the development of disorders such as acute withdrawal or wild attacks upon or ventures into his environment that are designed, however poorly, to restore his sense of well-being.

7. Although there is good reason for believing that creative

achievement is often motivated by insecurity, it is also possible that the individual possesses creative drives which can be expressed most fully (thereby giving rise to a sense of belonging) when he is free from the distraction of insecurity.

8. The state of dependence with which the individual begins life is related to seeking and continuing to seek support in interpersonal relationships in order to preserve a sense of belonging in the environment. Some principles concerning seeking support from others in order to preserve a sense of belonging are as follows:

a. The culmination of the seeking of personal affection in the marriage relationship in the American culture may be and often is blocked by affectional ties to parents.

b. Attachments to individuals of the same sex may block the seeking of personal affection in marriage and heterosexual relationships.

c. "Self-love" or "narcissism" may play a part in interfering with the culmination of the seeking of personal affection in marriage.

CHAPTER 3

Interactive Adjustment

Introductory Summary

Adjustment is the process of gaining, keeping, or regaining a sense of well-being. When an adjustive technique preserves the sense of well-being and at the same time fosters effective maintenance in the environment, it is adaptive. A series or sequence of adaptive adjustment techniques constitutes the adjustive process of interactive integration. While all adjustment processes are directed toward the preservation of a sense of well-being, an adjustive technique may preserve the sense of well-being but jeopardize effective maintenance in the environment. Such an adjustive technique is nonadaptive. A series of such nonadaptive adjustive techniques constitutes the adjustive process of interactive conflict which renders the continued preservation of well-being combined with effective maintenance in the environment more and more difficult.

The necessity for using adjustive techniques arises because of the existence of demands that the environment makes upon the individual, demands that he makes upon himself, and demands that he makes upon the environment. Various adjustive techniques can be considered in relation to these three types of demands.

THE ADJUSTIVE PROCESS

It is reasonable to infer, as was suggested in the previous chapter, that the individual strives to preserve a sense of well-being as he interacts in his environment. *Adjustment refers to the proc-*

ess of gaining, keeping, or regaining this sense of well-being. This
adjustive process includes techniques such as flight, attack, thinking or refusing to think, compromising or holding fast, coöperating with others or opposing others, and so on.[1] The necessity for
using such adjustive techniques arises because of the existence of
demands that the environment makes upon the individual, demands that he makes upon himself, and demands that he makes
upon the environment.[2] The demands of the environment can be
illustrated by the pressure that is brought to bear upon the individual to follow customs and obey laws. To preserve his sense of
well-being, the individual must find some method or technique of
adjustment that will enable him to cope with this pressure. The
adjustment process might include obeying the laws and following
the customs or finding some way of avoiding or minimizing the
penalties if they are not observed. In some instances an individual
may seek punishment for violating customs, laws, or moral standards. The demand for punishment in such a case is a demand
upon the environment, and the seeking of punishment is an adjustive technique in response to this demand. Such a demand for
punishment might arise from a guilty conscience which can be
thought of as a demand or set of demands that the individual
makes upon himself. Seeking punishment, then, could also represent a method of adjustment to a demand upon the self.

*Adjustive techniques that add to the individual's ability to main-
tain himself in his environment are adaptive.* An adaptive adjustment process employs techniques which preserve the sense of
well-being combined with fostering effective maintenance in the
environment. The man who reprimands a subordinate, when the
necessity arises, in a fashion that makes the point of the reprimand quite clear but also demonstrates his fairness, preserves
his sense of well-being by clearing up the problem at hand. He

[1] The term "adjustive technique" is taken from Cameron (*1947*).
[2] The concepts of environmental demand, demand upon the self, and
demand upon the environment are, like the Freudian concepts of id, ego,
and superego, a way of describing an interplay of "forces." Although they
have something in common, the present concepts do not correspond to the
Freudian concepts. The mode of conceptualization was suggested by the
Freudian framework, however.

at the same time maintains himself effectively in his environment by being clear and by demonstrating fairness which will be to his future advantage in relationships with the subordinate. *A sequence of adaptive adjustment techniques constitutes the adjustive process of interactive integration.* Reprimanding a subordinate clearly and fairly which is followed by productive discussion of some other problem—which is more likely to take place as a result of the subordinate's feeling he has been treated fairly— would be a sequence of two adaptive techniques that continue the preservation of well-being combined with effective maintenance in the environment.

All adjustive techniques are directed toward the preservation of a sense of well-being. However, an adjustive technique, while preserving or partially preserving a sense of well-being, may jeopardize effective maintenance in the environment. Such an adjustive technique is nonadaptive. The man who does not reprimand a subordinate clearly and fairly might add to a sense of well-being or relieve the lack of a sense of well-being simply by shouting and thereby expressing feeling, but he might not contribute much to effective maintenance in his environment. *A sequence of nonadaptive adjustment techniques constitutes the adjustive process of interactive conflict which renders the continued preservation of well-being combined with effective maintenance in the environment more and more difficult.* Shouting, which is neither clear nor fair, being followed by an unproductive discussion of a problem—which is more likely to occur as a result of the subordinate's feeling he has not been treated fairly—would be a sequence of two nonadaptive techniques rendering continued preservation of well-being combined with effective maintenance in the environment more and more difficult. Various behavior disorders can be analyzed by means of the concepts of nonadaptive adjustive technique and interactive conflict. The suicide of a depressed patient is a nonadaptive act that may relieve his lack of a sense of well-being, but reduces his maintenance in the environment to zero. The man who believes that he is Napoleon is probably adding to his sense of well-being in so believing. However, the premises he adopts do not add to his effectiveness in coping with his environment. The extreme to which he has had to go in preserving his sense of well-being can, in fact, be understood as an end point of interactive conflict or sequences of interactions that have rendered his continued preservation of a sense of well-being combined with effective maintenance in the environment more and more difficult.

ADJUSTIVE TECHNIQUES CONSIDERED FROM THE POINT OF VIEW OF ENVIRONMENTAL DEMANDS

In order to meet the demands of the environment, the individual must know what the demands are and be able to act in accordance with them. An employee must know what an employer expects of him and must have or acquire the skills necessary to carrying out what is expected of him. Problems in meeting the demands of the environment arise when the individual does not have knowledge of these demands because of lack of information or misinterpretation and when there are barriers of one kind or another to acting in accordance with the demands. The employee might not know the demands of his employer because he has not been given information about his employer's policies or because he misinterprets the information he has been given. He may not have been told what hours he is supposed to keep, for example, or if told, he may not believe that he is really expected to keep such hours. Barriers to acting in accordance with his employer's expectations might take many forms. If it is a matter of keeping certain hours he may have transportation difficulties which make it hard for him to keep such hours, or he may lack the habit of getting up on time in the morning, or he may think that the hours he is expected to keep are ridiculous and resist keeping them as a matter of principle. Various adjustive techniques in relation to environmental demands can be considered in the light of the individual's knowledge of these demands and the presence or absence of barriers to acting in accordance with them.

Withdrawal

Relief from environmental pressures that are disturbing to the sense of well-being can be gained by withdrawal. Such withdrawal may or may not be adaptive. If noise is disturbing, one may withdraw in order to be able to think without distraction and his thinking may enable him to solve important problems. When a schoolboy withdraws from a challenge to fight, on the other hand, he may invite his schoolmates to make him a scapegoat which will, of course, complicate his problems. The conclusion cannot be too readily drawn that a schoolboy's withdrawal from such a challenge would be nonadaptive, however. One boy might be able to withdraw without being made a scapegoat whereas another could not, just as one adult can withdraw gracefully from an argument without gaining a reputation for not having the courage of his convictions whereas another cannot.

Withdrawal often occurs when one is not familiar with a situation or does not know what is expected or demanded of him in a particular situation. One may remain relatively quiet or withdrawn when thrown in with a new group of people until he has learned what topics of conversation he might pursue that will be of mutual interest, or what kind of adjustive techniques he will have to use in the group if he does one thing rather than another. Such "sizing up" of one's social environment may be highly adaptive and is sometimes done with great skill by good listeners who learn a good deal about others by "drawing them out." Adaptive withdrawal of this kind is not particularly encouraged in the American culture even though the recommendation is often made that one should keep his mouth closed and his eyes open. Active social participation in the form of "mixing," "joining," "being one of the gang," etc., is highly esteemed, and the tendency is to evaluate an individual as "odd" if he does not readily join with others. The individual also tends to make this evaluation of himself if he is not a "good mixer," and many who appear to be "strong, silent types" in the American culture probably react to their silence as personal weakness rather than as strength.

Withdrawal occurs because of inability and resistance to meeting environmental demands as well as because of lack of knowledge or unfamiliarity with such demands. A man may withdraw from his wife or a wife from her husband because the marriage partner makes demands that cannot be met or that are found distasteful. A husband might demand that his wife entertain people in ways that she has not learned or the wife may resist entertaining people in the fashion that her husband desires even if she has learned how to do so. Many marriage problems arise because demands are not modified in the light of the marriage partner's ability or willingness to meet them. A wife may demand that her husband make more money than he is able to, for example, and a husband may insist that his wife bake apple pie the way his mother did when she is not able to do so or has different ideas about baking. When such demands are not modified, there is often a tendency for husband and wife to withdraw from one another by not talking to one another, not sharing their problems, and not spending time with each other when it can be avoided.

A history of interactive conflict often lies behind withdrawal because of inability to meet environmental demands. The seclusive adult who is ill at ease with people and does not have the social skills necessary to talking with them, fighting with them, enjoying their company or enduring their company when it is not enjoyed, was the child who did not learn to talk, play, and fight with other youngsters. Withdrawing during childhood prevented learning how to deal with others which predisposed the individual toward further withdrawal and so on. It is this kind of sequence of nonadaptive adjustive techniques that constitutes the adjustive process of interactive conflict. It can readily be seen that fantasy or dreaming would tend to be employed more and more as nonadaptive withdrawal (that would prevent the individual from gaining satisfactions in coping with his environment) continued.

Fantasy

The individual who does not have the social skills necessary to meeting the demands of his social environment frequently dreams of himself as having such skills. The boy who has not met a challenge to fight, for example, may go home and dream about "beating up" his tormentors. A similar kind of fantasy is engaged in when one has not been able to think of a cutting retort to an insult or slighting remark, but thinks of it later and in fantasy "cuts down" his antagonist with this retort. Fantasies of this kind in which one meets and triumphs over environmental challenges and pressures have been called "conquering hero fantasies." Dreams of becoming a great athlete, statesman, industrialist, orator, lover, actor or actress, etc., are all examples of conquering hero fantasy. Movies and novels that have plots of the hero or heroine winning out over obstacles and mastering their environments have conquering hero themes and provide what Shaffer (1936) has called "ready-made fantasy." The success story in which the hero makes a fortune or becomes a great man, or the heroine marries a rich man or wins her lover's affection in competition with another woman, is a popular form of conquering hero fantasy in the American culture. In contrast to the conquering hero theme in fantasy is that of the suffering hero in which one dreams of how sorry people will feel that they have treated him poorly after a great misfortune falls upon him. The man who has been nagged by his wife, for example, may see her in deep remorse in fantasy after he has met his death in an accident. The fantasy has the effect of bringing an end to her demands upon him—while the husband is engaged in the fantasy. Suffering hero and conquering hero fantasy often blend, of course. Thus, if the husband dreams of dying heroically he conquers through his heroism and at the same time achieves the result of making his wife feel remorseful for her mistreatment of him.

Conquering hero fantasy may become an adjustive technique that virtually dominates a person's whole life. Thus, one may be preoccupied for weeks at a time with dreams of fame, fortune, and triumph. The seclusive individual spoken of above whose withdrawal cumulatively led to further and further withdrawal may come to rely on fantasy almost exclusively in order to preserve a sense of well-being. Thus, he may be spending most of his time in bed lost in his world of fantasy in which he is satisfying his needs for recognition and affection and at the same time meeting the demands of his environment with superb efficiency. In reality he is, of course, not approaching such effectiveness in meeting the demands of his environment. A sequence of interactions that reduce this effectiveness is taking place because the individual is relying on fantasy more and more and gaining no actual experience in contending with reality. Such a sequence of interactions is not irreversible, however. That is, it does not necessarily have to continue as it is. The individual may begin to experiment to the best of his ability with coping with his environment, and, in so doing, set in motion interactive integration or a sequence of interactions that increase his ability to meet environmental demands and to preserve his sense of well-being at the same time. The seclusive individual, for example, may begin to experiment with talking with people, being in their company, and so on and thereby begin to gain greater and greater skill in dealing with people. Imaginative activity, it may be added, can be used to facilitate this experimentation as when one thinks about how he might talk with people, handle himself in their company, and so on. In such imaginative activity, which is not too far removed from fantasy, barriers or difficulties are anticipated and the techniques used in dealing with them may, then, be used in real situations later.

Curiosity

When environmental demands are unknown the adjustive technique of holding a questioning and observant interest in one's surroundings can, of course, serve the purpose of discovering what these demands are. A soldier who is new to Army life is appropriately curious about when he is supposed to salute, when he can take leave legally (or when he can take it illegally without getting caught), and other rules and regulations with which he is unfamiliar. Whether one meets particular demands of his environment or acts in accordance with other demands, he is in a better position to cope with them if he knows what they are. Curiosity about one's wife or husband, one's employer, one's neighborhood, and one's culture can, therefore, have adaptive significance for the individual.

One can be curious about modes of meeting environmental demands as well as the demands themselves. Thus, if a man enters a new employment situation and finds that his associates are interested in something such as baseball in which he has had relatively little interest, curiosity about baseball terminology and baseball teams can enable him to learn how to discuss baseball. Such curiosity can be more adaptive than the automatic adopting of responses such as talking about baseball in an attempt to impress others without knowing anything about it. This kind of automatic adopting of reponses is frequently done in an effort to "make an impression" in the American culture. While the impression is sometimes made, it is also true that effectiveness is often lost as the result of trying to "make the impression" without knowing what one is talking about. The individual who develops a large vocabulary, for example, but who seldom has a helpful or original idea comes to be regarded as a fool rather than as a smart man because of his vocabulary.

Curiosity is not always adaptive because acting rather than continuing to be curious will function best at certain times to enable one to maintain himself in the environment. The contractor who must know all the details before he is willing to put in a bid often loses a contract to an individual who is willing to risk action and commit himself with limited but relevant information. The adaptive value of curiosity cannot be underestimated, however, because it is an adjustive technique that can be of considerable help to the individual in meeting new situations. In present day American culture the individual is likely to meet a fairly large number of new situations with which he has had relatively little experience and he is, therefore, by no means completely prepared for all that he encounters. Specialization does not contribute to preparation for future experiences either, it might be added. One person with a considerable amount of advanced training in a particular field, for example, bought a house and commented that with all of his education he had never learned anything about making such a purchase. In a culture that values individual initiative and resourcefulness, curiosity about matters that one has not learned about previously can strengthen considerably the individual's feeling of capability of acting on his own.

Regression

An individual may fall back upon earlier adjustive techniques when his ability to meet present environmental demands is out of reach. One may break down and cry like a baby, for example, when external stress is very great. Such an adjustive technique may be employed when a man loses his job and cannot find a new one or when a soldier has been under the stress of combat for a prolonged period. The reversion to earlier adjustive techniques, such as that of breaking down and crying like a baby, is called "regression." It may or may not be adaptive.[3] When the immigrant to a new country is learning the language of that country and does not know the demands of his new environment, it may be very adaptive for him to revert to his native tongue for purposes of talking to somebody who also knows his native language about the attitudes and expectations of people in the new country. Returning to his native tongue on other occasions, however, may add to his sense of well-being temporarily, but add nothing to his ability to get along efficiently in his new environment. The immigrant's learning a new language, it might be added, makes it unnecessary for him to regress to his native tongue except when he chooses to do so for purposes of recreation or keeping in touch with the general feeling and attitudes of the country he came from. Many problems of preserving a sense of well-being while at the same time maintaining oneself effectively in the environment can be solved by means of such learning. The person who reverts to dependence upon others, in the way that a child runs to a parent, can learn self-reliance techniques that make such regression unnecessary. This learning may depend upon the individual's being able to acknowledge the existence of regressive adjustive techniques that he is using. In one case, for example, a student reported that he did not realize that a somewhat persistent habit he had of running to superiors to ask questions was a regression to childhood habits. When the realization came about, he began to learn habits of acting more independently. His dependent tendencies, it might be noted, were in part continuations of earlier adjustive techniques and in part reversions to such techniques. Regressions frequently have both of these parts, and it is difficult to distinguish between the element of returning to earlier

[3] Regression is sometimes used to refer only to nonadaptive reversions to infantile or childish phases of development. It is used in a different way in the present discussion, as will be clear from the context.

adjustive processes and the mere continuation of earlier adjustive processes.

Although learning new ways of coping with one's environment may make regressions unnecessary, as pointed out above, regression can also facilitate learning. A good mathematics tutor, for example, may take his pupil back to first principles in order to deal with more advanced principles later. A willingness to play a childlike role can also contribute to learning as when one seeks the counsel of an experienced person and thereby profits from the latter's experience. Such profiting does not exhaust the adaptive values that can be found in regression. Relaxation which prepares one to meet problems more effectively is another adaptive effect that regression can have. When one plays "like a kid," for example, he is often better prepared to carry on with occupational responsibilities. The relaxation that such playing can produce is amply demonstrated by the keen pleasure that American fathers derive from joining their sons in running toy trains. In addition to serving the purpose of relaxation, regression can also restore a feeling of confidence through demonstrating to oneself that he is still competent to handle situations characteristic of an earlier period of life. The man who rides his son's bicycle when he comes home from work, for example, gains confidence from demonstrating his skill. This increased feeling of confidence may enable him to cope more adequately with future situations.

Negativism

Resistance or negativism in response to environmental demands occurs when they are reacted to as unreasonable or distasteful. Children are often negativistic about going to bed, for example, when their parents inform them that the time has come for them to go to sleep. Many other instances of negativistic behavior in children can, of course, be cited. They do not see why they cannot pull lamps off the wall or tear books, and often persist in doing so in negativistic response to their parents' commands or pleas not to do so. A certain amount of negativism, it seems reasonable to assume, is to be expected in the behavior of most children. The amount of it depends on a number of factors. Parents sometimes invite it by telling their children not to do things that had not previously occurred to the children. Once the suggestion is made to keep out of the flower bed or not to spill the root beer, the child is often inspired to proceed with forms of negativism that had not occurred to him. Parents may not permit any mischief, however, and when this occurs the child may become so passive that his ability to resist is minimized. Instances have been known, for example, of parents' using sedatives to make sure that a child would go to sleep. When such a practice is followed it is not hard to imagine that similar measures might be employed to keep the child from being a "nuisance." Reprimands for getting dirty or noisy that make the child feel guilty might also be methods used to control the child and eliminate any negativism. It might appear in one fashion or another in spite of parental efforts to eliminate it. Children have been known not to talk, for example, when they have given indication of being able to talk and not retarded in their speech development. Their refusal to talk often turns out to be a negativistic adjustive technique in response to parental overcontrol. Lack of attention from the parent also results in children's using negativistic techniques to gain the attention they desire. A child may knock a glass off the table, wet his pants, play with mud, or pull his younger sister's hair in an effort to gain attention. Even though the attention may be punishing, the need for attention may be so great in such instances as to make the punishment insignificant in comparison to the rewarding aspects of the attention itself.

Adults as well as children employ negativistic reactions, needless to say. A man may be negativistic about mowing his lawn, painting his house, balancing his books, carrying out a suggestion of his employer, shopping for his wife, or not making a left-hand turn. Even though he does all of these things, he may do them with a considerable amount of resistance. The nonadaptive aspects of negativism can be illustrated by the effects it can have upon interpersonal relationships. If a husband is highly resistant to helping with household responsibilities he creates strains in his relationship with his wife that are of no help in preserving his sense of well-being and at the same time fostering effective main-

tenance of himself in his domestic environment. Adaptive negativism can also be illustrated by its effects upon interpersonal
relationships. If a husband and wife refuse to gloss over differences until they have argued them out and found a workable
basis for reconciling them, they make their relationship more
harmonious.

ADJUSTIVE TECHNIQUES CONSIDERED FROM THE POINT OF VIEW OF DEMANDS UPON THE ENVIRONMENT

The various adjustive techniques that have been discussed
thus far in this chapter have been considered in relation to demands of the environment. All of them can be used to deal with
demands upon the environment as well as to meet demands of the
environment. Withdrawal and fantasy, for example, occur when
the individual cannot meet the demands of the environment and
also serve the purpose of getting what is wanted from the environment as when the individual retires from social participation
and dreams of glory and recognition. In his fantasy, at least, he
gets what he wants from the environment. Curiosity not only enables a person to learn the demands of his environment as well
as the modes of meeting such demands, but it also can function
to find ways of getting food, money, prestige, and the objects of
other demands that the individual makes upon the environment.
Negativism, which was also discussed from the point of view of
the demands of the environment, similarly can function to deal
with demands that the individual makes upon the environment.
One may persist in refusing to agree with another, for example,
as a way of trying to get the other person to submit. Negativism,
in fact, is a way of pressing one's own demands upon the environment rather than yielding to demands of the environment. The
members of a football team, for example, are resistant to the demands of the opposing team and press their own demands upon
the opposing team. A similar kind of phenomenon is seen in labor-
management disputes. Regression, which occurs in response to
environmental pressures, may also be a response to demands
upon the environment as when the older child reverts to baby
talk to get the attention the newborn baby is receiving. Many

other adjustive techniques can be considered from the point of view of demands of the environment as well as demands upon the environment. Compensation, duplicity, sublimation, interpersonal opposition, interpersonal dependence, and restriction can be conveniently considered from the point of view of demands upon the environment.

Compensation

Compensation is an adjustive technique of making up for a condition that is felt to be a deficiency or inadequacy. It can take many forms such as swaggering, boasting, dreaming, or lying, all of which can be used to counteract a felt deficiency or feeling of inferiority. A direct form of compensation is found in attempts to remove the condition that is reacted to as a deficiency. Thus, if one does not have athletic skills and feels inferior about not having them, he may try to develop them. An indirect form of compensation is found in the substitution of a new goal, the attaining of which helps to reduce the inferiority that is felt about not being able to attain some other goal. Rather than trying to become a good athlete, for example, one might try to become a good student as a way of counteracting his feeling of inferiority over being a poor athlete. Whether the compensation is direct or indirect, it is an adjustive method that can serve the purpose of meeting demands upon the environment. Trying to become a good athlete or trying to become a good student can both serve as ways of getting recognition from one's social environment.

Direct compensation or attack on what one feels to be a deficiency in oneself in an effort to get what one wants from his environment tends to be considered as praiseworthy in the American culture. The Declaration of Independence asserts that all men are created equal, and although the statement may not be taken literally, it expresses a fairly widespread attitude that a man can make of himself what he chooses. The so-called self-made man is admired and the "underdog" who wins out is accorded great respect. The student with poor scholastic aptitude struggling to prepare himself for a profession and the weak boy lifting weights are examples of direct compensation that illustrate the belief in the possibility of acquiring the ability necessary to get whatever one wants from his environment.

Indirect, as well as direct, compensation is found in the American culture. As with direct compensation, it is to be expected when the individual does not have traits or skills that are highly esteemed in the culture. The boy who cannot play football can easily feel inferior because of the importance that is attached to athletics in the American culture. The girl who does not "measure up" to the cultural standards of sexual attractiveness may also fall into attitudes of inferiority toward herself quite easily. In either case indirect compensation may be used as an adjustive technique to relieve the feelings of inferiority and to get what is wanted from the environment. The girl may come to seek attention through professional or occupational achievement as a substitute for attention from men. A similar sort of substitution may take place with the boy who was a poor athlete and turns out to be an able orator.

Direct compensation is adaptive insofar as it enables the individual to develop ability to make demands upon the environment successfully. Theodore Roosevelt is said to have converted physical weakness into strength by means of direct compensation, and grew up to become a vigorous participant in his environment. Such direct compensation might not prove to be so adaptive when there is little prospect of the environment's yielding to the means employed to satisfy one's demands. The young man who wishes to become an aeronautical engineer, for example, without having had opportunity to acquire minimal scholastic skills stands relatively little chance of achieving his goal by means of direct compensation, i.e., scholastic success. In such an instance, indirect compensation by means of preparation for another occupation would prove more adaptive in all probability.

Although the substitute achievements gained by indirect compensation diminish feelings of inferiority, they do not necessarily alter to any great degree the individual's susceptibility to such feelings. These feelings stem from cultural expectations. As long as these expectations are deeply rooted in the individual's personality, he will feel inferior when he does not live up to them, and the fact of the matter is that they are likely to be deeply rooted in the American culture. A girl cannot help but take seriously, for example, the cultural emphasis on feminine beauty. A boy in the American culture cannot help but take seriously the identification of athletic prowess with masculinity. It is also difficult to escape being imbued with a considerable amount of success-striving in the American culture, particularly if an individual comes from a middle-class background. Some emancipation from cultural expectations is possible, however. Some women do reconcile themselves to remaining single without bitterness in spite of the fact that the culture does not make it easy for women to accept the idea that they may never marry. Many people reconcile themselves without severe psychological "scars" to positions carrying only limited prestige in spite of growing up in a culture giving fairly serious emphasis to the idea that any boy can become President. Although substitute achievements do help to sustain self-esteem, the foregoing examples make it clear that the culture will permit an individual to live without making all of the demands that he has been taught to make in growing up in the culture. A man who is not outstanding in his profession might prize highly his skill in golf and offset feelings of inferiority in that way, but they will probably be counteracted in greater measure if he can release himself to some extent from the idea, which prevails to a considerable degree in the American culture, that occupational success is the principal justification for living.

Duplicity

Deceit or duplicity in interpersonal relationships can, of course, be employed as a means of satisfying desires or demands upon the environment. A considerable amount of sanction is given such duplicity in present-day American culture. It is often recommended, for example, that a person develop a winning smile and an ingratiating manner in order to be able to manipulate people and get what he wants from them, although the recommendation may not be made as baldly as this. While out and out deceit or insincerity is not recommended, the emphasis on the importance of the "front" that one presents strongly suggests that sincerity is not as important as the impression that is made. The salesman, lecturer, politician, and professional man endeavor to say the right thing at the right time, tell the appropriate joke, and know the right people. Popular acceptance of duplicity in interpersonal relationships is shown by the belief that is often held to the effect that "it is not what you know, it's who you know," the implication being that one can be a fraud if he knows the right people. There are, of course, limitations on such deceit and duplicity in the American culture, as Green (1943) points out:

A clergyman, without censure, may dance attendance on a wealthy widow to insure her continued generous contributions to his church, and, in turn, to his career; but if he misrepresents to her the use he is making of her money, he must keep secret that fact from her and his congregation. A physician may simulate a high regard he does not feel for a wealthy hypochondriac, and collect exorbitant fees for that service alone; but advising an unnecessary operation violates the ethics of his profession. The office worker may dissemble an affection for his employer he is far from experiencing, with no too severe inner conflict; but painting a rival subordinate as incompetent, in order to secure the one raise available, may cause the betrayer psychic distress.

Duplicity can prove nonadaptive when it is practiced in such a way as to inspire more distrust and suspicion than anything else. "Many men," as Green also points out, "resent unalloyed fawning, much preferring the other to adopt a pose of forthright self-assertion." Being too polite and accommodating, then, in an effort to manipulate another to one's advantage can be a form of duplicity that is actually self-defeating. It may occur when one does not know the reactions of particular individuals in his environment to such an adjustive technique. Such lack of knowledge might, of course, result when one has been taught to believe that everyone prefers to be treated by others with obsequiousness or excessive politeness. A considerable amount of such teaching takes place in the middle-class American culture.

When the individual possesses demands that his environment is not inclined to tolerate, duplicity may prove highly adaptive. The labor organizer who enters a section of the country that is very hostile to unions, for example, may do well not to advertise his purpose until he has support. The businessman, similarly, who wants to set up a plant or store in territory in which competitors are located may gain advantages in such things as purchasing land cheaply if he is sufficiently deceitful to keep his purpose from being known. Both of these examples illustrate the significance of knowing the environment's reaction to one's demands. Neither the labor organizer nor the businessman of the foregoing examples could act adaptively without such knowledge.

Sublimation

Sublimation is an adjustive technique by means of which socially acceptable expression is given to desires or demands upon the environment that might otherwise be expressed in a socially unacceptable way. Thus, a desire to injure someone who is hated might be expressed by hating the enemy of one's country. Hating the enemy is socially acceptable, whereas hating a member of one's family and desiring to injure him is not as socially acceptable. Reading romantic poetry is often cited in psychological literature as an illustration of a sublimated or socially acceptable expression of sexual desires. Whether sublimation always gratifies the desires that motivate it, as many writers have implied, is open to question. In some instances it apparently does. An unmarried woman who has a desire for children of her own and finds socially acceptable expression of her desire to play the mother's role by becoming a kindergarten teacher, rather than by becoming a mother out of wedlock, probably actually finds satisfaction of her maternal impulses in her work. Whether reading poetry gratifies a sexual desire or merely distracts an individual from impulses to express such desires in socially unacceptable ways, on the other hand, is not too clear. It may depend upon the individual and the significance the poetry has for him, but enjoying poetry could be just that and not a gratification of a sexual desire; it could at the same time serve as a distraction from such a desire. Similarly, hating the enemy of one's country may not gratify the desire to injure a member of one's family so much as it distracts him from the desire, although it might have both effects to some degree.

Sublimation is, of course, highly adaptive at times. The penalties for murder do not enable a person to maintain himself in his environment, and sublimating desires to kill into chopping wood, hunting animals, and verbal lashings, therefore, is more adaptive than murder. Various forms of institutionalized aggression or vicarious aggression such as those associated with prize fighting, football, political contests, and so on may also be adaptive sublimations of impulses to maim people. Sublimation, or an adjustive reaction very similar to it, may prove nonadaptive, however, when a direct expression of a demand rather than a seemingly socially unacceptable expression of it would go far toward maintaining oneself more effectively in the environment. Thus, a wife might "clear the air" by demanding that her husband argue with her or discuss a problem with her, whereas the air will not be cleared if she expresses her resentment by means of vigorous house-cleaning, which she has learned to consider more socially acceptable than arguing with her husband. Many marriage problems, as a matter of fact, seem to stem from a tendency to try to sublimate or avoid direct expressions of irritation and resentment. The chief task of the marriage counselor very often is to teach married couples how to make use of fighting to settle difficulties rather than to teach them not to fight. This instruction may require that a married person learn that his demands upon his environment will not necessarily be reacted to unfavorably by the environment. His previous learning may have made any consideration of the idea that he could demand that someone listen while he "got something off his chest" unthinkable.

Interpersonal Opposition

Since the American culture is a competitive one, there is a certain amount of idealization of opposition to others in attempting to get what one wants from the environment. The ruthless businessman, for example, is sometimes admired and envied for his daring when he runs competitors out of business or "buys" a town and runs it to his liking. He does not earn complete approval, needless to say, because ideals of fair play, honesty, and brotherly love exist alongside the idealization of opposing and fighting others as means of seeking power. Gaining the feeling of power may be done in many ways. Older individuals can get it by ridiculing children, or telling them "I didn't think you had it in you" when they accomplish something unusual, or by comparing them unfavorably to themselves at a particular age as with statements to the effect that "when I was your age, I was doing such and such" with the implication that the younger person is not doing as well. The individual who is accomplished in making cutting remarks similarly gains some feeling of power in so doing. The strategy of making others feel insignificant may be used to gain concrete advantages as well as a general feeling of power. An employer who really intends to hire a man, for example, may tell him that he does not have a very good employment record in order to put himself in a superior position for purposes of bargaining over salary.

Interpersonal opposition can be an adjustive technique involved in a series of adaptive techniques. One instructor, for example, related that his colleagues had been in the habit of ridiculing his field before he went to a certain college to teach. He, therefore, made it a point not only to defend his field but also to attack those who ridiculed his specialty by exposing weaknesses in their logic and information. This opposition resulted in respect for him and his field, although it was sometimes given grudgingly. The respect thus gained put the instructor in a better position to be listened to in faculty meetings, and when he talked in these meetings to a respectful audience he was able to further the interests of his department. This whole sequence of adaptive interactions, of which interpersonal opposition was one, illustrates the adjustive process of interactive integration.

Interpersonal opposition may also be involved in a nonadaptive series of adjustive techniques. One married couple, for example, was in the habit of constantly ridiculing other people both in their presence and not in their presence. Their direct attacks on others produced antagonisms, as when the woman of this couple would make disparaging remarks to another woman about the latter's husband's occupation. The slandering of other people resulted in a feeling on the part of the couple's friends that they too might later be discussed in a highly uncomplimentary way. The outcome of these attacks on others was to leave this couple without friends. After losing the friendship of one couple they would take up with another. An apparently budding friendship would soon cool off and then another would start until the couple was rejected anew by prospective friends. The antagonism that this couple aroused in others did not facilitate maintaining themselves in their social environment effectively, and the taking up with another couple and then losing their friendship being followed by a similar sequence with still another couple affords a clear illustration of the adjustive process of interactive conflict. Failure to perceive the consequences of the environment's reaction to an adjustive technique is also illustrated by the behavior of this couple, in that they were puzzled about why they didn't keep friendships longer. They attributed it to other people's not being bright enough to keep their interest alive, or to the inability of others to have the friendliness and love for people that they possessed in saintly quantities.

Interpersonal Dependence

To get what one wants from the environment, it is often necessary to get help from others. The adjustive technique of seeking help from others can be called interpersonal dependence. It can, of course, take many forms. A man may get another to help him build a house or to loan him money to pay for a house. Illness can also be a form of getting help from others. Recovery from physical illness is sometimes retarded by inability to give up dependence upon others. A person may actually have made a good physical recovery from an illness that has kept him flat on his back, for example, but find it hard to walk because of inability to give up his dependence. Functional ailments or illnesses, which are physical symptoms that do not have any organic basis in infection or injury, frequently develop as a means of satisfying demands upon the environment through dependence. A person may develop a headache that is largely functional, for example, as a way of getting attention as well as service from members of his family by means of apparently justified dependence. The woman who has or nearly has a heart attack everytime her children do something contrary to her wishes also puts herself in a seemingly justified position of dependence that enables her to make demands upon her environment in accordance with her whims. People receiving pensions for either physical or functional illnesses similarly sometimes hang on to their ailments as a way of retaining a justified position of dependence. Such adjustive techniques, it might be added, often function without the person's being aware of what he is doing. The woman who is always about to have a heart attack, for example, tends to believe that she really has a weak heart. Furthermore, it would in all likelihood be very disturbing to admit to herself that she was controlling her children by means of functional complaints. It is also true that such a technique can function automatically with the result that a person has no more awareness of it than he does of how he goes about tying his shoes when he gets up in the morning.

Adaptive interpersonal dependence is shown by the use made of it to gain ability to maintain oneself effectively in his environment. An individual might seek help in order to learn from others, for example, as when the young carpenter consults the older carpenter about tricks of the trade. The child similarly seeks help when he needs it in order to learn to do things better for himself. One might also seek help from a nurse or doctor only when necessary, with the objective of no longer needing such help. Psychotherapeutic help, in particular, can be thought of as the kind of help that can be sought to become independent. To take an illustration from an earlier part of the chapter, a married couple might learn from a psychotherapist how to fight in such ways as to settle their differences and get along without needing the therapist's help.

The nonadaptive qualities of dependence can be seen in the undermining of ability to cope with demands upon and from the environment that can result from its prolonged use. The child whose mother never lets him do anything for himself becomes the adult who has great difficulty in doing anything for himself because of the cumulative effect of a long sequence of dependent interactions. In one instance a mother continued to wheel her child in a buggy, for example, until she was 3 years old. The child was, of course, predisposed to be dependent as a result of this treatment and continued to receive encouragement to cling to her mother throughout childhood. When her mother died after the girl had grown up she was literally thrown into a panic because of the helplessness she felt in facing life without her mother's aid.

Restriction

An athlete often restricts his activities during rest periods in order to conserve his energy and make more vigorous demands upon his environment as the athletic contest continues. A man may also restrict his expenditures and save his money in order to be sure that he will be able to make demands upon his environment at a later time. Restricting or limiting oneself as an adjustive technique has many varieties. It sometimes takes the form of miserliness as in instances, reported in the newspapers from time to time, of a person's dying in an old shack and thousands of dollars being found under the floor boards.

The miser's restriction of expenditures is presumably designed to make it easier for him to meet the demands of his environment and to make demands upon it. The demands he makes upon it are themselves restricted, however. A restriction of demands and activities somewhat similar to the miser's is found in limitations that people place upon what they seek from the environment when they are insecure and unsure of their ability to cope with their environments. An insecure person might stay home rather than take a trip across the city or to another town because of his uncertainty about getting along in strange places and coping with what impresses him as the hazards of travel. Being unsure of one's ability to cope with the environment can also, of course, lead to withdrawal and restriction of demands that takes the form of listlessness and never really expecting to get what one would like to have. Much so-called laziness, in fact, is in reality a matter of discouragement and lack of confidence in one's ability to meet demands from and make demands upon the environment, just as excessive sleeping is frequently not so much a result of physical exhaustion as it is a form of restricting demands upon the environment to a minimum and at the same time avoiding demands from the environment.

The restriction of demands to a minimum can be adaptive in that it can lead to more effective making of demands at a later time. It is nonadaptive when it does not prepare one for future effective maintenance in the environment. Sleep, accordingly, can be adaptive or nonadaptive. It may furnish an individual with new energy to meet demands of the environment and to make demands upon it, or it may serve as a kind of drug that removes the necessity of meeting and making demands for the time being but only creates problems because it is an escape, rather than a method of learning how to maintain oneself in the environment more effectively.

ADJUSTIVE TECHNIQUES CONSIDERED FROM THE POINT OF VIEW OF DEMANDS UPON THE SELF

The individual's social environment is made up of the influence of other people, but as he interacts with his environment he influences it himself. His own influence, therefore, must also be considered a part of his environment. Accordingly, demands of the environment, demands upon the environment, and demands upon oneself cannot be sharply differentiated. When one demands exertion from himself to achieve a certain goal such as submission from others he affects the environment and the demands that the environment make upon him. If others do submit, for example, they may in so doing encourage further domination and such encouragement is a demand from the environment requiring that the individual make some further demand upon himself to meet this environmental demand. Because of this blending of demands from and demands upon the environment and demands upon the self, all of the adjustive techniques can be considered adjustive reactions to all three types of demands.

The blending of the different types of demands spoken of above is also shown by the fact that the individual's expectations of himself are to a large extent taken from his environment. One is trained in cleanliness habits by his social environment, for example, and adopts cleanliness expectations or standards for himself just as one is trained in standards of honesty, competence, and sexual conduct and learns to make these standards demands upon himself. Various adjustive reactions arise in response to such demands upon the self.

Repression

Evasive adjustive techniques are avoidances of facts that the individual finds difficult, disturbing, humilating, or unpleasant to face. If a man is scrupulous about honesty in business dealings but has on some occasion cheated someone, it is painful for him to recall the occasion and he will tend to avoid thinking about it. Similarly, if a boy is afraid of the school-ground bully, but wants to think of himself as brave, he will find it difficult to admit to himself that he is actually afraid. Still another example of evasion is a student's blaming the instructor for doing poor work in a course when he has actually failed to do the necessary studying himself, or an instructor's blaming students for being "dumb" when he has actually not been able to present material clearly. All of these examples indicate that evasion is employed as an adjustive reaction to demands upon the self to be honest, brave, competent, etc.

One type of evasion is repression. It is usually described as "shoving out" of consciousness feelings or thoughts that the individual does not want to admit to awareness. It can be thought of somewhat more clearly probably as perceptual avoidance or not "seeing" what one does not want to "see." It is evident, for example, that there are some events and feelings that people do not care to be reminded of. An appointment with a disliked acquaintance is easily forgotten as is an appointment with the dentist. Dislike of an individual upon whom one is dependent may also fail to be perceived. The true feeling may manifest itself in some fashion, nevertheless. Thus, if one contends that his employer, Mr. Cutler, is a "nice guy," but really has a strong underlying dislike for the gentleman, he may inadvertently refer to him as "Mr. Cutter" and thereby betray his true feeling. The development of repression as an adjustive technique for dealing with feelings is shown in the following case presented by Symonds (*1946*):

Mr. R. is a gentleman who is liked by everyone in his community because of his forbearance, courtesy, thoughtfulness, and fairness. These characteristics represent an almost complete inhibition, at least in social relationships, of tendencies toward taking advantage of another person and outdoing another person in a business deal. The origin of these tendencies can be traced back to early childhood when Mr. R.'s mother and father would show their displeasure when he showed normal masculine aggressiveness. They were horrified when he came home with a bloody nose after a fight and made him feel that to be self-effacing was good and to assert oneself against another person was bad. Now when Mr. R. opposes another person as, of course, he is forced to do on occasion, he feels as though he had committed some sin, and a sense of unworthiness comes over him.

The reference to "an almost complete inhibition, at least in social relationships, of tendencies toward taking advantage of another person" in the foregoing account makes it clear that repression does not have to be an all-or-none process. Mr. R. may not have entirely avoided perception of his own aggressiveness, but it is apparent that he was strongly inclined toward such avoidance. His guilt in relation to such feelings illustrates how an attitude toward one's own tendencies can develop and come to function as a demand upon oneself to disown these tendencies.

The adaptive function of a process similar to repression is shown by the fact that distraction from, or perceptual avoidance of feelings can at times be of considerable assistance to maintaining oneself effectively in his environment. Distraction from anger may save one his job, for example, when he is tempted to "tell the boss off." It has been contended that such an inhibition when one actually knows that he is angry is more properly designated as suppression than repression. As stated above, however, repression does not have to be thought of as an all-or-none affair and when it is not so conceived, the distinction between suppression and repression can be considered one of degree. When one simply distracts himself from anger, still knowing that he is angry, he for the moment at least does not know it as well.

The nonadaptive features of repression are illustrated by the difficulty it can create in finding the reasons for self-defeating forms of behavior. The aggression of Mr. R. of the above case, for example, might be taken out on a member of his own family by long-suffering silence rather than by saying anything when he was displeased. He could in this way make a member of the family feel guilty for having offended him which would be a method of punishing or expressing aggression toward this other member of the family. His failure to perceive it as aggression, however, would stand in the way of recognizing how his own behavior was causing difficulties in family relationships based upon his long-suffering silence.

Rationalization

Rationalization is still another evasive adjustive technique. It enables the individual to avoid recognizing the real desires behind his behavior. The student who tells himself that it will do him good to get out and see a show rather than study is rationalizing if his real reason for not studying is that he simply prefers shows to studying. He avoids acknowledging his desire not to study by giving himself some other reason for going to the show. Rationalization consists of substituting acceptable reasons for real reasons. It involves various degrees of self-deception. The student would probably not have to reflect for long to acknowledge that he preferred shows to studying and that he was "kidding himself" in believing that getting out to the show would do him any particular good. The individual who constantly slanders others, by means of brutal frankness, however, and justifies himself if this behavior is called to his attention by saying that he is only being honest with people, must, it seems likely, "cover up" his own bitterness and hostility to a greater extent than the student must conceal his real reason for going to the show. The difficulty of acknowledging one's own "meanness" because of demands upon oneself to be otherwise, and the rationalizing of the "meanness" are brought out nicely by Fisher (1937) in the following example:

The gossip is a person who gains great egoistic gratification from ferreting out and exposing ghosts in other persons' closets. But unless our gossip is a completely demoralized person she must conceal from herself the true reason for her gossiping activities. She does this by an act of rationalization. Thus, she has just learned of a dark and delectable secret concerning Mrs. Smith's past life. She was told this secret by another gossip, whom she secretly detests, and up to the present moment she is quite guiltless of any reprehensible behavior of her own. But she aches to pass the secret on; for it is only by passing it on that she can procure that tingling satisfaction of a deflated ego's coming to life. Her problem now is to justify the act which she is strongly inclined to commit. She thinks—thinking is as much in the service of a vicious motive as a friendly motive. That is, she rationalizes. Notice her line of thought. She must have someone to whom to tell her secret and she must have a laudable reason for telling it to this person. She runs over her different acquaintances as she washes her dishes. Most of them will not do and besides she has a score to even with Mrs. Jones; for Mrs. Jones recently told her the most shocking secret about Mrs. Edwards. She is only vaguely aware of her envy of Mrs. Jones. But Mrs. Jones persistently recurs to her thoughts. In the intensity of her concentration she drops a dish and ignores the lusty crying of her infant in the adjoining room. Then she has it! Why, Mrs. Jones' son is paying attention to Mrs. Smith's daughter. There is simply no way to avoid it, Mrs. Jones simply must be told what Mrs. Smith was like before her marriage. Conveying the secret to Mrs. Jones is now a moral obligation which devolves upon our poor gossip. "Mrs. Jones, I just hate to tell you this but I feel I must. . . ."

In the above episode it is pointed out that the gossip thinks. Thinking, a process which is involved in rationalization, as Fisher makes clear, can, of course, be highly adaptive. A form of thinking similar to that found in rationalization proves adaptive when an individual has done something that he cannot "undo" and then presents himself with reasons for accepting conditions as they are. It may have been unwise to spend money for a particular purpose, for example, but if deliberation enables the individual to accept his present financial status, and turn his energy to problems at hand, it may be adaptive. The nonadaptiveness of rationalization is illustrated by the fact that the gossip of the above case is prevented from discovering how her own "meanness" and the behavior associated with it can make for strains in her relationships with people.

Reaction-Formation

The evasion of impulses that an individual finds unacceptable to himself may take the form of reaction-formation, the manifesting of behavior that is in keeping with an impulse or desire opposite to the unacceptable impulse.[4] An everyday example of reaction-formation is the urging of guests to stay awhile longer when the urger really has an impulse to yawn in their faces. In such an instance a high degree of awareness of the unacceptable impulse is usually retained. In other instances little awareness of it is retained. A woman who is oversolicitous of her child's welfare may be employing reaction-formation in order to evade recognition of impulses she has to escape the responsibilities of being a mother. There would ordinarily be less awareness of the unacceptable impulses in this case than when an individual has the impulse to yawn in his guests' faces. Strong expressions of protest or disgust furnish additional illustrations of reaction-formation. Protesting that one is really fond of somebody, for example, may be an evasion of a desire to vent his resentment or dislike of this person. Extreme disgust with immoral behavior may similarly reflect evasion of such immoral urges in oneself, urges that are inconsistent with demands upon oneself to be moral.

Reaction-formation is adaptive when it functions primarily to enable the individual to control impulses, the expression of which might only produce difficulty in maintaining himself effectively in his environment. Controlling an impulse to yawn in the faces

---

[4] "Reaction-formation" is sometimes used to refer only to the manifesting of behavior that is in keeping with an impulse or desire opposite to a deeply repressed, unconscious impulse. In the present discussion, the definition is not made dependent upon the unacceptable impulse's being deeply repressed.

of guests by urging them to stay longer might prove adaptive when the guests would take offense at the yawning. Manifesting behavior that is in keeping with an impulse that is opposite to the unacceptable impulse can also be nonadaptive. A case in point would be that of the oversolicitous mother who displays behavior that conceals her impulses to avoid the responsibilities of motherhood and in so doing only increases these responsibilities through making it impossible for the child to learn to take responsibility for himself. Furthermore, the concealment from herself of the impulse considered unacceptable would only render it difficult for the mother to acknowledge rejecting behavior on her part as such. In spite of her oversolicitousness she might reject the child in various ways. Invariably getting the child to bed at a certain time without deviating fifteen minutes or a half hour from that time, for example, could be a method of getting the child out of the way even though not acknowledged as such.

Whether reaction-formation is employed primarily to conceal an unacceptable impulse or to control behavior in an adaptive way depends upon whether it is generated by mild or acute fear. The latter creates a sense of helplessness and predisposes the individual to get away from what is feared at any cost. Mild fear also predisposes the individual to get away from what is feared, but does not carry a strong sense of helplessness with it. The presence of whatever is feared can be tolerated when there is mild fear. The mother who has mild fear or apprehensiveness about her own impulses to escape the responsibilities of motherhood can still recognize these impulses. In so doing, she can engage in reaction-formation in an adaptive way. She might feed her baby, to take a simple example, even when she feels like doing something else. Her impulse to do otherwise is reacted against and evaded or excluded to a slight degree from awareness. The mother who has more accute apprehension over her own impulses to escape the responsibilities of motherhood, on the other hand, becomes strongly preoccupied with evading these impulses. Oversolicitousness may then be employed as a measure that serves the purpose of evasion; that is, it serves to demonstrate to herself that she is a "good mother." This demonstration has the effect of ruling out (and thereby evading) any impulses to reject the child.

Projection

Projection is the attributing of one's own impulses, desires, attitudes, or feelings to others. It serves the purpose of evasion of unacceptable tendencies of one's own when they are attributed to others but not perceived in oneself. Thus, one may attribute his own dishonest inclinations, which are unacceptable because of his demands upon himself to be honest, to others but not perceive them in himself. Hostile impulses that are found unacceptable in the self are often attributed to others and not perceived in oneself. Thus, a married person may contend that his mate does not love him when it is he who does not love his mate. Similarly, an individual may attribute hostility to others by means of a belief that there is a conspiracy against him without perceiving his own hostile and destructive impulses. Such an individual entertains delusions of persecution and might be found in a mental hospital. He might also be found outside of a mental hospital doing quite well in warning others of nonexistent conspiracies on the part of international bankers, Catholics, Episcopalians, or Jews to take over the world.

Projection can be very useful in understanding another person.[5] The best doctor for a sick person may be one who has himself had the sickness he is consulted about because he can understand the person consulting him by attributing feelings he has or has had to a patient who has the same feelings. An older person can also make use of his experience to understand younger people by attributing feelings and desires he had at an earlier period to younger people who have the same desires and feelings. The effort to recall these feelings and desires is frequently not made, as many young people who fail to find understanding from their elders know.

Projection proves nonadaptive when impulses and tendencies of one's own are blindly attributed to people who do not have

[5] "Projection" is sometimes used to refer only to nonadaptive "disowning," or evasion of impulses one finds unacceptable in himself. It is used in a broader sense in the present discussion.

these tendencies. The married person who attributes hostility to the wife or husband that the latter actually does not have may in so doing block manifestations of affection that would otherwise be present. The possibilities of working with the mate to foster the effective maintenance of the family unit would also tend to be eliminated or reduced by such projection. Nonadaptive projection can also be illustrated by a general's guessing wrong when he blindly puts himself "in the enemy's boots" or attributes his own ideas to the enemy when the latter has different ideas. Seeking information about the enemy, on the other hand, might enable a general to project his ideas to the enemy with a high probability of guessing what the latter's next move might be. In such an event, projection would, of course, be adaptive.

Self-Understanding

A girl's demand upon herself to believe that she is a reasonable person might prevent her from recognizing that she is actually hostile in her attitude toward men. Self-understanding would enable her to acknowledge this attitude. Such self-understanding is not easily attained because various demands upon the self give rise to evasive adjustive techniques that prevent recognition of impulses or behavior that is out of keeping with such demands. An understanding of this effect of evasive techniques can in itself be of some value in fostering self-understanding. If a mother can detect her projection of hostility to a child so that she can say, as in a case reported by Rogers (1942), "I suppose I've worked so hard at trying to correct him that I haven't taken time off to . . ." she begins to understand herself. In such an instance she also begins to see what to do about a problem in interpersonal relationships. Similarly, a supervisor who can detect his rationalization of his real desires to dominate others when he says that he does not praise his subordinates because he wants to keep them "on their toes," may solve a problem in his relationships with others. In these examples mere textbook knowledge of definitions of projection and rationalization would not necessarily enable the mother or supervisor to detect their own use of these adjustive techniques. One reason why this would not be true in the

American culture is that it is competitive and individualistic. In such a culture it is important to the individual's sense of well-being to believe that he is competent and outstanding. He cannot preserve this feeling by acknowledging problems that arise because of his own behavior and, therefore, might be expected to evade recognition of the nature of his own behavior to a considerable degree in many instances. The degree of evasion will depend upon the amount of fear or anxiety giving rise to it. Whether the fear is relatively acute or mild, the evasion may fit a cultural pattern so well that it is strongly supported by the sanctioning of the evasive technique employed. Thus, the "sweet" girl may actually have a great deal of anxiety over her own hostile impulses. Her "sweetness," then, could be understood as reaction-formation designed primarily to conceal her hostility from herself. As such it would in itself relieve her anxiety over her hostility, and this relief would be greatly reinforced by the sanction and approval given to her "sweetness."

SUMMARY OF PRINCIPLES

The concepts of environmental demands, demands upon the self, and demands upon the environment furnish a framework for discussing various kinds of adjustive techniques. Although some of the adjustive techniques have been considered primarily in terms of one of these three types of demands in this chapter and some in terms of another of these demands, they can all be analyzed from the point of view of all three types of demands. The demands themselves, furthermore, cannot be sharply differentiated, but they are of value in formulating or suggesting principles, such as the first one stated below, concerning the adjustive process. Two basic principles concerning this process proposed in this chapter are as follows:

1. The necessity for using adjustive techniques arises because of the existence of demands that the environment makes upon the individual, demands that he makes upon himself, and demands that he makes upon the environment.

2. All adjustive processes are directed toward the preservation of a sense of well-being.

Principles pertaining to various of the particular adjustive techniques are as follows:

3. Withdrawal tends to occur in response to environmental pressures that are disturbing to the sense of well-being.

4. Fantasy tends to occur when one does not have the skills necessary to meeting the demands of his social environment.

5. Curiosity tends to be more adaptive than the automatic adopting of responses.

6. Regression tends to occur when the individual does not have the ability to meet current environmental demands.

7. Negativism arises in response to environmental demands when they are reacted to as unreasonable.

8. Both direct and indirect compensation tend to occur when the individual does not have traits or skills that are highly esteemed in his culture.

9. Duplicity can prove nonadaptive when it is practiced in such a way as to inspire more distrust and suspicion than anything else, but may prove adaptive when the individual possesses demands that his environment is not inclined to tolerate.

10. Sublimation is adaptive when direct expression of impulses would incur serious social penalties, but under certain conditions direct expression is more adaptive than sublimated expression of impulses.

11. Interpersonal opposition and interpersonal dependence facilitate interactive integration under certain conditions but foster interactive conflict under other conditions.

12. Laziness, excessive sleeping, and indifference may be evidences of an adjustive process taking the form of restriction.

13. Repression, rationalization, projection, and reaction-formation are employed to evade recognition of impulses not in accord with the individual's ideals or standards.

14. Self-understanding tends to foster interactive integration.

a. Self-understanding tends to be thwarted by cultural demands upon the individual to be outstanding and free of faults.

CHAPTER 4

Interactive Adaptability

Introductory Summary

The word *intelligence* has strong cultural bias. Intelligence tests weight scholastic performance heavily and have not been free from cultural bias. There has also been a tendency to think of them as measuring an inherited capacity. The difficulties that arise from this assumption can be avoided by employing a concept of adaptability, defined as the ability to maintain oneself effectively in his environment, that does not specify that it is inherited or acquired. Such a concept directs attention to the factors involved in an individual's interaction with his environment. Adaptability as defined is strongly influenced by past experience and anxiety and the exercising of curiosity is one of its most significant manifestations.

EVALUATING ADAPTABILITY

Various adjectives such as "dull," "bright," "stupid," "keen," "dumb," "smart," etc., are used in everyday speech for purposes of describing differences in "intelligence," a word that is loaded with strong cultural bias. When people exhibit the kind of resourcefulness and efficiency that is valued in our own culture or subculture we tend to regard them as "intelligent." When they do not we regard them as "dumb," although their resourcefulness may be impressive from another point of view. Porteus (*1937*) makes this point nicely in the following comparison of whites with African natives and Australian aborigines:

. . . I am quite ready to admit, on the basis of my experience, that, in his own environment, under his own cultural conditions, the African native or the Australian aboriginal is not only equal, but superior to the white man. He is a better animal—and that is saying a lot in his favor. He can endure the pains of existence with a fortitude of which I am utterly incapable. Anyone who has witnessed the victims' hardihood when suffering a circumcision or subincision operation by means of a stone knife will not doubt the stark courage of the native.

If humor be defined, not as the ability to see a subtle joke, but as the ability to keep a cheery spirit in the face of the most depressing circumstances of poverty and injustice, then the African has a decidedly superior sense of humor—and humor, after all, is the saving social grace.

If also the ability to support the rigors of a terrifying environment is everyday courage, then the Australian aboriginal is much braver than I. If the assurance that life is essentially worth living under any circumstances is more firmly set in the African native's mind than in mine, then I must give him credit for a more effective foresight and hindsight than I possess. There may be many other ways in which the black man be considered superior and his contributions on the credit side of living should be freely acknowledged. But when it comes to his ability to cope with the white man's environment, which by reason of so-called progress, or of the turn of circumstances, has been thrust upon Negro and aboriginal alike, then I cannot but question their adaptability, especially that of the Australian. The latter, in his natural surroundings is so far superior to the white man, that if he were even equal to the white man in the latter's environment it would be most surprising. If that were the case he would soon inherit the earth.

The cultural bias, suggested by Porteus in the above passage, that is likely to be present in a concept of intelligence, because of the tendency to regard people as "bright" when they exhibit the kind of resourcefulness that is valued in one's own culture and "dumb" if they do not, has existed in the history of intelligence testing.

Attempts to construct intelligence tests received their chief impetus from the work of Alfred Binet, a French psychologist. In 1904 Binet was named as a member of a commission, appointed by the Paris school directors, that was charged with the task of ascertaining which children would be able to undertake ordinary school instruction successfully and which would not. He began his work by looking for problems and information that would be fair to children from all walks of life and that would not be influenced by ordinary home or school conditions. He apparently thought of intelligence as an inherited capacity and his purpose was to find the kind of material that children had an equal chance to learn. If this could be done, a test could be constructed which would reveal differences in intelligence as he defined it, namely, as an inherited capacity. That he was not successful in selecting such material for his test, however, is pointed out by Davis and Havighurst (1948):

> Binet . . . considered the research of Decroly and Degand, which indicated that 47 children tested in Brussels, of "a social class in easy circumstances," showed an average advance in test level of one and one-half years over Binet's "working-class" children. . . . First, he himself conducted a better and more conclusive research, in which he had M. Morlé test one group of children of high socioeconomic status and another of low socioeconomic status. This research also revealed that the children of low socioeconomic groups did less well on Binet's tests, and that they also did less well in scholastic work . . .

It is pointed out above that "the children of low socioeconomic groups did less well on Binet's tests, and that they also did less well in scholastic work." Binet's successors have also constructed tests that equate intelligence and scholastic achievement. Terman (1916), who extended Binet's work in this country by developing the Stanford Revision and Extension of the Binet-Simon Scale in 1916, "followed Binet," as Davis and Havighurst put it, "in choosing only those problems highly correlated with school ratings and school progress." Terman also chose material for his test that distinguished between adjacent age groups. Since the problems were of a scholastic nature, however, it is clear that achievement at the higher age levels on the test would reflect scholastic training. This emphasis on scholastic ability has the effect of giving an advantage to individuals of higher socioeconomic status who do better in school. If it could be assumed that equal opportunity existed in the population at large for acquiring the ability necessary to doing well in school or on a test that reflected such performance in school, then it could be concluded that differences in the school attainment or the test attainment by children from different walks of life could be attributed to differences in hereditary capacity. This assumption is very doubtful, however. One of the reasons that it is doubtful is that scholastic skills and attainment are not taken as seriously or valued as highly by lower socioeconomic groups as by higher socioeconomic groups. People of lower socioeconomic status, therefore, would not be expected to acquire the ability necessary for high scholastic achievement as readily as people of higher socioeconomic status, inasmuch as they are exposed to quite different influences. The difference in such influences brings into question the equality of opportunity referred to earlier in this paragraph. Current intelligence tests tend, however, to be constructed in such a way as to differentiate between good and poor students and at the same time between higher and lower socioeconomic levels.

When intelligence is defined as an inherited capacity and a test is labelled as an intelligence test, it is easy to slip into thinking of the test results as indicators of such a capacity without consideration of the effects of learning on test performance. Binet's influence in thinking of intelligence as an inherited capacity has persisted. As has been pointed out, he began his work by attempting to get a measure of such a capacity by means of selecting material that would be fair to children from all walks of life. Although Binet and later test constructors did not achieve this goal, a tendency continued, nevertheless, to attribute differences in test performance to differences in hereditary capacity. For example, differences between Negro and white soldiers in test performance during World War I were so interpreted; the interpretation was later retracted by the psychologist who originally made it, with an acknowledgment that he had not taken into account environmental differences in background.

The difficulties that have stemmed from defining intelligence as an inherited capacity might be gotten around by thinking in terms of an individual's adaptability, defined as the ability to maintain oneself effectively in his environment, without specifying by definition that this adaptability is either inherited or acquired. For purposes of evaluating how well an individual functions in his environment, it does not matter whether this functioning has been determined primarily by heredity or environment. An analogy might be drawn to the physician's evaluation of the functioning of a man's heart. His interest for purposes of evaluation is not in whether the man inherited a "strong" or "weak" heart or whether he developed the kind of heart he has as a result of the kind of life he has led. Furthermore, when an attempt is made to go beyond the evaluation of functioning and to relate it to causes, it is not reasonable to eliminate either heredity or environment in advance. This consideration is still another reason for avoiding commitment to either heredity or environment in the definition of functioning. Moreover, a concept of adaptability that leaves open the question of heredity versus environment dispenses with the necessity of employing for purposes of evaluation only problems or information that everybody has had an equal chance to learn.

A concept of adaptability as the ability to preserve the sense of well-being while at the same time maintaining oneself effectively in the environment, in contrast to a definition of intelligence as innate capacity, also directs attention to the factors involved in the individual's interaction in his environment. A basic aspect of the nature of this interaction, it seems apparent, is the use made of stimuli as cues, which can be defined as "pointers," indicators, or signs. If a hammer is to be used to nail two boards together, it must be perceived as a cue to the pounding of nails. Perceiving the hammer as a cue of this kind depends upon having knowledge of it as such. Evaluating adaptability, then, would seem to require information about what the individual knows. Vocabulary tests of various kinds are one method of getting such information. In everyday experience, an attempt is also made to find out whether an individual has certain basic knowledge about a particular area before asking him to perform in that area. One does not engage a lawyer unless he has been admitted to the bar, which is presumably a guarantee that he knows something about law. One does not ordinarily engaged a plumber unless it is known, by hearsay at least, that he knows something about plumbing.

Information about what an individual knows does not furnish an adequate evaluation of his adaptability. It is also important to get an estimate of how well he makes use of what he knows. Two mechanics or two physicians might have equal or relatively equal knowledge of machines or bodies. One of the mechanics or physicians comes up with a "bright idea" as to what is wrong with particular machines or bodies more often than the other mechanic or physician, however. In everyday experience differences are noted between different mechanics, different truck drivers, different lawyers, etc., in respect to their ability to make use of what they know in meeting new problems. One personality test attempts to furnish an index of this kind of flexibility by noting among other things the extent to which an individual can perceive movement in material that is not suggestive in itself of movement or lack of movement. The assumption made is that the perception of movement is indicative of resourcefulness of thinking. While it is difficult to reduce an estimate of the ability to make use of stimuli as cues to a test, such estimates are made in everyday experience. Good students are sometimes at a loss when thrown on their own and it is remarked that they know a lot but don't know what to do with what they know. When such a comment is made, an implicit comparison is made between ability to solve new problems and the amount of information the individual has. This comparison might be thought of as an "adaptability quotient."[1] Thus, if one solved four new problems with only two units of knowledge, we might say he had a high adaptability quotient whereas if he solved only one new problem with two units of knowledge, his adaptability quotient would be lower. What has been know as the I.Q. or intelligence quotient that is derived from certain existing intelligence tests compares the individual's mental age (M.A.) which is gotten from test performance with chronological age (C.A.). The mental age divided by the chronological age is multiplied by one hundred. The intelligence quotient places emphasis on the individual's comparison to others of

[1] The "adaptability quotient," spoken of above, is a concept used to illustrate a point of view, not an actual measure or index employed in psychological testing.

his age. An "adaptability quotient" implies a different emphasis in that the individual's problem-solving performance is compared to his own knowledge.

A comparison of one's ability to solve new problems to the amount of knowledge he possesses might be expected to vary from one area of a person's life to another. Thus, one might solve four new problems in mathematics with only two units of mathematical knowledge but solve only one new problem in dealing with people with two units of knowledge about people. In evaluating adaptability, then, it is necessary to remember that it may vary from one area to another. Keeping in mind that adaptability does vary from one area of a person's activities to another becomes particularly important when it is remembered that attention has been directed primarily to scholastic performance in the history of intelligence testing. This scholastic performance can be viewed as only one aspect of adaptability. It has often been assumed, however, that only the activities involved in such performance are indicative of "intelligence." This assumption has been made by educators as well as test makers. The schools, accordingly, sometimes conclude with the support of test results that only those children who excel in scholastic performance are "intelligent." Children coming from homes in which scholastic performance is not highly valued, and who, as a consequence, do not strive to do good work in school nor perform well on tests of "mental ability," may be written off as "dumb." A recognition of the fact that scholastic performance is only one aspect of adaptability might not only alter such evaluations but also contribute significantly to the creation of educational programs that would attempt to develop students' resources in a more comprehensive manner.

Adaptive interaction is not confined to one area of life, but is manifested, whether in large or small degree, in any problem a person copes with whether the problem be scholastic or otherwise. Effective maintenance in the environment involves all areas of a person's life. *The manifestations of adaptability are strongly influenced by past experience and anxiety, and the exercising of curiosity is one of its most significant manifestations.* The following sections will, therefore, deal with the influence of past experience and anxiety upon adaptability and with curiosity as an aspect of adaptability.

THE INFLUENCE OF PAST EXPERIENCE UPON ADAPTABILITY

The relationship between adaptability and past experience is particularly clear in considering demands from the environment. If one has lived in a particular neighborhood or country, he knows from past experience what the demands, taking the form of social pressures, expectations, customs, laws, etc., of the neighborhood or country, are. In the absence of such experience he lacks cues to present demands. Thus, in a certain neighborhood strong social pressure might exist to keep one from associating with a certain family. The name of this family is a cue to the existence of this social pressure for a person who has lived in the neighborhood, whereas it has little or no significance for the newcomer to the neighborhood. Knowledge of the demand in such a case could have adaptive significance whether one chose to abide by it or not. If one associated with the ostracized family, he would be in a better position to maintain himself effectively in his environment by preparing to cope with the penalties that might come from such association. In the absence of the knowledge of the social pressure to avoid the family, such preparation would not be undertaken.

Past experience also affects knowledge of one's own demands upon the environment. From past experience, for example, one may have discovered that he possesses a certain kind of need or demand of which he had not had full knowledge previously. A man might take a certain kind of work that reduces considerably the amount of time he can spend with his family and find that it alters his life to a much greater extent than he had expected. As a result of such an experience he might, then, acquire a fuller appreciation or knowledge of the demand he makes upon his environment to have his family present a few hours each day. Knowledge of demands upon oneself can be acquired in a similar fashion. If one is scrupulous in business affairs but has on some occasion cheated somebody out of a small sum of money, he may discover from the intensity of his pangs of conscience that his demands upon himself to be honest are stronger than he had previously known them to be. Past experience that provides fuller realization of what one's demands upon the environment or upon himself are can, of course, contribute to adaptability. The man who fully knows that his conscience requires him to be honest can save the trouble of trying to rationalize his dishonesty because he realizes that no rationalization will satisfy him. The energy he might have used to little avail in such rationalization can be turned to activities that contribute to effective maintenance in his environment. Thus, rather than trying to justify an occasion on which he has been dishonest, he can simply admit that his behavior was out of keeping with his demand upon himself to be honest. Recognizing that he must take this demand into account in regulating his future interaction, he can then direct his thinking to matters at hand, such as occupational or household problems, that require attention if effective maintenance in the environment is to be fostered.

Past experience determines what skills the individual will use to meet or satisfy demands. If one has grown up in a family whose members entertain themselves by discussing controversial issues, he may acquire skills that he can use in later discussions. The learning of these skills in the first place comes about through significance being attached to stimuli as cues. In learning to debate an issue, for example, hesitation on the part of one's opponent is a stimulus (or combination of stimuli) that becomes a cue to pressing one's advantage. As experience is gained in pressing one's advantage, additional stimuli become cues; his own words constitute stimuli that become cues to enlarging or reemphasizing a point, or letting well enough alone if the total context of cues, including his own words, indicates such a course. When stimuli have acquired cue significance from past experience, they are then available for purposes of using the skills for which they have become pointers or indicators in the future.

The kind of environment in which past interaction has occurred can result in a person's being able to attach cue significance to some stimuli and not others. Rural and urban children differ in respect to their grasp of certain terms. Americans are likely to be "brighter" about automobiles than Europeans, since automobiles are more common in America, or to state the point differently, Americans have cues to the use of automobiles that Europeans do not. A child whose parents are highly educated is likely to know a larger numbers of words and be able to use words with greater facility than a child whose parents' vocabulary is more limited. Skill in the use of language provides a particularly good example of the effect of past experience upon the use of skills to cope with the environment, since the cues to the use of these skills are represented to a large extent in what the individual verbalizes to himself as well as in what others say to him. The language cues available to him depend upon his past experience, and every language has subtleties and nuances which are grasped only through prolonged opportunity to acquire intimate experience and familiarity with the language. Even within the same country, opportunity will exist in one environment to learn more refined or exact language cues that will not be present in another. Sherman and Henry (1933) make this point clear in telling about the concept of distance as expressed by a boy living in an isolated region of the United States:

> Ability to make specific space and time differentiations also was quite undeveloped. When a boy nineteen years old was asked where the next family lived, he replied: "Ovar thar a piece."
> He didn't know what was meant when asked whether the distance was a mile or a hundred yards. Asked where another family lived, he again replied: "Ovar thar a piece."
> One of these families lived a mile and the other about a quarter of a mile away. He could not differentiate distance in definite terms. The nearest any child came to making such a differentiation was that one family lived "not a far piece over the hill" and that the other lived "a good piece through the woods."

Speaking in terms of miles and fractions of miles obviously provides more refined cues to perceiving distance as well as to the use of methods, skills, or techniques to be employed to cover distance than to refer to a "piece over the hill." Sherman and Henry also found that children's intelligence test scores became increasingly lower as the community in which they lived became increasingly remote from the larger culture. This finding suggests (and the suggestion is supported by the fact that the children in these communities were all of the same racial stock) that opportunity to become familiar with certain kinds of cues accounted for the differences in the intelligence test scores. Literacy and schooling, which were greater in the less remote communities, presumably afforded greater familiarity with the cues to the use of skills necessary for higher achievement on intelligence tests.

Studies by Gordon (1923) and Klineberg (1935) also demonstrate the significance of past experience in relation to the acquisition and use of skills. Gordon found that among canal-boat children in England indexes of intelligence test performance in comparison to others of the same age were considerably higher for younger children than they were for their older brothers and sisters. These children are not in close contact with the larger culture, and as they grow older the absence of stimulation from schooling and the training that comes from living in an environment that gives greater stress to reading and allied skills has a more and more retarding influence on performance on conventional intelligence tests. In a study of a somewhat different kind Klineberg found that intelligence test scores were clearly associated with the amount of time children had lived in the city. The higher scores corresponding to greater lengths of time lived in the city indicate that past experience affected the acquisition and use of skills that the intelligence test measured. It is not tenable, it might be added, to hold that the more intelligent individuals moved to the city in the first place; if this were true there would be no reason to expect a relationship between intelligence test scores and length of urban residence. Furthermore, it is just as reasonable to assume that the less intelligent individuals or those who were not interacting adaptively in a rural environment were the individuals who moved to the city. If this assumption is made, the higher test scores corresponding to greater length of time lived in the city demonstrate that "stupid" people are not necessarily doomed to stupidity for the rest of their lives.

Asher (*1935*) brings out the relationship between past experience and the use of skills in discussing the performance of Kentucky mountain children on intelligence tests in comparison to that of city children:

Different knowledge and skills are needed for successful adjustment to an environment where the spinning wheel is still used; where some of the inhabitants are still weaving fine woolen blankets and coverlets and making their own furniture; where churning, canning, butchering, etc., are routines in every home; where axes, plows, mules, etc., are many times as important as books, papers, and pencils.

All of these facts indicate that the mountaineers live in an environment that *differs* from an urban environment or even from other rural environments. In view of these facts, one can hardly conclude that these mountain children are mentally deficient because they make low scores on intelligence tests which were constructed for and standardized on children living in another kind of environment. . . . If the children in a mountain environment are given a test which measures the knowledge and skills in kind and amount of urban children, it seems obvious that the mountain children would be at a decided disadvantage unless they had had approximately the same opportunities to acquire this knowledge and skill as the urban children. The same could be said for racial comparisons. Of course such comparisons can be made, and one can conclude that mountaineers do not know what other children know or cannot do what other children can do, but it is just about as likely that the city children do not know some of the things that the mountain children know, things that may require as much ability to learn as the things which they do not know . . .

Asher's remarks make it clear that variations in past experience result in the possession of different kinds of skills. A mountain boy, for example, is much more likely than a city boy to have had the kind of past experience furnishing him with techniques used in getting a mule to move. The mountain boy is also more likely to be in possession of knowledge of general methods, modes of procedure, and principles having to do with the care and treatment of mules. Various studies demonstrate that such knowledge is a considerable aid to problem solving. Maier (*1933*) found that subjects succeeded better in arriving at solutions after a lecture on "How to Reason" than they did when no general modes of problem-solving were presented. A mountaineer's environment provides more opportunity to learn cues to general modes of handling a mule than a city person's environment. A mountaineer, then, who has knowledge of general methods of dealing with mules will seem "bright" if he is observed when engaged in handling mules, but may seem "dumb" when engaged in other kinds of activities. Conversely, a city person is more likely to seem "dumb" when handling mules, whereas he will appear "bright" when engaged in activities that have a closer relationship to his past experience. A further consideration is that the longer a person has employed general methods, principles, or modes of attack, the more automatic their use becomes. An adult who has had little or no experience with arithmetic may, therefore, seem nothing less than stupid to someone who has been familiar with the basic principles of arithmetic most of his life. Established patterns, moreover, can block the acquisition of more efficient modes of attack. If one's reading skill is so primitive that he has to spell out words and has been doing so for some time, he will have trouble in learning to deal with phrases as units when he reads, even though this general procedure will prove more advantageous in the long run. An adult with the primitive kind of reading skill described might easily be evaluated as a born moron by someone whose reading skills were much more highly developed. The real difficulty, however, would stem from the fact that more efficient general modes of handling written or printed material had not been acquired.

The most efficient use of past experience comes from learning general methods and principles. Many experiments have shown that mere drill or repetition in itself is not particularly effective as a means of improving one's ability to make use of past experience. Woodrow (1927) found that a group of subjects given instruction in general methods of memorizing combined with practice showed marked improvement in ability to memorize in comparison to a group that had merely practiced. The widespread idea that the experience gained in practice, drill, or "exercising the mind" in itself makes for much greater efficiency in future situations is not particularly tenable in the light of experiments such as Woodrow's. If one is able to form generalizations from experience or practice, on the other hand, the experience can contribute significantly to ability to deal with future situations. If a doctor can generalize from his experience with patients so as to recognize particular symptoms as belonging to certain general categories, his diagnostic skills will, of course, be much greater than if he cannot make such generalizations. Similarly, if one can generalize from his experience with people so as to recognize particular characteristics as belonging to general personality "categories" (which enable him to predict people's reaction to his behavior), his effectiveness in maintaining himself in his social environment will be increased. The individual who is at ease with people from all walks of life has been able to form generalizations, whether he has verbalized them or not, concerning personality characteristics that various men have in common. While such an illustration shows the values of generalization, it is also true that adaptability can be decreased by overgeneralization. The doctor who interprets every symptom as belonging to a certain category of illness will make many mistakes in diagnosis and treatment. Efficient use of past experience, then, comes from relating the truly common elements of past experiences to present situations by means of accurate generalizations. Overcaution may prevent a person from generalizing sufficiently; that is, his caution results in his treating every situation as new and different to make sure he does nothing wrong. The architect who has to find out all the building materials that are present in a certain locale before submitting a design when he should be able to generalize from past experience in this locale treats a situation similar to past situations as new and different; his overeagerness to do nothing wrong may result in indefinite postponement of drawing up the design and loss of business. Overconfidence, on the other hand, may lead to inaccurate generalizations as when a team that is too sure of itself overgeneralizes to the effect that all other teams are sure to lose to them; such nonadaptive overgeneralizing is, of course, often followed by rude awakenings.

A final observation to be made about the relationship between past experience and adaptability is that most experience makes possible the anticipation of social pressures or penalties that are brought to bear when one engages in certain kinds of behavior. Effective maintenance in the environment is facilitated considerably by such anticipation. If one does not know the laws and customs of a country he may become involved in difficulties that interfere to a considerable extent with adaptive interaction in his environment. If a man enters a town for the first time, for example, he may not know that certain streets are one-way thoroughfares and, therefore, fail to anticipate a fine and loss of time that comes from driving in the wrong direction. Just as difficulties can arise from not knowing the laws of a country or town and, therefore, not anticipating the effects of violating those laws, they can arise from not knowing people and not anticipating their reactions. One may jeopardize his job, for example, by not knowing his employer and not anticipating his reaction to one's actions. Many employers like to play the role of executive and are not particularly pleased by subordinates who display too much eagerness to play such a role themselves, although they will welcome ideas from subordinates if they can believe they are being consulted rather than "told." Some employers may prefer great outspokenness on the other hand. Accordingly, any rule of thumb for attempting to deal with people is doomed to failure. The personality of the particular individual must be known in order to anticipate his reactions. Green (1943) makes this point nicely in the following passage:

Many men resent unalloyed fawning, much preferring the other to adopt a pose of forthright self-assertion. A certain graduate student at a large eastern university, concluding that academicians must be weary of generation after generation of cringing students, inaugurated a campaign of exaggerated egalitarianism with his professors; he breezily rushed into their offices wreathed in blue smoke from long black cigars, called them "Doc," told locker-room stories with great relish, and invited them out to the local tavern. This treatment delighted younger renegade academicians, in revolt against the genteel tradition of professor-student social relations, but it failed dismally with one old 'gaffer' who, after being conditioned to years of the diffident student, found this upstart a bit unsettling. The student in question made the fundamental error of not modifying his tactics to the given personality.

Green makes clear the basic fallacy in many popular works on getting along with people. A good many such works recommend "greasy obsequiousness," as he puts it, or directing one's efforts toward friendly agreement with everyone. Aside from possible nonadaptive effects upon one's own personality resulting from concentrating excessively on being "nice" to people rather than thinking for oneself, such a rule of thumb practice may also prove nonadaptive because it will not work with many people. Tactics must be modified in accordance with the particular individual with whom one is dealing, as Green shows in the above quotation.

Knowing the effects of a course of action upon oneself as well as upon others has adaptive significance. When a man knows that he gets certain kinds of satisfaction from one work that he does not get from another, he may sacrifice a certain amount of income, because the effects upon him of doing one kind of work rather than another make for more effective maintenance in his environment. Thus, an office worker might be able to make more money as a salesman, but his dislike for salesmanship may aggravate his ulcers so as to reduce his overall efficiency considerably. To take an earlier example, a man might also accept a job that did not permit him to spend much time with his family. Anticipating the possible effects upon himself in the form of homesickness could enable him to pursue a different course of action or to try to do something about his homesickness, both of which could prove adaptive under particular circumstances.

THE INFLUENCE OF ANXIETY UPON ADAPTABILITY

Emotions or feeling states are intimately associated with the sense of well-being. In general they might be said to fall into three categories: (1) feelings such as contentment and pleasure that exist when the sense of well-being is neither threatened nor suddenly augmented or restored; (2) feelings such as joy, delight, and relief that are present when the sense of well-being is augmented or restored; and (3) feelings such as anger, fear, sorrow, guilt, and distress that are present when the sense of well-being is threatened. Anxiety falls in the latter category. A differentiation is sometimes made between anxiety and fear. Since all fear has an element of uncertainty as to what will happen to the individual, however, there is probably no clear-cut distinction between anxiety and fear. It is the sense of uncertainty and helplessness that is characteristic of anxiety. Furthermore, it cannot be too sharply separated from other feeling states that arise when the sense of well-being is threatened. That is, it overlaps with anger, sorrow, guilt, and so on.

Perhaps the most extreme way in which anxiety can affect adaptability is through driving the individual into such complete withdrawal that he becomes indifferent to his surroundings and the demands of his environment. Distortion of reality occurs in extreme cases and the individual cuts out his own world in fantasy in order to find relief from the intolerable pressures of social reality. In less extreme instances anxiety may restrict the individual's exploration of his environment so as to prevent his gaining knowledge of the demands of his environment or of demands that he can make upon the environment. A timid individual may be afraid of asking for directions with the result that he does not know what is expected of him. He fails to discover at the same time that it is possible to demand a hearing from his social environment. Knowledge of demands upon oneself can also be thwarted by anxiety. The demands upon oneself that are associated with sexual urges arouse anxiety when the individual has learned to be ashamed of them and the anxiety leads to their repression.

The lack of knowledge of demands that results from anxiety can have many nonadaptive consequences. A certain amount or what might be called an optimal amount of anxiety, however, can contribute considerably to efficient maintenance in the environment. One may not know with absolute certainty how far he can go in making demands on the environment. Cars might stop when he steps in front of them and raises his hand, but some anxiety about making this test is likely to make for better prospects of effective maintenance in the environment. The same observation can, of course, be made about exploring demands of the environment as well as determining what demands the individual can make upon himself.

Perception, a process of sensing cues, pointers, indicators, or signs, is influenced by sets or states of readiness to attend to particular kinds of stimuli. An interest in automobiles gives one a set to observe automobiles and to perceive indicators of its make, age, general condition, and so on. A set cannot only predispose an individual to attend to certain stimuli but also to exclude attending to others. Thus, one's desire to be accepted by others may furnish him with a set to perceive indications of others' laughing with him but not of their laughing at him. In such a case a demand from the environment would be misinterpreted. It would be perceived as an encouragement to continue certain modes of interaction as a means of gaining acceptance, whereas the actual demand would be to discontinue these modes of interaction if one desired to gain acceptance. Set can result in misinterpreting demands upon oneself and the environment as well as demands from the environment. Thus, one may not perceive his demands upon himself to gain acceptance from others which is at the same time a demand upon the environment for acceptance. These demands upon himself and the environment may be excluded from perception because of a desire, and the set that is dictated by the desire, to think of oneself as "strong," for example, and to attend only to indications of being "strong." Such demands for support from others are, then, excluded from perception because of anxiety lest one be in need of support, help, or coöperation from others. Thus, one may not perceive that he seeks help or that he requires help from another person in a coöperative enterprise but perceive only that he is giving help.

The ideals that an individual has for himself do not have to bias his perception of demands from the environment or upon himself or upon the environment. They can, in fact, be used to achieve a clearer perception of such demands. If one wishes to be "strong," for example, he can realistically consider how dependent he actually is on others and at the same time perceive that a certain amount of help from others is not necessarily a demand to give up one's own individuality. Such realistic perception of demands can be highly adaptive. The individual who knows that he needs help and that he can get help without necessarily "selling his soul" can get it when it is necessary to effective maintenance in his environment. On the other hand, biased perception of demands resulting from holding ideals for oneself in such a way as to limit perception often proves nonadaptive. The individual possessing an ideal of himself as one who stands out "from the masses" may not perceive that he makes demands upon the environment for attention, because making such demands would be out of keeping with his conception of himself as a "man of distinction" or as one who has no necessity for making such demands. He would not be able to "see" his ways of gaining attention, then, because they would signify that he actually desired attention, and perception of this desire would arouse anxiety. A nonadaptive method of gaining attention, such as posing as an authority when he actually was not and being exposed as a "fake," might, therefore, continue in spite of its nonadaptive consequences. To take still another illustration a conception of oneself as a "lover of mankind" can function in such a way as to block perception of one's demands upon himself to exploit or control others as well as his demands upon others to allow themselves to be exploited or controlled. These failures in perception frequently result in continued efforts to reform others or to get them to think in a certain way that results in greater and greater rejection of the reformer and more and more difficulty on his part in maintaining himself effectively in his social environment.

Anxiety may not only bias the perception of demands but the inability to shift approaches and appraise cues to the use of appropriate skills or modes of interaction can also be analyzed as a matter of being overly-intent upon relief from the pressure of anxiety. The frantic student may be so intent upon not failing an examination that he cannot think clearly. The examination he is taking symbolizes the possibility of failure and his tendency is to exclude from perception anything that he may be uncertain about, even though it may actually be the cue to the correct solution of a problem. In some instances the whole examination situation itself is so disturbing that it is responded to with acute indigestion or similar emotional upheaval which forces escape from the pressure of anxiety. The intentness upon relief from pressure, then, predisposes the individual to avoid situations rather than to entertain and evaluate stimuli as cues to adaptive modes of interaction.

The inability to evaluate stimuli as cues because of anxiety can be observed in many everyday activities. People get rattled in card games and make mistakes that they ordinarily would not make. They may also be consistently inept in certain activities, although quite proficient in others. An emotional block of some kind may prevent a man's improving his game of golf in spite of practice, even though he is generally regarded as highly competent in his occupation. The block might take the form of feelings of inferiority about athletics which result in constriction or "freezing" or a "drawing into one's shell," which is a kind of avoidance. This avoidance rules out an approach permitting perception of cues and experimentation based upon this perception that leads to improvement.

These examples suggest that emotional disturbance could be sufficiently general to affect a great many phases of a person's life in such a way as to result in his being evaluated as feeble-minded. In fact, such an explanation might account for those cases of feeble-mindedness, known as *idiots savants*, in which the individual excels in a given activity, such as building miniature boats or adding figures or telling one the day of the week of a particular date within the last hundred years, but is deficient in practically everything else. The outstanding performance in the limited area is suggestive of potentialities for broader adaptability that are blocked by emotional disturbance. Many other instances of low intelligence are quite possibly a function of emotional disturbance. One extreme form of emotional disorder, schizophrenia, is often confused with feeble-mindedness. This disorder is characterized by unresponsiveness and indifference which can easily give the impression of stupidity. It is differentiated from feeble-mindedness because evidence can be found from careful observation or from the histories of patients diagnosed as schizophrenic that they are not lacking in problem-solving ability. The possibility remains, nevertheless, that many cases of low intelligence are instances of schizophrenia that dates from an early age and results in the individual's being evaluated as of inferior intelligence. If the seclusiveness, which is another prominent aspect of the schizophrenic adjustment process, of such an individual takes the form of turning to books or other activities that are regarded as "intellectual," he is not considered "dumb" although he may be regarded as "odd." If the seclusiveness does not take such a turn the probabilities are that he will be considered "dumb" as well as "odd." In either case the seclusiveness indicates certain difficulties in adaptability. The active fantasy life, which is still another aspect of the schizophrenic adjustment process, suggests potentialities for adaptability that has not come about because of emotional problems.

The chairman, executive, or leader who succeeds in getting a group of people to work together, so as to gain maximum achievement from the group enterprise, and who impresses us as being far from "dumb," perceives cues to the moves he must make in order to maintain coöperation and productivity. His perception of cues to the right moves to make is comparable to the mechanic's perception of cues as to what must be done in order to repair a motor. After listening to a sputtering motor, the mechanic does not look at the tires of an automobile but looks under the hood instead. Knowing where to look is essential to perceiving cues to adaptive interaction. While this knowledge is dependent upon past experience, many situations arise which call for selection of the cues so as to make the correct move after getting into the situation. A general can plan his overall strategy, but must adapt his tactics to a particular situation after he encounters it. A salesman, likewise, knows the general merits of his product but will play up one of these merits more than another after he perceives the reaction of the particular customer he is dealing with. A speaker may also vary his emphases on different points or present them in any of a number of ways after perceiving how a particular audience receives him.

Effective maintenance in the environment consists to a considerable extent of the ability to perceive cues to the use of appropriate skills after actually meeting a situation. This ability is dependent, among other things, upon the individual's readiness to endure the discomfort of not being sure of how to handle a situation in advance. Adaptability, therefore, does not necessarily rest upon the individual's being perfectly sure of himself, but can arise instead from the uncertainty that is involved in waiting to see what action might be appropriate. Bettelheim (1947) describes an instance of this "wait and see attitude" very clearly in the following description of an experience in a German concentration camp:

The prisoners seemed convinced that the Gestapoman on duty could not see through their schemes. Moreover, they neglected to take into account the fact that he might be an individual with personal biases and that it might be advantageous to appeal to these. Finally they asked me about my plans. I denied having definite plans and replied that, instead, I preferred to observe the Gestapoman's behavior, particularly his way of dealing with other Jewish prisoners who suffered from frostbite as I did, and to proceed on the basis of these observations. I concluded that I thought it undesirable to follow a preconceived plan, because it was difficult to anticipate the reactions of an unknown person. The prisoners' reactions to this statement were similar to those in previous situations in which I had thus formulated my ideas on how to deal with Gestapomen. They asserted that one Gestapoman was like the other. They accused me of not wanting to share my plan with them, or of not having any plan and intending to use one of theirs. These accusations were couched in abusive language. It obviously annoyed them that I was ready to meet the enemy unprepared.

Waiting to perceive the cues to adaptive modes of interaction, as illustrated by the above passage, requires that the individual permit himself to be uncertain. Idealization of fearlessness can, of course, militate against the individual's permitting himself such uncertainty. An attempt to instill admiration of fearlessness is shown by one case which involved training a child in the attitude that "we are never afraid." This child's fear and shame over the fact that he did become afraid were so acute that he was virtually panic-stricken. Although idealization or training in idealization of fearlessness in the American culture may not ordinarily reach such an extreme, it is also true that shame tends to be associated with fear in this culture. When this shame is "learned too well," it can undermine what might be called adaptive uncertainty.

The anticipation of consequences of one's modes of interaction may not occur, because "self-esteem anxiety" has prevented the perception of these consequences. The man, previously discussed, who thought people were laughing with him rather than at him, did not perceive the consequence of the behavior that resulted in his actually becoming an object of ridicule. It can readily be understood that he would not want to think of himself as a person who could become an object of ridicule and would, therefore, tend to avoid perception of any indications that this might be the case. The protection of self-esteem, then, is one important reason for failure to perceive and anticipate consequences. The individual who takes pride in his ability to manipulate and control people may fail to perceive that he actually antagonizes others because his self-esteem is dependent upon his believing that he can bluff successfully or that he can "take people in" without their knowing it. His distorted perception of the consequences of his modes of dealing with people prevents his anticipating these consequences in the future.

Protection of self-esteem may not only take the form of failure to perceive how others react to one's behavior, but it may also take the form of not perceiving the behavior itself. Thus, a man might perceive that he is laughed at, but perceive little or nothing about the behavior that resulted in his getting laughed at. It is, of course, well known that we have trouble in seeing ourselves as others see us. This difficulty in being objective about oneself or perceiving one's own ways of acting can be a barrier to the anticipation of consequences. Thus, a parent may perceive that his child doesn't like him but fail to perceive what he is doing that results in the child's disliking him; the perception does not occur because it would arouse anxiety in the form of a blow to the parent's self-esteem. Being unable to perceive what he is doing tends to obscure the relationship between his behavior and its consequences, and the possibility of anticipation of the consequences of the behavior in the future is reduced at the same time.

It might be noted at this point that an individual may not only fail to anticipate the results of his behavior because of protection of self-esteem but also because the results were not "brought home" in the first place. Thus, if one has consistently broken laws or violated social conventions but has been spared any serious penalties for such behavior, he will not anticipate penalties for socially disapproved behavior. Furthermore, he may very well develop an attitude that penalties are not to be expected for such behavior. If penalties are finally encountered, they are perceived as unreasonable acts on the part of the social environment rather than as consequences of his own actions. Since they are not perceived as consequences of his own action, they will not be anticipated as consequences of this action in the future.

An optimal amount of anxiety, as has already been suggested, can function to enable an individual to anticipate consequences in an adaptive way. It might be adaptive for a man to consider with a certain amount of caution the consequences of asking his employer for a raise at one time rather than another. Strong anxiety, on the other hand, frequently results in "grasping at straws" rather than pausing to consider the consequences of a course of action. The "big operator" with million-dollar schemes, for example, is in reality often possessed of more anxiety than confidence in spite of his apparent assurance. His schemes are attempts to reassure himself and relieve his anxiety rather than brilliantly thought-out plans.

CURIOSITY AS AN ASPECT OF ADAPTABILITY

New situations can produce uncertainty because the individual does not know the demands or requirements of his environment in these situations. Curiosity and what has been called reality testing can enable the individual to ascertain these demands. Thus, a trial lawyer faced with an unusual courtroom situation may become curious, form hypotheses about the reactions of his witness, and proceed to test these hypotheses by trying various lines of questioning or by speaking in a certain tone of voice. The formulation and testing of hypotheses might be done later rather than at the particular time by means of observation, thinking, and talking with other lawyers. In the absence of becoming curious in the first place, no test could be made to determine what the behavior of the witness called for. The lack of curiosity about what one's environment calls for in such an instance might stem from an overgeneralization to the effect that all witnesses are alike, resulting in categorizing the behavior of a particular witness incorrectly. Just as lack of curiosity can prevent gaining knowledge of environmental demands, it can also prevent knowing what demands one can make on the environment. A boy might assume that a girl would not let him kiss her good night rather than being curious and subjecting to test the hypothesis that he might be able to kiss her. A reserved person, similarly, sometimes goes on the assumption, of which he may not be aware himself, that he could never be outspoken without being severely penalized when the fact of the matter is that he could often gain more consideration by such outspokenness than by remaining reserved. Such a person might find through curiosity and reality testing that he makes unnecessary demands upon himself to be reserved. An overly conscientious person also makes unnecessary demands upon himself and also misinterprets the demands of the environment. A zealous housewife, for example, would not necessarily be criticized by guests because her house was not always in perfect order, or even if she were, such criticism might not be as damaging as she assumes. Subjecting herself to such criticism, or the chance of getting it, would be a form of reality testing that could alter the demands she makes upon herself as well as her interpretation of pressures from her social environment. The individual who accommodates others to the extent of "being taken advantage of" might also discover through curiosity and reality testing that he can keep friendships without invariably sacrificing his own interests. This point was nicely illustrated in the motion picture, "The Snake Pit," in a scene in which the heroine who had made considerable recovery from a mental illness gave one cigarette rather than a whole pack of cigarettes to a fellow patient; her comment was that when one was mentally well he did not have to give away everything.

Curiosity, as was pointed out in the previous chapter, can be a highly adaptive adjustive technique or skill. It stands in contrast to relying on standard solutions to problems rather than finding one's own solutions. Thus, one might try to find out what everybody has said about a given subject rather than permitting oneself any curiosity about the subject. Curiosity can be dangerous, nevertheless, as the popular saying about its killing a cat suggests. Erich Fromm (1941) makes some very discerning observations concerning the way in which it can be blunted during the course of a person's development in the following passage:

> The suppression of critical thinking usually starts early. A five-year-old girl, for instance, may recognize the insincerity of her mother, either by subtly realizing that, while the mother is always talking of love and friendliness, she is actually cold and egotistical, or in a cruder way by noticing that her mother is having an affair with another man while constantly emphasizing her high moral standards. The child feels the discrepancy. Her sense of justice and truth is hurt, and yet, being dependent on the mother who would not allow any kind of criticism and, let us say, having a weak father on whom she cannot rely, the child is forced to suppress her critical insight. Very soon she will no longer notice the mother's insincerity or unfaithfulness. She will lose the ability to think critically since it seems to be both hopeless and dangerous to keep it alive. On the other hand, the child is impressed by the pattern of having to believe that her mother is sincere and decent and that the marriage of the parents is a happy one, and she will be ready to accept the idea as if it were her own.

The suppression of curiosity and critical thinking tends, of course, to go hand in hand with knowing or believing what it is safe to know or believe. It is safer for the girl to believe that her mother is not disloyal to her father, since any expression of this belief would bring punishment from her mother upon whom she is dependent and with whom she can get along only by not being critical of her.

Knowing or believing only what is safe to believe constitutes an exclusion of curiosity or a kind of rigidity that may run through a person's whole thinking. Rokeach (1948) tested the hypothesis that the rigidity characteristic of biased persons' thinking about social problems was not confined to thinking about social problems but would manifest itself in thinking about other problems as well. One method he used of testing the hypothesis was to have subjects "solve problems in which required quantities of water were obtained by manipulating three jars of given capacities." He goes on to point out that, "A set was established by presenting problems solvable by only complicated method. Then followed critical problems solvable both by a complicated and by a simple method." The results of this study supported the hypothesis that the rigidity of thinking about social problems was also present in handling other problems; the more biased subjects exhibited greater rigidity by not switching over to the simple method of solution as often as the less biased, for example. Rokeach also found that the more biased subjects made greater use of scratch paper in solving the problems, a greater use that could not be attributed to differences in arithmetical ability since his procedure ruled out such differences. The purpose in determining whether greater use was made of scratch paper by the more biased subjects, who were expected to be more rigid and automatic in their responses to the problems, according to the hypothesis, is explained as follows:

It seemed reasonable to suppose that the use of scratch paper might mean that the subject did not really perceive the problem as a whole but rather saw the problem as being composed of several parts which, when manipulated in a stereotyped temporal and positional fashion, would automatically and mechanically lead to the "correct" solution. It was as if the individual had to use a "crutch" in order to subtract one- or two-digit numbers from each other. It was as if the subject was asked to add 10 and 4 and, instead of giving the solution immediately, had to avail himself of an electric calculator, punch in the number 10, then punch in the number 4, and then read off the sum from the dial or printed tape.

The failure to perceive the problem as a whole that is spoken of in the above quotation can be thought of as resulting from lack of curiosity. An inquiring or curious estimating of a situation can put an individual into a position that enables him to perceive a problem as a whole and to select cues to the most efficient ways of dealing with the problem. Assuming, for example, that one did not know immediately the sum of ten plus four, he might proceed by raising the question as to what ten plus four would be likely to be, whereupon he might get a visual image of 10 + 4 which becomes the cue to 14. Simple as this illustration may be, it indicates the difference between a procedure based upon one's own curiosity and the stereotyped or rigid approaches to problem solving that Rokeach describes above.

Lack of curiosity leads to failure to anticipate consequences that is illustrated by the student who memorizes everything he is required to know but finds himself unable to use his information. One can memorize the multiplication table but if he cannot figure out that working for ten weeks at fifty dollars a week yields earnings of five hundred dollars, he cannot anticipate his future purchasing power. The lawyer, spoken of previously, who persists in stereotyped ways of handling witnesses, rather than becoming curious about the reactions of an unusual witness, does not anticipate courtroom problems that may arise in the future. Reliance on standard solutions or rules of thumb rests on the assumption that foresight is unnecessary or that the rule or standard practice will take care of any eventuality that might arise. The student who simply does what he is told without exercising his own curiosity or the lawyer who follows a stereotyped method of cross-examining witnesses proceeds on the assumption that these methods will take care of everything. Curiosity, on the other hand, implies a readiness to learn and a tentative attitude toward the techniques or skills one uses in coping with his environment. This very tentativeness constitutes an alertness to consequences that enables the individual to maintain himself effectively in his environment. The competent boxer has an alertness to what his opponent will do when he uses a certain style of boxing. He persists in this style when it is clear that his opponent is unable to defend himself effectively, but at the same time is sufficiently tentative about its use to shift to another style if his opponent begins to catch on to it. A similar alertness to consequences is found in the individual who places neither too much nor too little trust in others but adapts his modes of interaction to particular circumstances and particular individuals.

SUMMARY OF PRINCIPLES

1. Evaluations of intelligence tend to be biased by the values of the culture.

2. Adaptability tends to vary from one area of a person's life to another.

3. Adaptive interaction is facilitated by making use of stimuli as cues, "pointers," or indicators.

4. The manifestations of adaptability are influenced by past experience.

   a. Past experience is a factor determining what stimuli a person will attach cue significance to.

   b. The most efficient use of past experience comes from learning general methods and principles.

   c. The learning of general methods and principles varies with past experience.

   d. Past experience affects knowledge—which is of adaptive significance—of a course of action upon oneself as well as upon others.

5. The manifestations of adaptability are influenced by anxiety.

   a. A set or state of readiness, including a set based upon anxiety, can result in misinterpreting demands upon oneself and the environment as well as demands from the environment.

   b. Inability to shift approaches and appraise cues to the use of appropriate skills can be analyzed as a matter of being overly intent upon relief from the pressure of anxiety.

   c. Perceiving cues to the use of appropriate skills after actually meeting a situation is dependent, among other things, upon the individual's ability to endure the anxiety of not being sure of how to handle a situation in advance.

   d. Anticipation of consequences of one's modes of interaction may not occur because "self-esteem anxiety" has prevented the perception of these consequences.

6. The exercising of curiosity tends to facilitate adaptative interaction.

   a. Curiosity can function to enable the individual to ascertain demands from the environment and demands that can be made upon the environment.

b. The suppression of curiosity and critical thinking tends to go hand in hand with knowing or believing what it is safe to know or believe.

c. Rigidity in thinking or exclusion of curiosity may run through all aspects of a person's thinking.

d. Lack of curiosity tends to lead to failure to anticipate consequences.

CHAPTER 5

Interactive Learning

Introductory Summary

As the individual interacts in his environment he learns. He learns something no matter what he does. The learning may be planned or unplanned, or "positive" or "negative." The concept of learning environment has become more and more prominent in the thinking of psychologists, sociologists, and cultural anthropologists, all of whom are interested in man's behavior. One of the major reasons for seeking an explanation of differences between people in terms of learning is that cultural groups differ widely in their outlooks and ways of life. The great variations in ways of life that are found from one culture to another cast doubt upon a conception of man as having a basic, hereditary "nature" that will tend to make men alike no matter what their environment. Still another reason for directing attention to man's environment as a learning environment is that it cannot automatically be assumed, as has often been done, that a characteristic or mode of behavior is inherited simply because it runs in families.

The individual learns to interact in his environment in accordance with the influences upon his sense of well-being. These influences are rewards and punishments. Cultures and subcultures are learning environments that make provision for training the individual in socially acceptable modes of interaction through the use of reward and punishment. The values that a person has for himself are in large part values that are held in his culture, or some part of his culture, that he learns to adopt as values for himself.

Adaptive interaction in one's environment takes place when one can profit from punishment and continue to learn to get along effectively in his environment. An individual may not profit from punishment, because he has always been able to circumvent loss of support when he might have been punished. Profiting from punishment so as to continue to learn to get along effectively is dependent upon experiencing loss of support, but not to the extent of its creating disabling fear orientations. Punishment can be administered without disabling fear orientations arising. When one has not been able to circumvent punishment but has not been made to feel worthless, either, he does not develop strong anxiety over his own characteristics. Since he can profit from punishment and continue to seek rewards from his environment, he maintains himself effectively in his environment while preserving his sense of well-being. His interaction is, therefore, adaptive or integrative.

INTERACTION AS A LEARNING PROCESS

As the individual interacts in his environment he learns. As the child interacts with his parents he learns attitudes and feelings toward them that generalize to other figures of authority. As the parent interacts with his child he acquires modes of response to the child. These modes of response will already have been determined by previous learning to a large extent, but will still be affected by present and future learning. Thus, a father may have learned to be companionable to children but the total family situation, including the child's relationship to the mother, will affect his learning of attitudes toward and modes of companionship with a particular child. One learns something no matter what he does. If he changes a tire, he may learn a better method of getting a tire off a wheel or simply a stronger distaste than he already had for changing tires. Furthermore, the learning may be planned or unplanned or "positive" or "negative." A part of the learning that goes on in the classroom is ordinarily planned. Teachers plan the learning of the alphabet, American history, grammar, and so on, but a large part of the learning that goes on in the classroom is unplanned. Attitudes of liking or disliking teachers and subjects are learned without any formal arrangement having been made for them to be learned in advance. Whether learning is "positive" or "negative" depends upon the point of view that is adopted toward what is learned. If one learns to speak clearly, the learning is usually regarded as "good" or "positive." If one stutters, on the other hand, the acquisition of the speech mannerisms he has is usually regarded as "negative." Learning occurs in either case, and it is largely in terms of learning that differences between people in speaking, acting, and thinking can be explained. A Chinese individual growing up in America learns American attitudes, values, and mannerisms. An American growing up in China learns Chinese attitudes, values, and mannerisms. To state the matter differently, interaction in a Chinese learning environment results in one kind of personality, whereas interaction in an American learning environment results in a different kind of personality.

The concept of learning environment has become more and more prominent in the thinking of psychologists, sociologists, and cultural anthropologists, all of whom are interested in man's behavior. One of the major reasons for seeking an explanation of differences between people in terms of learning is that cultural groups differ widely in their outlooks and ways of life. Miller and Dollard (1941) cite an example, in this connection, of two tribes, one of which was warlike and the other peaceful. Environmental conditions can account for a whole tribe's becoming warlike or otherwise in its general mode of life. If a tribe has been subjected to attack from other tribes, for example, it might be expected that this tribe would learn to become warlike, and that the warlike ways of living would be transmitted from one generation to another through the younger generations' learning from the older. On the other hand, a tribe might have been repeatedly beaten in battle and learned to cope with attacking tribes by nonwarlike methods, because warlike methods have resulted in more loss than gain. Techniques of passive resistance, for example, might be learned and transmitted by a learning process from one generation to another.

The great variations in ways of life that are found from one culture to another cast doubt upon a conception of man as having a basic, hereditary "nature" that will tend to make men alike no matter what their environment. Homosexuality tends to be scorned in the American culture, for example, but it was regarded as an ideal love relationship in ancient Greek culture. It is interesting to note that homosexuality is popularly thought of as an inherited "defect" in the American culture when it can actually be explained by reference to the individual's learning environment. Probably the reason that it is thought of as inherited is that it is not the usual, ordinary, or accepted practice in the culture. The tendency, therefore, has been to assume that it is foreign to man's basic nature, and that when it does occur it can only be accounted for as an hereditary oddity. The fact that practices such as homosexuality are usual and accepted in other cultures is another reason that the concept of learning environment has become more and more prominent in the thinking of psychologists and other students of man's behavior.

Still another reason for directing attention to man's environment as a learning environment is that it cannot automatically be assumed, as has often been done, that a characteristic or mode of behavior is inherited simply because it runs in families. It is popularly believed that alcoholism is inherited, because both a father and a son or a grandfather and a grandson were drunkards. The fact of the matter is that fathers and sons and grandfathers and grandsons also speak the same language, as Maslow and Mittelmann (1951) have pointed out. It is generally recognized that the development of ability to speak a language is dependent upon having a certain kind of learning environment. There is also good reason for believing that alcoholism, "insanity," and many other forms of behavior that have been believed to be inherited are actually dependent upon the individual's learning environment. The life histories of two "insane" or psychotic individuals in the same family reveal that they have both had learning experiences that could result in the development of "insanity" or psychosis. Alcholism, similarly, can be traced to learning experiences that result in lack of confidence and the acquiring of drinking as a method of relieving the anxiety and insecurity accompanying this lack of confidence.

One last observation, of considerable practical importance, to be made about the concepts of heredity and learning environment is that individuals who bring social disapproval to a family are often written off as "black sheep" who have a "bad hereditary strain." Writing them off in this way tends to relieve the family of any responsibility for the unacceptable conduct of the "black sheep." The family's concern about its own good name being reflected upon, nevertheless, implies a fear that it might be thought that the individual became what he is as a result of the family learning environment. The fact of the matter is that identical twins, who develop from the same fertilized ovum and have the same heredity, may have very different personalities when they grow up in different learning environments. The fear that a family has about its own good name being reflected upon when one of its members goes "astray" is, therefore, well founded. The probability is that the family learning environment was largely responsible for the "black sheep"'s being what he is, just as different learning environments result in identical twins becoming different kinds of individuals. One example of personality differences between identical twins stemming from different learning environments is furnished by Newman (1940) in the following description of the twins, Mildred and Ruth:

Mildred was the foster child of a banker who was also the mayor of a medium-sized city. He was a well-educated man whose home was a gathering place of interesting and cultured people. Mildred entered into all of these activities. Ruth, on the other hand, was the foster child of a man of little education who was a foreman of laborers. The foster mother disapproved of Ruth's normal associates and kept her at home after school hours, with dolls as her only companions. On all the personality tests Ruth showed an inhibited character, shy, diffident, silent, with lisping speech and an unhappy expression, while Mildred was much more confident, unembarrassed, talkative, happy in facial expression and spoke without a trace of lisping.

Although the family learning environment often accounts for a "black sheep"'s becoming what he is, it does not follow that families deliberately plan to train their members as "bums," "crooks," "nuts," or "fools." As was stated earlier in this discussion, learning does not have to be planned. Nevertheless, it takes place as the individual interacts in his environment whether it is planned or not. The fact that learning of one kind or another does take place as the individual interacts and that it profoundly influences future interaction means that it must be understood if interaction itself is to be understood.

LEARNING WHILE INTERACTING IN THE CULTURE

As the individual interacts in his culture, he learns. The learning environments of the culture include the family, neighborhood, play group, gang, school, church, occupational organizations, and so on. Rewards and punishments are administered in these learning environments and result in orientations that dictate the individual's modes of interaction in the culture. Many of the orientations toward his culture that he learns are internalized values. These internalized values consist, in general, of ideals that the individual has for himself and restraints that he imposes upon himself that correspond to values, rules, and moral standards that exist in his social groups.

Reward and Punishment in Social Environments

In striving to preserve his sense of well-being, the individual seeks support or coöperation from his environment. When this support is not forthcoming his well-being is threatened, because goal attainment or preservation of his sense of well-being meets with interference. This interference constitutes frustration or punishment, and from the individual's point of view it is a lack of support or coöperation on the part of the environment in the enterprise of preserving his sense of well-being, an enterprise in which he is constantly engaged. Lack of support takes various forms, both direct and secondary. Imprisonment is a direct punishment. The threat of imprisonment is a secondary punishment. In and of itself it does not cut the individual off from his environment, but he has learned to attach an "ostracism significance" to such a threat. Having learned to attach this significance to it, it becomes a real interference because it reduces his sense of control over his environment by indicating that he is not able or might not be able to attain his goals. A frown from a friend or lover is another secondary punishment or frustration. The friend's or lover's frowning in and of itself does not constitute lack of support or acceptance any more than the threat of imprisonment in and of itself constitutes lack of support, but it has been associated with lack of acceptance in the past and has acquired the significance of rejection. Having acquired this significance, it is a real interference, punishment, or frustration, because it reduces the individual's sense of control. The many varieties of social punishment taking the form of disapproval and ridicule are secondary. They are painful to the individual because they signify real punishment, frustration, or lack of support from the environment, and having gained this significance they become real punishments or frustrations in that they reduce confidence in the ability to attain goals.

When support or coöperation is forthcoming from the environment, the sense of well-being is enhanced, because goals are attained or goal attainment is facilitated; in both cases well-being is preserved. Goals include food, water, bodily comfort, acceptance in one's culture, safety, and so on. *The attainment of goals or the facilitating of their attainment constitutes reward.* Rewards as well as punishments take many forms and are also both direct and secondary. Attending to the infant's bodily needs is direct reward. The mother's smile that accompanies the attention is a secondary reward. Originally the smile in and of itself does not constitute goal attainment or the facilitating of goal attainment. It acquires goal-attainment significance for the infant, however, and having acquired this significance it becomes a real reward for the individual because it preserves his sense of well-being by providing assurance that goals will be attained. The many varieties of social reward in the form of praise, recognition, and approval are secondary rewards. They signify goal attainment and having acquired this significance, they constitute real rewards because they add to the individual's sense of well-being by providing assurance that goals will be attained.

Cultures and subcultures are learning environments that make provision for training the individual in socially acceptable modes of interaction through the use of reward and punishment. Acceptable modes of behavior in one learning environment are not acceptable in another, and a form of behavior that is rewarded in one learning environment may be punished in another. Informality in interpersonal relationships, for example, tends to meet with approval in America, whereas it is more likely to meet with disapproval in England. Furthermore, rewards and punishments vary from one social environment to another within the same culture. This variation sometimes produces conflict as when a boy is rewarded for dressing in a certain way in the family environment and ridiculed for dressing this way in the neighborhood gang. Another example of behavior that is rewarded in one social environment and not another is respect for law enforcement agencies and officials. This respect tends to be encouraged and commended at one class level whereas it tends to be scorned at another. Social classes, then, can be conveniently thought of as learning environments. Socially acceptable modes of interaction vary considerably from one class to another. One way in which they vary is in respect to drinking habits and attitudes, as Miller and Dollard (*1941*) show in the following description of drinking practices based on data gathered on a small American town:

In the lower class, both men and women may drink, although the men seem to drink with much more freedom from criticism than do the women. There is little punishment for overindulgence and no urgency to "drink like a gentleman" among lower-class men. Getting drunk is not frowned upon. Lower-class individuals drink episodically —usually when they happen to have the money necessary to buy liquor. If these conditions were unknown, the drinking of a lower-class person might seem to be a very marked personality trait. Lower-middle-class individuals in the very same town drink little or not at all. They have religious scruples against it and are afraid that the habit of drinking would lead to their being confused with lower-class persons. Upper-middle-class people draw a distinction between men and women so far as drinking is concerned. The men drink quite freely, especially in their clubs, but they do not engage in mixed drinking with women. Upper-middle-class wives are expected to refuse alcohol when it is offered. In the upper class, by contrast, both men and women drink, and there is no moral significance attached to drinking.

There is, however, a code involved. While an upper-class individual is allowed to drink a good deal, he must "drink like a gentleman." He is punished with social scorn if he allows his drinking to lead to disorderly or aggressive behavior, such as is often characteristic of lower-class people.

If an individual moves from one of these social classes to another, he must change his habits with regard to the use of alcohol. If he moves into the lower-middle class from the lower class, he must learn to stop drinking or he will be thought vulgar. Lower-middle-class men who move into upper-middle class must learn to begin again, at least when they are with men. Upper-middle-class individuals who move into upper class must learn to become very liberal from the standpoint of their former upper-middle-class habits, or they will be thought stuffy. What is rewarded in one social class is punished in the other.

The fact that what is rewarded in one social class is punished in another might, as Miller and Dollard suggest, present problems to an individual as he moves from one class to another. These problems are somewhat comparable to those of an individual who has learned to type by looking at the keyboard and then begins to learn to type without looking at it. Old orientations are hard to relinquish. They are particularly hard to relinquish when the behavior that they dictate is directed toward the relief of fear or anxiety. When the individual is punished by threats of ostracism or lack of support from the social group, it is to be expected that he will acquire attitudes, beliefs, and habits designed to keep the support of the group. Even when the individual rebels against the standards of his group, it is often done against the resistance of anxiety. A college freshman who has been taught that drinking is wrong may rebel against this teaching by getting drunk, but the orientation toward drinking that he has learned in his earlier life may dictate strong feelings of guilt. Violation of standards that the individual has learned to adopt for himself in order to retain the support of the social group often results in seeking restoration to the group by "paying a debt to society," even when the debt may cost one his life, as when one gives himself up for murder. A similar example is found in the behavior of the rebel who always gets caught by the police when he advocates unpopular doctrines as a way of fighting against beliefs or standards of conduct that he has learned in earlier social environments.

If an individual learns the standards of his group without strong fears of ostracism or loss of support from the group, he can countenance other standards without fear, and at the same time is likely to have a friendly rather than a rebellious feeling toward his social group. Punishment can be employed to train an individual in the ways of the group without establishing strong fears of ostracism. This point can be illustrated by the fact that in strong friendships, friends can criticize each other frankly without the friendship's being disrupted. Criticism is a form of punishment, or lack of support or coöperation from the environment in maintaining the individual's sense of well-being, but can be offered in the context of friendship so as to leave open many possibilities of continuing rewards from the friendship. Thus, one might criticize a close friend for the way he treats his wife, but do it in such a way as to make it clear that the criticism has nothing to do with the mutual pleasure they get from going to ball games together on Saturday afternoons, or from many other activities that they enjoy in each other's company. A parent, similarly, may reprimand a child for breaking a neighbor's window, but do it in such a way as to make clear that no overall ostracism or lack of support is involved. He might scold him, confining the punishment to the act, then drop the matter, and let the child join in family activities that are rewarding. In contrast to this way of punishing the child, the parent might deprive him of dinner and send him to bed, a course of action that cuts off rewards from his social environment to a much greater extent, and is, therefore, more likely to establish strong fears of ostracism.

In a family environment that punishes the child by highly threatening withdrawal of support, orientations are learned that dictate abiding by the standards and beliefs of the family primarily on the basis of fear. Such punishment does not have to be physical punishment, and frequently is not. Many people boast of "never laying a hand on their children," but these same people sometimes send their children to their rooms and tell them to think of how much they are "hurting" their parents. When the child is banished in this fashion, there is an overall ostracism that leaves open little or no possibility of rewarding interaction in the social environment. If he is punished in such a way as to leave open possibilities of rewarding interaction, on the other hand, his environment remains comfortable rather than threatening, because it is clear to him that he can still get rewards from it. If a child is spanked for a particular act but not banished by complete disapproval or removal of affection, his fear is not likely to be as great as when he is told, in effect, by people upon whom he is dependent for support, to go away and think about how worthless he is. When one abides by standards and beliefs primarily on the basis of fear, new standards are difficult to accept or tolerate, because following them or even considering them conflicts with the standards to which the individual feels that it is necessary to cling in order to relieve anxiety. If they were rebelled against, strong feelings of guilt might be expected or even seeking restoration to good graces by repenting, as was indicated above. On the other hand, the individual who is subjected to sufficient punishment to know what his society permits and what it does not permit, but who is not subjected to strong threats of ostracism, can more easily countenance standards of groups other than his own or of new social groups that he must take part in. The fact that he is not burdened with strong anxiety orientations also makes it easier for him to appraise what is socially acceptable or non-acceptable in new groups. Although he may not choose to abandon old standards, neither does he have to cling blindly to them, or to clutch frantically at new standards in order to preserve his sense of well-being while still feeling guilty about giving up the old standards.

Learning Internalized Values

The ideals that a person has for himself are values that are held in his culture or some part of his culture that he learns to adopt as values for himself. They represent conceptions he has of the kind of person he would like to be. When a girl speaks of a movie actress as her ideal, she describes the kind of person she would like to be. In speaking of the movie actress in this way she also indicates that the valuing or prizing of the glamour of movie actresses that exists in the culture has become internalized. That is, the "glamour values" of the culture have become her own values. A businessman may have an ideal for himself taking the form of thinking of himself, or desiring to think of himself, as one who is able and keen in business tranactions. This ideal may have been learned in his family environment in which shrewdness in business was prized highly or it may have been learned later in his neighborhood, school, gang, or occupational environment. A clergyman, similarly, may have an ideal for himself, taking the form of desiring to serve others, that was learned in his family environment or in another learning environment in which service to others was highly valued.

Ideals are learned when the individual is rewarded by praise, recognition, approval, and other goal attainments as well as when he is punished by disapproval, ridicule, and other penalties. A girl learns to internalize the valuing of attractiveness and success in getting attention from men when she is rewarded with praise for being "cute," or with prospects that are held out to her of romantic experiences if she is glamorous herself, or by actual attention from men and recognition of her as someone who can attract men. Regardless of whether she is "cute" or able to attract men, the prospects of romantic experiences themselves have a quality of reward that can result in the girl's learning an ideal of attractiveness and "glamour." Punishment in the form of ridicule or lack of attention also contributes to acquiring the "glamour ideal," since it can result in learning an orientation to avoid punishment by becoming "glamorous." Warner, Havighurst, and Loeb (1944) illustrate the role of reward and punishment in the development of a boy's ideals in the following passage:

> Arithmetic is Tom's best subject. Doing well in it brings him many rewards. He wins approval from his teacher; his lateness is excused as soon as he says he had to go back for his arithmetic book; his father praises him because he is ahead of his class.
>
> For stopping to chat with a girl at recess Tom is immediately punished by the taunts of sixth-graders who are just older than he and

whom he admires and imitates. Tom is beginning to learn that boys should have nothing to do with girls. Not only does the school put girls on one side of the school to play and boys on another, but the boys who have learned to spurn girl companions taunt Tom whenever he is found talking to them. Part of this lesson having been learned, Tom refuses to walk to school with his sister.

The boys just older than Tom may make life pleasant for him with their approval or punish him with their disapproval. They can permit him to hang around their gang activities and to play sometimes in their games, and if he behaves like them he has a better chance of being accepted. Therefore he is impressed when he hears a group of older boys calling another a "goddamn Polack." His suspicion that there must be something not altogether right about the boy who is called a Polack is confirmed by his father's statement that Poles are ignorant people—not yet Americans. The principal sources of reward in his life —his parents and the boys just older than he—agree; and he unconsciously learns their attitudes toward Poles.

The formation of Tom's ideals by means of reward and punishment can be seen quite clearly in the above account. He will not want to be a "sissy" because of the disapproval which accompanies playing with girls, he will take pride in arithmetic achievement because it has led to reward, and he will not want to be like people who are said not to be Americans yet because of the ridicule they are subjected to and that he would be subjected to if he were like them. His ideal for himself will be compounded, among other things, of not being a "sissy," "having a head for figures," and being a "real" American.

The development of ideals emerges in no small measure from the child's interaction in the family learning environment. Overall withdrawal of support is punishing, and events accompanying this punishment come to arouse strong fear or anxiety. Thus, if parents withdraw affection and express contempt or disappointment when a child fails, failure itself will come to evoke fear. The child learns an orientation that dictates the avoidance of failure, and the ideal of success becomes strongly established. Success is rewarding because it relieves fear. This kind of valuing of success is not uncommon in the American culture. Good grades in school and promotion on the job are sought not merely for their value in fostering further preservation of well-being in one's environment, but because of the anxiety that is relieved by success. It would appear that an important problem faced by American educators is that of motivating achievement without fear. Parents also would seem to be wiser in rewarding the child for what he accomplishes rather than comparing him unfavorably to the child next door or reprimanding him for not doing better. The use of rewards rather than punishment, insofar as possible, tends to do away with the learning of fear orientations which are especially hard for the individual to tolerate in a culture in which he learns to idealize being unafraid. In an interesting experiment performed by Hurlock (1925) praise was found to be superior to other forms of motivation, including reproof, in motivating American children to achieve. Although learning results from both reward and punishment, fear orientations that dictate avoidance are learned when punishment occurs. These avoidance orientations can interfere with learning behavior that the individual is trying to engage in. Thus, if one is learning to drive, reprimands for mistakes may cause him to learn fear orientations toward the objects he is trying to learn to manipulate. These orientations result in tendencies toward avoidance that interfere with learning the correct things to do in handling the steering wheel, brakes, etc. If fear orientations are kept to a minimum, on the other hand, which is more likely to occur if primary emphasis is on reward for what is done correctly, the individual can more readily learn the correct things to do.

Various restraints that the individual learns are internalized values. Moral standards that forbid engaging in various kinds of behavior become standards that the individual adopts for himself. Learning to interact in a socially acceptable way in a culture requires that the individual develop an imposing number of self-restraints. In the American culture, the individual must learn to stop at red lights, to refrain from eating without benefit of silverware, to keep his hands off other people's property, to "keep a civil tongue" under a great many circumstances, etc. The role of punishment in the erecting of restraints is illustrated by the ridicule that a boy might be subjected to for crying. The ridicule for crying results in learning a fear orientation that dictates "not crying." Disrespect for one's elders may also be punished so that assertiveness toward superiors is restrained. Fear orientations dictating restraint are sometimes learned "too well." A culture not only has the problem of establishing restraints within the personalities of its members, but also of leaving them sufficiently free from anxiety to think and act for themselves. This problem presumably exists for a democratic society, such as the American culture, at any rate. A certain amount of punishment is probably necessary to the learning of restraints. If the child is not punished by actually being burned by a stove or by warnings that the stove can burn him, he is not likely to acquire the restraints that are involved in being cautious when in the vicinity of a stove. Punishment does not have to be severe, however, in order to establish restraints necessary to socially acceptable behavior. An understanding might exist in a family situation that if a youngster does not take care of his own clothes he will be punished by not being able to find a favored item of apparel, or by not having his clothes in the condition that he will often want them to be in. Punishment of this kind is not likely to be reacted to as unreasonable nor to result in the learning of fear and avoidance orientations toward the social environment. Reward can also be employed in the setting up of restraints and its use will tend to eliminate the learning of fear orientations. A rule that prevents people from doing something can be explained. The offering of the explanation is a reward in the form of recognition of the people to whom the explanation is offered, and can establish a willingness to abide by the rule rather than a fear of what will happen if one does not abide by it.

LEARNING AND ADAPTIVE INTERACTION

Adaptive interaction in one's environment takes place when one can profit from punishment and learn to get along effectively in his environment. Thus, a man who has failed in business, and failure is a form of punishment, might consider his mistakes so as to avoid making them again without becoming so afraid that he gives up efforts to make a living. If he did withdraw in this fashion he would not be able to learn how to get along effectively in the business or occupational world. If he did not become sufficiently afraid to consider what his mistakes had been, he would not profit from punishment nor would he be in a position to learn a more adaptive mode of interaction. Profiting from punishment so as to continue to learn to get along effectively is dependent upon the individual's experiencing loss of support but not to the extent of its creating disabling fear orientations. Strong fear orientations can be disabling because they result in leaving the environment or pushing it away rather than in using it in order to continue to learn how to get along effectively.

Circumventing Punishment

An individual may not profit from punishment, because he has always been able to circumvent loss of support when he might have been punished. Indulgent overprotection in the family learning environment makes this circumventing of loss of support possible. Thus, the child who is never "in the wrong" learns that he can "get around" punishment. If he bites other children so as to injure them severely, for example, and the other children begin to leave him alone, the parent might take the position that he "really didn't mean to bite" or that the other children "just don't understand," rather than making it clear to the child that being left alone is the punishment he must expect when he mistreats others. At a later time, this same overindulged child might skip school. Rather than allowing him to get punished by having to stay after school, the parent may lie for the child by saying that he was sick. When this child becomes an adolescent, the parent might furnish the money to cover a check that the child has written without money in the bank to cover it. A long series of such experiences result in the individual's learning to believe that he can "get around" punishment. He also learns orientations through reward that dictate ways of manipulating people to his advantage. He may be rewarded, for example, in lying or similar ways of circumventing punishment by being allowed to "get away" with it and proceeding to do as he pleases. Other means of manipulating people are crying or exhibiting great sincerity. The use of these techniques by the kind of individual under consideration is dictated by an orientation to gain one's ends rather than by sympathy or understanding. Sympathy and understanding are based on having experienced loss of support oneself; the individual who has not experienced this loss of support, because he has circumvented it, cannot have such feelings for others to any great degree. Moreover, when an individual has learned to believe that he can circumvent punishment and gain reward in doing as he pleases, he learns to expect that his environment will applaud him as an exceptional or great person. When he actually encounters punishment after having learned that he is never "in the wrong," he tends to react to his environment as unreasonable, to pay little or no heed to the punishment which he regards as no fault of his own, and to continue his pursuit of "greatness." The kind of interaction resulting from learning to expect that punishment can be circumvented is nicely demonstrated by Fisher's report (1937) of the following case:

George T. was a young married man twenty-six years old, the father of one child. He was of superior intelligence. For the three years which he had been married he had contributed nothing to the support of his wife and child.

. . . He was liar, swindler, egotist, sentimentalist. Once when asked if he loved his wife and child he immediately began weeping and declared that they were the only thing in life that meant anything to him whatever. A few minutes later he tried to borrow five dollars from the writer "in order to secure a position that he might support his family." George was nomadic. He went to Florida where he became the self-invited guest of a family in very modest means. He represented himself as a colonel of the American Army on leave of absence from India. He induced the man with whom he was staying to dispose of his property, assuring him that much greater fortunes awaited him in India—with the aid and guidance of the colonel. He borrowed part of the money which the man had realized from his property and disappeared.

George next came to life in New York again. He went to one of the better hotels representing himself as an advance man for a group of middle-western buyers. He complained about the service until he had the manager of the hotel in a state of constant distress. After a couple of weeks he left the hotel, leaving his two large trunks packed with newspapers in lieu of his bill which he had neglected to pay.

Then George bedecked himself in uniform and went away for the summer to a citizens' army training camp. One day his wife received a telegram advising her that her husband's body was arriving at the Grand Central Terminal at a certain hour. She scarcely had read the telegram when George walked in. He stoutly denied that he knew anything whatever of the source of the telegram. He affected an almost convincing perplexity concerning the whole matter.

George next came to the attention of his acquaintances through a middle-western newspaper. He had given a lengthy interview on conditions in India to the paper. The "Colonel's" picture occupied a full quarter of a page. George went from there to California. He is avoiding New York at the present time inasmuch as the police of that city are very desirous of meeting him.

The abandon with which George of the above case repeatedly misrepresents himself is striking evidence of a firm belief that punishment can be circumvented. Lack of sympathy and understanding combined with manipulating others to one's own advantage is shown in George's case by his indifference to his wife and child, in spite of protests to the contrary, as well as by his swindling. Learning to manipulate others in a self-centered way is a part of the process of learning to "get around" punishment. Although George is avoiding New York, it is obvious that he does not believe in the reality of punishment in relation to *his* behavior, and it also appears that he expects to be applauded rather than penalized for what he does. In spite of getting into difficulties repeatedly he continues to employ the same modes of interaction time after time, because he does not profit from punishment.

The individual who has always been able to circumvent loss of support when he might have been punished has not learned what can actually lead to loss of support. He might write a check without money in the bank to cover it with little appreciation of the actual consequences of doing so. Whereas somebody else would anticipate imprisonment for forgery with qualms, such an individual would abstractly realize what might happen but not actually feel many qualms about it. His very limited experience with punishment has not given him a basis for experiencing such qualms. That is, cues to the punishments that his culture administers have not been learned. When punishment is encountered, it is not perceived as his fault, and not related to his own behavior which he perceives as faultless. Since *he is not burdened with fear orientations,* he is often effective in getting along in his environment, and this effectiveness is reason for continuing to perceive his behavior as faultless. Even if put in prison he can still be effective in getting along there. Nevertheless, in any environment he tends to "trip himself up," because although effective a good share of the time in securing rewards from his environment, he does not learn or continue to learn to get them without getting into trouble. The trouble reduces his efficiency in getting along in his environment, and his interaction is, therefore, not adaptive or integrative. Although he does succeed in getting rewards from the environment, his behavior is not integrative, because his effectiveness in getting along in his environment is reduced by the trouble he repeatedly gets into as a result of failing to perceive cues to punishment or to relate punishment to his own behavior. Since he is often effective in getting along in his environment, his interaction might be called *pseudo-integrative.*

Disabling Punishment

Profiting from punishment so as to continue to learn to get along effectively, as was said earlier, is dependent upon experiencing loss of support, but not to the extent of its creating disabling fear orientations. Strong fear orientations can be disabling, because they result in preoccupation with avoiding punishment rather than continuing to seek cues to "more positive" rewards. This process of seeking cues or learning new cues to the attainment of goals can be thought of as "coöperation" with the environment. If a man looks for a tool with which to chop down a tree and finds an ax or learns a new method of chopping down the tree, he is coöperating with his environment through having gotten a cue to an orientation that dictates a sensible way of attaining his goal. If he became highly anxious about getting the tree out of the way, his anxiety orientation might dictate avoiding the punishment, resulting from the tree's still standing, by walking away from it or, conceivably, by beating at it with a stick. In neither case would he be coöperating with his environment by getting cues from it to orientations dictating effective ways of getting the tree out of the way. The absence of such coöperation interferes with continuing to learn how to get along effectively in one's environment. If a man who has failed in love (through an unhappy relationship with his mother or some other woman) avoids women, he cannot learn or continue to learn how to get along with women. The avoidance might take the form of leaving women alone or of "pushing them away." The latter could be accomplished by making fun of women in their presence. While such behavior is in the nature of attack, the attack itself is designed to get away from or to avoid "the enemy" by "annihilating" him. An overreadiness to avoid the environment or persons in the environment, whether by withdrawal or attack, can block the learning of adaptive interaction. In both cases the individual fails to coöperate with his environment by using it in order to learn how to get along in it more effectively.

An important factor affecting how strongly an individual reacts to punishment is his *frustration-tolerance, which is the ability to endure anxiety.* One may react strongly, but also "put up" with the loss of support entailed in punishment so as not to "lose his head." The "strong" individual, in fact, is often anxious but has learned to "keep his head" while "sweating out" crises or trying circumstances. In so doing, he continues to learn how to get along effectively in his environment. The homesick person who can tolerate his homesickness, in spite of its painfulness, continues to add to whatever efficiency he already has in getting along in his environment. There are limits to anyone's frustration tolerance. If loss of support has been overwhelming and continues to be in spite of determined efforts to get along in one's environment and endure one's anxiety, "cracking at the seams" is to be expected. It is less likely to occur if the individual has had opportunity to learn to tolerate loss or absence of support. Thus, if a family is subjected to threat to its economic welfare, a learning environment in which parents remain relatively calm and are oriented to meet the environment rather than to avoid it provides opportunity for children in the family to learn how to withstand anxiety. Such behavior on the part of the parents furnishes support and also demonstrates the possibilities of getting support from the environment under trying circumstances. *Frustration-tolerance is based on the conviction that there are such possibilities of support or reward.*

Just as a learning environment can provide opportunity to learn how to withstand anxiety, it can also provide punishment which indicates errors without intimidating the individual. It was pointed out earlier that a parent could explain to a child when other children left him alone because he bit them that such punishment is to be expected for such behavior. The parent might even spank the child, for that matter, but spanking him for a particular act rather than spanking him as though he were totally worthless entails a different degree of loss of support. In the first case the child is given enough loss of support to profit from punishment. In the second case, he is more likely to learn disabling fear orientations that dictate avoidance of his environment rather than "staying" in his environment and continuing to learn how to get along in it.

An individual cannot only learn to avoid others but he can also learn to avoid recognizing himself. Loss of support in the form of ridicule, rejection, or negative evaluation of the individual can result in his becoming anxious about his own characteristics and protecting his self-esteem by not recognizing these characteristics. Thus, the individual, spoken of previously, who makes fun of women might not admit that he is actually hostile toward women, because his self-esteem requires that he think of himself as friendly toward everybody. The stronger his anxiety over not being friendly, the more essential it will be for him to protect his self-esteem by avoiding recognition of his hostility. His inability to recognize the nature of his own behavior would deprive him of a cue to the difficulties that it could easily create in getting along in his social environment. He, therefore, would not profit from the punishment provided by these difficulties. Coupled with failure to recognize his behavior there might be failure to recognize the results of the behavior itself. He might perceive women as thinking of him as "daring," for example, rather than as obnoxious. In this case he would also fail to profit from the punishing results of his behavior. Experiences that result in strong "ego-anxiety" or fear in connection with preserving self-esteem produce disabling fear orientations, and make it difficult for the individual to recognize his own behavior or its consequences. "Ego-anxiety" often accompanies a generalized anxiety or lack of confidence in one's resources which combine to block the individual's understanding of himself and the experimenting with new forms of behavior. This combinition is illustrated in the following case:

John Appleton is a 25-year-old man currently employed as a shipping clerk. He has shifted from one occupation to another and has usually been dissatisfied with his work because it has not seemed important enough to him. He moves from one job to another with the vague hope that the next one will be more promising and thinks of going back to school from time to time but has little confidence in his ability to do satisfactory work in spite of the fact that he got along all right during the 2 years of college work he did complete. His lack of confidence in his ability to do satisfactory work in college extends to all phases of his experience. He is uncertain about being accepted by friends and doubts if they do or could find him congenial and is hesitant about "holding up his end" of an argument even when he is as well informed and logical in his thinking as the person with whom he disagrees.

John's difficulties can be traced to a childhood background that held many uncertainties for him. He had been strongly encouraged to "make something of himself" and had learned to aspire to be like his father who was a successful engineer. His father's principal technique for "making something" of John, however, consisted of pointing out the error of his ways and exhorting him to be strong, manly, and courageous. Since his mother was submissive to the father and taught John to be similarly submissive, he tended to feel "deep down" that his father had the monopoly on manliness in the family. He, therefore, did not feel equal to his father, but desired, nevertheless, to be as strong a man as it seemed to him that his father was. The feeling seldom arose, because his father's approval was sparse. If John built a good model airplane, played a good game of tennis, or wrote a good essay, his father always pointed out how he could have improved his performance rather than praising him to at least some degree for what he had accomplished.

When John finished high school he decided to follow in his father's footsteps and become an engineer. The feeling of being unequal to his father continued to plague him and became more acute as his college work progressed. John didn't think of his doubts about himself as a matter of feeling unequal to his father, but he did feel more and more unequal to the demands of the course of study he had undertaken. Matters were not helped by his father's urging him to "shoot for the stars" and pointing out the discrepancies between the actual level of John's performance, which was adequate, and "the stars."

When John went to work he did not get on too well with his fellow workers. He was friendly enough, but a certain amount of horse play and gruffness was taken for granted in his new environment. His submissiveness and retiring manner were not suited to the forthrightness and aggressiveness that he found in the new setting.

He corresponds with his parents and yearns for some word of support and encouragement from his father in particular. Since his father is not very pleased with John's dropping out of school, he leaves all correspondence with John to John's mother. John goes on managing to earn a living, and to outside appearances seems to be getting along all right. His confidence in himself and his corresponding ability to get along are limited by his dependence on his father's approval. If he could rid himself of this dependence he would be a more self-sufficient person. With a greater degree of support and approval from his father earlier in his experience he would probably have derived sufficient security in his own right to be relatively self-sufficient now. As matters stand, the development of John's self-assurance would seem to depend on learning how to approve of his own efforts to get along rather than always subjecting himself to his father's point of view. Constructive relationships with others, moreover, could contribute to his assurance by providing some of the elements of support and positively expressed interest in John that were not present in his relationship with his father.

Loss of support far in excess of enough punishment to profit from one's mistakes is illustrated in the preceding case. Furthermore, the absence of support from his father that was so essential to John's self-esteem undoubtedly resulted in anxiety about his own worth. It can be imagined that he would have difficulty in facing any characteristics in himself that did not approximate the ideal he had for himself. His desire to be a capable man of the world, for example, could easily lead to anxiety and shame over the very fact that he was afraid and lacked confidence. He might, then, fail to recognize withdrawal, growing out of his lack of confidence, as withdrawal. In not recognizing it, he would not get a cue to the difficulties that it led to such as its preventing the learning of aggressive modes of interaction that could have proven useful. This result of his withdrawal, namely, not learning more assertive behavior, might not be perceived as a failure to learn, but as a matter of superiority to "lower breeds of men." He would, then, again fail to profit from the punishing consequences of his own behavior. The overwhelming lack of support that John had been subjected to and the anxiety over preserving his self-esteem combined to make it impossible for him to learn, or to continue to learn to get along effectively in his environment.

John's family learning environment provided few possibilities of reward. There was, therefore, little opportunity for him to develop frustration-tolerance. The ideal he had of being like his father was learned through the punishment that his father administered in rejecting him. This punishment resulted in an orientation to avoid "being no good," and his pervasive anxiety included fear of any characteristics that were not in accordance with his ideal. *The interaction resulting from overdeveloped anxiety is nonintegrative,* because preoccupation with it tends to prevent securing rewards from the environment. In John's case, "ego-anxiety" combined with generalized anxiety or lack of confidence to prevent understanding of his behavior and the "courage" to try new forms of behavior, such as experimenting as best he could with more aggressive ways of acting, which such understanding might have led to. In the absence of such understanding and experimentation John is, of course, limited in his ability to secure rewards from his environment. Since this ability was undermined by anxiety, the interaction of a person such as John might be spoken of as *anxiety-dominated.*

Optimal Punishment

Punishment can be administered without disabling fear orientations arising. When one feels sure that a friend is loyal to him, as suggested earlier, he can take severe criticism from the friend, because he knows that the fundamental security or reward inherent in the friendship will still be there in spite of the criticism. Similarly, the child who has experienced no overall ostracism when punished, but knows that he is still liked, in spite of the disapproval he is being subjected to at the moment, can take the punishment without developing strong anxiety. He learns, at the same time, that his environment does hold punishment, and that he can be "in the wrong." When he is not able to circumvent punishment but not made to feel worthless, either, he does not develop strong anxiety over his own characteristics. He, therefore, does not have to protect his self-esteem by failing to perceive the nature of his own behavior or its consequences. Thus, if he is failing to carry out his responsibilities in a coöperative enterprise, and this is pointed out to him, he can perceive his own "laziness," and he can also recognize the social disapproval that ensues from his "laziness" as disapproval rather than envy. Through being able to make such perceptions he can relate his behavior to consequences, and thereby profit from punishment. In seeing his "laziness" as "laziness," for example, rather than as "dignified leisure," he can relate his indolent behavior to difficulties that it leads to in getting along with his coworkers. In seeing disapproval as disapproval, and not writing it off as envy in order to protect his self-esteem, he also relates the consequence of his behavior to his behavior, rather than disregarding the consequence and failing to profit from punishment. Since he can profit from punishment and continue to seek rewards from his environment, he maintains himself effectively in his environment while preserving his sense of well-being. His interaction is, therefore, *adaptive or integrative.*

The adaptive individual learns and continues to learn adaptive modes of interaction, whereas the anxiety-dominated and pseudo-integrative individuals learn modes of interaction that make it more and more difficult to maintain themselves effectively. The adaptive or integrative individual has learned to react to his social environment as rewarding, and is oriented toward gaining positive support and coöperation from his culture in attaining his goals. *In order to gain coöperation from his culture, he must observe the limits that it imposes upon him.* That is, he must be oriented to avoid the loss of support that will ensue if he does not conform to cultural standards. *However, his fear or avoidance orientations are not so strong as to be disabling* or to result in preoccupation with anxiety, rather than with developing his resources for "getting the most out of life."

While an individual's personality may correspond quite closely to the "normal" personality of his culture, it does not necessarily follow that he is an integrative individual. One may abide by cultural standards rigidly, or may do so with a certain tentativeness and readiness to modify or discard them when they are not adaptive. In both cases his behavior may correspond quite closely to the patterns of behavior that are considered "normal" in his culture. This point can be illustrated by reference to two individuals in the American culture, both of whom would be considered as falling within the range of behavioral characteristics considered "normal." These individuals are described in a study of fairmindedness by G. B. Watson (*1925*). An acquaintance makes the following comments about one of them:

I consider this man one of the most prejudiced individuals I have ever known. He is so much of a fundamentalist that he gleefully condemns to the nethermost hell any person who suggests that heaven is not up above the clouds, a real, existing place. He has been a leader in finance, connected with one of the greatest banking institutions of the country. He said to me at one time, "I should like to see every socialist with a millstone around his neck thrown into the deepest part of the ocean."

The impression gained of the man described above differs from the impression gained of a woman who writes of herself:

Eight years of comparative leisure in a cosmopolitan city, abroad, gave me the advantage of a wide variety of friends of different races, classes, beliefs, and interests, from every part of the world. The complexity of social conditions and the genuineness of widely diverse points of view came home to me vividly.

With such a nature, schooling, and experience is it strange that I should reserve decisions, reconsider all kinds of arguments, and make all possible allowances. . . . The "All" or "No" response is utterly foreign to me. . . .

The comment, "The 'All' or 'No' response is utterly foreign to me," indicates a characteristic of the integrative individual. He is flexible enough to reformulate his point of view and to consider new solutions to problems rather than clinging to fixed or ready-made solutions. He is also capable of having a point of view. To put the matter succinctly, he is not afraid to make up his mind nor is he afraid to change his mind. The man described in the first of the above passages, who "is so much of a fundamentalist that he gleefully condemns to the nethermost hell any person who suggests that heaven is not up above the clouds, a real, existing place," is apparently a "normal" individual in that his behavior is in accord with the patterns of behavior accepted as "normal" in his culture. Since he has been a leader in finance, he would be considered "successful" and "being successful" is considered "normal" in the American culture. It appears that he has learned many of his beliefs through punishment which has created fear orientations that make it necessary to cling to these beliefs. In view of the dependence upon fixed solutions resulting from these fear orientations, one would hesitate to describe him as highly integrative, even though he is "normal." One can be "normal" as well as integrative but "normality" is no guarantee of integration.

SUMMARY OF PRINCIPLES

The fundamental theme of this chapter has been that as the individual interacts in his environment he learns. The following principles have played a central part in the development of this theme:

1. Cultures and subcultures are learning environments that make provision for training the individual in socially acceptable

modes of interaction through the use of reward and punishment.

a. When the individual is punished by threats of ostracism or lack of support from the social group, he will tend to acquire attitudes, beliefs, and habits designed to keep the support of the group.

b. If an individual learns the standards of his group without strong fears of ostracism or loss of support (punishment) from the group, he can countenance other standards without fear, and at the same time is likely to have a friendly rather than a rebellious feeling toward his social group.

c. Social values are learned when the individual is rewarded by praise, recognition, approval and other goal-attainments as well as when he is punished by disapproval, ridicule, and other penalties.

2. Profiting from punishment so as to continue to learn to get along effectively is dependent upon the individual's experiencing loss of support but not to the extent of its creating disabling fear orientations.

3. Frustration-tolerance is based on the conviction that the environment holds possibilities of reward.

4. Punishment can be administered without disabling fear orientations arising.

CHAPTER 6

Interactive Integration

Introductory Summary

The integrative individual is one who preserves his sense of well-being while continuing to get along effectively in his environment. He is able to "grow" by learning new adaptive orientations and to conform to cultural standards tentatively rather than tenaciously. The "normal" individual is not necessarily integrative because the inflexible use of adjustive techniques prescribed by the culture furnishes no guarantee that the individual will preserve his well-being and at the same time maintain himself effectively in his culture. Although the "normal" individual is not necessarily integrative the integrative individual tends to be "normal." Conforming to the patterns of behavior considered "right" and using the adjustive techniques prescribed as normal are necessary to effective maintenance in the culture.

Problems in reorientation arise when the individual is not adaptive or integrative. In order to learn integrative modes of interaction, it is necessary for the pseudo-integrative individual to experience punishment and to perceive that it has something to do with his own behavior. The anxiety-dominated individual must come to feel at ease in interpersonal relationships if he is to acquire more adaptive modes of interaction. Psychotherapy is a process of enabling the individual to learn integrative modes of interaction when his socialization has not resulted in such interaction.

THE INTEGRATIVE INDIVIDUAL

The integrative individual[1] *is one who preserves his sense of well-being while continuing to get along effectively in his environment.* Both the pseudo-integrative and the anxiety-dominated individual act to preserve the sense of well-being, but do so at the expense of getting along effectively in the environment. *Although the pseudo-integrative individual does not suffer to any great degree from anxiety or feelings of helplessness, he does not get along effectively because (1) he has not learned what leads to punishment and (2) when punishment is encountered, it is not related to his own behavior which he considers faultless. The anxiety-dominated individual does not get along effectively because (1) he has encountered disabling punishment resulting in his feeling helpless and worthless and (2) his feeling of worthlessness leads to protecting his self-esteem in ways that prevent relating his behavior to its consequences. The integrative individual has learned what leads to punishment but not at the expense of being made to feel worthless.* His self-esteem is not so shaky that he avoids relating his behavior to difficulties that it leads to in getting along in his environment. He can continue to learn to get along effectively because in relating his own behavior to consequences, he selects for learning those modes of interaction that make for efficiency in maintaining himself in his environment. Thus, the woman who has competitive attitudes toward men and can relate her difficulty in getting along with men to her own needs for "showing them up" tends to select and learn more adaptive modes of interaction with men.

The integrative individual is able to "grow" by learning new adaptive orientations. "Growth" of another kind takes place when the individual clings to old orientations, regardless of their adaptive value. In so doing, he continues to learn old orientations better but does not learn new adaptive orientations. The woman who clings to an old method of cooking, for example, perfects that

---

[1] Although the term "the integrative individual" is employed in the present discussion for purposes of exposition, there are varying degrees of integration in the behavior of different individuals.

method of cooking but in clinging to it she excludes the possibility of learning new methods that may serve her purposes better. The woman who has learned a method of cooking that serves her purposes but holds the orientation to cook in the way she has learned tentatively is able to pick up more effective methods. Similarly, a scientist might hold to a particular theory tenaciously. In so doing he might fit in or assimilate many facts to his theory, even if they had to be forced, but fail to develop a more adequate theory. Similar observations can be made about political, social, and economic beliefs.

The integrative individual is able to conform to cultural standards but holds to them tentatively rather than tenaciously. He conforms, to take a simple example, to the regulation to drive on the right-hand side of the road, but can react to an instruction to drive on the left-hand side when the right-hand side is being repaired. No high degree of adaptability is involved in such an example, to be sure. To take a somewhat more pertinent example, the integrative individual would not have great difficulty in learning to drive on the left-hand side all of the time if the regulation to drive on the right-hand side all of the time was changed to a regulation to drive on the left all of the time. The integrative individual can also be sufficiently tentative to refrain from abiding by cultural standards when it is not adaptive to abide by them. If tact is highly valued in his culture, for example, he can, nevertheless, become blunt when it is necessary to effective maintenance rather than clinging to tactfulness at any cost.

Readiness to learn new adaptive modes of interaction and to hold old orientations tentatively is probably particularly important when a culture is changing rapidly, because many old standards cannot be completely relied upon. Many sociologists hold that present-day American culture is in a process of rapid change. It has been pointed out, for example, that the family as a unit in the society does not have the stability that it did when the society was more agricultural or "closer to the soil." The standard that "woman's place is in the home" can no longer be counted upon as it could at one time as a way of life. A husband who clings to it tenaciously without making any concessions to his wife's desires to play roles outside of the home may overlook possibilities of adaptive interaction in the family. Similarly, the wife who "latches on" to the idea that woman's place is no longer in the home, rather than orienting herself in terms of the old standard as well as the new one concerning woman's "place," may overlook possibilities of adaptive modes of getting along with her husband as well as other men. Training the individual to orient himself according to new as well as old standards and to continue to seek more adaptive modes of interaction is perhaps more essential today than in many previous generations, as Gillin (*1946, 1948*) suggests very clearly in the following comments:

It seems to me that the dilemma in which we find ourselves in present-day North America is a serious one, but not incapable of solution. The problem is essentially this: to train the members of the next generation to rely upon their own inner resources as distinct from external props for the solution of life's problems, but at the same time to develop personalities capable of social coöperation and sufficiently flexible to appreciate the values of, if not to originate, new cultural patterns of more permanent functional value than those we now possess. For the time will come when the culture will once again provide more adequate security props for the individual. Taking the societies of mankind as a whole, this is one of the universal functions of cultural systems. But at the moment—and it is not unlikely that this moment may stretch into several human generations—our Western culture is not fulfilling this function. The individual must consequently be socialized in such a manner as to find his own way about his world and to make the most of it, not only from the individual, but also from the social point of view. The modern man or woman must depend upon his own analysis of the situations which confront him, and the hope of the world lies in modern man's ability to invent and establish a type of cultural definition of such situations which will make the lot of his successors less difficult.

Depending upon one's own analysis of the situations which confront him, as Gillin puts it in the above quotation, is a matter of neither blindly rebelling nor conforming. When standards are held tentatively the individual is prepared to abide by them when it is functional to do so and to discard them when it is functional to do so. Blind conformity does not permit discarding standards when they are not functional and blind rebellion does not permit accepting them when they are. The point can be illustrated by reference to parental practices in the American culture in training children. One might conform slavishly to the belief that "children should be seen and not heard" or rebel against it blindly and insist that children be given complete "freedom." Neither of these standards is likely to prove functional when followed blindly, since training a child to live in the American culture involves preparing him "not to be heard" at times as well as to be "free" enough to think for himself. Blind conformity and blind rebellion are actually not essentially different, since the one involves clinging rigidly to old or existing standards and the other involves clinging rigidly to their opposites. It is interesting to note in this connection that "modern" practices and "keeping up with the times" are often highly regarded in present-day American culture. It is probably to be expected that modernity will seem desirable in a rapidly changing culture, but modernity for its own sake is just as "blind" as "old fogiess." The integrative individual is willing to look at new "fads," but is also willing to look at so-called "tried and true" methods, beliefs, standards, and values. Rather than relying on pat solutions, old or new, he is creative. That is, he can originate modes of interaction or learn orientations that better serve the purpose of maintaining himself effectively in his culture. It is this creativeness that Gillin refers to when he speaks of training people to originate "new cultural patterns of more permanent functional value than those we now possess."

Continuing to learn so as to maintain oneself effectively in his environment may occur more readily in certain areas of a person's experience than in others. A chef may pick up more and more "know-how," for example, in preparing food but not in taking care of his automobile. The individual who is integrative "on a broad front" tends to acquire know-how in many activities. If mental ability is thought of as being composed of general as well as specific factors, as Spearman (1927) has suggested, the integrative individual might be considered one who has a general ability to acquire know-how that can "reach into" many kinds of experiences. This ability is probably dependent, among other things, upon frustration-tolerance or ability to endure anxiety, because the learning involved in picking up know-how is often painful. New situations and problems that provide opportunity for learning to get along more effectively are painful because of the uncertainty that they carry with them. If the individual can endure his anxiety and accept new situations as challenges as he endures it, he can add to his adaptability. Enduring his anxiety requires that he accept the limitations that any human being has. That is, in order to become more capable, one must permit himself the awkwardness that is involved in new learning rather than expecting of himself that he will be a superman in handling every problem that he meets. The anxieties that one must endure as he engages in new learning have been called "growth pains." The integrative individual can subject himself to such pains in order to become adaptive "on a broad front."

The willingness of the integrative individual to subject himself to "growth pains" implies foresight. That is, he can put up with immediate discomfort, pain, or anxiety for the purpose of "growing" or learning new adaptive orientations. The scientist who can relinquish a pet theory in order to develop a more adequate theory, for example, will find it discomforting to give up a theory that he has come to "cherish," but foresight enables him to give it up in order to develop a new theory that will more adequately explain the things that he is concerned with explaining. The scientist of our example can accept the discomfort of giving up his old theory in order to secure the gratification that ensues from developing a new theory. The immediate satisfaction that would seem to be involved in sticking with his old theory is actually not satisfying because his readiness to subject himself to "growing pains" has resulted in alertness to the punishing consequences of clinging to an inadequate theory. The integrative individual, then, is often dissatisfied. His alertness to the punishing consequences of existing orientations toward life means that he will be dissatisfied. On the other hand, he exploits his environment to the utmost in securing rewards from it that are produced by "growth" or continuing to learn new adaptive modes of interaction. In order to do this, he must regard his environment as a playground on which he may be uncomfortable at times but from which support and coöperation can be gained. The support and coöperation that he is able to exact from it in preserving well-being indicate that "growth pains" are means to ends. They are not ends in themselves, as many popular ideas about "improving one's mind" would seem to suggest.

INTERACTIVE INTEGRATION AND "NORMALITY"

Every culture prescribes certain patterns of interaction among its members. The individual whose behavior corresponds to these patterns is considered "normal," and the one who does not is considered "abnormal" or "subnormal." Normality is a somewhat confusing concept because of two related but not identical meanings that are attached to it. A person is sometimes said to be "normal" when he is at least "up to average." He may still be considered "normal" when he goes beyond the average. In other cases he is considered "normal" when he is neither below or above average. The acuity of his vision may be well above average; it is regarded as "normal" or "right" when it is. To have a "normal" amount of suspicion in our culture, on the other hand, means that one is neither so suspicious that he distrusts everybody—if he did he would be considered "crazy"—or so lacking in suspicion as to be "simple." In both instances, the individual must fall within a certain range if he is to be evaluated in his culture as "normal." The range may be fairly broad as in the case of vision, since anything above average is presumably "normal," but even one's vision cannot be too good and still "rate" within the normal range. If it is, the tendency is to react to it as "abnormal." An oculist might, accordingly, fit a person with glasses to decrease the exceptional acuity of his vision, even though no visual defects could be discovered. Similarly, one can be "bright," but if he is too "bright," the conclusion is that he must be "abnormal" in some way. If nothing very "abnormal" can be found, wonder never ceases or it is believed that his "abnormality" has simply not been discovered yet.

Standards of normality vary from one culture to another. It is difficult to be too self-effacing in some cultures, and difficult to glorify oneself too much in other cultures. In still other cultures, the normal individual is neither too modest or too immodest. The normal individual in one culture, therefore, does not look like a normal person from the point of view of another culture. Ruth Benedict (1934) makes this point in her descriptions of behavior that is evaluated as normal in different North American Indian tribes. Concerning the Kwakiutl of the northwest coast of America, she says: "The object of all Kwakiutl enterprise was to show oneself superior to one's rivals. This will to superiority they exhibited in the most uninhibited fashion. It found expression in uncensored self-glorification and ridicule of all comers. Judged by the standards of other cultures the speeches of their chiefs at their potlatches are unabashed megalomania." An example of one of these speeches runs in part as follows:

I am the first of the tribes,
I am the only one of the tribes.
The chiefs of the tribes are only local chiefs.
I am the only one among the tribes.
I search among all the invited chiefs for greatness like mine.
I cannot find one chief among the guests.

In contrast to the normality of the Kwakiutl Indians described above, Benedict furnishes the following description of normality among the Zuni of New Mexico:

Personal authority is perhaps the most vigorously disparaged trait in Zuni. . . . The ideal man in Zuni is a person of dignity and affability who has never tried to lead, and who has never called forth comment from his neighbors. Any conflict, even though all right is on his side, is held against him. Even in contests of skill like their foot-races, if a man wins habitually he is debarred from running.

It is clear from the foregoing descriptions of contrasting patterns of life that different cultures select far different personality "types" as normal.

While an individual's personality may correspond quite closely to the normal personality of his culture, it does not necessarily follow that he is an integrative individual, as was pointed out in the previous chapter. The reason that the "normal" individual is

not necessarily integrative is that the inflexible use of adjustive
techniques prescribed by the culture furnishes no guarantee that
the individual will preserve his well-being and at the same time
maintain himself effectively in his culture. Thus, the overly conscientious student who employs the adjustive technique of working hard and worrying about his schoolwork is considered normal.
If worry and anxiety mount sufficiently and result in his "cracking
up," he is no longer considered normal, but his previous behavior
was so normal that people are often astonished that such an
individual has a "nervous breakdown." It is interesting to note
the results of a study of Wickman (1928) in this connection. He
had teachers and psychologists rate the seriousness of various
behavior characteristics and found discrepancies in their ratings.
The teachers tended to evaluate behavior as serious when it did
not correspond to patterns considered acceptable, normal, or
right. The psychologists were not so much concerned with "right"
behavior as they were with evidences of the individual's being
under stress that would prevent his functioning effectively in his
environment.

Although the normal individual is not necessarily integrative,
the integrative individual tends to be normal. Conforming to the
patterns of behavior considered "right" and using the adjustive
techniques prescribed as normal are necessary to effective maintenance in the culture. Working to become successful in one's occupation is a mode of interaction considered normal in the American culture, or in those groups in the American culture in which
people are born neither to poverty nor to wealth. It is a way of
maintaining oneself effectively in these groups. The individual
who spurns occupational success as nothing but "social climbing"
or as of no importance in comparison to "personal happiness" may
ignore effective ways of maintaining himself while preserving his
sense of well-being. Thus, if he does not exert himself to "get
ahead" in his occupation, he does not achieve a position that
makes it easier to maintain himself in the culture. When he can
maintain himself more easily, it might be added, he also removes
obstacles to the preservation of well-being. Hence, maintaining
oneself effectively and preserving well-being go hand in hand.

The individual who is so intent upon "getting ahead" that he "drives himself into the ground" does not add to his ability to maintain himself effectively nor to the preservation of well-being. The integrative individual can work toward occupational success, and in doing so he conforms, but can do it without conforming so rigidly to the normal idea of success that he thwarts his own effectiveness in maintaining himself and preserving his well-being.

The individual who is a member of a group in the American culture that is closer to poverty is not as likely to be considered normal in his group when he strives toward occupational success as the individual who does so in a group that is neither close to poverty nor wealth. The individual considered normal in the sub-culture that is closer to poverty lives from day to day. Aspirations toward occupational success beyond making a living as best one can tend to be considered unrealistic and abnormal. The integrative individual in this culture conforms in that he does live from day to day, because it is the effective way of maintaining himself in his environment. That is, he is concerned with finding work "right now," and cannot be too concerned about the future. He does not conform so rigidly, nevertheless, that he fails to look to the future for possible opportunities for the kind of work or working conditions that would enable him to maintain himself more effectively.

Although it is difficult for anyone to move from his own culture to another and learn the normal patterns of the new culture, the integrative individual can do so more easily because he conforms adaptively rather than rigidly to the patterns of his own culture. In order to get along in any environment one must have "mental maps" of what leads to reward and what leads to punishment in that environment. Since what is "right" in a culture is rewarded and what is "wrong" is punished, these maps are guides to "right" and "wrong." The integrative individual has these maps so far as his own culture is concerned, and, therefore, has moral standards. He abides by these standards not only because he has learned that not doing so leads to punishment, but also because he has learned that his environment holds rewards. In reacting to it as rewarding, he is disposed to have friendly feelings toward his environment. He respects rather than fears the "commands" of his own culture, and accepts them as guides rather than as whips. He can, therefore, respect the standards of other cultures as guides which presumably have their reasons for being as they are just as he feels that the standards of his own culture are reasonable. If he cannot respect them, he can still react to them more as guides than as whips. Thus, many American men cannot readily accept the standards of military life that call for obeying authority without question, but many can use this standard as a guide for purposes of getting along effectively without either cringing or rebelling. The integrative individual in the Army tends to conform to its standards of obedience, but not so much because of an overwhelming fear orientation as because he would defeat effective maintenance of himself while preserving his well-being if he did not. His conformity is normal. Intergration and normality, therefore, can converge in meaning when they both refer to conformity. They diverge in meaning, on the other hand, because conformity is not necessarily integrative. The soldier who obeys so well that he cannot think for himself may be a normal soldier, but his inability to think for himself means that he is by no means integrative.

INTERACTIVE INTEGRATION AND REORIENTATION

Problems in reorientation or relearning arise when the individual is not adaptive or integrative. Pseudo-integrative interaction does not result in effective maintenance in the environment because fear orientations are underdeveloped and indicators of punishment in the social environment are not heeded. Anxiety-dominated interaction does not lead to effective maintenance in the environment because fear orientations are overdeveloped and interfere with rewarding modes of interaction. When pseudo-integrative or anxiety-dominated modes of interaction exist, reorientation resulting in integrative modes of interaction can often be brought about by altering the learning environment.

Pseudo-Integration and Reorientation

The pseudo-integrative individual has not learned what leads to punishment, and is not able to relate punishment to his behavior when it is encountered. He, therefore, is not able to get along effectively in his environment because he has to spend a large share of his time getting out of trouble. While he may be skillful in getting out of the trouble, he does not profit from having gotten into it, but proceeds to get into further difficulties from which he must extricate himself. These characteristics are nicely demonstrated in Luella Cole's account (*1936*) of the following case:

Joseph Brown is a man of about thirty-five. . . . His father, while a successful artist, was a dissolute individual from whom his mother obtained a divorce when Joseph was about three years old. The mother herself was an irresponsible person who boarded Joseph and his sister with their grandmother out in the country while she worked rather intermittently in the city. She visited the children only two or three times a year and never contributed regularly to their support. When Joseph was about eight the grandmother died, and he and his sister (who was five years older) continued to live alone on the farm. The mother was not willing to have the children with her in the city because they would interfere too much with her good times, and there was no other relative to whom they could be sent. Joseph's sister was not old enough to control him, and for the next few years he did practically what he pleased. At that time his mother made a second marriage and arranged for the two children to live with her. The sister did not like her stepfather; after living with the family for a few months she eloped.

Joseph continued to live with his mother and stepfather, and seemed to be making a reasonably good adjustment. Although he had attended country school most irregularly, he quickly made up the work he had missed and entered high school at fifteen. A year later he was severely injured in football practice. For months he was in the hospital, and was subsequently in bed for about two years. During this time he was the center of lavish devotion from both his mother and stepfather. When he was finally well enough to return to school he felt himself too old to be a high school sophomore, so he took some tutoring and entered a trade school.

There his irresponsibility first became prominent, although it had probably always existed. His earlier environment, first on the farm with his grandmother, then with his sister, and then at home in bed had permitted irresponsibility without serious consequences. For the first time, in the trade school, he was meeting normal competition and difficulties. He remained only one semester and left without taking the final examinations. He complained that the instructors were unfair, that the work was uninteresting, and that nobody liked him. He next held half a dozen odd jobs, from none of which he was actually fired because he walked out of his own accord after giving his superior a "piece of his mind." In fact, he was always proud of having "bawled out" his superiors and of leaving his jobs voluntarily.

He next got employment as salesman for a hardware company. He had always like to travel about and talk to people, and he usually made, at first, a rather favorable impression. For several months all went well, and Joseph's family believed he had found himself at last. During this time, he married a naive and not very intelligent country girl from a tiny hamlet in his district. She regarded Joseph as a brilliant and rising young man, much too good for her. While she was totally unsophisticated, she was completely reliable and not afraid of hard work. The marriage started off well, and the girl's dependable nature seemed to have a stabilizing effect on Joseph's personality. Gradually, however, he became dissatisfied with his work, got into arguments with the head salesman, failed to keep appointments with customers, and became a general nuisance. As usual he sensed almost to a minute when he was going to be discharged, wrote an angry letter to the head of the concern, marched into the head salesman's office, criticized everybody, and loudly resigned his job. After this emotional flurry he again settled down for a few months as an insurance salesman. But this job also was drawing to a close when the depression threw him out of work completely.

His wife had a horror of living on charity; she therefore got a part-time job as sales girl during rush hours in a large store and spent the rest of the time raising vegetables, which she sold to neighborhood markets. Joseph sat around the house, nursed his grievances, and made no effort to get any kind of work. At about this time he met some Italian friends who were Fascist supporters and became greatly interested in Italy. While his wife worked fourteen hours a day, he read every book on modern Italy he could find, talked with his enthusiastic friends, and made plans for a visit to their relatives in Italy. All of this seemed a mere daydream, but at this moment an uncle died and left him $500. In spite of his wife's pleading, he spent this money making a visit to Italy. As he had been warned by others before he started, his friends' relatives did not like him and he did not like them. It annoyed him that they talked no English and that the Italian he had studied for three or four weeks before leaving home proved so inadequate! He remained less than a week, terminated his stay with an emotional display, and returned home. In the meantime, his wife determined to leave him, but upon his return he became repentant, promised her to be more responsible in the future, and persuaded her to take him back. One cannot blame her too much, for Joseph is the one colorful experience in an otherwise drab life.

Since that time he has alternately lived with his mother, who is now a widow, and with his wife. At present, at the age of thirty-four, he has decided to become a doctor. Joseph undoubtedly has the mental capacity to enter one of the professions, but he cannot understand that he has an inadequate preparation, that his characterological defects may prevent his success, or that he is too old now to start on such a long program of work. He is at present taking premedical courses in which he does no more than average work. He will never be allowed to enter medical school because his grades are too poor. The money for this work has been paid jointly by his mother and wife, the former out of her meager inheritance from her husband and the latter out of her daily earnings. As Joseph nears the end of his premedical work, he is realizing the impossibility of becoming a doctor. He is beginning to cut his classes and to project the blame on everyone but himself; he is gradually working himself up into a rage, at the height of which he will undoubtedly deliver an emotional blast to the college officials and then withdraw from his classes.[2]

Joseph Brown is clearly an individual who goes on the assumption that he can do as he pleases without regard for the difficulties that doing as he pleases lead to. His early learning environment apparently did not contain punishments for behavior that would ordinarily lead to punishment. Although no specific information is given about his relationship with his grandmother, it might be

[2] In a subsequent report Cole (1948) states that "since this study was first published, this man has held several clerical jobs, each for a short period. He was called up but rejected by the Army because of his personality, his age, and his previous history of unemployability."

inferred that she was indulgent toward him, as grandmothers often are toward their grandchildren. If she did not "spoil" him too actively but simply failed to demonstrate that "no" sometimes meant "no," he would be able to do as he pleased and to circumvent punishment. At the same time he would be in the process of developing the conviction that he "could do no wrong." His sister, as Cole points out, was not old enough to demonstrate later that "no" meant "no," and it is also possible that she would not be inclined to. Since she was left alone herself with her younger brother, it would be understandable if she were indulgent toward him in order to appease her own loneliness. The devotion that his mother and stepfather lavished upon him after he was injured, while also understandable, would reinforce the conviction (that, it seems reasonable to infer, had already developed) that he "could do no wrong."

In order to learn integrative modes of interaction, it is necessary for the pseudo-integrative individual to experience punishment and to perceive that it has something to do with his own behavior. He does encounter punishment by getting into trouble repeatedly, and, therefore, does not continue to circumvent it entirely. However, he has skills in minimizing it and in extricating himself when it is encountered. When Joseph Brown knew that he was going to be fired, he resigned before getting fired and probably left his employers in doubt as to whether they were wrong in the first place in thinking of firing him. The skill with which the pseudo-integrative individual minimizes punishment and extricates himself from difficulties is learned through the reward that has come from being able to "get away" with doing as he pleased. He is not only skillful in extricating himself from difficulties but also in other ways which he has learned and continues to learn because such learning is not blocked by fear. Joseph, for example, had the social skills enabling him to make a good impression on people—at first. The success that the pseudo-integrative individual has in extricating himself from trouble as well as in other ways is sufficient to maintain his conviction that his behavior is faultless. The trouble that he gets into, then, does not have the effect of changing his behavior.

If the pseudo-integrative individual were placed in a learning environment in which it was consistently impossible for him to "wriggle out" of the difficulties that he repeatedly gets into, he would presumably acquire a better idea of what led to punishment. The problem is not simply one of learning what leads to punishment, though, because he has not learned to relate punishment to his own behavior. His tendency to perceive his behavior as faultless and his conception of himself as a "great person" cause him to regard punishment as an unreasonable act on the part of his environment. Simply encountering consistent punishment for "misbehavior," then, would tend to develop feelings of persecution. If the part that he plays in bringing on the punishment can be pointed up, there is not the opportunity to attribute the punishment to something other than his own behavior. In order to perceive the part that his behavior plays in bringing on the punishment, it is necessary to make clear repeatedly the relationship between the punishment and the behavior and to provide opportunity for alternative modes of interaction. Repeated opportunity for alternative modes of interaction in a situation that consistently punishes "misbehavior" and consistently makes clear the relationship between the behavior and the punishment is difficult to arrange. It is for this reason that the individual with highly developed pseudo-integrative trends does not usually change. Joseph of the above case went from one job to another. If his misdemeanors on a particular job could have been consistently penalized with clear indications of why they were penalized, and he could remain on the job so that alternative modes of interaction could be tried, he might have changed. The only problem would be confining Joseph to the job and finding an employer sufficiently interested in problems of behavior to cooperate!

Confining an individual like Joseph to a situation in which he cannot escape the penalties of his "misbehavior" is not easy because he is adept in setting up new situations and developing new schemes. Joseph could make a good impression on people at first and get started with new ventures. Even if such an individual could be confined, it is not the confinement in itself that can bring about reorientation. When confined, he must experience punishment in combination with the pointing up of the relationship between his behavior and the punishment, and have opportunity for alternative ways of interacting. If Joseph Brown could have been kept from going to Italy and had to abide by certain agreements through behaving differently or facing punishing consequences if he did not, with clear indications of how his own behavior led to these punishing consequences, he might have changed. It might be understood, to take a simple example, that if he got home for dinner at a certain time he would have dinner waiting, and that if he did not get home by that time, he would not have it waiting. Sticking to this agreement with an explanation of the fact that the consequence of doing completely as he pleased about getting home was "no dinner" would provide experience in relating his behavior to consequences. Simple as this example is, it illustrates the kind of experience needed to develop reorientations that counteract pseudo-integrative trends. As matters stood, Joseph's wife took the role of an indulgent parent figure—understandably enough in view of her own drab existence, as Cole points out. In the example used, the pointing up of the relationship between not getting home and not getting dinner might be ignored, to be sure, but a regular series of such clarifications would tend to make a dent when the consequences of the misbehavior could not be avoided. If they were regular and clear, they would also tend to burst the conception of himself as a "great person," because it would be evident that doing as he pleased did not always work, and that it did not work because he could be "in the wrong." Provision for alternative ways of acting that could be rewarded would tend to be adopted because they led to reward and avoided punishment. If a patient employer, to whom he had to stick, had the understanding with him that mistreating a customer involved certain penalties but that reward ensued for other ways of dealing with customers, opportunity would be provided for learning the other ways. If this understanding was consistently followed, acceptable interaction in this social environment might gradually ensue. As said before, the only problems would be finding a fantastically patient employer with a remarkable interest in problems of behavior and confining Joseph to the job.

Anxiety-Dominated Interaction and Reorientation

The anxiety-dominated individual is handicapped in securing rewards from his environment because of preoccupation with anxiety or fear. The anxiety may manifest itself in many ways. The sharp-tongued person, for example, is frequently one who is actually following the motto that the best defense is a good offense. His defense takes the form of pushing away his environment rather than running from it, but it is, nevertheless, a form of avoidance. Preoccupation with fear and avoidance, whatever form the avoidance takes, interferes with rewarding modes of interaction. The individual whose fears of people result in his lashing out at them tends to be too preoccupied with protecting himself to find rewarding modes of interacting with them. If somebody puts him at ease, he can relax, and when he relaxes he can begin to see ways of enjoying himself. Anxiety and the resultant difficulties in finding rewarding modes of interaction are illustrated in the following case:

Jack C. complains of headaches, insomnia, and feelings of discouragement. He is a mild-mannered individual who answers questions clearly and coherently but with a certain amount of hesitation and stuttering. He has worked for the same company for 3 years and there is no evidence of frequent change in employment prior to that time. If anything, he seems to prefer the security of a particular job to risking any change in employment. He lives alone and has not been active in any social organizations recently. He is a member of a fraternal organization and knows many people in his town. Although he is on good terms with them, he does not have any close friends as far as can be determined. He goes to work regularly and to a movie occasionally. He is also interested in amateur radio with which he spends a certain amount of his time. Most of it is spent alone. He has gone out with girls occasionally, but currently he has no girl friends nor any close friends among his male acquaintances.

Jack comes from a large family with whom he lived during the first five years of his life. He remembers his father as a kindly but irresponsible man who did not contribute regularly to the support of the family. The mother and father got along well together, he says, in spite of his father's irresponsibility. He was also happy with the other children and remembers an older sister particularly who seems to have taken a motherly interest in him. His mother died when he was five years old, and the father was unable to keep the family together. He and the older sister went to live with relatives. These relatives could not support them, and after a year's time, Jack and his sister were separated and sent to different homes. After living with another family of relatives for a year, this family apparently felt that it had done its share. When a neighboring farm family expressed interest in Jack's living with them because he got along well with one of their youngsters, it was agreed that he could live with this family. This new move did not work out, because he did not "warm up" to the new family as it had been expected he would. After several months time with them, he went back to the relatives he had been living with and stayed with them for the next 2 years. His father then reappeared and tried to reunite the family, but this proved unsuccessful. He and his older sister managed to stay together this time, but only because they were sent to an orphanage together. He remained in the orphanage until he was 14 and has supported himself ever since that time.

In reviewing his background with him Jack says that he used to be very aggressive. If he was pushed on a street car, for example, he made sure that he pushed back. On one occasion he got into a fight and nearly killed a man. Since that time he has made it a point not to fight, and he now gives the impression of being a rather quiet and subdued person. In spite of his apparent shyness he works hard and has been promoted on his job. He also takes correspondence courses and does fairly well in them; his idea is that they will help him to continue to advance in his work. Recently he has become increasingly tense and apprehensive about the future and has not kept up with his courses. He is also concerned about his symptoms because they make him less efficient in his work.

The shifting about from one family to another and the attendant uncertainty about support from or security in his environment were not designed to make Jack feel particularly comfortable in it. His avoidance at one time took the form of aggression and more recently has taken the form of withdrawal. Although he is effective in getting along in his environment in many ways—he has earned promotions in his work, for example—it is also evident that his ability to gain rewards from his environment is limited by his anxiety. He is virtually isolated from people, and is not finding rewarding modes of interaction with them. In failing to find them, he is not adding to his ability to maintain himself effectively nor to preserving his sense of well-being. The disturbance in his sense of well-being taking the form of headaches, insomnia, and feelings of discouragement might be understood as reactions to the limited channels he feels he has for maintaining himself in his environment and preserving his sense of well-being. That is, his environment is reacted to as one that provides support through working hard, but not in other ways. He must, then, demand of himself that he work hard while feeling that he would be "lost" if he didn't. His headaches, insomnia, and discouragement are, therefore, not surprising.

Reorientation leading to more rewarding modes of interaction in Jack's life would require a learning environment in which "pointers" to such interaction could be found, but bluntly pointing out to him the "error in his ways" or simply telling him that he should "get out and mix with people more" would be of little help. The bluntness would in all probability be reacted to as another form of punishment from his social environment. Since he would probably already be feeling inferior about his difficulties, the bluntness would also only tend to add to his feelings of inferiority. Adding to his feelings of inferiority would, in turn, make it harder for him to perceive how his own behavior limited his possibilities of finding more rewarding ways of getting along, because protection of his self-esteem and combating the inferiority feelings would result in avoiding recognition of the shortcomings in his own behavior.

If Jack came to feel at ease with someone who did not engage in bluntness, but encouraged him to talk about his problems, this in itself would be a relearning experience that would counteract his avoidance of people. In discovering that he was not going to be censured, he could also talk more and more freely, and in doing so gain "pointers" from his own verbalizing as to the difficulties that his present behavior led to. Furthermore, the confidence placed in a person who did not censure him would make it possible for this person to suggest difficulties with present modes of interaction. Through being able to perceive the difficulties with his own behavior, then, as the result of a learning situation in which he was not censured, he would be in a position to begin to "see" more rewarding ways of handling his life. As he saw them, he would also be in a position to act in accordance with them. In so doing he would learn further ways of finding rewards in his environment. Thus, if he saw for himself that "mixing" could bring rewards that he was not finding and then began to "mix" he would learn additional ways of finding rewards in interpersonal relationships.

Assuming that Jack began to discover for himself that new modes of interaction could be more productive of rewards from his environment, he would still have to continue to go through the process of learning these new ways of living. He might begin to exhibit interest in people in ways that he had not been doing, for example, and do such things as engage them in conversation more often. In doing so, he would learn new ways of evoking positive reactions to himself on the part of others. Since his avoidance of people had been a fairly well-established practice, interacting with them in new ways would not be easy. It would not be easy because it would be in conflict with the established patterns of avoidance. Reorientation, then, would not necessarily be smooth sailing, and in achieving it Jack would have to engage in procedures with which he would not be too comfortable. If he started to try to take an active part in the fraternal organization to which he belonged, his tendency might very well be to continue to avoid participating in its affairs. The conflict between this tendency and the new-found inclination to participate would be disconcerting. An important part of his reorientation, therefore, would be learning to endure discomfort while finding more rewarding ways of living.

Jack's reorientation would not necessarily be dependent upon a learning situation in which he discussed his problems with someone else, and proceeded from there to develop more effective ways of getting along in his environment, as described above. If he happened to be thrown in with a group of people who put

him at ease (because they were at ease themselves), he would
be in a learning environment that would tend to counteract the
avoidance orientations he had acquired in previous learning environments. In being at ease he would be less preoccupied with
anxiety and could learn ways of becoming more at ease. In being
at ease, he would also tend to see himself more clearly, because
the acceptance he found would diminish feelings of inferiority.
As they diminished, he could "look at himself" and the shortcomings in his attempts to get along in his environment. This
"seeing of himself" would not have to be a highly conscious
process, but could instead take the form of sensing, without definitely knowing, what was wrong with his adjustment processes.
Thus, reorientation might occur without his knowing exactly
what had happened.

A final point to be made about reorientation in the direction of
interactive integration and away from anxiety-dominated interaction is that as more rewarding methods of acting are learned, the
individual uses his environment as one in which he can learn to
get along effectively. As anxiety diminishes or as one learns to
withstand it, he can "look around," and as he "looks around" he
finds leads to reward that he would not have found otherwise.
Thus in looking around Jack might find that a bid for attention
from a girl, when followed by certain behavior on his part, could
lead to a rewarding friendship. In looking around he could also
observe the behavior of others, and in doing so, get leads to rewarding modes of interaction himself. He might note, for example, that somebody else found satisfying relationships with
women that he had not been finding. In observing their behavior,
he would "pick up pointers" as to how to get along with women
himself.

INTERACTIVE INTEGRATION AND PSYCHOTHERAPY

Socialization is the training or preparation of an individual for
participation in his culture. The ideal socialization process prepares an individual for adaptive or integrative modes of interaction. It is frequently far from ideal because of rejecting or overprotecting parent-child relationships, such as those discussed in

Chapter 1. Conditions equivalent to those provided by a rejecting or overprotecting parent may exist when the individual has no parent (or, in effect, has no parent). The general social environment may be rejecting, as when a child is shifted about from one family to another. Someone other than the parent, such as a guardian, grandmother, or aunt who plays the role of the parent or has considerable influence over a child, may also reject or overprotect a child. When an individual is not interacting in integrative ways, he has frequently not had a relationship with a parent, or someone in the role of a parent, that has prepared him to maintain himself effectively in his environment. Psychotherapy is a process of enabling the individual to get along more effectively when his socialization has not prepared him to do so. It involves a relationship with another person comparable to a child's relationship with a parent who prepares the child to leave home and to get along effectively after he has left. In order to get along effectively, the individual must have independent experiences in handling his own problems and must be able to relate his behavior to its consequences.

The Therapist as a Nonpunitive Parent

If a child is to have the confidence necessary to effective maintenance in his environment, he must neither fear a parent nor be overdependent upon him. Similarly, the individual who lacks confidence must neither fear nor overdepend upon a therapist if he is to profit from the therapy. The amount of dependence involved in the therapeutic relationship will vary from one person to another, because the amount of confidence that people have when they enter the therapeutic relationship varies. Fear of the therapist will not be conducive to acquiring confidence regardless of the extent to which the person lacks confidence. One of the objectives of therapy, then, is to establish a relationship in which the person whose lack of assurance interferes with getting along effectively in the environment, feels unafraid. Therapy with children consists in large part of demonstrating that they need not be afraid. Toys that they can destroy, if they choose, without getting punished may be made available, for example. Somewhat similar methods are sometimes employed with seriously disturbed adults. A therapist may establish a friendly relationship with a mental patient, who pays little attention to what goes on around him, by such devices as gradually persuading him to play a game of ping-pong with him. Still different methods are employed with individuals whose problems may be serious but who are in better contact with their surroundings, as Alexander (1946) shows in the case of an individual he describes as follows:

The patient's attitude was, in a sense, similar to that of an intimidated animal—a combination of rebellion and fearful, grudging submission. The jerking of his arms were abortive rage attacks, inhibited blows. The irritability toward his family and friends was a sign of insecurity. Then, too, his needs for dependence were frustrated because his inferiority feeling and hostility would not allow him to lean on anyone. His impotence was the expression of his adolescent insecurity, since all sexual expression was linked in his mind with "parental veto."

Alexander relates the way in which this individual became less fearful and hostile in their relationship in the following passage:

An unusually tolerant attitude was maintained. . . . Where the father had been extremely critical of the patient, the analyst openly acknowledged admiration of certain of the patient's qualities—his quick mind, his physical skills, his sophistication. He also expressed interest in the patient's business and social activities. Of particular importance was the fact that the therapist's tolerance extended to sexual matters. It became apparent that the straitlaced father had had a very intimidating effect upon the patient concerning any sexual expression. The therapist had ample opportunity to display the opposite attitude, since the patient's sexual yearning and attempted adventures took an important place in his associations.

In response to the treatment described above, the patient became considerably more comfortable in his relationships with people in general. It is evident that the therapist was in the role of a parent but that he took this role differently than the real father had taken it. In taking it as he did, he furnished the patient with preparation for more integrative modes of interaction. Still different ways of demonstrating that fear in the therapeutic relationship is unnecessary would be appropriate with other individuals. Whatever the particular procedure, the eliminating of fear from this relationship is an important factor in the fostering of greater assurance when an individual lacks confidence.

Dependence and Independence in Psychotherapy

Lack of confidence is not only diminished by means of the individual's discovering that he will not be punished in the relationship with a therapist but also by discovering that he can be independent of the therapist. This process is similar to that of a child's finding that he can do things for himself and not needing and not wanting his parent's help in doing them. The parent who prepares his child to get along effectively furnishes his child with help as he needs it, but also encourages his doing things for himself. The therapist has a similar role, and encourages independence as the individual is ready for it. This point can be illustrated by the following summary of a series of therapeutic interviews:

When Mr. M. first came to the therapist, he said that he had "kept himself going by keeping a bottle around the house." He ordinarily did not drink during the day, but when he got home at night he found that he could "let down" from tensions that had built up during the day by means of "a few drinks." He was also troubled by a skin rash that a doctor had told him resulted from nervous tension. It was at the doctor's suggestion that he had come for psychotherapy.

In recent months Mr. M had been given a position in his firm that he had been glad to get but that differed considerably from the work he had previously been doing. His previous work required considerable skill, and he had been very competent at it. It was because of this competence that he had been given the new position. In the new position he had to allocate work and direct others, whereas he worked alone and according to the direction of his supervisor before. It was since he had been promoted that he had been troubled with the skin rash and had been drinking at night. He was sufficiently familiar with his work to do it fairly well in spite of his "nervousness," and had not become so distraught at any time that he did not perform satisfactorily on the job. He was not sure how long he could continue to perform satisfactorily.

Therapy with Mr. M. took the form of explaining that the uneasiness in his new position was not surprising, since he had not had previous experience with the type of work he was doing. It was suggested that he, therefore, had to make allowances for the discomfort that he was going through, and that if he could make allowances he would learn to handle the position more easily as he gained experience. This idea seemed to strike home. He offered the observation himself that he had had to go through a period of training before he was able to do the work that he had been doing before, and that what he was doing now was actually similar to a period of training. One of his problems was that he occasionally had to dictate to a secretary, and felt embarrassed about his English, which was not perfect, as well as about often not knowing exactly how to say what he wanted to. It was suggested that he was perhaps trying too hard to impress the secretary, and that he might even ask her how something sounded or if she could think of a better way of putting it. Since she had had a good deal of secretarial experience, she was able to help him considerably, and was also pleased because he had asked for her help. He at the same time became surer of how to express himself and did not have to depend upon her help as much as he had at first. As incidents of this kind were discussed with the therapist, he also found that he needed his help less and less and came into his office one day with the buoyant but friendly announcement, "I don't think I will need your services any longer." He added that he was no longer keeping a bottle around the house and didn't think he would have to have it around in the future.

In the above case the therapist, in effect, acted as a parent preparing and encouraging his "child" to do things for himself. The analogy to the parent-child relationship does not imply condescension on the part of the therapist. The parent who enables his child to get along effectively on his own is not condescending but respects the child's potentialities for handling his own life. The effective therapist has the same respect for the individual. An indefinite period of dependence upon the therapist was not involved in Mr. M.'s case. When a person's ability to handle his own life is more completely undeveloped in the first place, a more prolonged dependence is often necessary. In some instances a relationship with a therapist continues for years, because the individual's limitations in getting along on his own are like those of a young child. Even in such cases, however, alertness to the individual's potentialities for doing things for himself, and working out ways in which he can gain experience in doing them for himself, can reduce the period of dependence. In view of these considerations, the assumption that has sometimes been made that therapy must necessarily extend over a period of years can be seriously questioned. This assumption is that all of the details of a person's background must be reviewed and "brought to light" before he can "get well."

While it is true that reviewing the ways in which a person learned his modes of interaction is, in general, an important part of therapy, the purpose of this "review" presumably is to enable the individual to get along more effectively now. The details of how he became the kind of person he is are not always of great importance in bringing about new orientations. Mr. M.'s difficulties in dictating to his secretary, for example, could be considered from the point of view of what he might do about it and how he might gain confidence in doing it, without too exhaustive an exploration of why he was overly concerned with "making an impression on her" in the first place. Overpreoccupation with why an individual is what he is can, in fact, be a detriment to reorientation in his present life experience. If Mr. M. had directed his attention primarily to the conditions in his childhood that had interfered with the development of his self-confidence, he might have understood himself better, but still not have any clear ideas about what he could do now to develop greater confidence. Competition with an older brother who always achieved more than he did might have resulted in discouragement and feelings of inferiority on his part. He might come to understand that the competition was actually encouraged by his parents, and in understanding it lose resentment toward his brother. The clearing away of this resentment would make for greater comfort and effectiveness in handling his life in all probability because he would not have to be distracted by it any longer. His effectiveness in getting along in his environment might not actually be increased too much, though, because the steps necessary to displacing his habits of discouragement would still lie ahead of him. Taking these steps requires that the individual be willing to achieve something less than perfection as he is getting underway with working out new modes of interaction. One function of the therapist is enabling the individual to be willing to make step-by-step progress with his problems, as Shaw (1949) brings out in the following quotation:

> What role can the therapist play in manipulating conditions in such a way that the client will meet with reward or success in his attempts at readjustment? While he cannot control the life experiences of the client, the therapist can influence his motivation and levels of aspiration. More specifically, he can assist the client in accepting himself, which will in turn affect his evaluation of his attempts at readjustment. A timid college freshman might consider himself a failure if he had a date but found his conversational efforts somewhat inept. From another point of view the fact that he had the date might be considered an important step in the direction of reorientation. If he can adopt this point of view, he is in a position to reward himself, as it were, for the progress he has made. The motivation based upon self-acceptance, in short, is much different from that based upon unrealistic levels of aspiration, and the prospects of reward accompanying the former are much greater.

The therapist cannot only enable the individual to be willing to make step-by-step progress, as discussed in the above passage in which it is indicated that the freshman must have some dates before he can learn how to talk to girls and get them to talk to him, but can also consider with the individual general ways of going about things that he does not know how to go about. It might be in order, for example, to discuss with the freshman ways in which a girl might be asked for a date. The freshman has to do the asking himself, however, if he is to become independent in handling his own life, just as birds must leave their nests and try their own wings.

Relating Consequences to Behavior in Psychotherapy

From what has been said thus far about the therapeutic relationship, it can be seen that the therapist's function is to foster the growth of confidence when it does not exist. It is also his function to enable the individual to relate his behavior to consequences. The problem of the pseudo-integrative individual (such as Joseph Brown, who was discussed earlier in the chapter, or George T., discussed in the previous chapter) is not lack of confidence, but inability to relate consequences to his behavior does exist. Since the pseudo-integrative individual does not associate consequences with his own behavior because his behavior is perceived as faultless, it is necessary to define the ways in which it leads to difficulties. The analogy to the parent-child relationship can be seen by returning to an earlier example. It was pointed out in the previous chapter that when a youngster bites others so as to injure them severely, and the other children then leave him alone, it could be made clear that being left alone was the consequence of his behavior. The pseudo-integrative individual has not had the experience of the consequences of his behavior being brought home to him in this fashion. Since he does not believe in the reality of punishment, he is uninhibited and proceeds without regard for consequences. A college student with such tendencies might cheer for a team that was opposing the team of his own college, an act not designed to endear him to his classmates. His perception of what happened would be that he was simply having fun, and the disapproval he received from others would be seen as the behavior of "stupid people." It would not be perceived as a consequence of his own behavior.

A therapist who consistently pointed out to the college student, mentioned above, the way in which his behavior made for difficulty might bridge the gap between behavior and consequences. The procedure would not consist of defending others but simply pointing out that whether people reacted in a "stupid" way or not, they did react as they did and that noting how one's own behavior could evoke their "stupidity" might prove more effective in the long run. Such a procedure would tend to prevent writing off the therapist's observations as further stupidity. Alternative ways of acting would be implied at the same time, and might be adopted because they would prove more rewarding in the long run.

The individual with strong pseudo-integrative trends would probably not consult a therapist in the first place. If he did, it would in all probability be done as a means of avoiding punishment. That is, he might try to use a therapist as he previously used an overindulgent parent. The college student mentioned above, for example, might get drunk and disrupt the quiet of the library with loud and obscene language, whereupon he would face the prospect of getting expelled from college. He might then endeavor to get a college doctor to "come to bat" for him on the grounds that he had psychological problems. While it would be true that he had problems they would stem from his skill in using people to get around punishment as he would be trying to use the doctor. Since such an individual is often successful in getting around punishment, or in proceeding to new ventures which work for awhile at least, he would not ordinarily continue to consult a therapist even if he had started to see one.

Enabling the individual with anxiety and lack of confidence to relate his behavior to consequences involves putting him at ease. When he is at ease, the therapist can point out relationships between what he is or is not doing and the problems he is having. They can be pointed out because assurance has been gained after the individual is at ease that the purpose of the therapy is not to punish, but to work out more rewarding modes of interaction. This is shown in the following passage from Shaw (1949) in which the difficulties with present behavior and more rewarding modes of interaction are both indicated, the first indirectly and the second explicitly:

One individual complained of the stupidity of people's conversation about such things as the weather. Further discussion led to the observation that idle conversation was often an attempt to be friendly at least even though it might not be very meaningful in itself. At this point the client was receptive to the idea that he himself might do more to manifest his good will toward others. During the subsequent interview he told with obvious pleasure of the satisfaction he had gotten from engaging people in conversation about the weather. Apparently the previous interview had suggested ways of acting that brought rewarding consequences which in this instance consisted of friendliness shown by others toward the client.

The expression of feelings is an important aspect of therapy, because the individual can discover in the therapeutic relationship that he will not be punished for having certain feelings. Shame and anxiety over sexual and aggressive feelings, for example, can be relieved, and in finding release from this shame and anxiety, the individual can function more effectively. In addition to the diminishing of fear by expressing feeling, its expression also functions to enable the individual to relate his behavior to consequences. Thus, a woman who actually resents being married to her husband, but can't openly admit that this is the case, can get this feeling out in the open in the therapeutic relationship. In doing so, she can more easily relate absence of affection on her part to the difficulties that exist in the marriage relationship. Similarly, if a person can openly admit fear of which he has been ashamed, he can see the relationship between the behavior growing out of the fear and the consequence of this behavior. This behavior might take the form of never making a concession in an argument even when more would be gained by making the concession than by not making it. Being able to acknowledge the fear underlying the refusal to make concessions would amount to relating the "bullheaded" behavior to its consequences. Since the expression of feeling not only relieves shame and anxiety but also facilitates relating behavior to consequences, a therapist must be willing to listen as an individual "gets things off his chest." The analogy to the parent-child relationship can again be drawn. The parent who prepares a child to maintain himself effectively in his environment encourages open discussion rather than bottling up of feelings.

As an outside observer, the therapist is in a position to make clear to the individual the nature of his behavior when he may not be able to see it for himself, because he is too close to it. This idea is expressed by Shaw (1949) in the following quotation:

Still another procedure the therapist can use to make available to the client the unfortunate consequences of his behavior is enabling him to define his modes of adjustment. Let's say that a client reports that he sleeps excessively, prefers to spend a large amount of his time alone, and seeks instruction about his work even when it isn't necessary. Any one of these items of behavior by itself may baffle him. If they are all seen as manifestations of dependence or withdrawal growing out of his dependence they become more comprehensible and the client is able to define them as parts of a total mode of adjustment. In so doing he at the same time has a reaction which can be described as "I see what I am doing" or "I see the relationship between my behavior and my difficulties." In short, the punishing consequences of the behavior have been brought home.

The defining of an individual's behavior, spoken of above, might seem to constitute a serious blow to the individual's self-esteem. It need only be pointed out, however, that the child who has genuine confidence in his parent can take constructive "criticism" from him.

SUMMARY OF PRINCIPLES

In this chapter it has been pointed out that the integrative individual abides by cultural standards and modes of interaction tentatively, but can discard them when it is adaptive to do so as well as conform to them when such conformity is adaptive. The principles of any field of knowledge must be held tentatively in a somewhat similar fashion if more accurate and comprehensive generalizations are to be developed. It was believed for some time, for example, that forgetting was a function of the passage of time. With further investigation, however, it was concluded that although forgetting occurs as time passes under certain conditions that often exist, forgetting was not a function of the passage of time as such but of what happens in time (see Mc-Geoch, 1932). Some of the principles of interactive integration, tentatively proposed in this chapter, are as follows:

1. The pseudo-integrative individual does not get along effectively because (a) he has not learned what leads to punishment and (b) when punishment is encountered, it is not related to his own behavior, which he considers faultless.

2. The anxiety-dominated individual does not get along effectively because (a) he has encountered disabling punishment resulting in his feeling helpless and worthless and (b) his feeling of worthlessness leads to protecting his self-esteem in ways that prevent relating his behavior to its consequences.

3. The integrative individual can continue to learn to get along effectively because in relating his own behavior to consequences,

he selects for learning those modes of interaction that make for effectiveness in maintaining himself in his environment.

4. The reason that the "normal" individual is not necessarily integrative is that the inflexible use of adjustive techniques prescribed by the culture furnishes no guarantee that the individual will maintain himself effectively in his culture.

5. When pseudo-integrative or anxiety-dominated modes of interaction exist, reorientation resulting in integrative modes of interaction can be brought about by altering the learning environment.

a. In order to learn integrative modes of interaction, it is necessary for the pseudo-integrative individual to experience punishment and to perceive that it has something to do with his own behavior.

b. Reorientation leading to more rewarding modes of interaction in the life of the anxiety-dominated individual requires a learning environment in which "pointers" to such interaction can be found, but bluntly pointing out to him the "error in his ways" or simply telling him what he should do is of little help.

6. The individual who lacks confidence must neither fear nor overdepend upon a psychotherapist if he is to profit from the psychotherapy. Additional principles concerning the therapeutic relationship are as follows:

a. One function of the therapist is enabling the individual to make step-by-step progress with his problems.

b. Enabling the individual with lack of confidence to relate his behavior to consequences involves putting him at ease.

c. The expression of feeling in a therapeutic relationship functions to relieve fear and to enable the individual to relate his behavior to consequences.

d. Just as a child who has genuine confidence in a parent can take constructive criticism from him, so an individual who has genuine confidence in a therapist can take constructive "criticism" from him.

CHAPTER 7

Protective Interaction

Introductory Summary

Protective modes of interaction result from the sense of help-lessness that is implicit in any state of fear or anxiety. These protective modes of interaction can be considered from the points of view of turning away from the environment, turning toward the environment, and turning against the environment. Protective turning away from the environment is found in flight as well as in loss of identity, seclusiveness, autistic wish-fulfillment, and motivational apathy. While all protective interaction implies avoidance, it also implies seeking safety or coming to terms with one's environment. Among the protective measures employed in coming to terms with the environment or turning toward the environment are atonement, conformity, bolstering, submission, and ascendence. The clearest example of protection by means of turning against the environment is attack or aggression which occurs when the individual feels threatened or endangered. Suspicion and self-aggrandizement are also forms of turning against the environment and holding at a distance the dangers that the individual feels it contains for him.

ANXIETY AND PROTECTIVE INTERACTION

In order to maintain oneself effectively in his environment fear or anxiety must not be so strong or intolerable that it stands in the way of employing rewarding modes of interaction, but the individual must have enough fear to avoid punishing modes of interaction. One must have enough fear of fire to avoid being

198

burned by it, but not so much that he refuses to use it to cook a meal. When fear is not intense, it functions to give the individual pause and to cause him to "proceed with caution." *A sense of helplessness is implicit in any state of fear or anxiety and becomes stronger as the fear or anxiety mounts.[1] The protective modes of interaction resulting from this sense of helplessness can be considered from the points of view of turning away from the environment, turning toward the environment, and turning against the environment.[2]* The clearest instance of protection by means of turning away from the environment is headlong flight in the face of danger. Protective turning toward the environment can be understood in the light of the fact that flight from danger is flight toward safety. Thus, when one conforms he is avoiding the penalties associated with nonconformity and at the same time seeking safety through turning toward the social environment and abiding by its dictates. The achievement of safety through turning against the environment is a matter of protection through pushing danger away or holding it at a distance. Aggression toward others and suspicion of others are examples of this kind of protective interaction.

PROTECTIVE TURNING AWAY FROM THE ENVIRONMENT

As stated above, the clearest instance of protection by means of turning away from the environment is headlong flight in the face of danger. Protection through turning away from the environment also occurs when the individual does not literally take to his heels. Thus, one might get "fed up" with a dreary existence and turn away from it or try to forget it. This forgetting carried to the extreme becomes loss of identity. Seclusiveness is still another kind of turning away from the environment that the individual employs when under stress. A frequent accompaniment of

[1] In the present discussion no distinction is made between fear and anxiety. Both are thought of as feelings of helplessness that may be of a greater or lesser degree.

[2] The concepts of turning away, turning toward, and turning against the environment were suggested by Karen Horney's concepts (1945) of moving away, moving toward, and moving against others. The present concepts do not correspond completely to Horney's concepts, however.

seclusiveness is autistic wish-fulfillment. Just as seclusiveness and autistic wish-fulfillment are employed as protective measures, motivational apathy or indifference, similarly, can be seen as a form of protective turning away from the environment that is adopted when the individual is under the pressure of anxiety.

Flight

A traumatic event is an experience to which an individual reacts with an overwhelming sense of helplessness and urges toward flight. Combat conditions during war frequently prove traumatic, particularly when a soldier has been exposed to these conditions over a prolonged period of time. Automobile accidents and train wrecks are also examples of situations that have been traumatic for many individuals. As a result of such experiences the individual becomes strongly predisposed to protect himself by turning away from environmental stimuli that are reminiscent of the traumatic incident. Soldiers who have been exposed to intense or prolonged combat, for example, may react with fright and tendencies to seek cover when they hear a tire explode. A person who has been in a traumatic automobile accident may display similar reactions when riding in an automobile if it exceeds a certain speed. Flight from a threatening environment, then, is clearly illustrated by the protective reactions resulting from traumatic experiences.

The impulses toward flight that occur in connection with traumatic experiences are a basic feature of fear, helplessness, or anxiety. The individual's principal motivation in the face of such stress is to relieve it. This pressing need for relief implies instigations to seek protection, and the seeking of protection constitutes a flight from danger. The pressure of the need for relief will, of course, vary with different individuals. The person who has acquired a considerable amount of security, confidence, and self-reliance (all of which are related to frustration-tolerance) will be less predisposed to react to stress with strong anxiety. Instigations to fly from danger can be discerned in such protective measures as clinging to others or attacking others. They can be even more clearly discerned in the actual flights that sometimes occur in response to traumatic events. McDougall (*1926*), for example, reports the case of a soldier who found himself far from the scene of battle without knowing how he had arrived there or what had happened to him. Under treatment it was discovered that the soldier had taken flight when a shell exploded near him. Although unaware of his actions, he had been "driven on," according to McDougall, "by the single strong impulse of fear, taking the form of a desire to get away from the danger-zone."

In the foregoing case the explosion of a shell resulted in fear's mounting to the point where the predominant aim became that of escaping from danger at any cost. It is this mounting of anxiety that produces extreme or acute forms of protective interaction such as the amnesia that accompanied the soldier's flight. The anxiety functioned in such a way that possible consequences of the behavior, such as court-martial, were excluded from awareness. Furthermore, some individuals will be more predisposed to react with strong anxiety under stress than others. The soldier in question, therefore, was undoubtedly reacting to the explosion of the shell on the basis of insecurities he brought to the situation as well as in accordance with the stress of the moment. The same principle is illustrated in far less dramatic experiences than that of the soldier. Any number of students experience tendencies toward "fleeing" from difficult examinations. Some experience the tendency toward flight more strongly than others because of the effects of past experiences which they bring to the examination situation. These past experiences, moreover, need not relate specifically to examinations. If one's past experience has been generally productive of uncertainty about himself, this uncertainty may then be reflected in an examination situation. The effects of past experiences, however, can be counteracted by present and future experiences so that uncertainty about oneself and tendencies toward flight are not necessarily "fixed quantities."

Loss of Identity

In the case discussed above, the soldier forgot who he was or lost his identity for a short period of time. Such loss of identity is a method of protection taking the form of turning away from a hopeless or threatening environment. A milder counterpart of loss of identity is found in the inclination to give up one's mode of life when it seems futile and unrewarding. Army enlistments are sometimes attempts to get away from a dull, boring, or frustrating existence. Dissatisfied people from small towns seek out the big city and unhappy people in big cities swear that they would "give it all up" for the peacefulness of a rural environment. The actor, physician, or engineer who cannot meet the standards of performance he sets for himself also frequently reacts to his disappointment with the desire to "forget it all." Actual forgetting of the circumstances of one's whole life, or loss of identity, is sometimes employed as a protective measure in the face of acute stress. A person may, accordingly, disappear and later be found in another part of the country going by another name without recollection of his previous life. Some crisis, such as failure or an imminent scandal, usually precipitates this loss of identity which can be comprehended as a protective measure in the face of the crisis. Since differences in past experiences predispose people to react differently to crisis situations, a crisis situation in and of itself will not necessarily precipitate a forgetting of one's identity. The degree of security and the adjustive habits that one brings to the crisis will determine the mode of interaction set off by the crisis.

Some inclination toward the dropping of one's old life and taking up anew is probably implicit in reactions to crises since they disrupt existence and threaten values that the individual holds dear. Failure or an imminent scandal might have this effect. Similarly, the soldier's reaction to the explosion of the shell, discussed above, probably involved values of honor and courage; as he began to flee and these values were violated by his fleeing the tendency toward loss of identity may have become stronger and stronger. (This interpretation seems quite plausible in view of the fact that McDougall reported that the soldier had a good record and held a responsible position. Values of honor and courage were probably taken seriously.) The experiencing of the inclination to drop one's old life, in any case, does not mean that one is necessarily strongly predisposed to forget his identity in the face of crisis. The actual loss of identity can, at the same time, be understood as the extreme of a tendency that is not unusual.

Seclusiveness

A milder, everyday form of protective interaction is found in staying at home rather than going out. A college student who is not comfortable with a particular teacher, or with his classmates, or with the ideas that are discussed in the class may stay in his room rather than go to class. He may also oversleep. If he does, he is not the first person in the world to employ oversleeping as a method of protective interaction. Oversleeping and laziness go hand in hand, and the latter is another kind of protective seclusion. The individual who appears to be lazy and unambitious is often a person who is not without ambition but one whose fears of failure keep him from trying to fulfill his ambitions. The student who stays away from a particular class, for example, may want to succeed in the subject that this class is concerned with, but profess indifference and not do what is necessary to succeeding. He may tell himself that he can do the work if he wants to or that the subject matter taken up in the class is really not important. Among other things, an ideal of himself as somebody who does not have to work in order to succeed in his class work may result in laziness rather than "applying himself," because working disturbs this ideal. Failing as a result of not working could also disturb the ideal, to be sure, but it could still be preserved by the student's telling himself that he was really capable of doing the work if he wanted to.

The student mentioned above might continue to go to his class even though he was uncomfortable in this class. Protective seclusion in this case could take the form of remaining quiet while in class or adopting a spectator's rather than a participant's mode of behavior. The behavior of the spectator often appears to be that of a cool observer. Very frequently the "coolness" is more apparent than real. Thus, one who goes to a football game and views his fellows as "idiotic fools shouting their heads off over matters of no consequence" is likely to have fears of not being accepted by others. His "superior" conduct toward them is protective seclusion in the nature of standing off from people rather than letting himself participate with them.

The "superior" conduct toward others found in observing, rather than participating, is somewhat like the behavior of the "lone wolf." The individual who gains a reputation as a lone wolf is not necessarily a person who fears or distrusts others, but may be simply one who is competent enough in his work not to have to depend on others. Nevertheless, even such competence is sometimes striven for or developed as a form of protective seclusion. Thus, one may work on the assumption that if he is successful or competent enough, he will be "above criticism." In the meantime, he protects himself by not getting too close to anybody and not letting anybody get too close to him. This maintaining of distance from others is, of course, a kind of seclusiveness. Highly successful people as well as individuals who have not attained a high level of success become known as lone wolves or as people "you can never get next to." Lone wolf behavior motivated by fear may manifest itself as hard-bitten "toughness" of the kind that Humphrey Bogart portrays in the movies or as the quietness of the "strong, silent type" that Gary Cooper's roles are better known for. While neither of these characteristics of an individual's personality are necessarily indicative of protective seclusion, neither are they necessarily indicative of completely "calm, cool, and collected" reactions, as is so frequently assumed to be the case.

The milder forms of protective seclusion have counterparts in more extreme forms. The individual who stays in his room and day-dreams for an hour differs in degree from the individual who spends weeks at a time in fantasy. Staying at home with a sick headache occasionally to avoid unpleasant events differs in degree from staying in bed for months at a time with ailments that have developed as protective reactions against a fear-inspiring world. The superiority of the withdrawn spectator at the football game differs in degree from that of the emperor in the mental hospital who rules the universe from the vantage point of his "throne." The individual who does not permit himself to "get too close" to anybody differs in degree from the mental patient whose suspicion is manifested by a delusion of persecution to the effect that harmful and invisible rays are being directed at him.

As fear mounts and possibilities of rewarding modes of interaction decrease, the milder forms of protective seclusion tend to become more acute. In simple form this progression can sometimes be observed as a person becomes increasingly unresponsive and has less and less to say as he is overwhelmed by an adversary in an argument. In more complex form, and over a longer range of time, more acute forms of withdrawal sometimes replace earlier forms of withdrawal that are less striking. A person who is noted as "never having too much to say" may become virtually uncommunicative, for example, when thwarting of his life goals becomes pronounced. Such an individual may come home after losing a job and sit in a chair quietly, looking up only occasionally. Suggestions or questions from his wife may be received with apparent indifference or even with a seeming resistance to considering any form of positive action. The seclusive behavior, accordingly, gives the impression not only of quietness but of refusal to interact in a "give and take" fashion with an unrewarding environment.

Negativistic refusal to interact in a "give and take" fashion of the kind described above not only involves the erecting of a wall between the individual and his environment but also often seems to partake of efforts to anticipate all of the dire things that might happen. It is as though the individual not only does not want to venture forth again into an unrewarding environment but also remains utterly still in order to be prepared for punishments or misfortunes that may descend upon him at any moment. Protective seclusion, therefore, may sometimes consist of severing positive ties with the environment but retaining touch with it in order to anticipate further disaster.

Just as milder forms of protective seclusion tend to become more acute as fear mounts and possibilities of rewarding modes of interaction decrease, so more acute forms of seclusiveness may diminish as fear lessens. This lessening of seclusiveness is often apparent in the behavior of children as they become more familiar with new surroundings and increasingly certain that they will be given a "friendly reception." The more uncertain the child is in the first place the more reassurance he will need before relinquishing his tendency to withdraw. Perceptive adults can often win a child's confidence by awaiting opportunities to demonstrate their friendliness without trying to persuade the child to give up his shyness prematurely. As the child gradually discovers that it is not dangerous to enter into active interplay with others he relinquishes his shyness. As he relinquishes his shyness he also gains confidence from the acquiring of new modes of contending with his environment. He may learn to joke with others, for example, when chided himself and the acquiring of the ability to joke equips him to deal with greater assurance with situations that might otherwise prove frightening.

Just as the child can gain confidence from acquiring new modes of contending with his environment, the adult, similarly, gains confidence as his resources for dealing with his environment are enlarged. In the normal course of development, this enlarging of adjustive resourcefulness tends to take place. As experience is gained the ability to meet new demands and assume new responsibilities tends to grow. This growth process appears to be a matter of graded increases in facing challenges. The imposition of very heavy responsibility upon an inexperienced person may undermine his confidence and make him fearful of a lesser degree of responsibility. The imposing of responsibility in proportion to his experience and the resources that he does possess, on the other hand, can foster further development of his resourcefulness. In general, it might be said that challenges that are graded so as to be somewhat difficult but not overwhelming make for a relatively steady increase in the development of the individual's ability to maintain himself effectively in his environment. Recognition of this principle seems to be implicit to some degree in the practice of training men for future positions of responsibility in government, education, and industry by graded increases in responsibilities assigned to them. A more explicit recognition of it might lead to even better provision for developing human resources. Recognition of this principle by the individual, in any case, furnishes him with a means of planning the development of his own adjustive resourcefulness to some degree. Even when strong predispositions toward protective seclusiveness are present graded challenges can be planned which enable the individual to dispense increasingly with the necessity of seclusiveness.

Autistic Wish-Fulfillment

Autistic thinking is a form of imagination or fantasy that is not restrained by the facts of existence.[3] One kind of autistic thinking is found in the wish-fulfilling daydream of wealth and prestige engaged in by the individual who in reality has little status or wealth. A more extreme form of autistic wish fulfillment is found in the delusion of the individual "without a nickel" who actually believes himself to be a millionaire. Autistic wish-fulfillment serves the purpose of gratifying desires through fantasy when they are not gratified in reality and providing the individual with a context of interaction other than the actual setting in which he lives. As fear mounts the individual is more prone to seek protection by means of selecting a substitute setting for his life activities. As with seclusiveness, the milder forms of autistic wish-fulfillment tend to become more acute when rewarding modes of interaction in the environment become less and less accessible to the individual. The adopting of more extreme forms of autistic wish-fulfillment in the face of reduced possibilities of support from the environment is illustrated by the following case:

A young man of outstanding intellectual attainment complained that he dreamt away a few hours each day and was not working efficiently. In his day dreams he received recognition and applause from huge audiences for brilliant achievements, and was troubled by an increasing preoccupation with the idea that he possessed an extraordinary talent as a military strategist. He stated that there was no good reason for holding this idea but life seemed empty without it.

[3] It might be pointed out that creative thinking also goes beyond facts. It differs from autistic thinking in that it goes beyond facts in order to explain them rather than to ignore them.

He reported that neither his father nor mother had had any active social life as he was growing up. The mother was a retiring person and the father, although not as retiring, was ill at ease with people. The father was an intellectually able man, and the patient's own intellectual attainments and aspirations indicated strong identification with the father. The father was also perfectionistic and consistently pointed out defects in the patient's accomplishments even when these accomplishments were above average according to any reasonable standards. As a child he had not learned to play with other youngsters who regarded him as odd, and had been pathetically grateful to the few youngsters in the neighborhood who had been friendly. Long periods of time had been spent in solitude and fantasy during childhood and adolescence.

In spite of this young man's seclusiveness he had managed to establish a romantic relationship with a young woman who liked him and shared various interests with him. She was one of the few people by whom he felt thoroughly accepted and from whom he gained affection that had never been present to any high degree in his experience, except in relationships with an imaginary playmate during childhood. It was after this young woman became engaged to another man that he began to dream away a few hours each day.

The attack on the problem consisted of a gradual fostering of understanding of needs for affection and of how his daydreams of applause and admiration represented needs for affection and responsiveness from others that required satisfaction in his everyday experience. Gradual experimentation in associating with people more actively for purposes of finding warmth in his every day relationships with people was undertaken at the same time. Preoccupation with fantasy gradually became less intense and the social adjustment slowly improved.

The above case illustrates the learning of a particular form of protective interaction. The family environment did not provide models for the child to imitate in dealing with people. The parents, on the contrary, set the example of seclusiveness themselves. Without the ability to participate actively in his social environment and with the strong uncertainty about getting approval from others resulting from his father's perfectionism, it can be seen that the individual might turn to autistic wish-fulfillment for gratification. The satisfaction that he found from it would lead to its acquisition as a characteristic adjustive technique. When he was thwarted in his ardent desires for affection and acceptance as a young man engaged in trying to establish a love relationship, it would, then, be expected that he would fall back on this adjustive technique.

Motivational Apathy

The members of a losing football team are inclined to walk from the field in a dejected and dispirited fashion. Their discouragement can be described as a turning away from the environment with a loss of zest for further active participation in it or as motivational apathy.[4] The tired housewife, the salesman who has worked long hours without making a sale, the worker who cannot make ends meet react with similar apathy. The degree of this apathy corresponds to the intensity of an individual's disappointment. The members of a football team are more disappointed by failure to win a game with a traditional rival than with some other opponent, and the worker who finds no prospect of satisfying ardent desires for a better life is, of course, more profoundly affected by such disappointment than by the loss of a card game. Motivational apathy is a method of protection from stress by means of surrendering to "odds" rather than continuing to meet them as challenges. As disappointment and stress mount, more extreme forms of such apathy appear, as shown by the following case:

A young woman who ordinarily impressed her friends and associates as a cheerful person exhibited what was for her unusual apathy. She had been married for only a short time and believed that she had found "what she was looking for" in the marriage. When she found that her husband was having an affair with another woman she became depressed and seemed to lose her usual interest in living. Since she was ordinarily an apparently cheerful, self-reliant individual, her reaction to her husband's unfaithfulness did not seem to be in keeping with her usual modes of behavior. The unexpected strength of her

[4] Motivational apathy might be considered simply an expression or manifestation of an emotional state. It is viewed here as having adjustive or coping aspects as well as expressive aspects. For the distinction between expressive and coping phenomena, see Maslow (1949).

reaction could be traced to the fact that she had left home when she was only 12 and had managed to support herself quite successfully since that time, but had also always yearned for intimate companionship with another person. She believed that she had found this companionship with her husband, and his disloyalty, therefore, resulted in strong stress and depression. The apathy was an acting out of her feeling that there was little reason for continuing her active interest in daily activities. In spite of her problems her insecurities were not so strong that she did not begin to regain her zest for living and participating in her customary life routines. She at the same time began to gain insight into the conditions leading up to her depression and to learn to make allowance for reactions she might be expected to have to disappointments in love relationships. No serious recurrence of her depression had occurred after several months.

It was pointed out in the above case that the individual's reaction to her husband's unfaithfulness did not seem to be in keeping with her usual modes of behavior. A consideration of her life history suggests that in reality it was in keeping with earlier reactions. Her desires for intimate companionship had existed previously and it is probable that she periodically became depressed over the absence of such companionship. The depression with which she reacted to her husband's disloyalty, then, can be understood as a more pronounced recurrence of depressive reactions that had occurred before.

PROTECTIVE TURNING TOWARD THE ENVIRONMENT

Protective interaction is directed toward relief from the stress of anxiety. It is a flight from danger and a flight toward safety. While all protective interaction implies avoidance, it also implies seeking safety or in some way coming to terms with one's environment. Among the protective measures employed in coming to terms with the environment or turning toward it are atonement, conformity, bolstering, submission, and ascendance.

Atonement

Atonement is a method of restoring a sense of security and well-being by means of suffering penalties for what a person reacts to as his misdeeds. Thus, a child sometimes confesses a misdemeanor to a parent at the risk of being punished when the misdemeanor might have gone undetected. In atoning the individual turns toward his environment and seeks restoration to good standing in it. Many acts of so-called self-punishment can plausibly be attributed to such seeking of restoration. The criminal who gives himself up makes a gesture toward restoration to good standing by seeking punishment. He may at the same time be seeking attention as a kind of substitute for affection by means of his misdeed. A person might, accordingly, commit a robbery, then confess, and gain attention and a feeling that he is significant enough to be given such attention. In such cases the need for attention is ordinarily not understood by the individual, and feelings of guilt for the misdeed are often present even though it was engaged in in the first place for the purpose of getting attention. In other cases the misdeed was not engaged in for the purpose of getting attention, but guilt over the misdeed does impel the individual to atone by seeking punishment. Greene (1948), for example, relates the case of a murder in which the body was left in open view and the murderer drove around in the victim's car and wore his clothes. All of these acts were well designed to receive punishment for the crime. This is not to say that they were planned with awareness on the part of the murderer that they more or less insured his getting caught. These acts lend themselves to an interpretation of seeking punishment for the crime, nevertheless. The victim had asked his assailant, "Why don't you quit drinking and make a man out of yourself?" The question had aroused the fury that the defendant's own father aroused on various occasions when he reprimanded him and actually used the phrase, "Make a man of yourself." In his rage the defendant shot the victim and his subsequent behavior, as has been said, appears to have been motivated in large part by guilt over his act.

The atonement for hostility that is indicated by the case discussed above seems to be an important factor in many instances of depression. In one case, for example, a woman went into a deep depression beyond the bounds of ordinary grief when her mother died. The facts of the matter were that she had supported the mother and lived with her for a great many years. Apparently nothing but fondness for one another existed in the relationship between the mother and daughter. Actually, the daughter had repressed deep resentment toward her mother who had thoroughly dominated her life. When the mother died, then, the daughter's depression seemed to result from the hostility she held toward the mother. It was as though she had been responsible for her mother's death because of her hostility. The depression could be understood as a kind of atonement or as a manifestation of needs for atonement, although it also involved grief that would be expected in any case over the loss of a person to whom there had been a strong affectional tie. It was at the same time a more acute outcome of guilt that the daughter had experienced when the mother was alive on occasions when she had not acted in accordance with the mother's wishes.

Many instances of everyday behavior offer fairly clear suggestions of atonement. Thus, a man may conceal his pause for a moment of relaxation with his cronies as his reason for getting home late but then inadvertently let his wife know that this is his real reason for being late. The "inadvertence" in such an instance may be motivated by guilt over getting home late and serve the purpose of atonement, since the man brings punishment upon himself when he reveals why he was late. Similarly, a student may cheat on an examination but do so in such an obvious manner that he makes sure, as it were, that he will get caught. He might also copy words directly from another rather than introducing his own variations and then double the probability of being caught by handing in his paper immediately after the individual from whom he copied handed in his; the proximity of the similar papers will then make it quite evident to the grader that there has been cheating. The man who "inadvertently" reveals to his wife the real reason for getting home late and the student who "inadvertently" gets caught cheating can both be understood as abiding by standards of conscience. Having violated the standards they then make amends by atonement or by bringing punishment upon themselves. Since the development of standards of conscience of one kind or another is an integral part of the individual's preparation for living in society, tendencies toward atonement are to be expected when these standards are violated. When the actual seeking of punishment is understood in this light, it is less likely to be regarded as "abnormal," as is true of many other forms of "abnormal" behavior when considered from the point of view of the process underlying the behavior. Atonement, moreover, can be employed deliberately rather than more or less unknowingly. Thus, a person may deliberately decide to make a "clean breast" of something and accept whatever penalties go with this course of action as more tolerable than a guilty conscience. While standards of conscience may be overdeveloped and destructive from the individual's point of view, it is also true that living in society ordinarily involves training in such standards. The deliberate use of atonement may, therefore, often prove useful and adaptive since the individual must contend with his own conscience as much as with events external to himself.

Conformity

Conformity is another method of turning toward the environment as a means of protection when anxiety impels the individual to seek protection. It is, of course, an aspect of atonement since the individual conforms to social standards that he has made his own when he atones. Since penalties exist for violating laws and social customs, conformity is a realistic method of maintaining oneself in his social environment. It is also true that the anxiety associated with failure to conform can and does become so strong that the individual is compelled to devote so much of his energy to relieving this anxiety that his efficiency in maintaining himself in his environment is considerably reduced. A well-known example of such reduction of efficiency in psychological literature is the compulsion to wash one's hands repeatedly as a symbolic way of ridding oneself of "sin," and thereby conforming, when the sense of sin is based on the violation of a moral code. In such instances large amounts of time are given over to the compulsion and strong distress is experienced if it can't be carried out. As with atonement, the symbolic gesture toward ridding oneself of "sin" can be understood as turning toward the environment in that it signifies an attempt to restore, or a concern with restoring oneself to good standing.

The conformity that can be discerned in the hand-washing compulsion described above is also present in a more generalized kind of compulsiveness taking the form of excessively strong inclinations toward orderliness. The housewife who must have everything in "apple pie order" at any cost as well as the shop-keeper who is overly obsessed with the motto, "A place for everything and a thing for everyplace," are frequently people who have learned to anticipate severe disapproval if their behavior does not please others. Their orderliness and perfectionism, then, are forms of conformity designed to insure approval. Perfectionism and orderliness, furthermore, serve the purpose of distraction from what are reacted to as antisocial or unacceptable desires or impulses. The shopkeeper who is overly intent upon orderliness, for example, can distract himself from irritations that his cus-tomers provoke by his obsession with orderliness. Such obses-siveness, furthermore, often symbolizes a person's attempt to bring order into his own life or to understand himself when conflicts associated with repressed impulses exist. The elaborate schemes that some mental patients have for curing the world's ills, and thus bringing order into chaos, can be partially under-stood in this light.

The relationship between anxiety and conformity is illustrated by anxiety attacks, episodes of extreme fright, which seem to occur when the individual feels that he is confronted by the danger of ostracism for the desires he holds. These desires are not understood by the individual but retaliation for their socially unacceptable nature is, nevertheless, anticipated. The anxiety attack occurs when circumstances are such as to arouse the anticipation of disapproval to a high degree. In one case, for example, a woman had been carrying on an affair with a married man and had an anxiety attack when it appeared that this affair would be exposed. Her attitude toward marriage was on the one hand cynical because of the shock and disillusionment she had experienced when her own parents were divorced after she had been taught that marriage was a "sacred institution." On the other hand this teaching had instilled fear of the consequences of immoral conduct. This fear was deep-seated in spite of the attempt to discard the reverent attitude held toward marriage and the family by having an illicit affair with a married man. When it appeared that this affair would become known to a great many people, there was not only concern, which might have been expected in any case, but a strong anxiety reaction involving fear that her heart would stop, that she would not be able to get her breath, and so on. Underlying this anxiety was the desire to defy the moral standards that had become deeply instilled but which she had also learned to despise because of their violation by the very people from whom she had learned them. The anxiety attack seemed to be an acute anticipation of ostracism precipitated by the danger of being caught in having gone as far as she had in her defiance of the moral standards. Defiance, or urges toward defiance, are not an uncommon basis for anxiety attacks. In another instance a man experienced such an attack after reprimanding a waiter. Prior to this he had himself been reprimanded by his employer and, although believing that he had accepted the reprimand with good grace, he had become somewhat depressed. The anger displayed toward the waiter set off the anxiety attack because it was closely related to defiance of the employer. The employer was a figure of authority, and desires to rebel against authority were reacted to as dangerous and productive of ostracism and retaliation for such rebellion.

Conformity need not be motivated by strong anxiety, of course, but simply by the necessity of abiding by laws, customs, and regulations. The degree to which it is motivated by anxiety would appear to be a function in large part of past and present relationships with authority figures. The effects of interaction with harsh figures of authority can be counteracted by relationships with "more reasonable" figures of authority. Understanding teachers, for example, are often successful in helping frightened children to become less fearful of offending authority. Adults as well as children make authority attitudes a part of themselves, however, and the diminishing of strong fear as a condition motivating conformity or over-conformity can often be considerably facilitated by understanding the nature of these attitudes. Exaggerated anticipations of disapproval from authority may be present, for instance, and the individual making this anticipation may, in fact, be unable to "give himself a break." A simple mistake may, accordingly, evoke relatively strong feelings of guilt or worthlessness. When this happens, it is as though the individual was acting as his own severe judge. While it is no simple matter to talk himself out of his own severe judgments, it is also true that some comprehension of the part played by his own attitudes can contribute to reorientation. One might take note of his reaction to a mistake, for example, evaluate how proportionate or disproportionate it is to what has actually happened, and proceed as best he can without exaggerating the consequences of his error. The individual who is not unduly burdened by fears of disapproval interacts in this fashion habitually when the occasion for doing so arises, and the individual who is more heavily burdened by conformity anxiety can learn to do so. Here, then, we have another illustration of the modifiability of acute forms of protective interaction. Although they may take striking and even bizarre forms, they are subject to change through relearning processes as is true of most forms of human behavior.

Bolstering

Bolstering oneself is a method of seeking to be on equal terms with one's environment by distraction from anxiety. A well-known example is whistling in the dark when a person is actually afraid. The whistling is, of course, an attempt to persuade oneself that everything is all right and that "the situation is under control." Another common form of bolstering oneself and distracting himself from anxiety at the same time is excessive eating, although it is not as generally recognized as a method of handling anxiety. In one case a man told about grabbing food that was at hand and "stuffing it down" when a crisis arose in his business. While this activity was not in itself effective in doing anything about the crisis, it can be understood as an attempt to quench anxiety and as a kind of preparation for meeting a crisis. This same man had an inclination to gain weight during periods of domestic or business stress. His excessive eating was, therefore, a characteristic way of trying to "hold a position in his environment" when under pressure. Sexual activity also sometimes serves the purpose of bolstering oneself by means of distraction from anxiety. Masturbation may be engaged in, for example, as a means of reducing feelings of distress and providing, temporarily at least, feelings of security or of being on equal terms with one's environment. The consumption of alcohol can serve a similar purpose. That is, it can function to offset anxiety and feelings of inadequacy and at the same time to give the individual a feeling of strength or assurance in dealing with his environment, as shown by the following case:

One patient more or less consistently asked his physician for medicine that "kept his nerves under control." When unable to secure this medicine, or in combination with securing it, he drank regularly. During a period when he had been in the Army he had gotten along quite well with no outstanding episodes of emotional disturbance. The Army had in certain respects provided him with a kind of sheltering and relief from responsibility. After getting out of the Army he had attempted to go into business for himself, but seemed to become afraid of whatever he attempted and resorted to "medicine" or drinking whenever he could not see his way clearly to success in whatever he undertook. His home background had been characterized by a constant economic struggle to keep the various members of the family clothed and fed, and the father and mother were impatient people who made no particular effort to conceal their own anxieties from their children. In view of this background, the patient's need for the support that he gained from alcohol was thoroughly comprehensible. During periods of achievement he drank less, but his confidence was seldom sustained. He consistently returned to the use of alcohol and demands for drugs from his physician. Improvement in his condition began to occur, however, and seemed to result, in part at least, from a prolonged relationship with another person who assumed a supporting role and made it possible for the patient to go through a comfortable period of dependence while gradually "weaning" him toward independence at the same time.

In the above account the absence of a supporting relationship can be seen as the basis for learning the bolstering techniques, taking the form of use of drugs and alcohols, in the first place. If the individual's background had provided him with the support that he was in need of while learning to stand on his own, it does not seem likely that basic doubts about his ability to cope with various life demands would have existed to such a high degree. As matters stood, these doubts were present and the use of drugs had been learned as a means of blotting them out in an effort to deal with his environment as though he were sure of himself.

Submission

Submission is a method of protective interaction taking the form of turning to others and placing oneself in their hands. An everyday illustration is found in the attitudes that are often adopted when people consult a physician and look to him as an all-knowing parent who will relieve them of responsibility and make everything come out all right. These attitudes are to be expected to some degree during a period of sickness when one's energy is depleted and there is a corresponding sense of weakness or helplessness. They may also be characteristic of an individual's usual mode of life and exhibit themselves in a readiness to take directions or to turn to superiors for a solution of problems. These inclinations to seek protection from more powerful figures have a basis in childhood experience during which the individual learns to look to parents and other adults for direction, support, and guidance. They persist into adult life and can be observed among the disciples of intellectual leaders as well as the followers of political leaders. One columnist analyzed Franklin Roosevelt's popularity with the people during his presidency in terms of his ability to adopt the role of a benevolent father to the people. The inclination to seek protection through submission is most pronounced when one has not learned to act independently and has not acquired an assurance concerning his ability to make out in his environment. Milder manifestations of protective submissiveness tend to become more acute as stress and anxiety mount, as is shown by the following case:

A young man became emotionally disturbed after a period of a few months during which he had been away from home for the first time. He had been working and trying to accumulate money so that he would be able to go to school and prepare himself for a professional career. His associates were a friendly group of men but "razzed" him about his desire to go to college and also tried to teach him "to live" through escapades involving liquor and women. The patient reacted to the interest of his new friends by falling into the submissive role of a younger brother seeking to be one of the "guys" and to gain the approval of people whom he admired. He, at the same time, had no preparation for his new life and became more and more anxious about his ability to carry on in his new environment. At this time he met another young man whose adjustment took the form of "leadership" of others. He diagnosed people's problems, told them what they would have to do to solve them, and proclaimed his ideas for bringing peace to the world all at the same time. The young man under consideration followed the "leadership" of the other young man by listening intently to his ideas, holding towels for him when he washed, running errands for him, etc. While his submissiveness was evident before, it was now even more striking. It again diminished, however, as he became more comfortable and self-assured in his new environment in somewhat the same fashion that a college senior exhibits greater confidence than a college freshman.

The submissive interaction of the person described above, employed as a protective device, can be found in many forms. Although this person was a "follower," leaders themselves often display a similar submissiveness in their dedication to doctrines or causes. Their devotion to a cause is in many ways comparable to one's putting himself in the hands of a physician who is looked to as one who has all of the answers. A school of thought or point of view, whether political, economic, psychological, sociological, biological, or otherwise can, of course, be seized upon in a submissive fashion as the answer to various problems by the leaders of these "schools" themselves as well as by their followers.

Ascendance

Ascendance[5] is a form of protective interaction directed toward relieving anxiety by mobilizing one's energy so as to gain

[5] "Ascendance" is not used in the sense of dominance in this discussion; the latter meaning is often attached to the term in psychological literature.

control or mastery over the environment. Engaging in a burst of activity in order to clear away obstacles and to provide oneself with the conviction that he can achieve his goals is an outstanding characteristic of protective ascendance. The person who actually feels inferior sometimes undertakes a hundred and one projects and provides himself with the impression that he is highly capable and possessed of unlimited resources for getting along in the world. This striving toward capability also frequently underlies high aspirations. The struggling artist or writer who is intent upon creating a painting or writing a novel that will "end all" paintings or novels is likely to be an individual who is striving to prove himself. The businessman, politician, or scientist who struggles toward building financial, political, or research empires or projects also frequently has needs for demonstrating his capabilities. These needs may eventuate in highly creative achievements. The frustration of strong needs may also lead to forms of protective ascendance that persuade the person that he is doing all right or that all is well, but accomplish little more. Maslow and Mittelmann (1951), for example, report the case of a woman who was advised by the physician of a man she was going to marry to postpone the marriage. On the following day, she "became over-active and over-talkative," according to Maslow and Mittelmann, and talked in an excited and elated way to the man about their forthcoming marriage. Maslow and Mittelmann say that "in this instance, the postponed marriage was evaluated as a threatening catastrophe, depriving her of hoped-for help and dependence, and rescue from her state of helplessness and abandonment."

In the case described above, the woman's becoming overactive and overtalkative illustrates a surge toward ascendance over the environment and a burst of activity designed to make everything come out all right. She had previously idealized the man she had hoped to marry. This idealization can be understood as protective interaction in the form of submissiveness since he was quite obviously regarded as someone who would take care of her in a thorough-going fashion. When this submissive solution to her life problems was thwarted by the advice of the physician, she adopted another form of protective interaction involving an ascendant approach to her environment. This ascendant reaction is somewhat comparable to a man's cheerfully announcing that he is not going to be bothered by a failure in a business transaction that he had set high hopes upon and proceeding to throw a party as though he had consummated a hoped-for contract.

Protective ascendance tends to be associated with underlying feelings of inadequacy or inability to cope with a situation. A clear illustration is provided by a man's proclaiming in the face of reverses that he has the best business in the world, when actually consumed by doubts as to whether he can keep the business going. Conditions may change so that the need for protective ascendance may diminish. The man's business might improve, for example. A similar kind of diminution of the need for protective ascendance after it had appeared can be discerned in the following case:

A young woman of rural background secured a job as a clerical worker in a firm in a large city. She had not had business-college training but had managed to complete a commercial high school course in spite of circumstances which militated against her finishing high school. She came from a poor farm family that actually had difficulty in providing itself with adequate clothing during cold weather. The help of the children was also needed at home and it would not have been surprising if she had dropped out of school relatively early.

After finishing high school, she secured the clerical position through the help of an older person who had "connections" in the city and whose attention was brought to this young woman as a "very deserving person." The head of the office in which she worked took a similar view and could be described as adopting a fatherly attitude toward her. Under the influence of his interest and constant reassurance she did well in her work. The impression of her as a "deserving person" was confirmed, then, and it was no doubt gratifying to her superior to believe that he was helping such a person and was in a position to reward her for her good work. He, therefore, promoted her to a position of greater responsibility, but overlooked the fact that she might not be prepared for this responsibility. Such proved to be the case, unfortunately. The new position required that she make decisions about scheduling her own work as well as that of some of the girls she worked with in addition to other decisions, as opposed to cut and dried routines which she had been able to follow in her work before.

In the new position this young woman worked very conscientiously but took unduly long to make decisions and would then frequently reverse herself after making them. Her superior once again reassured her and encouraged her as he had done previously but called her into his office to talk to her rather than casually offering his encouragement in normal everyday contacts as he had done previously. She responded to this well-intended gesture as an ultimatum to improve her work and "went forth" into the office encouraging the other girls to work hard and became extraordinarily active herself. Her superior then saw that the responsibilities of her new position were "too much" for her and arranged to relieve her of some of them without detracting from the importance of her position. With this turn of events the young woman calmed down, did good work again, and ultimately went on to more responsible work after having opportunity to learn more gradually how to assume increasing responsibility.

In the foregoing case it is evident that the ascendant behavior was associated with feelings of inadequacy and inability to cope with a situation. It also diminished when conditions which had aroused these feelings changed. The gradual learning to take increasing responsibility, moreover, would appear to be the kind of learning that had not occurred earlier, and that is likely to lessen the pre-disposition to adopt acute modes of protective interaction.

PROTECTIVE TURNING AGAINST THE ENVIRONMENT

The clearest example of protection by means of turning against the environment is attack or aggression which occurs when the individual feels threatened or endangered. Insults probably occur more often than not when a person anticipates being embarrassed or ridiculed himself. Just as an insult "pushes away" danger or is designed to fend it off, suspicion is also a form of protection through holding anticipated danger at a distance. Self-aggrandizement designed to gain a sense of power over others is still another form of turning against the environment and pushing away the dangers that the individual feels that it holds for him.

Aggression

Aggression is a method of protection by means of offense or attack. Although the expression of anger and aggressive impulses often brings relief from anxiety, as when one relates to a friend how he was enraged by some experience, it is also true that anxiety is intimately related to aggression. Impulses to attack arise when the individual feels threatened. They cannot be differentiated too sharply from impulses to flee. In both flight and attack the individual is concerned with getting away from a dangerous environment, but does it by running away from the environment in the one instance and pushing it away in the other instance. The anticipation of negative evaluations or contempt from others constitutes an interpretation of one's environment as dangerous. Striking back at such an environment is, of course, a protective or defensive measure. Thus, the individual who expects to be criticized often criticizes his "assailants." The expectation of criticism is given added strength by the individual's own contempt for himself. The short man, who actually dislikes being short, although protesting that a short man is as good as any other man, expects to be held in contempt by others. In order to guard himself against "injury," an aggressive mode of behavior toward others, which is designed to forestall attack on himself, may be adopted. Similarly, the individual whose estimate of his own ability is in reality low anticipates corresponding estimates of himself or his work from others. An aggressive defense of his work taking the form of finding flaws in the work of others may, accordingly, be launched. A part of the explanation of lawyers, plumbers, doctors, dentists, grocers, psychologists, and chemists berating the accomplishments of their colleagues can probably be found in lack of confidence in themselves and the doubtful estimates they hold of their own ability. A somewhat similar relationship between aggressive behavior and a low estimate of oneself can be discovered in the joke about the man who thinks about borrowing a lawn mower from his neighbor. On the way to his neighbor's house he imagines that the neighbor refuses and by the time he gets there and speaks to his neighbor he tells him to keep his lawn mower before the neighbor has a chance to realize what he came to his house for. This joke is an exaggeration of reactions that do occur, but one can imagine how a person lacking confidence in himself, or not having too high an estimate of himself, might anticipate being turned down and then feel aggressive.

In extreme instances an individual might attribute his own unacknowledged negative evaluations of himself to others and then actually assault the individual or individuals he believes to be responsible for "taunting" him. Thus, one might unknowingly hold his own sexual desires in contempt but attribute his contempt of himself to others, believe that he is being ridiculed, and then actually make an assault upon someone he believes to be a persecutor. It is only in the extreme instance that actually assaultive behavior would occur. Nevertheless, a relationship between this acute kind of protective aggression and lesser manifestations of it, as in the case of the man telling his neighbor to keep his lawn mower, can be seen. While this observation does not mean that the lesser instances of protective aggression signify that a person is likely to become violent, it does indicate that both the lesser and more acute forms of protective aggression, which appears to be a very positive form of behavior, are associated with insecurity.

Suspicion

Suspicion is a form of protective interaction in the nature of guarding against a dangerous environment or what the individual interprets as a dangerous environment. It can also be defined as caution or mistrust that arises when one is afraid. A snarling dog, for example, is approached with a certain amount of hesitation if approached at all. A somewhat similar distrust is found when people learn to anticipate negative evaluations of themselves and to hold themselves in contempt at the same time. Contempt for oneself has many origins. It may stem from economic impoverishment which has the psychological effect of making the individual feel unwanted or "not worth feeding" when it is evident to him that others in his society are better off economically and are apparently "worth feeding." The negative evaluation of oneself might also result from being "kicked around" a good deal during childhood as in the case of an individual who is shifted from one family to another without ever feeling accepted in any environment. It also occurs when one does not feel that he measures up to cultural standards, even though he does not admit to himself that he feels this way. Thus, a basically timid man may have doubts about his masculinity because timidity is not in accord with cultural standards (that the individual adopts for himself) of masculinity. Whatever the source of the negative evaluation the individual makes of himself, the tendency is to anticipate this same evaluation from others and to be suspicious of them because of the injury, harm, or ridicule that is expected from them. Thus, if one feels funny about his clothes or makes a negative evaluation of his own manner of dress, he anticipates being looked down upon by others and is leery of the attitudes they might hold toward an individual who is dressed as he is. His tendency is to feel that people are looking at him or referring to him, even though they may be paying no attention to him. The most acute or extreme form of suspicion is found in delusions of persecution, convictions that one is being plotted or conspired against when no plots or conspiracies actually exist. In less extreme forms of protective suspicion the individual is guarded in his relationships with people. A basis for such guardedness can be found in the case below:

Benjamin was a second child whose mother had declared that she did not want any more children after his older sister was born. To many outward appearances Benjamin was treated as well as his sister. His parents spent as much money for his clothes, for example, and the children were treated equally in the dispensing of gifts. In many other ways Benjamin was not treated as well as his sister. The mother gave her attention more readily to the sister, showed greater interest in her school work and·play activities, seemed more eager for her companionship, and so on. The father was away from home a large share of the time. When he was home, he exhibited a kindly but detached attitude toward his children and Benjamin's efforts to secure from him any sustained affection of a kind that is meaningful to a child were fruitless.

As a consequence of the conditions of his childhood life described above, Benjamin was something less than a buoyant, cheerful youngster. His "moodiness" was attributed to an "unpleasant temperament," and Benjamin himself learned to feel that he was always at fault. Having acquired this conviction, it was impossible for him to feel that any resentment he harbored toward his mother and sister was justified. His resentment was, therefore, repressed, and going hand in hand with its repression there developed an apparently strong devotion for the members of his family. This "devotion" to people he actually resented detracted from an already negligible sense of self-respect. The underlying feelings of worthlessness, in turn, predisposed him to feel that no one could actually be fond of him.

As Benjamin grew older, it became increasingly difficult for him to believe that others could actually like him. When others were genuinely friendly, it was believed that they were really only grateful for some favor he had done rather than fond of him as a person or that they would not be as friendly if they knew him better. This distrust of others was not apparent to the casual observer to whom Benjamin seemed a likable person. However, there was a tendency among his acquaintances to feel that he was a difficult person to know even though he seemed cordial enough in the contacts they did have with him.

The relationship between negative evaluations of oneself and suspicion in interpersonal relationships can be traced in the above case to damaged self-respect based upon rejection in the early family environment. Benjamin developed a conviction, which he was in all probability unaware of himself, that anyone as despicable as himself could not be liked by others. Although he seemed friendly enough on the surface, he actually anticipated that others would have as little regard for him as a person as he had for himself. The remedy to this state of affairs, needless to say, would consist of the development of more positive evaluations of himself. While the individual cannot simply talk himself into adopting such feelings, it is also true that negative self-evaluations are subject to change. Benjamin, for example, might be in the habit of accepting other people's judgments about him rather than bringing his own judgment to bear. A habit of this kind can be displaced to a considerable degree as the individual learns that his own judgment of himself can be employed realistically without regarding himself as either hopeless or perfect. As this learning takes place, the individual is less subject to negative evaluations of himself.

Self-Aggrandizement

Self-aggrandizement is a protective measure taking the form of exalting oneself over others and striving for power. The woman who prides herself on the number of men who have fallen in love with her demonstrates self-aggrandizement. A corresponding exalting of oneself is found in the man who fancies himself an unusually accomplished lover. Other examples of endeavoring to hold power over others and to exalt oneself are found in the efforts of some orators to control the feelings of an audience, attempts to influence others through calculated adopting of poses, and subjecting others to one's beck and call through a position of influence. Self-aggrandizement is designed to furnish the individual with a feeling of power and offsets the feeling of helplessness that is implicit in anxiety. Thus an individual who actually feels insignificant himself reduces such feelings by being able to have someone do his bidding. Sending someone on an errand, for example, can function so as to enhance one's own feeling of significance. One former Army officer admitted that he had derived considerable gratification from assigning enlisted men to onerous and menial tasks.

Seeking symbols of prestige is a form of self-aggrandizement. Clothes, cars, houses, titles, etc., are employed as symbols of prestige. A title can be sought, for example, as a way of proclaiming one's importance and an expensive house may be desired not only as a comfortable place to live but also as a sign of one's status. Since prestige furnishes an individual with security and acceptance in a social group, it is to be expected that the symbols of status in that group would be valued by its members. The more uncertain and anxious an individual is about himself and his acceptance by others, however, the more preoccupied he is likely to be with prestige. This preoccupation with prestige and power is found in extreme form in the position of importance that patients suffering from delusions of persecution sometimes give to themselves. Such a patient may believe that he is the rightful heir to a throne but is being kept from the throne by a conspiracy. His belief that he is heir to a throne can be understood as a form of self-aggrandizement and his conviction that there is a conspiracy against him would appear to be a form of protective suspicion.

Self-aggrandizement, of course, does not ordinarily take on the proportions of a delusion in the form of a belief that one is a great and famous person. Moreover, some degree of preoccupation with one's own importance is to be expected in a culture in which the individual learns to strive for distinctiveness as an individual. A desire to be an "important person" is, therefore, not necessarily an indication of extreme insecurity or anxiety. The preoccupation with it may be greater, as was pointed out above, when the individual is uncertain about himself, but the desire for recognition of one's distinctiveness as a person is likely to figure prominently in the psychological make-up of relatively secure as well as insecure individuals in a culture in which the importance of the individual is stressed. The needs of "normal" and "abnormal" people do not differ essentially, but the pressure to gratify them is ordinarily greater and more intolerable for the "abnormal" person. Provision for their gratification is important to the welfare of the individual in any case. Accordingly, the office worker is disgruntled when his need for recognition is not gratified by praise from a superior, and mental patients have been known to object when doctors address them by their first name but do not expect to be addressed in turn by the first name.

A final observation to be made about self-aggrandizement is that individuals who have learned to evaluate their own behavior as faultless might be expected to react with strong feelings of persecution and intensified beliefs in the faultlessness of their own behavior when thwarted. In the case of Dr. Franklin (pp. 7–9) it was evident that she interpreted her behavior as faultless. She would violate ordinary social conventions such as not fulfilling the everyday responsibilities of a position she held, for example, with no apparent conception of there being anything wrong with her behavior. When exception was taken to such conduct, she was convinced that she was being persecuted and developed more intense beliefs in the correctness of her own conduct, a reaction comparable to self-aggrandizement. Many modes of interaction combining self-aggrandizement and feelings of persecution might, therefore, be explained by the hypothesis that they are the outcome of the individual's having been trained to perceive his behavior as faultless.[6] In such instances the self-aggrandizement is perhaps not so much a function of anxiety within the personality as it is of the individual's having too little anxiety over, or responsibility for, his own behavior.

SUMMARY OF PRINCIPLES

In this chapter the concepts of turning away from the environment, turning toward the environment, and turning against the environment have been employed to suggest the nature of defensive or protective processes. The fundamental principles concerning these processes that have been proposed in this chapter are these:

1. Protective interaction is motivated by anxiety.

2. As fear, anxiety, or helplessness mount and possibilities of rewarding modes of interaction decrease, milder forms of protective interaction tend to become more acute.

3. The person who has acquired a considerable amount of frustration-tolerance will be less predisposed to employ the more acute forms of protective interaction under stress than the person who has acquired a lesser degree of frustration-tolerance.

4. When underlying negative evaluations of oneself exist the tendency is to anticipate these evaluations from others and to employ protective measures as a defense against what is perceived as a hostile social environment.

[6] According to this hypothesis, "true paranoia" might be the outcome of the thwarting of a "psychopathic personality," sometimes spoken of as a "moral imbecile."

CHAPTER 8

Interaction in Age Positions

Introductory Summary

Practically any term used to refer to an individual's position in a social group implies at least some age range. Expectations exist of what the individual's interaction will be in various age positions, and these expectations are not only the basis of attitudes that others have toward the individual but they also become internalized or become the basis of attitudes that the individual has toward himself. Failure to reach certain goals at particular ages is, of course, more of a blow to self-esteem when one has learned to evaluate his personal worth in terms of promotion, prestige, recognition, and social position. This kind of evaluation of personal worth varies with different social groups.

In spite of the valuing of youthfulness in the American culture, the earlier periods of life are by no means free of pressure, and the child, adolescent, and young adult engage in a struggle to achieve full adult status and interaction on equal terms. Preparation for future age interaction is carried on in many ways. Older person–younger person relationships and practice in future age activities in play groups are two of the principal means the culture provides for such preparation.

INTERACTION IN SOCIAL POSITIONS

Throughout the preceding chapters attention has been directed to the relationship between the individual's interaction and his social environment. The concept of interaction in a social position furnishes a convenient way of thinking about this relation-

230

ship. Social positions are "places" in the social structure and can be designated by terms employed in everyday speech. Thus, there are the positions of mother, father, child in the family, worker, employer, policeman, officer in a club, etc. Expectations exist of what behavior in these positions should be. A father is supposed to be a good provider, a worker is expected to be punctual, and it is anticipated that an officer in a club will take more responsibility than the ordinary member for carrying on the activities of the club. While no two fathers, workers, or club officers may attempt to meet social expectations of interaction in their positions in the same way—one father may provide for his family in one way and another in a different way, for example —the behavior of each of them may be designed to meet social expectations. Even behavior that does not meet social expectations having to do with interaction in particular positions is usually influenced by these expectations. A worker might not be punctual, for example, but still show the influence of the expectation that he should be punctual in one fashion or another. The individual's life activities, then, take place in social positions and within frameworks that are defined by social expectations.

Since age, sex, and hierarchy positions can be found in any society, a consideration of the behavior associated with these positions is essential to a full understanding of the individual's interaction in his social environment.

AGE-BEHAVIOR EXPECTATIONS

Practically any term used to refer to an individual's position in a social group implies at least some age range. The range may be broader or narrower but certain limits are usually suggested. A grandfather under 40 years of age, for example, is relatively rare, and our concept of grandfather is determined in part by some such limit. Actually, of course, the word "grandfather" usually brings to mind an age range that begins with an age beyond 40. There is no upper limit in this instance as there is when we use the term "adolescent." The range in this instance would run from the early teens to the early twenties. "Child," "young man," "middle-aged woman," as well as terms such as "pop," "uncle," "kid brother," and so on, all designate age positions. Expectations exist as to what the individual's behavior will be in these positions, and these expectations are not only the basis of attitudes that others have toward the individual but they also become internalized or become the basis of attitudes that the individual has toward himself. Thus, a commanding officer is frequently spoken of as the "old man," which conveys attitudes of deference or "looking up" and readiness (which need not be willingness) to do as told by one in his position. In order to function in his position the commanding officer must adopt attitudes toward himself which correspond to the attitudes held toward him. How exalted an opinion he has of himself depends upon his particular personality, but interaction in a position requires that the individual, if he is to fulfill expectations of such interaction, must to some extent adopt counterparts to the attitudes held toward him in the attitudes he holds toward himself. The commanding officer, for example, must be ready to give orders and this readiness corresponds to the readiness that subordinates have to carry them out. One commanding officer may have attitudes of condescension toward subordinates and another may not, but both must have an attitude toward themselves that enables them to give orders.

While an individual must hold certain attitudes toward himself in order to function effectively in a given position, he is not always able to fulfill the expectations relating to interaction in the position for one reason or another. The reaction to this state of affairs may be a feeling of inferiority. In recent years, for example, many veterans who have families of their own, and who are not "young kids" any more, have grown restive and felt somewhat inadequate as they continued their education after World War II. Being in school has appeared to them to be inconsistent with their expectation that men of their age should hold jobs, own their own homes, provide for their families without relying upon relatives, etc. The fact that these expectations may not be satisfied too well even after completing their education indicates that economic, social, and political problems have important psychological counterparts. If a man is not able to buy a house, for instance, he not only faces the highly important practical problem of providing shelter for his family, but if he has learned to expect that a man with a family should furnish the family with a house, he also reacts to himself as inferior. One of the most striking inferiority-provoking circumstances associated with age behavior, it might be added, occurs when the young adult is forced through rapid growth of his family, low income early in his occupational career, little or no financial reserve, and so on, to seek help from his or his wife's relatives. If the relatives are willing to help, feelings of immaturity may only be reinforced, since their very willingness may have the effect of putting the young adult into an adolescent position.

Many additional examples of feelings of inferiority arising when the individual is not able to meet the expectations relating to his age position can be cited. Although no exact age can be stated as to when girls hope to marry, it is evident to the most casual observer that indefinite postponement beyond the age of 25, let us say, does not add to self-esteem. One 24-year-old woman whose prospects of marriage were not bright remarked that she was tired of being "good old Aunt Mary" as she played with her nephews and nieces while her married relatives and friends were preparing to go out for the evening. Similarly, for a man, feelings of worth are undermined when a certain amount of occupational stability and success has not been attained by the age of 30 or thereabouts. This undermining may be particularly strong with college graduates when their occupational future does not look too bright, inasmuch as there is a strong belief in the American culture to the effect that amount of education and occupational success have a definite positive relationship to one another. A person with a relatively high level of education is, then, likely to anticipate, or hope for, a corresponding level of occupational success. Not attaining such success when this hope exists can, of course, detract considerably from the individual's good opinion of himself.

The above examples illustrate how expectations associated with age positions produce what might be called an attitude lag in respect to age in our culture. By attitude lag is meant a tendency to think of oneself as younger than he is or to consider oneself from a point of view that makes it possible to act in as youthful a way as the circumstances permit. This tendency is ordinarily not present during childhood and adolescence when the individual is striving for adult status, but it becomes increasingly strong as one approaches the thirties. Individuals in their early thirties, for example, take pleasure in still being referred to as young mothers, fathers, etc., as they were in their twenties. Goals are set that one hopes to achieve by certain ages, and in a competitive culture one measures his own worth by his progress in attaining these goals in comparison to others. If this progress is retarded, it is necessary to protect one's self-esteem. The veteran who has had to postpone his education because of the war finds reassurance in the fact that many others have had to do the same thing. The business man whose income is not much greater than it was 20 years ago continues to dream of making his fortune, and tells himself that many have not attained financial success until late in life, or learns to adopt other values that make financial success less essential to maintaining his self-esteem. In addition to this tendency to compare oneself with others of the same age who have achieved no more than he, is the further tendency to undervalue achievements of those who are younger. Thus, a young man who has risen rapidly in his field is frequently referred to by older individuals as "still wet behind the ears." This young man may at the same time exhibit the assurance he has gained from his achievements in ways that cause others to say that his success has "gone to his head," even though the remark is often motivated more by envy than anything else. Expressions such as "If things had been different, I could have been there too," "still wet behind the ears," "gone to his head," etc., all represent the function of attitude lag in respect to age which is to protect self-esteem against the demoralizing forces of increased age without the increased prestige, success, and security that the individual had hoped to attain by the time he is as old as he is. The economic disadvantages that come with advancing years, such as greater difficulty in securing employment, furnish a basis, needless to say, for the antagonism that older people sometimes exhibit toward younger people who have achieved prestige, success, and security.

The attitude lag in respect to age mentioned above is probably stronger in the American culture with women than with men. This feminine attitude lag is most evident in noting how long some women stay 29. The transition from 29 to 30, incidentally, probably requires certain readjustments for most people which are similar to the psychological "shifting of gears" that takes place at 40, even though 40 is more often talked about as a significant transition point in growing older. Neither men nor women, to be sure, are immune to gratification stemming from other's underestimating their age as they grow older. It must be recognized, however, that below a certain age category, which we might approximately classify as 21 to 25, another attitude comes into play. The 21-year-old does not like to be taken for a 15-year-old and the 15-year-old is pleased to be taken for older. Beyond 25, or in that vicinity, the underestimating of age becomes increasingly flattering. It is of less importance to men because the culture supplies greater means for men to reinforce self-esteem as they grow older.

Men have occupational activities available to them as they grow older by means of which they can demonstrate their "worth" to a greater extent than women. Furthermore, greater importance is attached to physical attractiveness in women than in men. A man can even convert his "homeliness" into an asset. Abraham Lincoln was loved all the more, so far as we know, for not being handsome. Although it is not impossible, a woman cannot as easily make this conversion. Since physical attractiveness is defined as a youthful characteristic in our culture, it is no wonder, then, that women greatly prize youthfulness.

Both men and women are confronted by conflicts as they grow older, because of the value that is placed upon remaining young in the American culture. This conflict is strengthened by economic circumstances that make employment harder to secure as one grows older, but even with economic security assured in old age, psychological security does not necessarily follow. The retired business or professional man is often unhappy with his lot and the woman who has spent her life raising a family is not always content when she no longer has family responsibilities, even though personal financial problems may not exist. Psychological security in a position is dependent upon the recognition and prestige that the culture gives the position, and greater prestige tends to be given younger positions than old-age positions in our culture. It is for this reason perhaps that men and women often go through a period of depression and melancholia during middle age and beyond middle age as they realize that they are growing older and moving out of prestige-laden positions. It is not surprising, for example, when all of the circumstances are considered, to find a woman somewhat dispirited and listless when her children have grown up and have families of their own, since she is left without a function. She will be particularly without a function if her husband has been financially successful enough to make it possible for her to have a maid and to insist perhaps that it is in keeping with their social position for her to have a maid. Her function is somewhat restored when grandchildren arrive and she can assist in looking after them. She may also find a new function, which is not too far removed from motherly activities that she has already learned, in organizations which are devoted to helping others by means of raising money for scholarships for younger people, equipping hospitals with medical supplies, assisting with civic improvement projects such as improving public parks, etc.

Avoidance of the depression and melancholia that may come with growing older, or recovery from it, seems to be dependent upon acceptance, through acquisition of new points or view (or through reformulation of expectations relating to old age) toward the activities for which the culture does provide approval for older people. When a person does not expect to be as active physically and when he can make concessions in a spirit of understanding to the desires of younger people to be "in the limelight" themselves, or when he can acknowledge and realize that "the world changes," he is prepared for the older age activities that are approved and that are characterized by mellowness, sympathetic appreciation of the problems of younger people, and keeping out of the way to a greater or lesser extent. The function of wise counselor in the ways of the world is perhaps the one that has the greatest sanction for older people. In taking this function an older person may be fairly active, particularly when he does not attempt to compete with or dominate younger people who are trying to "run things" themselves. A retired minister, for example, who makes it a point to let a younger and newly appointed minister administer the affairs of the church without interference may still be asked to participate in important ways in many of those affairs. Similarly, when Herbert Hoover was no longer politically active himself, he was asked to head a government reorganization commission, and the work of this commission was widely recognized, commended, and respected by Democrats as well as Republicans.

FAILURE IN MEETING AGE-BEHAVIOR EXPECTATIONS

Failure to reach certain goals at particular ages is, of course, more of a blow to self-esteem when one has learned to evaluate his personal worth in terms of promotion, prestige, recognition, and social position. Self-esteem rests heavily in the American culture upon recognition from others. Pats on the back, congratulations rendered by shaking a person's hand, praise for a "job well done," all have more than a casual significance. They indicate that one is "doing all right." The yearning for such recognition is probably somewhat stronger in the middle class than in the lower or upper classes. Middle-class children are taught to strive for good grades in school and their scholastic standing in comparison to the neighbors' children is a matter of some importance. Promotion on the job later in life is very comparable to making the honor roll for high grades earlier in life. Becoming captain of a team, president of a school organization, or having the lead in a play can also be compared to becoming the head of a lodge, president of a bridge club, or chairman of a literary organization. Lower-class children learn from the time that they are young that working is a way of making a living, but do not necessarily expect prestige, promotion, or satisfaction in their work. Upper-class children learn to take it for granted that they are at the "top of the heap," and do not have to be too anxious over their achievements; they can pursue careers as a matter of spending their lives in an interesting way rather than because of pressure to "amount to something." "Amounting to something" is no idle phrase, however, to a middle-class child who brings home a report card on which is recorded all "A"s except for one "B," and is asked why he didn't get *all* "A"s. Getting a bicycle or something else that is highly prized may also depend upon how good his report card is. Failure to be elected to an office in a student organization or to get a part in a play does not necessarily pass by, either, without his parents responding to it with a certain amount of concern. Striving to get ahead is rewarded and indifference to such striving brings disapproval. The basis is, therefore, laid for a sense of failure in later life in case promotions and symbols of success are not forthcoming. Symbols of prestige are much more easily available to the upper-class individual from the time he is young, and the lower-class individual tends to be more or less reconciled to the improbability of securing such symbols for himself from the time he is young.

Arthur Miller's Pulitzer Prize-winning play (*1949*), *Death of a salesman*, illustrates clearly the striving to "get ahead" in the middle class and the subsequent disillusionment of the central character, Willy Loman. Loman is a salesman who is advanced in years, and has never been able to attain sufficient income to maintain his family and home as he desired. At one point he says, "Whoever heard of a Hastings refrigerator? Once in my life I would like to own something outright before it's broken! I'm always in a race with the junkyard! I just finished paying for the car and it's on its last legs. . . . They time them so when you finally paid for them, they're used up." Willy, despite this discouragement, encourages his sons to get ahead, complete with advice on how to do so. "Don't be so modest. You always started too low. Walk in with a big laugh . . . personality always wins the day." It is only when one of the sons forces Willy to face the true picture of his failure, according to middle-class standards, by saying, "Pop! I'm a dime a dozen, and so are you! . . . I am not a leader of men, Willy, and neither are you," that Willy is forced to face himself and discover that, according to age-position expectations for men of his class, he is a failure.

The comparisons made above of the lower, middle, and upper classes are oversimplifications, inasmuch as wide differences will be found within the different class levels. They do represent trends, however, and anxiety over "amounting to something" tends to be stronger among middle-class individuals. Growing old, therefore, presents an emotional problem to members of the middle class that can very easily take the form of taking stock as to "how far one has gone." If one has "not gone too far," a sense of failure may haunt his later years.

The sense of failure that can go with old age when one has not attained what he hoped to attain is frequently offset, of course, by new perspectives. Entertaining the grandchildren often becomes more important than dreams of fame and fortune that did not materialize. It must be recognized, nevertheless, that one of the functions of having children and grandchildren often seems to be that of reaching goals that the parent or grandparent did not reach. The child is looked at as a younger edition of the self who will succeed in the things that the older generations failed in. Hence, one frequently hears, "I want my child to have things I did not have." The father and grandfather with the letter of the successful young man in his hand or the child on his knee gains the satisfaction of success, or potential success, that he did not have for himself.

Another influence that probably functions to some extent to counteract a sense of failure in later years is the provision the American culture makes for keeping everybody young, as it were. When Northern veterans of the Civil War held their last convention, they were referred to as "the boys in blue" although none of them was under 100 years old. American Legion conventions are famous for their boisterousness and the most boisterous "boys" sometimes are past their teens by a few decades. Women's bridge clubs may be made up of grandmothers, but it is always "the girls" who get together on Wednesday afternoon, not "older women."

AGE-POSITION ATTAINMENT

In spite of the glorification of youth in the American culture the earlier periods of life are by no means free of pressure. The child, adolescent, and young adult engage in a struggle to achieve full adult status and participation on equal terms. Young people are told that when they are older, or when they have more experience, they can expect certain kinds of consideration but not until then. In the absence of such consideration they seek symbols of full adult status, and at the same time prepare for adult interaction. The little girl dresses up in her mother's clothes, for example. The adolescent boy is diligent in his quest to use the family car independently, and the young professional man cherishes his brief case. The pressures to achieve adult status are not diminished by the tendency to disapprove of achievement that comes too early. It is immoral, as it were, "to arrive" or "to get there" too soon. The young person who does so, as pointed out earlier, is said to be "still wet behind the ears." Furthermore, a certain amount of emotion often goes into the assertion that "he had the breaks." There are, nevertheless, privileges that go with "arriving," needless to say. Income is not only likely to be greater but less caution is necessary in everyday conduct as well. As a partner in a business or law firm, a young man can express ideas that he would be more inclined to keep to himself if he weren't a partner, lest they be considered "harebrained." A successful young author, similarly, need not be as concerned about the literary merit of whatever he happens to be writing as one who is still striving for recognition. Once having attained literary success, the chances are that literary merit of one kind or another will be found in subsequent writings. Even if it isn't, the success tends to insure that subsequent writings will be given a hearing.

The chances that the subsequent writings of a successful author will be found to have literary merit suggest a tendency for the culture to sustain recognition of high status once this status has been conferred upon an individual in order to justify the granting of the high status in the first place. Not only do authors have a good prospect of remaining "successful," but men in influential positions in government and industry are often gotten rid of by being "kicked upstairs." This phenomenon was nicely illustrated in a movie portraying the life of Woodrow Wilson in a scene in which local politicians were delighted with the prospect of his becoming President because it would get him out of New Jersey. The active manager of a department in a business firm may also be made less active by being promoted to a vice-presidency. Reorganizations are also sometimes brought about which result in men being shifted to positions of less influence but positions of high status, nevertheless. The prospects of maintaining high status once it has been achieved is an important incentive for those striving to "arrive."

Since there are privileges that go with "arriving," we can readily understand why young people would have considerable eagerness to achieve the sense of maturity or confidence that adult status can bring. Furthermore, the earlier one achieves such status in a competitive culture, the more he "proves himself." Young people in our culture are, therefore, in the somewhat strange position of being pushed toward achievement before they have had too much chance to gain the experience and skill necessary to achievement. Practice in activities similar to later interaction is provided, to be sure, but the eagerness to succeed that exists in a competitive culture does not always make this practice too comfortable. The college debater gains practice for later public speaking roles, but if his performance is at all halting he reacts to his imperfection as a strong threat to the success he hopes to have as soon as possible. Similarly, the young salesman does not regard his mediocre record as something that might be expected and that has had the value of furnishing him with practice in selling, but tends, instead, to have a sense of personal failure over his undistinguished performance. These examples suggest that those in our culture who are responsible for training young people to engage in adult activities that maintain the culture as a going concern might do well to consider the amount of pressure that is most conducive to learning such activities. Instructors in public speaking have been known to employ alarm clocks that go off whenever their students pause. The effects of this practice upon learning to appear before audiences when interacting in later positions as lawyer, teacher, supervisor, committee chairman, or toastmaster are probably not altogether constructive so far as large numbers of students are concerned. An occasional suggestion that one simply do the best he can rather than giving him a "pep talk" might also facilitate learning to take later functions to a much greater extent than is ordinarily expected. Such facilitation is not expected because the belief is fairly strongly entrenched in the American culture that one can do anything he wants to do when inspired by a "pep talk."

Not only is there a tendency for young people in the American culture to be pushed toward achievement before they have had the opportunity to gain the experience and skill necessary to such achievement, but it is also true that after a person "arrives" he is often moved out of the position in which he could make the best use of his hard-won skills. In educational circles, for example, it is not uncommon for a man who has made a reputation through research and writing to be selected for an administrative position in which he can make relatively little use of his research and writing talents. Similarly, in industry a man who has gained recognition as a production manager who knows machines and handles men well is promoted to another executive position in which he has much less direct contact with men or machines.

When a man is moved into a higher position after "arriving" he must learn a new mode of interaction of which an important aspect consists of acting as a father figure or someone who has gotten to the top and is looked up to by those younger than himself, or even by others of the same age in subordinate positions. Personal assurance and security is of great importance in taking this father-figure function if it is to be taken effectively. Just as the father who lacks confidence may bolster himself by ridiculing his son or "lording over" him, or treating him as a younger brother who competes with him, so a father figure or superior who is not sure of himself may create strains in his relations with his subordinates. One reason for such insecurity that is fairly prevalent in the American culture is that high goals are striven for, and although one may have "made the grade" in the eyes of others, he may not have done so in his own eyes. In such a case he will be too preoccupied with his own ambition to give adequate recognition to subordinates, and good work of subordinates may even be reacted to as competition or potential competition. Those who react to themselves as successes, on the other hand, have greater prospects of being secure in taking the father-figure function, inasmuch as their high status is consolidated in their own eyes and, therefore, cannot be threatened.

Security in father-figure interaction enables one to accept the dependence of others upon oneself that goes with such interaction to a greater or lesser extent. Even self-reliant subordinates must consult the "head man" and he must draw upon his experience, knowledge, and judgment to make the most effective use of their ideas. A head man must also frequently act as a kind of protective agent or representative of a subordinate and be prepared to defend him when necessary or to see that he is properly rewarded. The manager of a department, for example, may have to justify giving one of his subordinates whom he considers a "good man" a raise, or see to it that a subordinate is not too severely censured when he has made a mistake which anyone else might have made when all of the circumstances are considered. Still another feature of effective father-figure interaction in the American culture is dignity minus "stiffness." While dignity is approved, aloofness or "heavy-handedness" in father figures is not. The superior must, therefore, on the one hand have a certain restraint, but at the same time appear to be "one of the boys." A professor, for example, demonstrates that he is a "good guy" if he dances with a coed at a college prom, but if he dances with too many coeds he "makes a fool of himself." An executive may take part in a baseball game at a company picnic, but if he shouts too much during the game he loses status unless, of course, his position is sufficiently high for him to be regarded as "an interesting personality" no matter what he does. Even the latitude of behavior that a high position permits has limits, nevertheless. Perhaps the chief limit is the "ban" on behavior that belongs to a subordinate position when one is in the father-figure position himself. The coach can be informal with "his boys" but he can't hang out at the corner drug store with them without coming to be regarded by his peers, as well as "his boys," as immature. He, therefore, must be secure enough to be able to be relaxed and approachable on the practice field and at the same time to give up in large measure the comradeship of the team which he once enjoyed himself off the field. Since the balance is not always too easily achieved, we can see why the term "growing pains" might as readily be applied to psychological as to physical maturation.

PREPARATION FOR FUTURE AGE ACTIVITIES

Throughout life the individual is, of course, always faced with future age activities that lie ahead of him. The main business of education might be described as that of preparing students for future age interaction. Reading, writing, and arithmetic, the traditional basic ingredients of schooling, are skills of considerable use to subsequent participation in society. Aside from a person's formal education, however, a tremendous amount of preparation for future age interaction takes place in ways that go unnoticed. Children's play groups, for instance, are not often thought of as "training organizations," but it is quite apparent, when one stops to think of it, that rehearsal goes on in such groups for functioning as lawyer, doctor, nurse, teacher, merchant, soldier, policeman, and cowboy, and the counterparts of such functioning. Neither are relationships between older and younger people too definitely thought of in terms of providing training or instruction in future age activities, but they also serve that purpose. Older individuals are not only models for imitation by younger persons, but they also are tutors in the ways of the world, or at least in their ways in the world. Since the learning that occurs in play groups and young person–older person relationships does tend to go unnoticed, it is particularly deserving of consideration.

Perhaps the most important feature of the child's learning in a play group is the experience gained in interaction with others of similar status. The difference in size alone between adults and children has an implication of unequal status for the child. When he is with his play group, on the other hand, he has opportunity to feel that the odds are more in his favor, as it were, as well as to experiment more or less independently in dealing with others. When two boys choose up teams, for example, they pit a relatively equal degree of maturity, or immaturity, against one another, and at the same time exercise their judgment and estimation of the potentialities of their associates without adult supervision. Similarly, when youngsters of the same age fight for a toy there is a good probability that either one will get the toy and there is also experience gained in fighting on one's own. Adult protection or intimidation is, of course, sometimes so complete that the child does not feel equal to anyone, including others of his age, and is so lacking in confidence that he does not feel free to experiment on his own in coping with others. The play group, nevertheless, provides perhaps the only situation in which the child might interact on comparatively equal terms with others whose age status is actually similar to his own.

The function of the children's play group is by no means completely different from that of many young adult groups, such as the Young Republicans or Young Democrats or the Junior Chamber of Commerce. In all of these groups practice in later functioning can be gotten under conditions in which one is dealing with others of similar age status. Neither do the difficulties attendant upon such practice vary greatly from the nursery school level to the adult play group level. The 4-year-old who does not climb the jungle gym with other 4-year-olds displays the same reluctance that the timid committee member exhibits when he sits quietly at a committee meeting. Furthermore, the remedy for this timidity takes the same course that the child's introduction into the play group takes when it eventuates in active interaction. The child gradually gains confidence and social skill. His first ventures toward his playmates are tentative and awkward. If the aforesaid committee member is to lose his timidity, he must permit himself a certain tentativeness and awkwardness in his social interaction since it is a part of the learning process by which he, as well as the child, gains skill in social interaction.

The acquisition of skill in social adjustment through interaction in play groups is sometimes thwarted directly or indirectly by the play group itself. The younger child who must for one reason or another always play with older children may have difficulty in keeping up. The older children tend to leave him out of their activities because he cannot go on the big swing or ride a bicycle or play a certain kind of game. A similar exclusion occurs when a child is ostracized by others of the same age because he has not learned how to take part in the activities in which this group is engaging. A boy or girl, for example, who has been with older people a good deal has not had the opportunity to develop interests similar to those of his own age group, and finds it difficult to communicate with others of his own age group about dolls, marbles, baseball players, dresses, knives, or whatever the topics of conversation may be. Children are also left out of play groups because they do not "rate." A child who does not dress as well as other children is sometimes "looked down on." In adolescent "play groups" the girl or boy who is not "good-looking" or "smooth" or accomplished in athletics or some other activity that is valued by the group is not always readily accepted by the group.

The various forms of exclusion mentioned above reduce the individual's chances for learning social skills. If the exclusion has been fairly strong throughout an individual's earlier experience, the chances are increased that his later interaction will be characterized by withdrawal of one kind or another. The boy who was never accepted by his play group or adolescent crowd often becomes the adult who goes to parties only when he has to, but prefers to spend his leisure time alone or with his immediate family or close friends. Similarly, the woman who was left out of adolescent "giggle sessions" may not enjoy entertaining large groups. Seclusive social behavior earlier in life also apparently predisposes many individuals to fall back upon imaginative activities that are sometimes manifesteded later in writing, theorizing, or artistic or scientific pursuits. Individuals with such interests developed to a high degree for this reason are often spoken of as "intellectuals" and are thought of as having a rather special and unusual place in the culture. It is as though they were in a sense cut off from the larger culture, and the probability is that a good many of them were cut off from play groups of their own age to a considerable extent as they were growing up.

Whether a child has been cut off from play groups of his own age or not, there is ample opportunity to learn to compare oneself to others in the American culture. Competition is probably felt even more keenly by the child who is not "one of the gang," since he has more reason to compare himself unfavorably to others or to feel, although he may not admit the feeling to himself, that he does not "rate." It is virtually impossible for any child in our culture to avoid learning a competitive orientation, however. Even young children are taught to excel or try to excel one another in running, eating carrots, learning to go to the bathroom, getting to a toy, etc. Parents play any number of games with children involving the idea of "I'll beat you" in doing this or that, and they also take note of how soon a child walks, talks, or stands in comparison to other children. Children are prepared for competition even before they participate very actively in play groups, and it is, therefore, to be expected that the play groups themselves will engage in competitive activities. This play-group competition provides the child with opportunity to learn to expect competitive reactions from others. Comfortable functioning in an individualistic culture is, of course, aided by this expectation and acceptance of competition. Bargaining for a salary, carrying out a business venture, winning a girl (or a man) all involve rivalry. While such rivalry is sometimes learned so well that coöperative enterprises cannot easily be carried out, as was perhaps demonstrated by the difficulties in unifying the branches of the Armed Forces, it is also true that the individual who is not prepared to compete is likely to be somewhat ill at ease in the American culture. This point might be stated by saying that being "taken advantage of" is not as upsetting if it is taken for granted that it can happen. The boy who steals a base in a sandlot ball game learns something of the spirit of "taking advantage" as well as being "taken advantage of," and the girl who competes for a boy's attention learns that "all is fair in love and war," or that if it isn't, it is not always inappropriate to act as though it were.

At the beginning of this section it was pointed out that older person–younger person relationships, as well as play groups, serve the function of preparing the individual for later age activities. The influence of older people is particularly clear in relation to competition. Children's play groups, for example, are not particularly exclusive, but they become so when parents instruct their children that some youngsters are "nice" and acceptable as playmates and others are not. The latter fall into the category of those "you would not want to be like." Thus, the technique of exclusion as a means of competing with others in the achievement of social standing is learned. One of its most striking manifestations is seen in the striving to get into college sororities and fraternities, particularly one of "the better" sororities or fraternities. The various appeals that advertisers make on the basis of exclusiveness whether in respect to clothes, silverware, lodging, liquor, automobiles, or what have you, point to other forms of such striving.

Older persons are, of course, often motivated to influence younger individuals toward competitiveness, because they hope to gain through younger persons the competitive successes that they did not gain themselves. A parent who has not enjoyed the "exclusiveness" of a college education himself can enjoy it through his children. Furthermore, the parent who makes it possible for his children to go to college can see his own hand in his children's success. Teachers as well as parents have opportunity to see their own hand in the success of younger people, and this very opportunity is frequently presented as one of the rewards of teaching. The anger and disgust with which both teachers and parents sometimes react when younger people do not meet the expectations of success can probably often be attributed to the thwarting of the desire to detect their own "good work" in the achievements of the underling. The poor student, for example, may be berated as "dumb" at great length and to a greater extent than his merely being a poor student would seem to justify.

The vicarious satisfactions that older individuals can get through the successes of younger people are in many instances gained through the selection of younger people who seem to hold

promise. Those selected as holding promise will vary considerably from one older individual to another. The president of a
corporation will select a young man with different kinds of talents
than those displayed by the young man who finds favor with a
recognized poet. Two corporation presidents, for that matter,
will differ in their choices. One of the important factors determining the choice, it seems likely, is the similarity of personality
of the younger person and older person. The corporation president whose success rests principally upon his ability to plan, ana-
lyze, and foresee business trends will be inclined to select a
young man who may impress others as cold and calculating, but
who will be receptive to the kind of guidance he can give. A corporation president, on the other hand, whose success rests primarily upon skill in manipulating people will select a young man
who impresses others as an "operator" rather than a "cold fish."
In both cases the similarity between the older person and the
younger person lends itself to receptiveness on the part of the
younger person to learn from the older person, and in so doing
to give the older person an opportunity to see his hand in the
achievement of the younger person. The success of the younger
person at the same time becomes the success of the older person
in a very real sense, because the similarity in personality makes
it that much easier for the older individual to perceive himself in
the younger.

Similarity in personality not only determines the older person's
choice of a younger person in whom he can see himself, but it is
also a factor influencing the younger person's selection of an older
person to identify with. A contributing factor in this selection
may be a kind of justification, so to speak, of oneself, this justification taking the form of a feeling, of which the individual may
not be clearly aware, that "here is someone else even older than
I am who is like me; it is all right to be the kind of person I am."
It is also possible that the younger individual perceives mainly
the virtues of an older person like himself. If the older person is
at the same time successful and commands prestige, there is all
the more reason to identify oneself with him. The young trial
lawyer readily falls into a companionable relationship with the

older, successful trial lawyer, and the young physician interested in obstetrics idealizes the older obstetrician with a reputation in his field. It is also interesting to observe how students' evaluation of teachers often seems to be affected by the similarity or dissimilarity in personality between the students and their teachers. The student who likes order, exactness, and "facts" evaluates highly the teacher who lectures "clearly," whereas the student who is more interested in letting his own imagination run freely is fond of the teacher who throws out new ideas even though he is not always particularly "clear."

One aspect of what is ordinarily called "growing up" is the breaking of bonds with an older person. The young trial lawyer mentioned above, for example, finds that the older, successful trial lawyer has human weaknesses after all, and that he sometimes even misses important points in a case he is handling. The young craftsman finds that the man from whom he learned a good deal is set in certain ways that are not altogether efficient, and the student who has idealized a certain teacher discovers that he is not really as smart or as saintly as he had thought. This discovery of human failings, or of characteristics that are simply human but not necessarily failings, sometimes comes as a disillusionment, but may also have the effect of enabling the younger person to feel more adequate himself. He may come to feel that he is as good a man as his father, or someone who has had a fatherly relationship to him, after all. This feeling of equality in relation to individuals in older age positions is an important element in self-confidence and comfortable functioning in the culture. Since parent-child relationships are duplicated in many ways, as in teacher-student, apprentice-master, worker-boss, and junior partner–senior partner relationships, this feeling of equality can be fostered or not fostered during adolescence and adulthood as well as during childhood. While relationships to older persons during childhood are quite basic in one's development, it can also be seen from the considerations that have been reviewed in this chapter that the growing-up process is not confined to childhood, which is an illustration of the fact that an individual's personality remains modifiable in spite of the patterns established in childhood.

SUMMARY OF PRINCIPLES

As the individual interacts in his environment he occupies positions in the social structure and interacts in these positions. Throughout life an individual occupies age positions. Some of the principles of interaction in age positions proposed in this chap ter are as follows:

1. After childhood and adolescence there is a tendency in the American culture for an individual to consider himself from a point of view that makes it possible to act in as youthful a way as the circumstances permit.

2. In the American culture a sense of failure in later years is counteracted to some extent by the provision the culture makes for keeping everybody young.

3. Since there are privileges that go with "arriving" in the American culture, young people in this culture tend to be eager to achieve the sense of maturity or confidence that adult status can bring.

4. Training in future functioning is gained, among other ways, through play groups and older person–younger person relationships.

5. Similarity in personality not only determines an older person's choice of a younger person in whom he can see himself, but it is also a factor influencing the younger person's selection of an older person to identify with.

6. The feeling of equality in relation to individuals in older age positions is an important element in self-confidence and comfortable functioning in the culture.

CHAPTER 9

Masculinity and Femininity

Introductory Summary

The masculine and feminine aspects of social interaction enter into practically all of our activities. The fact that certain activities are prescribed for men and boys and others for women and girls provides an important condition for learning to adopt masculine and feminine modes of behavior. The individual whose activities have been channeled along lines inappropriate to his or her sex can easily become a misfit in his or her social environment.

Although the status of the family has undergone and continues to undergo change in our culture, it is, of course, a basic unit in the social structure. Family functions must be learned just as other kinds of functions, such as those having to do with an occupation, must be learned. Both the role of mate and the role of parent must be learned.

MASCULINE AND FEMININE INTERACTION

In every society, one must interact as a male or female, of course. *The masculine and feminine aspects of social interaction, furthermore, enter into practically all of our activities.* Speech, dress, work, recreation all have masculine or feminine qualities. Sex behavior, therefore, merits attention in the study of interaction. The culturally defined masculine "style" in our society can be characterized by such adjectives as *independent, forthright, assertive,* and *strong.* The culturally defined feminine "style," on the other hand, calls for adjectives such as *sympathetic, soft, modest,* and *devoted.* No individual man or woman corresponds

252

perfectly, to be sure, to these definitions of masculine and feminine "styles." There are, nevertheless, definite conceptions as to what is appropriate to being a man or a woman. These conceptions are reflected in such expressions as "the strong sex" and "the weaker sex." Furthermore, there are counterparts in the actual behavior, attitudes, and feelings of men and women to these conceptions as Terman and Miles (1936) make clear in the following summary of an exhaustive investigation of sex differences:

From whatever angle we have examined them the males included in the standardization groups evinced a distinctive interest in exploit and adventure, in outdoor and physically strenuous occupations, in machinery and tools, in science, physical phenomena, and inventions; and, from rather occasional evidence, in business and commerce. On the other hand, the females of our groups have evinced a distinctive interest in domestic affairs and in aesthetic objects and occupations; they have distinctly preferred more sedentary and indoor occupations, and occupations more directly ministrative, particularly to the young, the helpless, the distressed. Supporting and supplementing these are the more subjective differences—those in emotional disposition and direction. The males directly or indirectly manifest the greater self-assertion and aggressiveness; they express more hardihood and fearlessness, and more roughness of manners, language, and sentiments. The females express themselves as more compassionate and sympathetic, more timid, more fastidious and aesthetically sensitive, more emotional in general (or at least more expressive of the four emotions considered), severer moralists, yet admit in themselves more weaknesses in emotional control and (less noticeably) in physique.[1]

LEARNING MASCULINE AND FEMININE PATTERNS

The fact that certain activities are prescribed for men and boys and others for women and girls provides an important condition for learning to adopt masculine and feminine patterns of interaction. Miller and Dollard (1941) make this point very well in the following passage:

It is known that parents are aware of the biological sex differences of their children and that they respond differently to each sex from

[1] Quoted by permission from Sex and personality: Studies in masculinity and femininity by L. M. Terman and C. C. Miles, 1936. McGraw-Hill Book Company, Inc.

earliest infancy. The new father is invariably asked, "Is it a boy or a girl?" The name itself is chosen according to sex. Although considerable parallelism prevails in the treatment of boys and girls for a period after birth, by the time a child reaches his second year sex-typing has already begun. It becomes more marked as the years go on and is very apparent in the behavior of small boys and girls by the age of five. The apparent strategy is to provide children with a set of mental and social habits which will match their biological sex. Since these habits are incompatible at many points, although not, for example, in table manners or grammar, differential training conditions are set up. The little boy is punished or at least not rewarded for playing with dolls, but he is encouraged to be interested in trains, hammers, and the like. He is usually not permitted to wear girls' clothes, but he is allowed to take more risks and to be more expressive in a physical sense. The play of girls and boys is modeled (by the toys given them) according to sex, and the stories read to them emphasize the differential behavior of boys and girls. Punishment and discouragement prevent the boy from learning a girl's role and keep the girl from adopting masculine habits.

One would expect, in such a case, that there would arise a tendency not to imitate the other sex, to behave in an opposite or at least different manner. Life-history studies reveal, indeed, that this tendency is deep-rooted and vigorous, and that it remains throughout life a serious affront to accuse a man of effeminacy or a woman of masculinity. The punishments meted out to adults who actually exhibit such tendencies tend to maintain and strengthen the sex-typed habits acquired in childhood. Under these circumstances, imitation of the habits of the opposite sex would hardly be expected to be the rule. It does occasionally occur, however, and the exceptions are no less instructive than the usual behavior. In those cases where the own-sex role has been made to seem particularly dangerous or difficult, imitation of the opposite sex role may occur. Such individuals frequently learn to escape corrective social punishments by secretive behavior.

A male is expected to "keep his chin up," but it is permissible for a woman to cry. Girls can ask for dolls, but boys are ordinarily encouraged to ask for other kinds of toys such as tool kits or erector sets. Men and boys wear pants, women and girls wear skirts, although it must be admitted that pants are no longer as exclusively masculine as they once were. In short, men are re-

warded for engaging in certain kinds of behavior and women are
rewarded for engaging in other kinds of behavior. Furthermore,
punishment is the penalty for not conforming, and the fear which
it arouses becomes attached to various internal stimuli. A boy's
impulse to cry, for example, in itself comes to arouse fear of ridicule, and he learns to block his crying as a means of avoiding
ridicule as well as of maintaining his own self-esteem. The learning of emotional states akin to fear has considerable significance
in relation to the learning of sex behavior since such states motivate social interaction in no small degree. The girl who fears and
hates her mother may very well come to reject femininity which
her mother represents, and tend to pattern herself after her
father. Her development, accordingly, takes a masculine direction. An instance of this kind of development is seen in the following case:

Louise R.'s masculinity was evident in her manner of dress which
tended to be mannish. She was also strongly interested in business
and a career, although not indifferent to having a home and family.
Louise preferred men's company to women's, but her relations with
men tended to be platonic rather than romantic. It was also surprising
to her friends that she was adept in many masculine activities. She
knew more about motors than most men and was extraordinarily handy
with hammers, screwdrivers, and saws. Louise's relations with her
mother, who was a domineering, nagging person, had never been
cordial. She, accordingly, became her "father's daughter," a development that was not surprising under the circumstances since her father
was patient and companionable in contrast to her mother who was
abrupt and unable to establish a comfortable, affectionate relationship
with Louise.

Louise of the above case had reason to develop distaste for
her mother and things feminine which her mother stood for. It
is also apparent that she had reason to like her father and want
to be like him. It might be noted in passing that Louise would
not necessarily be totally unlike her mother. Children learn to
adopt attitudes and traits approved by a feared parent as a means
of avoiding anticipated disapproval or other forms of punishment. Our interest, however, has been in discerning the condi-

tions making for the development of masculine traits in the life history of an individual such as Louise.

In Louise's case fear and dislike of the parent of the same sex contributed to the development of masculine traits. These same feelings toward the parent of the opposite sex can also be productive of nonfeminine characteristics in a girl and nonmasculine traits in a boy. If Louise's mother had been warm and understanding and her father domineering and impatient, it can be seen that Louise could have acquired a distaste for her father that could generalize to other men and result in a preference for women's company and companionship. Although she would be feminine insofar as she patterned herself after her mother, she would be nonfeminine in her avoidance of men. It is also possible that she might have needs for competing with men and humiliating them in various ways. Masculine women sometimes learn to excel in such things as athletics and derive considerable satisfaction from beating male rivals. Some effeminate men also exaggerate their feminine gestures in such a way as to suggest mimicry or ridicule of women.

The preceding discussion requires elaboration, because the origins of fear and hatred of a parent are not always obvious. A girl who has such feelings toward her father, for instance, may have been taught that "men are beasts" by her mother and have learned the lesson thoroughly, even though her father endeavored to treat his daughter well. Nevertheless, the feelings toward the father that have emerged from her mother's indoctrination may generalize to other men. A boy's fear and hatred of his father may be based largely on an overly intense attachment to the mother and a corresponding tendency always to find his father in the wrong and to think of him as a devil or ogre. In such an instance, the dislike for the father may also stem from overreacting to him as a rival for the mother's affection. The feeling toward the father still exists in any event, and makes for a rejection of masculinity which his father stands for.

Comfortable relationships with both parents are productive of the greatest security in sex positions. A girl who likes her mother as well as her father does not have to turn away from femininity in her own development and neither does she have reason for disliking men. Similarly, the boy who likes both parents does not have to turn away from masculinity nor reject women.

No account of the learning of sex behavior would be complete without discussing the influence of models. Children take parents as models and pick up mannerisms, expressions, gestures, and attitudes that are characteristic of their mothers and fathers. It is the parents who attend to the infant's needs, of course, and the things that they do in looking after these needs take on reward value. Thus, if a mother sings when feeding her child the song becomes rewarding, and the child attempts to reproduce it and can be heard singing it to himself when the mother is not around. The infant and child reproduce other kinds of behavior of parents in a similar way. It is, therefore, to be expected that dominance of a feminine or masculine model in the child's environment will produce a personality corresponding to that of the model. Boys who have been brought up by their mothers without benefit of a father's influence are often somewhat effeminate. In such cases the femininity may not be extreme because other factors may offset it, but there may, nevertheless, be some tendency to adopt a somewhat more retiring pattern of interaction as opposed to the "rougher" patterns that are more in accord with masculinity. Overly possessive mothers often produce similar personality traits in their sons even when the father is a member of the household and family. His influence as a model is minimized because of the mother's possessiveness. Masculine traits in girls can, similarly, be observed when the influence of masculine models has been predominant for one reason or another.

The parents not only provide models but they also guide behavior in various ways that influence the learning of sex patterns. Whether certain activities will be engaged in and found rewarding depends greatly upon the parent's initiative. If a mother does not make cooking, shopping, etc., occasions for companionship with her daughter, the girl is deprived of rewards in connection with such activities. A boy is similarly deprived if his father does not include him in hunting and fishing expeditions or household chores such as building shelves. The guidance of parents is also illustrated by the fact that a mother will tend to channel interaction in one way and a father in other ways. A father will be less inclined, for instance, to engage in "playing house" with his children, whereas a mother will not tend as readily as the father to play "horseback riding."

That the channeling of a child's activities can make a difference is demonstrated in cases where boys have been brought up as girls even to the extent of being dressed like girls, being given presents suitable for girls at Christmas time and on birthdays, etc. A girl whose interaction is directed along masculine lines pretty completely will also find herself a misfit in many ways. The plight of such individuals will be treated in detail in the following section. Before proceeding to it, however, the following quotation from Davis and Havighurst (1947) seems particularly apt as a summary of many of the points that have been made in the above discussion:

It is clear . . . that the child's growing up is greatly influenced by the attitudes of the parents toward him, especially by what they expect or what they wish him to be. Parents can help a child to identify with his or her own sex—can help the *girl to become feminine,* the *boy to become masculine*—first, by their own inner wishes for the child, and, second, by their example.

The parents' inner wishes for the child are determined, of course, by their own history and personality. If their child is having a hard time patterning himself after his own sex, the parents should explore their own feelings about the child. The father, who in his disappointment that his daughter is not a son, treats his little girl like a boy; the mother who for some inner reason makes a girl out of her little boy, are well known in our culture, and all too frequent. There are many variations on this theme.

In such instances, the child is often thrown into psychological confusion. He does not know, let us say, whether it is better to be a boy or a girl. This conflict is rarely expressed consciously by the child, but it becomes evident in the child's fantasy life. It shows itself clearly, to the trained eye, in the child's activities and behavior. (Occasionally, a child may show striking behavior in this respect; for example, a little boy who runs away from home after his father's death, steals women's clothing, and dresses up in them.) When the child's confusion about his sex role is obvious, though not necessarily overt, it is well for the parents to seek psychiatric help and guidance.

Although the influence of the parents' personality is by far the greatest factor in determining the child's identification, there are many ways in which parents can *consciously* guide a child's growth toward manhood or toward womanhood. The mother can begin early to give the little girl household tasks of dignity (*shopping*, for instance—not just monotonous *dusting* that has influenced many a rebellious little girl against the role of homemaker). The mother can take her into a sort of alliance in household planning, finance, etc. She can enlist the girl's *interest* in the younger children; not as a burden, but as a dignified responsibility. It is common knowledge that the neighbors' children are often objects of a girl's solicitude, when her own little brothers and sisters are no more than tolerated. This attitude is usually the result of the mother's own feeling about the caretaking job. Fathers, too, have their part in helping to make a daughter feminine. A compliment on a new dress; occasional attention to the daughter when alone (not with the mother, who is her natural rival); an expression of pleasure in her feminine activities, all these contribute to the girl's wish to grow up to be a woman. They help her therefore on her way to a later heterosexual adjustment.

Likewise with the boy; the mother can help him to be masculine, by encouraging manly attitudes and activities. The father, too, can include the boy in his own interests, in sports, in hunting and fishing, in going on excursions together, and the like.

With boy or girl, the parent of *his own sex* should become the pattern. The parent of the opposite sex should join the other parent in helping their child find his place in the world.

SEX PATTERNS AND CONFLICT

The individual whose activities have been channeled along lines inappropriate to his or her sex can easily become a "misfit" in his or her social environment. Such an individual is involved in conflict between his or her own sex pattern and the cultural definition of acceptable sex patterns. An effeminate man does not act in the way that society prescribes for his sex. A masculine woman is "out of line" in the same way. Furthermore, cultural expectations become a part of the individual's psychological make-up, and the effeminate man and masculine woman are, therefore, often torn asunder by the clash between their actual tendencies and an underlying conviction that something is wrong with them. The conflict is likely to be more acute in men, since it is probably more permissible for a woman to be masculine than it is for a man to be feminine. Evidences of it can be found in both sexes, however. The boy who has been brought up under the overly protective wing of his mother shies away from play in which he might get hurt. He is labeled a "sissy" and reacts strongly to the label by making a negative evaluation of himself which manifests itself in feelings of inferiority. The girl who grows up as a "tomboy" may enjoy her association with boys and men, but also experiences some unhappiness because she does not get the kind of attention from men that more effeminate females command. The husband whose wife "wears the pants" may get some satisfaction from his dependence upon her, but also may have an underlying sense of inadequacy concerning the way in which he is interacting in the male's position. While his wife may also gain gratification from dominating her husband, yearning to be dependent upon him in a more conventional feminine fashion may exist at the same time. The professional woman can feel she has made her way in a "man's world," but she may also forego being treated as a woman by her associates, a state of affairs which can make for dissatisfaction.

Freud (1938) suggested that more extreme kinds of behavior disorders than those that have been mentioned stemmed from conflict relating to sex patterns. He had particular reference to those disorders characterized by delusions of persecution. His reasoning was that in such cases a person's development had been such that he was strongly attracted to members of his own sex rather than the opposite sex, but found it necessary to deny such feelings and did so by hating instead of loving. The hatred in turn was denied by the device of believing that others hated him and were persecuting him, rather than his hating others. Whether this explanation is accepted in its entirety or not, something of the kind quite possibly applies to many patients who are troubled by delusions of persecution. In clinical experience numerous cases are found of individuals whose sex patterns deviate from the cultural definition in that they are more strongly attracted to their own sex than the opposite sex and who also suffer from the belief that they are being persecuted in one way or another. One patient, for example, developed the delusion that he was being followed, watched, and whispered about after he had been told that he resembled a woman. The latter remark was reacted to as an accusation that he was, in effect, a woman (or that he was more strongly attracted to his own sex than to the opposite sex). This reaction to the remark as an accusation, rather than as nothing more than an observation, and the subsequent delusions had their origin in the conflict between the patient's own sex-pattern tendencies and the necessity he felt for denying these tendencies.

Even in the absence of strong attraction to members of the same sex and the necessity for denying such feelings, inferiority attitudes accompany inability to interact in ways expected of one's sex. The girl who has not learned how to dress and fix her hair in ways considered feminine is likely to feel "different," and perhaps be predisposed to think that people are talking about her or making fun of her, to a greater extent than actually occurs. The boy who has not learned to handle a hammer and saw or to hit a ball with much skill similarly feels inferior, and is not free from the conviction that others look down on him. Neither does the shy man fulfill the ideal of masculine assertiveness, and a sense of humiliation about himself is productive of the feelings that others don't have any respect for him. A host of problems of adjustment can, as a matter of fact, be understood in terms of discrepancies between actual sex patterns and cultural expectations as to what sex patterns should be. As stated previously, these expectations themselves become a part of the individual's psychological make-up, and if his behavior is not in accord with them he is the victim of a conflict within himself. This conflict can be illustrated by the following case:

Paul T. presented himself for psychological assistance because of a shortness of breath that troubled him on various occasions. He had consulted doctors about this symptom but they were unable to find any trouble with his heart or respiratory system that might be at the basis of it. He stated that the symptom took the form of panic and a feeling that he would not be able to get his breath. It seemed to trouble him particularly in group situations when he became the center of attention. He, therefore, did not like to recite in class, give speeches, or take front seats in audiences. As the interviews went on, Paul revealed that he had always wanted to take part in sports when he was younger but had not done so very often because of a tendency to "hang back." He remembered with acute embarrassment that he had been called "Pauline" in a gym class one time when he was afraid to jump over a hurdle. The label stuck with him for some time. Paul also reported that his father had died when he was still an infant, and that he had been brought up by his mother, who still tried to treat him as her baby. She wrote to him often and called him long-distance admonishing him to take care of himself, get enough rest, etc. The shortness of breath had started in Paul's freshman year in college. He first noticed it when taking examinations and when expecting to be called on in class. It became progressively worse and Paul gradually became obsessed with the idea that he might actually not be able to get his breath sometime.

It is not difficult to detect some of the events in the background of the individual discussed above that would undermine his confidence through lack of preparation to meet the demands placed upon men in our society. His mother's treatment of him gave him no opportunity to learn the behavior necessary to "being a man." He, accordingly, became the victim of a conflict between his lack of masculinity, or what is generally regarded as masculinity, and the aspirations that a boy develops to "be a man." It is not difficult to see that the feelings of inferiority and the fears that would result from his lack of experience in standing on his own could result in feelings of panic in exam situations or group situations where he was thrown into the limelight, since on such occasions he would be in the position of being on his own. A sense of inadequacy "as a man" would also be likely to run through his thinking about himself. He would be afraid and also be ashamed of his fear. A first step in dealing with such a problem, then, might be to relieve him of his shame about his fear or to enable him to look more objectively, and with less tendency to condemn himself, upon the discrepancy between his actual sex pattern and the pattern to which he has aspired. The major aspect of the problem in such cases, as a matter of fact, is not the discrepancy itself between the actual behavior and the culturally defined role so much as it is the attitude toward the discrepancy. The man who becomes afraid in certain situations, for example, but who is not humiliated over being "unmanly" because of his fear has far less conflict than the man who is humiliated over such "unmanly" behavior. In the light of this observation it can be seen why some men can permit themselves to engage in feminine activities more readily than others without intense conflict. Accordingly, the man who is not overly concerned about being "unmanly" can change diapers, sweep the floor, etc., without being disturbed over his nonmasculine activities.

Conflict relating to sex patterns as it applies to women can be illustrated by the case of Margaret M. who like Paul T. of the preceding case also had a physical complaint for which doctors could not find any organic basis.

Margaret M. suffered from persistent headaches which were not relieved very much by different kinds of medicine. The headaches were of fairly recent origin and seemed to have some relationship to difficulties with her studies. Margaret was enrolled in her first year of law school and her performance was such as to make it doubtful as to whether she would be able to finish law school and take her bar examinations. She had always been ambitious and had been a good student in both high school and college. Her ambition was apparently a reaction to growing up in a poor family. Her parents had relatively little status in the community and Margaret could not dress as nicely as she would have liked. She could get good marks in school, however, and received recognition for this in the neighborhood as well as from her teachers. Her parents also took pride in her doing well in school and were pleased when she managed to get through college by means of scholarships and outside work. Her interests and drives became pretty completely directed toward becoming a professional person, and she chose law because of an interest in social sciences that a friendly high school teacher inspired. The interest had grown and by the time she reached college she was determined to become a lawyer.

It can be seen that circumstances combined in such a way in the life of Margaret M. as to make for a masculine outlook on life. Neither is it surprising that she would develop headaches or similar symptoms when her professional ambitions were threatened, especially in view of the fact that she could not easily fall back on more feminine desires for herself. She in all probability would have already sensed a difference between herself and other girls with some misgivings about herself. In such a case an understanding of the origin of her modes of living and a new perspective toward childhood events, which would reduce the intensity of feeling she had had about such things as not being able to dress as well as other girls, could contribute to relieving the headaches. Some understanding of her neglect of feminine activities and experimenting with the possibilities of permitting herself to be more feminine might also make accessible satisfactions that had not been present previously.

The cases of Paul T. and Margaret M. illustrate conflict between actual sex patterns and cultural expectations of what the behavior patterns of a man or woman should be. There is another kind of conflict relating to sex patterns that is a matter of contradictions between patterns associated with a given sex position. Green (1948) treats this kind of conflict at length in a paper on "Culture, normality, and personality conflict." Concerning the Ojibwa Indians of southeastern Ontario, he says: ". . . only the individualized hunter who 'exerts power over people for his private ends' is highly regarded. Yet *goal-attainment is psychologically penalized,* for he becomes more vulnerable, instead of secure. The boy is trained not to rely upon the 'weak and competing human beings about him,' but to seek the aid of supernatural beings. Attainment of this power forces the respect of others, but they fear him, leave him alone, and other hunters, jealous of his power, direct *their* power against him." The penalizing of goal-attainment that Green refers to is an excellent definition of contradiction between patterns. He elaborates upon this point in discussing masculine and feminine patterns in the Ojibwa culture in the following passage:

The Ojibwa recognize two types of male deviants: those who fulfill the prestige and power drives in the culture beyond the statistical norm, and those who withdraw from all efforts to compete with others. Significantly, it is in the former that personality disintegration is most frequent, while the latter preserve a "coolness" in ignoring the "usual standards." In other words, *those who deviate most from the statistical and ideal norm* suffer less than those who fulfill the ideal to excess. The conclusion is inescapable that the source of male personality conflict is *in* the cultural imperatives, and not in overt behavioral deviation from them.

From a mental hygiene point of view, the Ojibwa female's culturally defined roles and goals are far superior to the male's. She works in company with others. Her appropriate sex role is not rigidly defined: under duress, she can take to the warpath if a relative's blood "is crying for revenge"; she can hunt if she is orphaned, widowed, or divorced, but this is a practical matter with her, free from power drives and with no stress on controlling the supernatural. Women do not "go windigo," i.e., develop neurosis or psychosis. Except that she must do all of the house chores, her training is more haphazard, allowing for a greater range of interest expression. Those women who follow masculine pursuits are honored rather than vilified. The only deviant type of behavior not tolerated for women is non-marriage.

Certain parallels to the plight of the Ojibwa male can be found in our own culture. The man who attains the masculine ideal of success in business or in a profession to a very high degree is often called upon to assume very heavy responsibilities. The emotional strain, accompanying these responsibilities, is a kind of penalty for success, and the highly successful American man can, therefore, be compared in a certain respect with the Ojibwa male who becomes more vulnerable when he attains the power that his culture encourages him to seek.

MARITAL INTERACTION

Although the status of the family has undergone and continues to undergo change in our culture, it is, of course, a basic unit in the social structure. It is permissible to remain single, but men and women ordinarily expect and are expected to marry. Individuals of both sexes, therefore, deviate from culturally defined "styles" when they do not marry. Their lives are affected accordingly. A prospective employer, for example, is often curious about why a middle-aged man has remained single. The attitude seems to be that it is not necessarily wrong to be single but remaining so may indicate personal peculiarities of one kind or another. Friends of a single woman, particularly if she is middle-aged or older, have difficulty in including her in parties, dinners, or similar social events. Old maids and bachelors are also considered "set in their ways" and different from married people who are assumed to be more flexible. The assumption may have validity, but even if it doesn't, the fact remains that the environment of the single person differs from that of the married person in that different attitudes are held toward one who does not marry than toward one who does. Furthermore, married and single people hold different attitudes toward themselves, and bachelors and old maids are susceptible to conflict within themselves unless they have reconciled themselves to being "different."

Just as there are pressures to marry, so are there pressures to remain married in spite of the fact that the divorce rate in America has led to speculation to the effect that marriage as an institution is seriously threatened. Divorce presents the very real possibility in many instances of jeopardizing economic welfare. Seldom do teachers and people in public office risk prospects of success in their vocations through divorce, since the culture demands that people in their occupational positions fulfill social expectations. Businessmen who must remain in good standing with their customers, employees who must maintain the good opinion of their superiors, and others cannot afford to violate these social expectations too readily, either. Taking a marriage partner "for better or for worse" is, therefore, a dictate that has some pressure to support it.

In addition to economic pressures supporting marriage vows, there is the general assumption that a newly married couple will live happily everafter. The possibility of divorce, separation, or dissatisfaction in the marriage is not contemplated by the couple or by the public at large. It, therefore, comes as a shock if the marriage fails, and the circumstances attendant upon the shock are usually unpleasant for the parties involved. Among these circumstances may be a feeling, shared—even if not acknowledged—as often as not by the couple itself, that one of the cul-

ture's stable institutions is being "let down." The going awry of
a social practice which we do not expect to fail can be disconcerting. Just as it is disconcerting when a respected citizen holding an important position misappropriates funds, so the breaking
up of a marriage can be disconcerting. The cultural expectation
is that the practice of investing a respectable citizen with responsibility as well as the practice of uniting people in matrimony
will work. When they do not work, some uneasiness is likely to
arise, and the uneasiness will be all the stronger if one has any
reason for feeling that he contributed to the failure. Whether one
has a high degree of guilt himself or not, discomfort may be
generated by disapproval from others. Anticipation of uneasiness on either score is one of the strong forces working against
divorce in the American culture.

Interaction in the Position of Mate

In spite of the conditions that militate against divorce, it does
occur, needless to say. One of the reasons is that adequate allowance is not made for learning how to interact in the position of
husband or wife. While people getting married may not literally
expect to live happily ever after, this phrase would seem to
describe more nearly the attitude with which marriage is undertaken than to say that "ups and downs" are anticipated. Practically everybody would consider it ridiculous to ignore the
necessity of gaining experience in an occupation, but the fact
that marriage functions, as well as occupational functions, must
be learned is not generally recognized. One of the reasons for
this oversight is not hard to find. Highly romantic attitudes are
held toward love relationships between men and women in our
culture. It, accordingly, comes as a revelation when the realities
of marriage demonstrate that husbands and wives can annoy and
hate each other as well as have more tender feelings for one
another. The fact of the matter is that irritation and quarreling
are to be expected in marriage. Learning this fact, as well as constructive ways of quarreling, constitutes a very important part
of becoming skillful while interacting in the position of husband
or wife. Learning how to handle marital friction in such a way

that issues are resolved and the air is cleared without lingering resentment might be analyzed as a process involving (1) the acceptance of quarreling as reasonable and even desirable, (2) appropriate participation in quarrels when they arise, and (3) the desire to restore harmony as the quarrel runs its course.

The acceptance of quarreling as reasonable can be fostered by considering that most interpersonal relationships involve conflict. Marriage, of course, is no exception. The formalities that exist in other relationships, moreover, can be dispensed with in marriage so that differences do not have to be glossed over to as great an extent. The kind of quarreling that can occur in marriage can, therefore, be regarded as a sort of privilege that relationships outside marriage do not offer. It does not follow, of course, that the marriage relationship is to be thought of as an everlasting battle. The airing of irritations and resentments, on the contrary, can go hand in hand with free expression of positive feelings that husband and wife have for one another. When antagonistic feelings are expressed and dissipated the capacity for holding and expressing positive feelings is that much greater.

Appropriate participation in marital quarrels when they arise requires, among other things, an assimilation of the partner's aggression. That is, one must permit himself or herself to be a "whipping boy" to some degree so as to provide opportunity for the partner to unburden pent-up feelings. On one occasion the wife will be sufficiently at peace with the world to let her husband "rave" without feeling any strong necessity of "lashing back" and on another occasion the husband will feel mellow enough to let his wife "rant" without answering her in kind. Some couples are, of course, better prepared than others for this kind of mutual assimilating of each other's aggression. Undue sensitivity may rule it out as unrealistic in many marriages. On the other hand, people learn to live together according to the testimony of any number of married people, and this learning probably often consists in no small part of relinquishing sensitivities that have thwarted the working out of marital conflicts. To the extent that marriage partners are relatively immune to "having their feelings hurt," they can ventilate their aggressions toward one another and assimilate each other's aggression at the same time.

A desire to restore harmony as a quarrel runs its course acts as a preventive device to forestall "blows" that cannot easily be taken in stride. Everyone retains certain sensitivities even when relatively immune to "having his feelings hurt." Thus, a husband may be able to take sharp criticism of some mistake he has made in handling his business but to be indicted as a poor husband or father because of this mistake may be more than he can take. A wife, similarly, may assimilate criticism of her housekeeping but recover far less readily from a jibe to the effect that she is a poor excuse for a wife. When husband and wife express themselves freely but refrain from taunts and jibes that wound deeply, marital quarrels function to clear the air and resolve differences. Quarrels, therefore, can be productive and useful, but the desire to restore harmony as they run their course is a condition that makes them useful.[2]

Learning marriage "skills" is, of course, influenced by what the individual has learned before he comes to marriage. Children who have lived with parents who have demonstrated that quarreling has its values as a means of clearing the air, and does not have to be reacted to as a threat to the marriage, are better prepared to cope with marital conflict as adults than children who have learned to look upon quarreling as symbolic of their parents' carrying prolonged grudges against each other. This assertion is supported by the findings of studies on marital happiness by Terman and associates (1938) and by Burgess and Cottrell (1939) which have shown that couples who are happy in their own marriages are likely to have come from homes in which their parents have been happy in their marriages. Similarity of background is another factor associated with happiness in marriage. This finding is not surprising, of course, since people with similar backgrounds are likely to behave in accordance with the expecta-

[2] The above discussion of marital quarrels was suggested in part by a similar discussion on pages 191–193 of *When you marry* by Duvall and Hill (1945).

tions of their marriage partners and are, therefore, less likely "to get on each other's nerves." Ort (1950), in fact, found a high relationship between the degree of marital happiness and the degree of agreement between expectations of participation and the actual role played in marriage. Two people coming from middle-class homes in which "good table manners" have been prized are less likely to annoy each other during meals than people coming from backgrounds that differ in respect to what is considered the right way of eating. Many other sources of incompatibility can stem from differences in background, of course. Accordingly, marriages between people from different religious and social backgrounds do not have the promise of marital harmony that marriages between people of similar background have, although there are many individual instances of such marriages working out quite well.

Although acting in accordance with the expectations of the marriage partner is related to marital happiness, a question might be raised as to how rigid these expectations can be and still permit happiness in the marriage. There is no conflict, of course, if a husband has the kind of table manners that his wife thinks he should have. If he doesn't happen to fulfill his wife's expectations on this score, however, they will obviously get along better if she can be somewhat flexible about her own standards. What is commonly known as "understanding" might in fact be defined as flexibility in respect to one's expectations of others. It is not easily attained because we are limited by the points of view and ways of doing things that have characterized our own backgrounds. Thus, people who have accents or other habits of speech that differ from our own seem "funny." Furthermore, prestige is attached to certain mannerisms, ways of dressing, talking, etc., and the striving for this prestige results in rejecting those who do not have the characteristics that enable them to "rate." Waller (1937) speaks in this connection of a "rating and dating complex" that exists on college campuses. In describing the qualities necessary to "rating" on one campus, he says:

Young men are desirable dates according to their rating on the scale of campus values. In order to have Class A rating they must belong to one of the better fraternities, be prominent in activities, have a copius supply of spending money, be well-dressed, "smooth" in manners and appearance, have a "good line," dance well, and have access to an automobile. . . .

The factors which appear to be important for girls are good clothes, a smooth line, ability to dance well, and popularity as a date. The most important of these factors is the last, for the girl's prestige depends upon dating more than anything else; here as nowhere else nothing suceeds like success. Therefore the clever coed contrives to give the impression of being much sought after even if she is not. It has been reported by many observers that a girl who is called to the telephone in the dormitories will often allow herself to be called several times, in order to give all the other girls ample opportunity to hear her paged.

It can be seen from Waller's remarks that relations with the opposite sex can become to a large extent a matter of seeking and maintaining status or prestige. Men seek women who "rate" as a means of gaining status for themselves and vice versa. The pattern is sometimes carried over into marriage so that the partner continues to be looked upon as an extension of the other's ego. A beautiful wife can be used as a symbol of status in very much the same way that an expensive car can support one's ego. A good-looking and successful husband can also be "shown off." The trouble is that husbands and wives who exploit each other in the fashion described may tend to look to each other for unqualified admiration as well. The beauty queen is exposed as human and petulant as well as "sweet and lovely" in marriage, however. The handsome and engaging young man reveals himself as surly and grouchy as well as charming. Since petulance and surliness are not consistent with unqualified admiration from others, difficulties can arise. Here is an instance, then, in which flexibility in expectations of the marriage partner may be called for. If a certain allowance can be made for human qualities, such as petulance and surliness, rather than holding rigidly to expectations of consistently agreeable behavior on the part of the marriage partner, the relationship will involve less conflict. The acquisition of this flexibility is another important aspect of the learning of marriage "skills."

To illustrate what has been called flexibility in expectations of the marriage partner let us use the following case:

Edward's and Ellen's early marital difficulties ranged from relatively minor conflicts over such things as Ellen's forgetting to replace the cap on the tube of toothpaste to more major conflicts provoked by such things as Edward's commenting too often on the attractiveness of other women. As in all marriages they had opportunity to become familiar with each other's sore spots. Edward learned, for example, that Ellen was not only sensitive about his commenting on the attractiveness of other women but that she also felt that she was unable to converse "intelligently" with his friends. Ellen learned that Edward not only became irritated over her not remembering to replace the cap on the toothpaste but that he was also afraid he might not succeed in his work. Since they were both eager to have a happy marriage, Ellen modified her expectation of cheerfulness on the part of her husband and tried to remember to replace the cap on the toothpaste. She also tried to understand the lack of confidence Edward had about his work rather than continuing to take it for granted that her husband would be sure of himself. Edward, in turn, did not insist that his wife be "broad-minded" about his comments on the attractiveness of other women, even though he had previously expected that she would be. Furthermore, he made an effort to understand her feelings of inferiority about talking with his friends rather than dismissing such feelings as silly—in spite of the fact that he was surprised to find that she had such feelings.

The modification of expectations of each other's roles in the marriage that Edward and Ellen were able to achieve illustrates the kind of flexibility that can foster harmony in a marriage relationship. Although the difference of opinion concerning the toothpaste may seem trivial, conflicts in marriage are often accentuated by such seeming trivialities. One need only consider the differences in attitudes toward the husband's helping with the dishes, the wife's getting up in the morning to get breakfast, who should control the family finances, etc., to realize that such problems are not actually insignificant in many marriages. A certain readiness to modify expectations can go far toward resolving such problems.

Interaction in the Position of Parent

Becoming a parent is, of course, deserving of attention as a part of interaction in marriage. How the parent assumes his function shapes the personality of his children, and also determines the kind of family life the parent himself will have. The most pertinent observation that can be made about parenthood is that the child tends to become like his parents. The significance of this process can be understood by considering some of the reasons for its taking place. In the first place, the child's needs such as hunger, thirst, and other physical discomforts are attended to by the parent. The parent's mannerisms and expressions accompany the satisfaction of these needs and thereby take on reward value for the child with the result that the child tends to reproduce these mannerisms and expressions. Thus, a child says things that Momma and Daddy say, sometimes to the embarrassment of Momma and Daddy. The parents also instruct and guide the child in various ways, and when the child follows the parent's lead he is rewarded with approval, or at least is less likely to receive disapproval. The child is often rebellious, of course, but the reason for this is that he finds it more rewarding to resist. It is sometimes more fun for the child to throw food around, for example, than to eat in a more orderly way. The fact remains that he is directly rewarded by praise when he eats as the parent wants him to, or indirectly rewarded by not being punished. The parent, furthermore, can withhold rewards whether they be in the nature of affection and praise, or gifts and food, or both. It, therefore, pays the child to do what the parent expects, and what the parent expects reflects the parent's values. When the child is doing as the parent wishes, he is learning these values and in that way becoming like the parent. Approval may be withheld when Johnny talks back to the teacher, for instance. To get approval he must refrain from being "sassy," then. When he learns this restraint he is acquiring the value that his parent attaches to "politeness." Furthermore, the parent is a powerful figure from the child's point of view. The parent's behavior, therefore, symbolizes power or a greater measure of control over the environment than he has. The child is, accordingly, likely to adopt this behavior himself in his efforts to cope with his environment. Thus, Mary "works" her dad for a new dress in the same way that her mother does. The child is not fully aware, of course, of his reproduction of his parents' values and modes of behavior in himself. Learning can and most certainly does take place, however, without awareness on the part of the learner as to what is going on. It is also in order to observe that the child patterns himself after both parents, and, therefore, does not become exactly like either one of them. He also patterns himself after others besides the parents. There are good reasons, then, for his being a unique individual, but the above discussion indicates that very powerful reasons also exist for his being like his parents.

Since the child's becoming like his parents is such a dominant factor in his development, it is evident that the parent who hopes that his child will have certain traits will do well to pay as much attention to his own behavior as to that of his child. A mother who wishes a happy marriage for her daughter is contributing nothing to that end when she constantly bewails her own marriage. A father who hopes that his son will be self-assured does not foster this assurance when he constantly exhibits anxiety about his business around the home. Parents can't help being as they are, of course, but neither are they completely powerless in controlling and changing their own behavior. If the foregoing father's anxiety is not too acute, for instance, he can submerge it to the extent of trying to be cheerful when he comes home at night. Similarly, the mother who is unhappy in her own marriage can give some thought to what she can do to work out a more congenial relationship with her husband.

While it may give a parent somewhat uncomfortable pause, unless he is thoroughly satisfied with himself, to reflect over the likelihood that his child will become like him, it must also be remembered that identification with the parent is "a powerful unseen ally in teaching . . . children proper habits," as Davis and Havighurst (1947) put it. They go on to say: "It is a salutary experience for parents to keep in mind this powerful aid, the process of *identification* in the child. With such a memento, they

will be less likely to overpress the child; they will reduce their
own tenseness and slacken their 'bombardment' of hourly demands in seeking to train the child. They will give him a chance
to learn to become like the parent in response to his inner pull,
rather than from outer driving." This apt reminder could undoubtedly relieve a good deal of distress on the part of parents
as well as children in many families in which excessive pressure
is brought to bear in training the child in acceptable cleanliness
and eating habits as well as in other kinds of behavior. Although
it is commonly recognized that the child picks up unacceptable
mannerisms through a process of imitation and identification, it
is also true that he learns acceptable modes of behavior without
formal instruction.

In view of the preceding remarks it must be acknowledged
that a parent's influence on a child will depend primarily on
what kind of individual the parent is. Nevertheless, there are
certain general principles of learning that can guide parents in
raising children in such a way that socially acceptable behavior is
established without excessive strain in the relationship between
parents and children. Some of these principles are as follows:

1. The responses the organism can learn are determined by its
level of physical maturation. The child cannot walk, of course,
until its musculature and nervous system have reached a certain
stage of maturation or growth. This much is generally recognized,
but it is not so generally recognized that a period of maturation
is also essential to establishing sphincter control. The child is,
instead, often hurried along in toilet training with little tolerance
for "relapses" which are to be expected not only because of earlier
established habits but also because of an early stage of maturation. Neither can the child speak precisely nor handle eating
implements with a high degree of coördination until he has
reached a certain stage of physical maturation. It is, therefore,
futile for parents to be overzealous in training young children to
do things in the "right" way. Not only is it futile but it can also
impose strains on the child that he cannot cope with. Tensions
and insecurities are thereby built into his personality that are
hard to displace.

2. If a response is to be learned, it must be made and rewarded. The significance of this principle is that it directs attention to the fact that punishment will not suffice to get an individual to behave in a desired way. It can inhibit undesired behavior, but it does not provide any substitute for such behavior. Parents can apply the principle by being on the alert for ways of rewarding desired behavior. The parent can make it a point, for example, to praise the child when it begins to dress itself and exhibits independence and self-reliance in other ways. The parent can also devise means of displacing undesired behavior by rewarding other behavior that will take its place. If a child likes to play with kitchen utensils such as knives that are dangerous for him to have, the parent can arrange for the child to put them away when they are washed, for example. The child's pleasure in helping the parent and in still being able to handle the knives under circumstances that are not dangerous to him are rewards for another kind of behavior that replaces his previous responses. Similarly, the child who likes to play with the telephone can be given a toy telephone of his own to play with.

3. Immediate rewards are more effective than delayed rewards. The child derives immediate reduction of excretory urges from using the floor rather than the pot for a toilet. He also gets immediate satisfaction of his activity drives by grabbing the nearest objects at hand which sometimes happen to be curtains and flowerpots. Parents cannot, therefore, expect to have exceedingly orderly households unless they make the child excessively guilty about behavior that his impulses are very likely to give rise to. Furthermore, it is to be expected that the child will not make perfect progress in learning behavior that involves postponement of immediate gratification. The child gradually learns to respond to delayed reward, however, if the parent consistently follows through on his promises as to what he will do in the future. If he says he will read to the child in a few minutes and then doesn't do it or that he will buy him an ice cream cone in the afternoon and doesn't, delayed reward does not have any reality for the child. The child has confidence in the parent who does keep his

promises, however, and this confidence predisposes him to have patience in foregoing immediate gratifications.

It will be recalled that the principles enumerated above have been presented as guides in raising children in such a way that socially acceptable behavior can be established without introducing excessive strain in the relationship between parents and children. The emphasis has, accordingly, been placed on the use of rewards rather than punishment in the training of the child. There are no simple rules that parents can be given, however, as to how to use rewards or as to what will be rewarding. It was suggested above, for example, that a child who plays with the telephone might be given a toy telephone of his own, but there is no guarantee that he will find playing with it as rewarding as playing with the real telephone. The parent, therefore, may have to exercise some ingenuity in figuring out ways of making it rewarding by inventing a game or using some other device for making it enjoyable for the child to play with the toy. Even then the toy telephone may arouse no interest. This is particularly likely to be the case if the child has gotten attention and affection by listening to Daddy or Grandma over the real phone and from being encouraged to talk to them over it. If it is crucial that the child leave the phone alone because important business calls come over it, the parent may be wise to refrain from rewarding the child's contact with it by having him listen and talk to Daddy and Grandma over the phone. If it is not so crucial that the child leave the phone alone, however, the parent must expect him to be interested in it and to want to play with it at times that are inconvenient for the parent if the child has been rewarded for attending to it at other times. From the child's point of view punishment for playing with it at inconvenient times is unjust. Accordingly, the parent who does not want to arouse feelings in the child of being unjustly treated must have some willingness to try to find ways of diverting the child, or finding substitute activities that will be rewarding, or reconcile himself to putting up with certain activities until the child learns that they are rewarding under certain circumstances but not others. To illustrate the last point, the child learns that he hears a voice over the phone some times but not others. He will probably become bored with the phone when he doesn't hear the voice and gradually learn that it isn't so much fun to attend to it except when he can hear and talk to Grandma or someone else.

In spite of the parent's efforts to use rewards rather than punishment, the parent will have to disapprove of some of the child's behavior. Disapproval need not necessarily create undue strain in the parent-child relationship nor have unfortunate consequences for the child. The child, in fact, is going to encounter disapproval and hostility from others outside the home and he can, therefore, gain preparation for such experiences by encountering disapproval in the home. It is again difficult to lay down simple rules as to how the parent should administer disapproval. One general guide that can be followed is that the parent can be firm without being harsh. When Bobby persists in pulling things off the stove which might have a pan of hot water on it on some occasions, there is obviously justification for trying to inhibit his behavior by punishing him. If the parent is guided by the general distinction between firmness and harshness, he can spank Bobby and impress him with the idea that he is not to pull things off the stove. This can be done without overwhelming the child by beating him as violently as one possibly can. The child senses the difference between being dealt with firmly and being bullied, and although this distinction may seem somewhat ambiguous, parents also know the difference in their own treatment of the child. When the child is dealt with firmly but not harshly, he has less reason to be overwhelmed by hostility when he meets it outside the home, and this is particularly true, of course, if other conditions do not foster his being overwhelmed. As has been pointed out elsewhere, the child who has been made overdependent is going to be more frightened by punishment, whether physical or verbal, than the child whose self-reliance has been encouraged.

Another general guide to the use of punishment is that the parent make clear the child's alternatives and then enforce them consistently and firmly but, again, not harshly. If the child is expected to pick up his toys after he is through playing with them but is not inclined to do so, the parent can make it clear that not picking them up carries penalties. He can pick them up or be spanked, for instance, but it is up to the parent to be consistent about insisting that the toys be picked up or the child will be spanked. The parent can also be "matter of fact," which is a part of being firm but not harsh; the spanking is a spanking for a particular incident. A procedure that stands in contrast to its being simply a spanking for a particular incident is the parent's acting woebegone and burdening the child with an overreadiness to feel guilty, or losing his "sense" and intimidating the child. Matter-of-fact punishment can teach the child responsibility for his own behavior and respect for social authority which are to be distinguished from overconscientiousness and fear of authority.

SUMMARY OF PRINCIPLES

An elementary but fundamental principle of social interaction is that in every society one must interact as a male or female. Some of the principles governing such interaction that have been proposed in this chapter are as follows:

1. The fact that certain activities are proposed for men and boys and others for women and girls provides an important condition for learning to adopt masculine and feminine patterns.

2. Significant adults in the child's environment have a profound influence upon his learning of sex patterns:

a. The child who fears and hates a parent may reject the femininity or masculinity that this parent stands for and tend to pattern himself or herself after the other parent.

b. Fear and hatred of a parent may generalize to other individuals of the same sex as the feared and hated parent.

c. Comfortable relationships with both parents are productive of the greatest security in interaction in sex positions.

d. Dominance of a masculine or feminine model in the child's environment tends to produce a personality corresponding to that of the model.

e. Parents not only provide models through their own behavior but they also guide behavior in various ways that influence interaction in sex positions.

3. The individual whose activities have been channeled along lines inappropriate to his or her sex can easily become a misfit in his or her social environment. Additional principles concerning the conflict are:

a. Delusions of persecution may be related to conflicts having to do with the individual's sex pattern.

b. Inferiority attitudes tend to accompany inability to adopt the patterns expected of one's sex.

c. Whether a discrepancy between a culturally defined sex pattern and the actual sex pattern constitutes a conflict for the individual depends upon his attitude toward the discrepancy.

4. The individual is faced with conflict not only when there is a difference between actual sex pattern and cultural expectations as to what the pattern of a man or woman should be but also when there are contradictions between sex patterns associated with a given position.

5. Individuals of both sexes deviate from culturally defined "styles" in the American culture when they do not marry. Further principles concerning marriage are:

a. The social expectation that a marriage will work tends to maintain the marriage relationship in the American culture.

b. The functions of husband and wife must be learned just as occupational functions must be learned.

c. There is a relationship between the degree of marital happiness and the degree of agreement between expectations of role and the actual role played in marriage.

d. Flexibility in expectations of a marriage partner tends to make for marital compatibility.

6. The child tends to become like the parent.

a. The child is motivated to become like the parent by approval as well as by disapproval.

b. The parent's behavior symbolizes power and the child

is likely to adopt this behavior himself in his efforts to cope with the environment.

c. The parent's mannerisms and expressions accompany the satisfaction of various needs and thereby take on reward value for the child with the result that the child tends to reproduce these mannerisms and expressions.

CHAPTER 10

Interaction in Hierarchy Positions

Introductory Summary

Hierarchies are those social structures in which there are higher and lower levels of authority, prestige, power, or privilege. Unitary hierarchies are organized for a specific purpose and confined to one segment of the population. Class hierarchy covers the whole population as does caste hierarchy. Cast differs from class in that an individual can move from one class level to another, whereas he remains in the caste in which he was born.

Social interaction is influenced by hierarchies in many ways. Expressions of aggression are affected by one's position in a hierarchy, as shown by the fact that a man does not talk back to the boss as readily as to his wife. Upward and downward mobility also occur in hierarchies, and the extent and manner of conformity as well as the attitudes an individual holds can be interpreted as a function of hierarchy position to a considerable degree.

THE CONCEPT OF HIERARCHY

Just as everyone must interact in the position of male or female, it is also true that virtually everyone in many societies must interact in hierarchies, which are social structures that have higher and lower levels of authority, prestige, power or privilege. Within the family the parents rank above the children as holders of authority. In a business firm the board of directors is at the top; management personnel next to the top—although there are several levels of ranking within it; and the workers are at the bottom of the hierarchy. Hierarchies of one kind or another are probably necessary to social organization. Warner, Meeker, and Eells (1949) suggest that even a simple society that relies largely on fishing to feed its members will make use of hierarchies in order to get its work done. Certain individuals will be placed in charge of boats, for instance, and others will be under their direction. In a more complex society, hierarchies are multiplied many times over. Lines of authority, for example, are defined by means of hierarchies in government, industry, education, etc. Hierarchies of the kind that exist in government, industry, and education are organized in a fairly clear-cut fashion for specific purposes and might, therefore, be called unitary hierarchies. Hierarchies of a somewhat different kind are found in the class and caste structure of a society. Before discussing hierarchy behavior as such, let us turn our attention to the three kinds of hierarchies that have been mentioned.

KINDS OF HIERARCHIES

Unitary Hierarchies

The president, vice-presidents, managers, supervisors, foremen, and workers of a manfacturing concern make up a hierarchy that is clearly organized for a specific purpose; this kind of ladder is an example of what is meant by a unitary hierarchy. In general, hierachies of this kind have policy-making bodies at the top, administrators, managers, or supervisory personnel that carries out policy at the next level, and workers at the lowest level. Educational institutions, for instance, usually have a board of education or board of trustees that assumes responsibility for policy. The president or principal of the school, deans, heads of departments, etc., are below the board of education or board of trustees, and the teachers make up the bottom rung of the hierarchy. In government, similarly, policy-making units, such as the President's cabinet or a county commission, are found at the top of hierarchies, bureau heads or other kinds of "chiefs" next, and office workers, janitors, etc., last. Unitary hierarchies exist in military organizations, labor unions, clubs and societies of various kinds, hospitals, professional associations, etc. All of them correspond more or less to the pattern that has been described. It is obvious that the individual's position in such hierarchies has an important relationship to his interaction in his environment. The president of a company, needless to say, is expected to behave and is likely to behave in ways that are not expected of a foreman or a worker under the foreman.

Class Hierarchy

Whereas a unitary hierarchy is confined to one segment of a society and does not take in the whole population, a class hierarchy covers the whole population. The concept of class is foreign to Americans because of ideals that are held concerning equality, democracy, and "everybody's being as good as everybody else." It is generally recognized, nevertheless, that some individuals have more prestige than others, and expressions such as "high society" and "the other side of the tracks" reflect the general recognition of higher and lower status of various people in American communities. Studies of the way in which people rank others as to their status reveal that a class system does in reality exist, and that it is pretty well defined by the people themselves even though they do not use the word *class*.[1] Warner and Lunt (*1941*) and others have found a prestige or status ladder in contemporary American life consisting of upper, middle, and lower classes with a subdivision of each of these classes into upper and lower. The ladder is, therefore, usually made up of about six rungs which run from top to bottom as follows: upper-upper, lower-upper, upper-middle, lower-middle, upper-lower, and lower-lower.

People at the upper-upper level are recognized by everyone as individuals who "rate." They come from old families that have had prestige for several generations and have considerable power and influence. Individuals at the upper-upper level are more than likely to be wealthy, but one can hold this rank without wealth if

[1] The discussion of class presented here was suggested by *Deep south: A social anthropological study of caste and class*, by Davis, Gardner, and Gardner (*1941*).

he comes from an old family. Belonging to the "old aristocracy" is, as a matter of fact, the most important qualification for being classified at the upper-upper level. The lower-upper level is also made up of "aristocracy," but the aristocracy in this instance does not have the quality of age, so to speak. People at this level also have considerable power and influence, and are often wealthier than people at the upper-upper level. They associate on intimate terms with the latter, and tend to differentiate themselves from people at the upper-middle level with whom they do not "have too much in common." That is, they do not associate on intimate terms with people at the upper-middle level to any great extent. Their cliques and clubs, for instance, will ordinarily not include many upper-middle-class people. The upper-middle class also enjoy considerable prestige in the community at large, however. In some instances they are wealthier than people at the two classes above them, and in any case, they are recognized as people whose livelihood comes from "working with their heads, not their hands." Professional people, administrative personnel in business and education, and teachers are usually to be found at the upper-middle level. Warner, Meeker, and Eells (1949) speak of the three classes that have been discussed thus far as being above the "common man" level.

The "common men" of the lower-middle, upper-lower, and lower-lower classes "work for a living," or are at least more likely to have to punch clocks regularly or put forth greater physical exertion in their work. People at the lower-middle level live in somewhat better homes than those at the two levels below them, ordinarily, and their occupations also carry greater prestige. Small shopkeepers, "white collar workers," foremen, and barbers are among the occupations to be found in the lower-middle class. Lower-middle class persons think of themselves as "poor but respectable" and as a notch above people who are poorer than they are but still above the "shantytowners." The people whom the lower-middle class refer to as poorer than themselves but above the "shantytowners" make up the upper-lower class. They live in somewhat better quarters than lower-lowers, and usually hold somewhat better jobs. They are more likely to be straw bosses or skilled workers than people in the lower-lower class. The latter speak of themselves as "just as good as anybody," but this expression itself belies some consciousness of their low status which is reinforced by constant reminders in the form of lowly jobs, poor shelter and clothing, and condescension or contempt from people outside of their class.

Caste Hierarchy

The concept of caste is foreign to Americans in the same way that the concept of class is. A democracy supposedly has no place for a caste system, but, as Myrdal (1944) has pointed out, Americans are faced with a dilemma. On the one hand, equal rights for all, regardless of race or religion, are cherished. On the other hand, distinctions are drawn on the basis of skin color, and being white or black actually defines a caste system in American society. As with a class hierarchy, a caste hierarchy covers the whole population. That is, everyone can be placed in respect to whether he belongs to a higher or lower caste. Caste differs from class, however, in that one can move from one class to another, whereas an individual remains, with rare exceptions, in the caste into which he was born. Dollard (1937) and others have shown that classes exist within both the Negro and white castes in American society. One may move up or down in his class position within either caste, but there are very strong barriers to his moving from one caste to another. Thus, either a Negro or white who comes, let's say, from a lower-middle-class family within his own caste might attain the level of education that qualifies him to become a professional person and in so doing move into an upper-middle-class position within his own caste. In both instances the individual remains in his own caste, however. The barriers to moving from one caste to another are illustrated by written and unwritten marriage restrictions. In some states it is illegal for Negroes and whites to marry, and even in those states where it is not, the individual who marries outside of his caste finds it extremely difficult to gain social acceptance from individuals in either caste.

Various minority or ethnic groups, that are in some way set

off from the population at large, are to some extent in the position of members of an "inferior" caste. So-called Italian-Americans, Polish-Americans, Syrian-Americans, and Jews, for instance, have a different status in the American culture from individuals of Anglo-Saxon or northern European ancestry. Marriage between individuals in these groups and individuals from other groups is not "frowned upon" to the same extent that marriage between Negroes and whites is disapproved, but neither is it completely accepted in spite of the pride that Americans take in their country as a "melting pot." Similarly, the individual who is born an Italian, Pole, or Jew continues to be identified as a member of his minority group to a greater or lesser extent, and although he is regarded as an American, his Americanism is not always given the ready recognition that is the case with an individual who does not belong to such a minority group. Expressions such as "Some of my best friends are Jews" imply, for example, a distinction drawn between Jews as Americans and others as Americans. Derogatory terms such as "wop," "hunky," "polack," etc., are also used in referring to members of minority groups, and these terms sometimes serve the purpose of distinguishing between such individuals and "Americans" or "full-fledged Americans" and others whose "Americanism" is not questioned.

INTERACTION AS INFLUENCED BY HIERARCHIES

An individual's interaction in a hierarchy position is, of course, influenced by various expectations, "rules," and social regulations. It is more permissible to kick the dog than it is to kick one's superior or to talk back to a brother or sister than to a parent or teacher. Many similar examples come to mind when these two are cited, and it is evident that expressions of aggression have a very definite relationship to hierarchy. "Social climbing" or upward mobility as well as losing status or downward mobility take place in hierarchies, and social mobility is, therefore, another kind of behavior that is related to hierarchy. Conformity is also governed by position in hierarchies, since acceptable behavior at one level of a hierarchy is not necessarily acceptable at another. Attitudes and the kind of behavior that corresponds to the attitudes, similarly, will vary from one status in a hierarchy to another; an upper-class person is more likely to be conservative politically than a lower-class person, for instance. In the sections that follow, the relationships between hierarchy and aggression, hierarchy and social mobility, hierarchy and conformity, and hierarchy and attitudes will be discussed.

Hierarchies and Aggression

When aggression arises it cannot always be expressed directly. As was pointed out above, the child can talk back to a brother or sister, but ordinarily he must be more careful about talking back to a parent or teacher. From such experiences the child learns to anticipate punishment for expressing aggression in some ways and learns that other ways of expressing aggression are not punished, and are, therefore, acceptable. The example makes clear that this kind of learning occurs in hierarchies. It is also true that when aggression cannot be expressed directly, it takes another course. The other course that it frequently takes is toward someone lower in the hierarchy. The captain suppresses his anger toward the major, but it comes out in full force when he talks to the lieutenant or sergeant. The captain might "take it out" on himself, for that matter, which would still be an instance of redirecting the aggression toward someone lower in the hierarchy, since his rank is lower than that of the major. It can be seen, then, that we are prone to anticipate punishment for expressing aggression toward "those above" but less prone to anticipate it for expressing aggression toward "those below." The mere fact that the child is smaller and weaker than adults who are "above" him predisposes the individual to a greater or lesser extent to be cautious about aggression toward "those above." At the same time, the child feels less necessity for caution in expressing aggression toward other children, particularly those who are smaller and weaker than himself.

The direction of aggression toward those lower in the hierarchy can be readily discerned in unitary, class, and caste hierarchies. In unitary hierarchies, such as a business organization, for example, one makes it a point to be "diplomatic" in dealing with superiors, but feels freer to be more direct with subordinates. Similarly, the higher one is in his class position, the more likely it is that he will be treated with deference, whereas there is much less deference toward those who are said "not to amount to much," or who are lower in their class position. The phenomena of race prejudice and prejudice toward minority groups, which are in a somewhat similar position to people in a lower caste, as has been pointed out previously, illustrate the direction of aggression toward "those below."

Aggression is not channeled exclusively toward those who are lower in hierarchies, of course. Prize fights, football games, violence in movies and comic strips, etc., all provide outlets for aggression. The expression of aggression by such means tends to involve identification with the "underdog" in our culture. Thus, the football team that is thought not to have a chance is highly celebrated when it wins. In the comic strip "Superman," the principal character has fantastic strength, but in everyday life he is a rather mild, retiring individual who might be described as an "underdog." Mickey Mouse of comic-strip and movie cartoon fame also seems to have strong appeal to the American public and is obviously a "little man" or an "underdog." We take special delight in his triumphs. A possible explanation of our tendency to identify with the "little man" is that traditionally America has been "the land of opportunity," and our class system is fairly flexible. "Coming up from the bottom" is considered commendable, and even the rich man's son who takes lesser jobs before assuming executive responsibilities gains admiration. The victory of the small man is apparently symbolic of American tradition, and it is, therefore, not surprising that a popular mode of expressing aggression is by means of identifying with the underdog.

In spite of the sympathy that Americans have for the underdog, it is also true, as has already been suggested, that Americans select groups with relatively little power as scapegoats and vent their aggressions on them. Race riots and lynchings, for example, are not unknown in American life. Less violent aggressions are reflected in the derogatory remarks that are consistently made about minority groups. Individuals as well as groups are, of course, used as scapegoats. Many comedians take the role of "stooges" and provoke laughter by poking fun at themselves or by having a partner who pokes fun at them. As stooges they are perceived as harmless or powerless. The laughter that accompanies the stooge's falling down, or getting hit on the head, or being the butt of a joke is quite possibly a release of aggression toward someone who is reacted to as more or less helpless. The mild-mannered and "harmless" member of a fraternity is also frequently the victim of practical jokes. The selection of helpless, powerless, or harmless individuals or groups as scapegoats can perhaps be interpreted as a matter of maintaining a sense of adequacy. Individuals encounter frustrations and thwartings that present them with a greater or lesser sense of their own limitations, particularly if anxiety already exists over their own limitations. Releasing aggression, wherether by laughter or by actual overt attack, toward those who are weaker, or who have even greater limitations, can serve the function of removing one's own sense of weakness or inadequacy. Finding weakness in those who have been reacted to as stronger and releasing aggression toward them probably serves this function even better. The intimidated school boy who finally "stands up" to the bully and discovers that he is not so terrifying after all gains new self-respect and confidence that he had not known it was possible to have.

Standing up to the bully, as was pointed out above, serves the function of restoring self-confidence better than taking out aggression on the younger brother. This is perhaps particularly true in our culture in which one is encouraged to "take a stand," or to "be a man" (and pressure is brought on boys particularly, of course, to be "manly"; it is more acceptable for a girl to be a "mouse"), or to "fight for one's rights." Margaret Mead (1941) states very succinctly and clearly the problem the individual in our culture is faced with when there are barriers to his taking a stand in the following passage:

An individual who has been taught that he must stand up, and choose, or else his parents will withdraw their love and punish him, cannot stand a situation in which the representatives of parents, teachers, and others in authority, suddenly deny all of his training, and start giving blind orders and expecting him to give blind obedience. With his delicately balanced personality structure, there is a shift in emphases, a rearrangement of affects; in proportion as he submits and toadies, he also will dominate and bully, to restore some sort of integration within his outraged personality.

The release of aggression as a means of restoring self-respect is used in psychotherapy with children as well as adults. A therapist may encourage a child to play with clay, for example, and to make dolls with the clay. In the course of manipulating the dolls that represent parents, teachers, or other children that the child hates, the child may pull off a leg and look furtively toward the therapist in anticipation of disapproval for "injuring" the person that the doll represents. When the therapist says something such as, "You really feel like hurting so and so sometimes," the child discovers that his expression of aggression does not meet with disapproval, and proceeds to get out more of his feelings of antagonism. It is frequently found that after the child gets out these negative feelings, he then begins to express more positive feelings toward others, and, in general, seems to be more at peace with himself and his world. The relationship between the child and the therapist is one in which the child discovers that an adult, who is a figure of authority for the child and, as such, "more powerful," accepts aggression. This state of affairs is comparable to the child's releasing aggression toward someone who is stronger, and in finding that it is possible to do so, feeling more adequate himself. Feeling more adequate within himself would seem to account for the positive expressions of feeling toward others, such as expressions of affection, which often ensue.

Barriers to expression of aggression toward more powerful individuals that have been referred to above result in various modes of dealing with authority. Children who have learned to feel ashamed of resentment, disagreement, or resistance to the extent that they become what might be called too well behaved are prepared for hierarchy interaction that can be described as overly conforming. Overly conscientious individuals are scrupulous about following rules and often tend to be at a loss without them. Some students consistently hand in papers well ahead of time, thus allowing more than enough margin for conforming (although such behavior is not necessarily a matter of overconformity) with the rule that they would be due by a certain date. They are also pleased with exact specifications of how long their papers should be and how they should be organized. Workers who are overly exact in filling out forms and making reports may also be exhibiting scrupulousness about rules. *Rigidity* is perhaps the best word that can be used to characterize the behavior we have reference to. The reader will note that the last sentence ends with a preposition. The writer was tempted to change it so as to read: "the behavior to which we have reference." The last phrase would be more grammatically precise than "the behavior we have reference to," and the temptation to make the change is a good example of rigidity, because the phrase employed adequately expressed the writer's thought. Rigidity is frequently not only a way of adjusting to authority in a subordinate position but it is at the same time a method of handling authority in a superordinate position. A supervisor may abide strictly by the rules, for instance, in order to avoid criticism from one of his superiors. In so doing he not only tries to avoid criticism from his superiors but also imposes the rules in a rigid way on subordinates.

While overconformity to authority and defiance of authority appear to be opposite kinds of interaction in the environment, they also bear a relationship to one another in the behavior of many individuals. The well-behaved child sometimes rebels. It is not surprising that he should, since his overconformity is based on fear or anticipation of disapproval. If parents or other figures of authority instill fear, they are also likely to be resented. The resentment may be repressed, of course, since children are taught that they are supposed to love and respect their parents. The exceedingly well-behaved child is particularly likely to have been indoctrinated in the shamefulness of expressing resentment. The resentment may occasionally break through, however, or at least be expressed in subtle ways. A child may stop doing his lessons, for example, when he has previously done them very conscientiously, or in some instances he may have trouble in mastering something like arithmetic. The trouble in such cases is not lack of ability, but an expression of resentment, even though it isn't recognized as such by the child or by his parents or teachers. Similar expressions of rebellion or protest can be found in the behavior of adults, of course. A worker, for instance, may let a foreman search for the reason a machine is not working when he knows the reason himself. A secretary may let her boss make a mistake in correspondence that she could have caught. A student wanting suggestions for a term paper, or similar project, finds something wrong with everything that his teacher proposes.

Needs for defying authority stem from overcontrol. It is sometimes exercised openly, as in the case of the parent who "lays down the law" and quells rebellion when it arises. Another kind of overcontrol takes the form of forestalling rebellion insofar as possible by making the child dependent. In the latter case, the child's fear of being on his own results in his looking for directions from superiors rather than even contemplating overt rebellion very seriously. His defiance of authority is, therefore, likely to be more indirect. Furthermore, the control that has been exercised over him is not as obvious or apparent, by any means, as in the case of the individual who has had "the law laid down" to him, and he doesn't know how to fight or defy authority, as it were, because authority has always been hidden. Parental overcontrol, in any case, is often duplicated by the child when he becomes a parent. One reason, perhaps, is that after the child becomes a parent, his own children become subordinates, and aggressions can be taken out on subordinates in the family as well as in the Army. In line with this observation, we can see how one might defy parental admonitions and control by defacing property, but be very severe in dealing with such an offense when in a position to punish such behavior. Similarly, a child or adolescent might resent parental overcontrol manifested by a parent who opens his mail, but do the same thing when he becomes a parent himself.

A clue to preparation for the kind of hierarchy behavior that is characterized neither by overconformity nor defiance is furnished by the distinction that Erich Fromm (*1941*) draws between rational authority and inhibiting authority:

. . . there is a fundamental difference between a kind of superiority-inferiority relation which can be called rational authority and one which may be described as inhibiting authority.

An example will show what I have in mind. The relationship between teacher and student and that between slave-owner and slave are both based on the superiority of the one over the other. The interests of teacher and pupil lie in the same direction. The teacher is satisfied if he succeeds in furthering the pupil; if he has failed to do so, the failure is his and the pupil's. The slave owner, on the other hand, wants to exploit the slave as much as possible; the more he gets out of him, the more he is satisfied. At the same time, the slave seeks to defend as best he can his claims for a minimum of happiness. These interests are definitely antagonistic, as what is of advantage to one is detrimental to the other. The superiority has a different function in both cases; in the first, it is the condition for the helping of the person subjected to the authority; in the second, it is the condition for his exploitation.

The dynamics of authority in these two types are different too: the more the student learns, the less wide is the gap between him and the teacher. He becomes more and more like the teacher himself. In other words, the authority relationship tends to dissolve itself. But when the superiority serves as a basis for exploitation, the distance becomes intensified through its long duration.

The relationship between superior and subordinate that is implied by what Fromm calls "rational authority" is one in which the subordinate is prepared for equal status. The security derived from such status is comparable to the new self-respect and confidence that the intimidated school boy gains when he stands up to the bully. In the rational authority relationship, the subordinate is consistently able to stand up to someone more powerful, since its purpose is to foster independent acting and thinking.

Such a relationship between student and teacher, for example, involves questioning rather than blind acceptance of the teacher's statements, as well as insistence upon the part of the teacher that students arrive at their own conclusions instead of expecting him invariably to furnish the "answer." Active questioning and thinking is, of course, not consistent with fear of or overdependence upon authority. Neither does it predispose the individual toward strong feelings of weakness and inadequacy in the face of frustration and thwarting that must be removed by venting aggressions toward those lower in the hierarchy.

Hierarchy and Social Mobility

Social mobility can be defined simply as moving up or down in a hierarchy. Expressions such as "getting someplace," "amounting to something," "going up in the world," etc., indicate what is meant by upward mobility. Everyday expressions for designating downward mobility are not as prevalent, because, in all probability, most people are preoccupied with "going up," or at least staying where they are, rather than going down, and they, therefore do not think, and do not like to think, in terms of "going down." Thinking in terms of "going up" is reflected in a tendency to estimate one's class position as somewhat higher than it is. Investigators frequently find such magnified estimates when studying the prestige structure of American communities. Thus, a person may rate himself as just below the "high society" group in his town, whereas his actual position in the prestige structure of the community, as indicated by the clubs he belongs to, the people he associates with, etc., is much closer to the "common man" level. This example makes clear the relationship between social mobility and class hierarchy. An individual can move up or down in a class hierarchy, as well as in a unitary hierarchy, whereas his position remains fixed in a caste hierarchy, as has already been pointed out in an earlier section of this chapter. Changes in position in a unitary hierarchy are likely to be accompanied by changes in position in class hierarchy. If a man is promoted in the organization he works for, which would be an example of his moving up in a unitary hierarchy, he is also likely to be "promoted" in class position. This correspondence in changes in position in unitary and class hierarchies is seen most clearly in the case of the office boy who ultimately becomes president of the company. In moving from office boy to president, he at the same time moves from a class position close to the "com-con man" level to one close to the "high society" level.

Movement up or down in a class or unitary hierarchy is likely to be accompanied by anxiety, as Allison Davis (1944) has pointed out. Anxiety exists lest one fail to move up, and is also provoked by the prospect of going downward in a class or unitary hierarchy. Furthermore, one can be anxious over simply maintaining the position he has. The reasons for this anxiety are clear when we consider the fact that the higher one's position in a class or unitary hierarchy, the greater his material and psychological security is likely to be. Conversely, his security diminishes as his position becomes lower. Aside from financial security, the assurance associated with "being somebody" is a strong incentive, and the insecurity associated with "not being anybody" constitutes an anxious prodding to be in a different position.

Upper-upper class individuals do not have the necessity for defending themselves or their children against the possibility of "not being as good as anybody." Their social position is assured by birth. Lower-upper class persons have a somewhat greater degree of anxiety about where they stand. They have reached "the top" or next to the top, which is upper-upper status, in their lifetime, and, therefore, have a greater sense of having something to lose. They may also either minimize the importance of family background which is a requisite to upper-upper status, or attempt to provide themselves with the symbols of old family status. An example of the latter would be searching through one's ancestry for the purpose of finding distinguished forebears. This kind of searching is not confined to the lower-upper class, of course, Middle-class people also exhibit hierarchy anxiety by engaging in it. Since middle-class persons have not come as close to "arriving" as either upper-uppers or lower-uppers, and since they have more prospects of upward mobility than lower-class people, their eagerness to "get ahead in the world" is intense. Education provides a means of "climbing," and is highly valued in the middle class. It is probably valued more highly at the middle class than at the upper- or lower-class levels. Lower-class people are more or less resigned to their low status in spite of the threat that it represents to their self-esteem. This threat to self-esteem is reflected in efforts to protect their children from it. West (1945) points out that "lower-class parents teach their children as a fundamental dictum regarding their status, 'You're just as good as anybody.'" Lower-class people hold little hope of going to college, and even finishing high school is considered only a remote possibility, particularly at the lower-lower level. Upper-class people, on the other hand, do not have to use a college education as a symbol of status. Hollingshead (1949), for example, in speaking of the upper-class evaluation of a college education in one community says, "Education is not highly regarded, either as a tool for a professional career or for knowledge in the traditional sense." He goes on to point out that a majority of the young people "attend good colleges or universities, but only about half of the men and a third of the women graduate."

The hierarchy-anxiety discussed in the above paragraph is handled in many ways. Defenses against it, as has been said, may take the form of asserting that one is just as good as anybody, looking into one's ancestry to find a distinguished forebear, etc. It also acts as a motivation to learn the forms of behavior that are appropriate to maintaining or raising one's status. If one encounters disapproval from those upon whom he is trying to "make an impression," for instance, when he shouts at a waiter, he may experience anxiety in response to the disapproval and modify his behavior toward waiters, accordingly, in the future. One may also dress in a certain way or drive a certain kind of car for the purpose of seeking higher status, and these modes of behavior can sometimes be interpreted as a response to anxiety about one's hierarchy position. The popularity of station wagons among people who can afford only one car is perhaps in part attributable to such anxiety. The purpose of a station wagon in the first place was presumably to serve as a kind of truck or service car for people who could afford more than one car and who had upper-class status. Possession of a station wagon, accordingly, became a symbol of such status, and their acquisition by people of lower status would appear to be a means of reducing anxiety about the lower status by behaving as though their position in the class hierarchy was higher. A similar kind of phenomenon is found in fashions of dress; the Duchess of Windsor's Easter bonnet finds its way to Main Street.

While imitation of the kinds described in the foregoing paragraph do not guarantee higher status, neither are they to be written off as entirely pointless or foolish. The child as well as the adult learns by imitation, and learning the behavior necessary to upward mobility is adaptive inasmuch as greater security is attainable as one moves up in social hierarchies. When a boy imitates a mannerism of his father's, the mannerism does not make him an adult, but if he at the same time learns how to handle a plow, win an argument, or flatter a woman, he is then becoming an adult in a real sense. Similarly, imitating the President's manner of dress does not make one a successful politician, but if one learns political and leadership skills of the President at the same time his prospects of leadership are considerably strengthened. An important, if not a necessary, requirement for imitation to take place is the availability of a model. The boy who grows up without a father is handicapped in learning a masculine role, because he is not in daily contact with a model after which to pattern himself. The individual who has little contact with superiors is in a similar position. This point seems to be recognized, at least implicitly, by some teachers and business executives who select young people they consider to have promise and turn them out in their own image by making themselves available as models through conferring with them, inviting them to their homes, confiding in them as the relationship becomes closer, etc.

Young people who are not considered so promising are not selected by superiors in the manner just described. Lower-class children in the schools, for example, tend to be excluded from close relationships with their teachers, not necessarily because of malice on the part of the teachers, but because they present traits that are not likely to result in their being evaluated as "promising" by their teachers who are largely middle-class persons. A lower-class child's grammar will not ordinarily be a "thing of beauty" to his middle-class teacher, even though it is appropriate to his background and the only mode of speech he could have learned. He is also likely to be more outspoken than his middle-class school mates, since outspokenness is accepted and approved among the people he lives with. It will not endear him to his middle-class teacher in all probability, however. The resulting distance that develops between himself and his teacher as well as other middle-class adults, who are likely to respond to him in a similar fashion, has the effect of making models in higher class positions unavailable. If he does manage to achieve upward mobility into the middle class later in life, he will have difficulty in acquiring modes of behavior appropriate to his new status. His outspokenness may not be easily modified, for example, and "tact," "diplomacy," and "polish" which are highly valued in middle-class life will not come easily because they have not characterized the models he has had available to him. He may pick up such traits from new models, but it will not be easy for him to find such models in the first place for the reasons that have been discussed, and social distance is, therefore, a formidable barrier to upward mobility.

Social distance separates middle-class and upper-class persons as well as middle-class and lower-class individuals. Private schools and residences that are set apart from the dwellings of people lower in the class hierarchy provide the upper class with a kind of insulation from the rest of the population. Servants also attend to many functions, such as shopping, which also helps to minimize association with middle-class and lower-class people. Middle-class people are, therefore, deprived of upper-class models in somewhat the same way that lower-class individuals are deprived of middle-class models. The middle-class person who achieves upward mobility into the upper class may very well have the same kind of difficulties, then, in learning upper-class modes of interaction that the lower-class person has in learning middle-class modes of behavior. Large contributions to charity which are given readily, for example, are approved and expected among upper-class people. A newly rich man in the process of moving into upper-class status from middle-class status may not have acquired appropriate upper-class attitudes toward charity from an upper-class model, however, and as a result not gain complete acceptance in the upper class until he adopts such attitudes. Assurance, poise, and relaxation are also valued in upper-class life. These modes of behavior are not entirely consistent with success-striving and modesty that are appropriate in middle-class life, and afford another example of traits that middle-class people do not have too much opportunity to learn from upper-class models.

Eagerness or anxiety to move upward in social hierarchies, and thereby achieve greater security, varies with different individuals, of course. Some are intensely ambitious, others are more or less content with whatever their lot happens to be, and still others are resigned to their status. Nevertheless, pressure toward upward mobility exists to a greater or lesser degree for most people in our society. While social distance operates to thwart such mobility, it is also true that admiration is given the person who rises from humble origins. A story is told of Theodore Roosevelt who was making a train journey with other high government officials on one occasion when several of them said that they were born in log cabins or modest farm-houses of the kind that could be seen as the train passed through the country side. Roosevelt is reported to have said that he was not born in such a place, but that he was as good as anyone in the group. The valuing of initiative and resourcefulness that is indicated by a story of this kind offsets to a considerable extent the barriers to upward mobility that have been discussed. The American culture makes allowance for individuality and innovation. "Build a new mouse trap and the world will beat a path to your door" is a slogan that is taken seriously. Superiors who squelch new ideas are boken away from and the breaking away is applauded. Members of minority groups also achieve distinction in spite of the fact that distinctions are drawn between "full-fledged Americans" and other kinds of Americans. Originality, therefore, does have a place in the American culture, and dependence upon models in higher positions for purposes of learning the behavior necessary to rising is strongly diminished by this acceptance of new ideas and new personalities.

Hierarchies and Conformity

The relationship between conformity and social hierarchies is readily understood when the expectations of behavior appropriate to different hierarchy positions are considered. We do not expect the office boy to slap the president of the company on the back usually, unless the office boy plans on seeking employment elsewhere. Expectations relating to the president's position also give him more freedom to indulge his personal whims. If he tells "shady" stories to the office girls, he is considered "quite a character." If a salesman in the organization does the same thing, he is more likely to be considered lacking in a sense of propriety, even though a certain amount of "breeziness" is expected from salesmen. Similarly an upper-class youth who wrecks a car when on a drunken spree has a better prospect of being taken home and put to bed by the police, rather than thrown in jail, than a young person of middle- or lower-class status. A scholar, scientist, or industrialist of distinction can also set forth opinions on subjects he is no better qualified to speak on than anyone else, and gain an audience. The same opinion from the mouth of someone of lesser prestige, if listened to at all, would be laughed out of existence. Many people disagreed with a famous industrialist when he said that history was bunk, but the assertion was not simply laughed out of existence. All of the foregoing examples indicate that need for conformity diminishes as one rises in a social hierarchy.

The decreased necessity for conforming to standard attitudes and practices as prestige is gained has an important relationship to social change. Social change is, of course, governed by a number of factors and cannot be reduced to a simple formula, but one of the ways in which it is brought about is through introduction of new approaches, ideas, and points of view by individuals in high prestige positions. Franklin Roosevelt's ideas of social security were strongly resisted, but he could force serious consideration of them in his position as President. He succeeded in not only forcing consideration but in translating the ideas into legislation. Less spectacular examples come to mind from everyday experience. A medical specialist's diagnosis may not differ from that of a local general practitioner's, but will often be more readily accepted than the local doctor's. One function of experts, specialists, and consultants would seem to be that of confirming what is already known. A student may be fairly sure of his choice of an occupation, for example, and learn nothing essentially new about himself by consulting a vocational counselor. He is reassured, however, if the counselor arrives at the same conclusions that he had already drawn. It is also true that a specialist or expert can set forth opinions, even though the specialist or expert himself may not consider his ideas as conclusive, with a good prospect of the opinion's being accepted as factual. An automotive engineer may predict that cars of the future will have a new type of engine—with the reservation that new fuel and metals will have to be developed before such engines are produced in large quantities; such an opinion from a specialist may then be taken as a definite prediction that the new engines will be on the market in a relatively short time in order to support one's own ideas about the rate of technological progress in the United States.

The fact that a position carrying prestige enables an individual to facilitate social change is of considerable interest in view of the relationship that usually holds between such positions and conservatism. Revolutionary leaders do not always come from the lower-prestige positions of a society. George Washington was an aristocrat in his day. Sigmund Freud, who revolutionized medical and psychological thinking by proposing that many symptoms of illness were manifestations of hidden personality conflicts rather than of infection or organic lesion, was a medical man and scientist. Tom Paine was a writer, thinker, and journalist; his mode of life came closer to that of an intellectual than to that of a citizen inspiring other citizens to revolt. The positions of aristocrat, medical man, and intellectual enabled

Washington, Freud, and Paine to have considerable influence upon their own and subsequent generations, and to modify the society that provided the positions in which their activities took place.

In the light of the foregoing remarks, it is clear that prestige positions are not invariably the strongholds of maintaining the culture as it is. It is interesting to note, however, that individuals such as Washington, Freud, and Paine conformed to the extent of taking or partially taking the culturally defined and accepted "parts" of aristocrat, medical man, and intellectual. Whether these "parts" were taken by design or accident need not concern us. The point is that in the instances cited, at least, conformity was involved to some extent in bringing about social change. While prestige positions decrease the need for conformity, the very playing of the roles corresponding to these positions represents conformity. Furthermore, the positions themselves require certain kinds of conformity. An aristocrat or upper-class person must act like an aristocrat if he is to be accepted as such, a doctor must conduct himself with assurance in dealing with patients or discussing medical problems, and an intellectual must have a superior vocabulary.

The kinds of conformity represented by the examples just given are all suggestive of the necessity of self-confidence in prestige positions. Conforming behavior, therefore, need not necessarily be motivated entirely by fear or disapproval. Any great degree of such fear, in fact, thwarts effective interaction in prestige positions. A greater or lesser degree of readjustment is, therefore, required in respect to the amount of this kind of fear that is entertained as one moves up a social hierarchy. It is not altogether unrealistic to have a certain amount of such fear while interacting in lesser prestige positions inasmuch as strong disapproval may seriously interfere with attaining a higher prestige position and the security that goes with it. One can afford to be less sensitive to disapproval after attaining the higher prestige position, but not before. The relinquishing of such sensitivity is, of course, a part of the security that goes with the higher prestige position.

Sensitivity to disapproval from superiors is particularly acute, but it tends to be obscured in our culture, particularly in the middle class. The reason for our confusion on this score is brought out by McGregor (1944) in the following comments on dependence upon superiors:

This dependence is not adequately recognized in our culture. For one thing, it is not consistent with some of our basic social values. The emphasis is usually placed upon the importance of the subordinate's own efforts in achieving the satisfaction of his needs. Nevertheless, the dependence is real, and subordinates are not unaware of it. Among workers, surveys of attitudes invariably place "fair treatment by superiors" toward the top of the list of factors influencing job satisfaction. And the extent to which unions have attempted to place restrictions upon management's authority reflects not only a desire for power but a conscious attempt to reduce the dependence of workers upon their bosses.

Green (1943) suggests still other factors, aside from the emphasis upon the importance of the subordinate's own efforts spoken of above, that contribute to the glossing over of dependence upon superiors and sensitivity to their disapproval:

With his superiors, the inferior's most effective technique is voluntary submission. This may masquerade as bluff fellowship, if the inferior infers that is what his superior wants, but the inferior's personality inevitably dances to the tune played by the superior's. For career purposes the inferior allows his superior to invade his ego. He consults, he defers, he flatters. He may raise some straw objection to an issue at hand, in order to allow his superior to state a positive position, and then agree wholeheartedly with him. Above and beyond presenting his work in as favorable a light as possible, the inferior intrudes himself socially, to the upper limits of the given situation and his superior's attitude toward him. Always, however, and because Western society has not structured master-slave relationship between whites, the inferior must pretend it is the *friendship* of his superior he is seeking. The folk speech of the new economy is rich with indications of the real basis for that friendship: "contacts"; "yes man"; "the fair-haired boy"; "polishing the apple"; "You've got to sell yourself first"; "It isn't what you know, it's who you know."

The last two quotations strongly suggest that although individuals do not entirely escape perception of striving for the approval of superiors and anxiety concerning their disapproval, the recognition of such striving and anxiety is not as explicit as it might be by any means. Perhaps the underlying reason for failure to recognize dependence upon superiors is that social hierarchies are subject to a considerable amount of disapproval in the first place. The concepts of class and caste are foreign to Americans, as was pointed out earlier in the chapter, because class and caste distinctions tend to be regarded as morally wrong. Similarly, "big shots" in business, educational, or government hierarchies who indicate in some fashion that they are "really just like everybody else" or "one of the boys" or "in touch with the common people" gain approbation. This valuing of equality is in many ways inconsistent with interaction in social hierarchies. One cannot feel equal and at the same time be too anxious about a superior's approval. It is no wonder, then, that this anxiety is not too readily recognized. Knowing that it is relatively common and not altogether unrealistic would probably reassure any number of people who have experienced it, but have been unable to admit such fear to themselves because of the humiliation associated with not feeling equal.

While the humiliation associated with not feeling equal may be relieved by knowing that it has been experienced by others, and that the anxiety occasioning such humiliation is not necessarily unrealistic, interaction in a hierarchy in which such humiliation is not evoked, or is minimized, probably does far more to relieve it or prevent it from arising in the first place. In the ideal family situation in the American culture, the child is secure in his feeling that his parents are behind him and can be depended upon. At the same time, he is encouraged to think for himself and to take responsibility for himself as he is ready for it. Clinical experience seems to indicate that a child coming from such a background is likely to be a comfortable and secure adult in the American culture. This knowledge of the conditions within the family hierarchy that are necessary to comfortable functioning in the culture has implications for other kinds of hierarchies, as McGregor points out. His central theme is that just as the child must be secure in his parents' affection, support, and approval, so the subordinate must feel that his superiors are "behind him," and that when the subordinate feels this assurance he is prepared to take responsibility and initiative himself, providing the superior, like the parent, encourages his doing so.

Hierarchies and Attitudes

It is, of course, well known that political and economic opinions and attitudes vary with economic position. Although the correspondence is by no means perfect, there is a tendency for wealthier individuals to be more conservative than less wealthy individuals. Many studies have found that people in higher occupational strata tend to favor private ownership of property and individualism and to oppose more power for working people to a greater extent than people in lower occupational strata.

Although it is not surprising to learn that political and economic conservatism is more prevalent at higher occupational levels, it is probably less well known that attitudes toward child-rearing practices vary from one class level to another. Ericson (1947) compared such practices among lower-class and middle-class people and found certain characteristic differences. Some of her findings are summarized as follows:

In the middle-class families, fewer children are breast fed than in the lower-class families; where they are breast fed, they tend to be breast fed for a shorter period of time than the lower-class children. Many fewer middle-class children than lower-class children are completely breast-fed. Middle-class children also tend to be bottle fed for a shorter period of time than are the lower-class children. Three times as many middle-class children as lower-class children were reported as thumbsuckers.

While political and economic attitudes and attitudes toward child-rearing may seem to have relatively little in common, the fact that they shift from one hierarchy level to another suggests that hierarchies provide a ready-made basis for the acquiring of attitudes. Thus, if an individual moves from one occupational stratum to another he finds new points of view and opinions which he may adopt for himself or which influence him to modify his previous attitudes, to at least some extent, in the direction of the new opinions. Similarly, a child growing up at a certain class level tends to adopt the attitudes of people of that class. The middle-class male child is more likely to acquire an attitude that women should be treated gently, for example, than a lower-class male child, since gentleness in relationships between men and women is valued highly in the middle class but not as highly in the lower class.

Differences in attitudes toward gentleness in relationships between men and women indicate that the administering of rewards and punishments varies from one level of a hierarchy to another. The middle-class male child is rewarded for being "respectful" toward women and strongly disapproved for failing to be "respectful." The lower-class male child, on the other hand, is more likely to be rewarded or praised by means of smiles or laughter, if not open praise, for being somewhat rough with women. Such behavior makes him a "man." If he does not display a certain amount of such behavior, he is punished by being called a "sissy." Similarly, people at higher levels of the occupational hierarchy tend to approve of associates who favor "private enterprise" as opposed to "governmental interference" and tend to disapprove of associates who do not hold to this opinion.

In spite of the administering of rewards and punishments in ways that support certain attitudes as opposed to others at different hierarchy levels, it is also true, of course, that differences in attitudes and opinions exist within any one level. Furthermore, some individuals deviate widely from generally accepted attitudes among others at their level. Some people at the upper levels of socioeconomic hierarchies, for instance, are considered radical in their political outlook and some people at lower socioeconomic levels are staunch defenders of the status quo. One explanation offered of such deviations in attitudes is itself based on hierarchy concepts. According to this explanation the radical son of conservative parents is seen as one who rebels or protests against the authority of his parents who have, of course, occupied a higher position in the family hierarchy than he, as a child, has or had occupied. Such an explanation of deviant attitudes, when carried to the extreme, implies that all new ideas, "slants," points of view, or opinions are the product of protest against authority or the prevailing and accepted ideas. While such an account of originality and new attitudes is probably an oversimplification, it is a fact that original thinkers have often had to "swim against the tide." As every schoolboy knows, Fulton and the Wright brothers were laughed at when they proposed the ideas of the steamboat and the airplane, respectively. We cannot help but be reminded as well of the opposition to Columbus's conceiving of the earth as round, or of Pasteur's struggle to gain acceptance of the possibility of infection by bacteria. In the light of such examples, it is evident that many original thinkers have certainly departed from conventional modes of thought, and the hypothesis that they have been motivated by protest against authority, which corresponds to a higher level of a hierarchy, does not appear completely implausible.

If the latter hypothesis is valid, it throws light on the interaction of geniuses, intellectuals, inventors, and certain kinds of college professors who are considered "screwballs" by the population at large. Such individuals are nonconformists in their thinking, and although labeled as "radicals," which is another way of saying that they protest—as the hypothesis under discussions holds, their discoveries, nevertheless, often prove useful. It is perhaps for the latter reason that they are accorded a place in the culture in spite of the fact that they are looked upon as "funny" or "strange" or in reference to whom it is often said that there is a thin line between genius and insanity. The actual physical place or places provided for them in the culture are illustrated by the existence of Greenwich Village in New York, which is well known as a center for aspiring literary geniuses, research centers and laboratories which are often found in universities, old garages where potential inventors experiment, and attics and cheap rooms where writing is done. The psychological place or places provided for such people is found in the attitude of indulgence the public holds toward absent-minded college professors and attic dwellers for whom, it is generally believed, a certain allowance must be made. (The latter may decrease when the rent on the attic is due, however.) Even the nonconforming original thinker often conforms to the extent of taking a culturally defined "part" and influences society in this "part," as was pointed out in the previous section of this chapter. In the light of the present discussion, it seems reasonable to think of the behavior of intellectuals, geniuses, inventors, etc., as behavior that occurs in culturally defined ways.

SUMMARY OF PRINCIPLES

Although the complexity and nature of hierarchies vary from one culture to another, the individual must interact to a greater or lesser degree in hierarchies in any culture. The individual's position in a hierarchy, therefore, bears an important relationship to his interaction in interpersonal relationships. Principles concerning social interaction in hierarchies proposed in this chapter are as follows:

1. The expression of aggression in hierarchies tends to be directed toward "those below." Additional principles concerning the relationship between the expression of aggression and hierarchies are:

   a. The higher one's position in a hierarchy, the more likely it is that he will be treated with deference.

   b. Identification with the "underdog" in the American culture tends to offset expression of aggression toward "those below."

   c. Direct expression of aggression toward "those above" tends to serve the function of restoring self-esteem to a greater degree than taking out aggression on "those below."

   d. Children who have learned to feel ashamed of resentment, disagreement, or resistance to the extent that they become what might be called too well behaved are prepared for hierarchy interaction that can be described as overly conforming.

   e. Needs for defying authority tend to result from overcontrol by individuals in positions of authority.

2. Pressure toward upward mobility exists to a greater or lesser

degree for most people in the American culture. Additional principles concerning social mobility are:

a. Changes in position in a unitary hierarchy are likely to be accompanied by changes in position in class hirarchy.

b. Social distance between individuals in higher positions in hierarchies and those in lower positions presents a barrier to upward mobility on the part of those in lower positions.

3. The need for conformity diminishes as one rises in a social hierarchy. Additional principles concerning conformity in relations to hierarchy positions are:

a. One of the ways in which social change is brought about is through the introduction of new approaches, ideas, and points of view by individuals in high prestige positions.

b. It is not altogether unrealistic to have minimal fear of criticism while interacting in lesser prestige positions, inasmuch as strong disapproval may seriously interfere with attaining a higher prestige position and the security that goes with it.

4. Just as the child in the American culture must be secure in his parents' affection, support, and approval in order to take responsibility and initiative effectively himself, so the subordinate in an adult hierarchy in the American culture must feel that his superiors are "behind him" in order to take responsibility and initiative effectively himself.

5. Attitudes tend to vary with hierarchy position.

6. Deviations from prevailing or conventional attitudes in a social group may stem from protest against authority.

CHAPTER 11

Adaptive Interaction
in Social Positions

Introductory Summary

Learning to interact in social positions adaptively requires (1) practice or experience, (2) analysis and understanding of expectations of such interaction, and (3) the selection of modes of social interaction that are uniquely suited to one's own resources. Experience in various forms of social interaction is gained in many ways and is influenced by the individual's perfectionistic or nonperfectionistic expectations of himself. Expectations can be analyzed in terms of (1) one's expectations of his own interaction, (2) others' expectations of one's interaction, (3) one's expectations of the interaction of others, and (4) others' expectations of their own interaction. The popular expression "Everybody must lead his own life" expresses the significance of uniqueness in social interaction. The conditions of everyone's life differ and their modes of behavior, therefore, must be unique in certain respects. The mode of interaction that is adaptive for any one individual is determined by his particular resources, and the feeling he has about his resources functions to produce or eliminate defensiveness in his interpersonal relationships.

ASPECTS OF ADAPTIVE INTERACTION IN SOCIAL POSITIONS

Learning to interact in social positions adaptively, or in such a way as to maintain oneself effectively in his environment while at the same time preserving a sense of well-being, requires practice or experience. Just as one does not become a skillful carpenter,

311

musician, or merchant overnight, neither does one learn other social functions such as those of husband, wife, leader, student, etc., skillfully without a considerable amount of experience. *In addition to practice, adaptive social functioning requires analysis and understanding of behavior expectations.* An employee, for example, can function more adaptively when he knows what kind of interaction his employer expects of him in his position as employee; similarly, knowledge of his expectations of himself as well as of his expectations of his employer can contribute to a realistic orientation in his social environment. *Still another aspect of adaptive interaction in social positions is uniqueness. Every individual must select the particular pattern of interaction that is appropriate to his limitations, abilities, and the circumstances of his life if he is to maintain himself effectively in his environment.* A younger person in a position of responsibility, for example, cannot function effectively in exactly the same way that an older person in the same position can. Similarly, a younger person cannot follow exactly in the footsteps of an older person, but must find the modes of interaction that are best suited to his particular talents and the situations in which he finds himself.

EXPERIENCE IN INTERACTION IN SOCIAL POSITIONS

Experience in various forms of social interaction is gained in many ways. Young children gain experience in adult activities in playing games that call for the function of parent, teacher, doctor, storekeeper, etc. Adolescents and young adults gain experience in later activities in a somewhat similar way by engaging in "amateur" activities of various kinds. Practice trials are held in law schools, for example, in which "parts" are taken that correspond to "parts" taken in actual courtrooms. Engineers in training in industry are, likewise, presented hypothetical situations having to do with production techniques, handling of personnel, etc., which involve practice in later functions in that they are confronted with the necessity of determining how they would carry out actual functions of the future. Experience in social interaction is also gained vicariously as when one listens to another relate an experience or watches another interact in a certain position and imagines himself doing the same thing. Vicarious experience in acting in a position is clearly illustrated by certain aspects of medical training: medical students observe operations, but do not perform surgery until some time later in their training. There are various ways, then, of gaining experience in interaction in social positions. How profitable such experience is depends, among other things, upon the individual's expectations of himself as he gains the experience. If he can regard flaws in his performance as a part of the learning process, for instance, he will not only be more comfortable with himself, but will also be more inclined to try to gain further experience with the attitude that his mistakes are something to be profited from rather than reasons for adopting a defeatist outlook.

Rehearsal in Interaction in Social Positions

As stated above, there are various methods of gaining experience in social interaction. Play, "amateur" activities of various kinds, and imagining oneself acting in a position are among these methods. They can all be regarded as forms of rehearsal in interaction in social positions or practice for purposes of preparation for future social interaction. Although such rehearsal is probably ordinarily engaged in without much awareness of its being rehearsal, adaptability can be facilitated by awareness and planning of practice in social functions. Thus, the law student who understands that practice trials held in law schools provide opportunity for rehearsal in future functions in his occupational position can avail himself of the opportunity to engage in such trials for purposes of gaining experience. Even in the absence of the opportunity provided by these trials, the law student can to a certain extent provide opportunities for himself in gaining practice in future functions, and is perhaps more likely to do so if he understands that these functions are learned through rehearsal. He can make it a point, for example, to try to organize his thinking in ordinary conversations and to present his ideas to others clearly. In so doing, he gains experience in thinking "on his feet" which his future function as a lawyer will involve. One of the important purposes of rehearsal of functions is the making of mistakes without undue concern about them. The law student of our example, therefore, need not expect perfection in his performance as he avails himself of opportunities, or provides himself with opportunities, for practice in his future occupational functions.

Rehearsal in interaction in a position can be obtained not only through overt activities of various kinds, such as the law student's actually taking part in practice trials, but also through imaginative or fantasy activities. Thus, as one watches a play or reads a book he engages in fantasy, the content of which is provided by the author of the play or book, and imaginatively takes the parts of characters in the play or book. While this kind of fantasy can serve the purpose of escaping from reality, it can also serve the purpose of preparation for actual social interaction, or of understanding forms of interaction that are in reality engaged in by other people. A good deal of literature is misleading, to be sure, in that it idealizes, distorts, or oversimplifies actual experience. Presumably one of the criteria of "great" literature, nevertheless, is that it portrays modes of interaction as they are or might be actually experienced by particular individuals. Reading about such modes of interaction or watching them acted out in plays provides a kind of experience in engaging in the behavior oneself. While one would not necessarily contemplate actually taking many of the parts portrayed in plays and novels himself if he could avoid doing so, the understanding of various kinds of social interaction that can be gained from literature can be of value in gaining insight into one's own behavior. As one places himself in Hamlet's position, for example, he is to some degree able to discern the effects of his own inner conflicts, and in the process of detecting them in himself he can more readily approach an adaptive resolution of them (in somewhat the same way, for example, that an individual can simply check expression of his anger when he knows that he is angry, but does not express it because of the disadvantages it might have for him in a particular situation, rather than becoming paralyzed with fear when his anger arises because he does not dare discern it in himself). Similarly, placing oneself in Lady Macbeth's position can serve the purpose of detecting the part that ambition plays in one's own experience, even though it might not function exactly as it did with Lady Macbeth by any means.

Somewhat similar to the rehearsal in social interaction that results from watching a play or reading a novel is the observing of others' interaction and imaginatively interacting in a similar way oneself. The imaginative interacting in a position in a manner similar to the mode of interaction employed by another may be followed by overtly acting in the same way. In one instance, for example, a socially retiring person noticed that another person who wanted to borrow a book spoke up to the other people in a group with which he was working and asked if anybody had this particular book. The retiring person in question imagined himself doing the same thing, although this was done with a certain amount of difficulty, and then actually did the same thing later himself when the appropriate occasion arose. In such a case the imitation may or may not be blind. That is, one might observe another's mode of interaction, and then attempt to adopt it as one's own without evaluating its suitability for oneself. Blind imitation might be distinguished from experimental imitation, the latter consisting of a tentative trying out of another's "style of acting" to determine its suitability for oneself. In the example that has been used, the socially retiring person might find that he couldn't "wisecrack" in the same way that the other person did when asking for the book. He would perhaps also discover that he could at least ask for it with no terrible consequences resulting from such nonretiring behavior. The latter discovery would, of course, be more likely to result from experimental rather than from blind imitation. Experimental versus blind imitation of social interaction can also be illustrated in marriage as well as in many other interpersonal relationships. In one instance, a newly married husband required that his wife give up her own religion and attend his church in a kind of blind imitation of the patterns of his own subculture. It was only after his wife began to exhibit fairly acute emotional distress over the conflict that he had precipitated that he gave up his demands that she adopt his religion. A higher degree of experimental, rather than blind, imitation of traditional behavior of husbands might have proven much more adaptive.

The blind imitation spoken of above is based upon a limited and superficial understanding of the nature of interpersonal relationships. A fairly widespread uncritical acceptance, in the American culture, of the prescription "Be a good fellow, all will go well, and you will succeed" illustrates this limited understanding of the nature of human relationships in many instances in which the prescription is followed. Imitating an individual who pats others on the back, eats and drinks with them, etc., may leave out the essential element of this friendly behavior, namely, the exhibiting of genuine warmth toward others through such activities. While blind imitation that left out this essential element might succeed for a while, because it is at first reacted to as a demonstration of real liking of others, it will no longer be responded to in this fashion when it becomes apparent that the back-slapper is "putting on an act," and is actually so preoccupied with "making an impression" that he cannot really "lose himself" in genuine expression of interest in those around him. Blind imitation of this kind is frequently motivated by a high degree of anxiety which impels the individual to look for quick and easily adopted forms of interaction that will relieve the intolerable anxiety, or what is experienced as intolerable anxiety. Such an individual feels that he cannot take time to try various forms of behavior, but that he must get an immediate solution. Experimental imitation, on the other hand, presupposes anxiety- or frustration-tolerance. Thus, one might imitate another's back-slapping to determine whether it "feels like" an appropriate form of behavior for him, and to find out whether he can really express interest in others in this way. This trying out of a particular form of interaction involves anxiety because the individual is not sure that it will work for him, but the anxiety is endured for purposes of learning how to function adaptively in the social environment, and is also relieved through experimentation rather than by the frantic and blind adopting of "solutions."

"Making an impression," "being smooth," "winning friends," and "wearing a smile" are among the prescriptions of the kind mentioned in the above paragraph that are often found in the American culture as guides to getting along effectively in one's social environment. The fact that they are offered as prescriptions is suggestive of the seeking of relief from what is experienced as intolerable anxiety. While they are not always accepted as pat solutions or sure remedies for problems in interpersonal relationships, they do have a widespread popularity, and this popularity probably often reflects underlying anxieties about being liked by others, anxieties which have perhaps been established in the first place through seemingly innocuous means of training children by withdrawing affection. Such withdrawal of affection may actually provoke anxiety to a very high degree, however. Thus, if a mother says, whether verbally or by means of the whole attitude displayed toward a child, that she won't love him if he acts in a certain way, or that people won't like him, rather than reprimanding him in a fashion that does not involve such threats of ostracism, it can be seen how being liked by others would become a matter of great concern. This concern might, then, come to be handled by such devices as "wearing a smile" and back-slapping rather than through experimental exploring of forms of social interaction that would prove more adaptive for the individual. Since there is considerable emphasis in the American culture upon "standing on one's own feet" and "being an individual," it is perhaps particularly important to prepare individuals to engage in experimental social interaction through which they can find the unique patterns of behavior that are suited to their particular personalities. Overdeveloped anxiety over being liked by others, stemming from threats to the effect that mother or people in general "won't like you," is not conducive to such experimentation. Furthermore, simple remedies for "making people like you" have less value for the individual's handling of interpersonal relationships than an understanding of the nature of experimental interaction.

Experience in Social Interaction and Expectations of Oneself

Experience in interaction in social positions is sometimes thwarted by perfectionistic expectations that an individual sets for himself. The young woman who aspires to be the perfect hostess may only be discouraged by her ventures in entertaining others because of her imperfect performance. With a different kind of expectation of herself, she could feel rewarded for having gained the experience in entertaining, even though her party may not have been as enjoyable to everyone concerned as she had hoped it would be. Furthermore, with this latter orientation she would be more inclined to entertain again and gain further experience in interacting in the position of hostess. Similarly, the inexperienced actor or actress who can permit himself or herself mistakes can feel rewarded in what he has done right and even in the opportunity to profit from the mistakes. Even the person who has had considerable experience in acting in a position, whether of worker, parent, mate, professional person, or whatever, is not immune from mistakes. An acceptance of this fact stands in sharp contrast to perfectionistic expectations of one's own social interaction. Principles of learning would seem to indicate, in fact, that the individual who learns to interact in various social positions effectively is the individual who can allow for a margin of error in his experiences and activities, since he is in a much better position to reward himself for what he does correctly and to continue to profit from experience without undue discouragement when he does make mistakes. Furthermore, the difference between the self-confident and the insecure person is probably not entirely a matter of assurance versus lack of assurance but is a difference in respect to perfectionistic expectations. The person who can allow for a margin of error is not necessarily completely sure of himself, but imposes much more reasonable expectations upon himself than the perfectionistic person. A greater degree of confidence is, of course, likely to accompany the holding of more reasonable expectations.

Perfectionistic expectations of one's own interaction not only impose demands upon oneself that are likely to result in discouragement, but also present barriers to profiting from others' experience. One reason is that the discouragement resulting from such expectations does not predispose the individual to observe others' modes of interaction and try them tentatively in one's own experience. Another is that perfectionism tends to produce the

conviction that profiting from others' experience is an indication
of inadequancy in oneself. While the latter conviction is probably
rarely put into words, it might be expressed in this way: "If I
really measure up, I have nothing to learn from others." The individual who does not impose perfectionistic demands upon himself, on the other hand, can permit himself to learn from others or
to "tap" their repertoire of social "skills" for purposes of becoming
adaptive in his own functioning. Thus, one young instructor who
had come into conflict with a class, because the members of the
class openly revolted against his assignments, did not know exactly what to do when he met the class the next time and, therefore, consulted a colleague. The colleague suggested that he open
the class with a light remark to the effect that "now that we have
cleared the air, let's proceed with the benefits of a fresh atmosphere," and go ahead with his lecture. Treating the incident in
this manner had not occurred to the instructor. Through consulting his colleague he was able to evoke a response that presented
him with a part of the behavioral repertoire of another. It remained for him to evaluate the suitability of this behavior for
himself, and to decide whether to use it in his own way and in
accordance with his own manner of speech, and so on. Through
consulting his colleague he was able to take stock of the latter's
behavioral repertoire. With more perfectionistic expectations of
himself, he might not have consulted the colleague in the first
place, and even if he had, his perfectionism could have blocked a
genuine consideration of the possibility of trying the suggested
procedure or any other procedure that he had not thought of
himself.

In addition to readiness to examine the behavioral repertoires
of others, without being blocked by perfectionism, the individual
must have means of making these repertoires open to consideration. One important means of doing this is group discussion and
group meetings. One function of conventions, whether of rug
cleaners or of chemists, is presumably that of bringing together
the occupational repertoires of many different people in a given
field and opening them to inspection, although it is well known
that conventions serve other purposes as well. In group meetings

of administrative personnel of government organizations, educational institutions, business firms, labor unions, etc., "unsolvable" problems are brought up for discussion, and the individual bringing them up is then able to consider the problem-solving repertoires of his associates in the handling of such problems. In less formal group meetings, the individual is also exposed to the modes of problem solving employed by others. A well-known example is the selection of a way of handling a wife or husband that emerges from a discussion of a particular domestic problem with a group of "one's peers." Thus, a man might say that he "just let his wife rave" upon a particular occasion when she seemed jealous of another woman, and that she seemed to feel better when he didn't argue with her. Another might say that he tried to explain to his wife why she did not have to be jealous after she had "gotten her gripe out." In listening to and engaging in such a conversation, a husband might pick up a mode of interaction suited to his own relationship with his wife by synthesizing the contributions of the others. Thus, he might make use of what he has learned from the one husband in "letting his wife rave" and of what he has learned from the other in explaining to his wife. Participating in group situations, then, provides an opportunity for learning to enlarge one's own behavioral repertoire. As has already been suggested, ready-made solutions cannot necessarily be found in such situations, but an experimental rather than a blind exploration of various possibilities of social interaction can be undertaken through group participation.

ANALYZING EXPECTATIONS OF INTERACTION IN SOCIAL POSITIONS

Interpersonal relationships involve four kinds of expectations: (1) one's expectations of his own interaction, (2) others' expectations of one's interaction, (3) one's expectations of the interaction of others, and (4) others' expectations of their own interaction. It is when discrepancies exist between the first and second or the third and fourth kinds of expectations that problems in interpersonal relationships arise. An analysis of expectations of interaction in social positions, therefore, has adaptive significance because it furnishes a means of identifying sources of difficulty in one's social relationships. The kind of problem that arises when there are discrepancies in such expectations can be illustrated by a disagreement between a man and his wife in respect to who should control the family finances. This disagreement involves a difference between the husband's expectations of his own interaction and his wife's expectations of his interaction as well as of his expectations of her interaction and her own expectations of her interaction. In coping with such a problem, the individual can approach it from the point of view of possible modifications in any of the four kinds of expectations involved.

Modifications in Expectations of One's Own Interaction

Modifications in expectations of one's own interaction occur when the changed expectations are acceptable to the individual or when they do not threaten his self-esteem. Altered expectations of occupational behavior came about in one instance after an individual had gained experience in teaching which he had declared he would never engage in. The experience was rewarding to him and his expectations in relation to his occupational behavior changed to include the possibility of teaching, because this experience produced satisfaction and enhanced his self-esteem. In another instance a woman reported that she was better able to accept the necessity of housekeeping tasks herself after trying to include her young daughter in household activities in a way that would make the little girl feel that these activities were useful and important to the family as a whole, rather than simply being "chores." The little girl, as a result, evinced keen interest in such things as setting the table. The mother also altered her expectations of her own domestic interaction, because in defining certain expectations of such interaction for her daughter in a way that made them acceptable to the daughter, she at the same time made these expectations acceptable to herself.

Conflict concerning an individual's expectations of himself occurs when such expectations are established but cannot be fulfilled. The resolution of such a conflict is frequently dependent upon the modification of some aspect of one's self-conception.

The woman, mentioned above, who felt that household duties were "beneath her," but was faced with the necessity of performing them anyway, found a resolution of the conflict in a new conception of herself as a person who contributed to the welfare of the whole family through her domestic activities. The resolution that she found illustrates that the working out of problems in interpersonal relationships need not necessarily depend upon altering the environment or the attitudes of others, but can also emerge from a modification in one's self-conception.

The resolution of conflicts by means of modifying self-conceptions can be illustrated by reference to conflicts having to do with age positions, sex positions, and hierarchy positions. A frequent conflict occurring in connection with interaction in age positions in the American culture, as has been pointed out previously, is the expectation that one will be able to continue to act young when he no longer has the energy and stamina to do so. This expectation can be inferred from the behavior of "young" men in their late fifties when attempting to dance several fast numbers in a row with women considerably younger and finally retiring to their "corners" because of physical exhaustion. When struggling with such a conflict over remaining young, there is relatively little that the individual can do about changing his physical capacities and resources. He can, on the other hand, change his expectations of himself, and when he is able to accept a new orientation and expectations of a different kind of behavior from what he has been accustomed to, the conflict over growing older no longer exists. Conflict in relation to sex positions occurs when the individual is not able to fulfill the cultural definitions of masculinity and femininity. Here again the individual can modify these cultural definitions as they relate to his conception of himself. A man can learn to take it for granted, for example, that he will not always be as masterful as the cultural definition of masculinity would seem to call for. A woman, similarly, can learn that ideals of physical attractiveness cannot always be met, and do not necessarily have to be met in order to interact in feminine positions effectively. She might learn, for example, that there are still possibilities of being treated "like a woman" without trying to smother the first appearance of a wrinkle with several layers of rouge. In interacting in hierarchy positions, a common conflict is that between the individual's expectations of being able to deal comfortably with figures of authority, which are likely to be learned through a considerable amount of cultural emphasis on equality between superiors and subordinates, and the actual discomfort experienced when he does deal with authority. When the individual can learn to expect that feelings of tension may arise in handling authority, but that they do not have to destroy his self-esteem, the conflict is diminished and he is also less handicapped in gaining greater assurance in dealing with authority.

The learning of new expectations of one's interaction in social positions occurs when the anxiety that motivates the holding of existing expectations is diminished, or when the holding of the new expectations is rewarded, or when both occur. Thus, the anxiety of the man who feels that he should control the family finances is diminished when he no longer interprets his wife's handling of the family budget as a threat to his masculinity or as a threat to living within his income, as the case may be. The diminution of the anxiety depends, of course, upon its source, and one does not necessarily have to consult a psychologist to find its source. The man of our example can take stock of his own expectations and of their basis in his outlook. While he cannot automatically relieve his anxiety by such taking stock, he can present himself with alternative expectations of his acting in the position of mate which may prove as acceptable to him as the expectations that he holds. If the source of anxiety is fear of "wild" spending on the part of his wife, he may be able to discuss this very fear with her, and endeavor to work out a plan with her that permits her participation in handling the family finances, and that also does not have to give him undue concern over living beyond their income. In the working out of this plan in the manner indicated, provision is made for rewarding the holding of new expectations by making it possible for the wife to participate in a mutually satisfactory way in the handling of the family finances as well as by exhibiting a willingness to consider her wishes, which is likely to result in her responding to her husband in a manner that will prove more rewarding to him than would have been the case if he did not exhibit this willingnes.. It is interesting to note in relation to this example that Ort (1950) found in a study of marital happiness that 82.5 percent of happily married couples used discussion in resolving differences whereas only 29 percent of unhappily married couples used it. While he also found that the happily married couples were apparently happy in the first place because role expectations and actual roles played agreed, it is also possible that the maintenance of the happiness in the marriage relationship was based upon their use of discussion in resolving differences when they did arise. As suggested above, such discussion makes possible rewarding new expectations because of the advantages that can be seen as a result of the discussion of holding the new expectations, as well as because the participants in the discussion recognize one another as individuals and respond to one another in mutually satisfactory ways as the expectations are altered.

Modifying Others' Expectations of One's Interaction

Adaptive interaction requires that the individual appraise other's expectations of his interaction, regardless of whether modifications in these expectations are likely or not. In many cases, such modifications cannot realistically be anticipated. It is not realistic to anticipate that the expectations embodied in laws, customs, and moral standards will change in a short time. One must, accordingly, learn to live in "the world as it is," if he is to maintain himself effectively in his environment, although he does not necessarily have to believe that he is living in "the best of all possible worlds." If one has to contend with traffic jams on his way to and from work, an acceptance of the necessity of coping with them will, of course, relieve the annoyance they produce and the decrement in one's efficiency that can result from this annoyance, even though one does not come to believe that a traffic jam is "a thing of beauty and a joy forever." Simple as this illustration is, it demonstrates the distinction between what might be called a demanding as opposed to a realistic orientation toward "the world's" expectations of one's interaction. Implicit in the existence of traffic jams is the expectation that one will put up with them. To throw one's energies completely into protesting their existence and acting as though the only thing to do is "demand" their removal when they have to be dealt with is obviously unrealistic. Unrealistic as such behavior may be, one does not have to look far to find many instances of it.

A good deal of righteous indignation is as "righteous" as it is because of the presence of a demanding rather than a realistic orientation. A certain amount of irritation might be expected when one is reprimanded by a traffic officer. To become highly incensed and righteously indignant over such a reprimand, on the other hand, reflects a failure to perceive the traffic officer's expectations of one's interaction in the position of citizen and a tendency to believe that expectations of this kind do not exist—or that one can demand that his environment be as he wishes without regard for the way it actually is. No very tragic consequences are apparent in connection with the demanding orientation associated with righteous indignation over a traffic officer's reprimand. If this orientation should carry over to a time when the circumstances of one's life took a drastic turn for the worse, its consequences might seriously jeopardize the individual's ability to "carry on." A sudden and sharp reduction in income, the outbreak of war, a death in the family, or any other number of shocking and depressing events are not easily taken in stride, but they are much less crippling when the individual who is affected by them can react to them as events that can and do occur, rather than as conditions that "had no right" to occur and the absence of which he is entitled to demand.

A realistic orientation, in contrast to a demanding orientation toward "the world's" expectations of one's behavior enables the individual to find the most rewarding modes of interaction in situations where rewards are limited. A reprimand from the traffic officer (and a possible ticket as well) is not rewarding, needless to say, but seeing the humor in the situation is. A demanding orientation does not permit a perception of anything funny in such a situation. Furthermore, a realistic grasp of the possibility of the traffic officer's acting as he does, rather than preoccupation with one's indignation and the conviction that the officer should act otherwise, results in greater likelihood of the individual's presenting his case to the officer in a way that might reduce his chances of getting a ticket. Similarly, a certain resignation (as distinguished from defeatism) to a sudden and sharp reduction in income enables one to proceed that much more readily to doing what is necessary to coping with the new circumstances as well as to restoring a better income.

Although adaptive interaction requires that the expectations of one's environment must often be accepted as they are, it is also true that others' expectations of one's behavior can be modified, and that their modification can have adaptive value for the individual. This modification may result from explaining one's modes of interacting in a position. A subordinate might expect directions from a superior, for example, when the superior is willing to have the subordinate act independently on many matters concerning which the subordinate expects directions. If the subordinate is not overly dependent, an explanation from the superior of his willingness to have the subordinate act independently may suffice to change the latter's expectations of his superior's modes of interaction. If the superior reinforces his explanation by refraining from interference with the subordinate, there is, of course, greater likelihood of the subordinate's expectations changing in accordance with the explanation. The actual demonstration of a particular kind of behavior is, therefore, also essential to the modification of others' expectations. The wife whose husband expects her to have nothing to do with the family finances may modify his expectations of her "financial role" in the family (if a plan is worked out whereby she handles the household money) by demonstrating that she does not spend money "wildly"—if that is his concern—or by demonstrating her willingness to let him occupy the position of head of the family—if that is his concern—through consulting him about some of her expenditures.

The modification of others' expectations of one's behavior is sometimes accomplished by an assertive demonstration of one's own expectations of his interaction. The American Colonies modified the expectations of England through assertively demonstrating their independence. In person-to-person interpersonal relationships a similar assertion is found in children's breaking away from their parents in order to "lead their own lives." A son may defy his father to follow the occupation of his own choice or a daughter may defy her parents in order to marry the man of her choice. The parents' expectations of their offspring continuing to follow their lead in a childish manner are modified by the assertion of independence on the part of the children. Such assertiveness also modifies expectations in interpersonal relationships other than parent-child relationships, of course. Dominant individuals, whether parents or not, often refrain from trying to dominate only when they discover that others can be just as insistent in "pressing their points." When possibilities of compromise are exhausted, combativeness may prove adaptive. The American Colonies presumably "came of age" through combativeness.

The combativeness discussed above may be employed inappropriately and to the individual's disadvantage, of course. This point may be particularly applicable when modifications in others' expectations of one's interaction can be achieved through gaining acceptance. An older person may modify expectations of his "sitting on the side lines" by gaining acceptance and thereby being invited to participate actively in community, business, or family affairs. When such an invitations is offered, it indicates that the expectation is no longer that the older person will sit on the side lines. Conversely, when older people expect a younger person to act in a subservient way, the younger person may modify these expectations through presenting his ideas in a way that does not antagonize his elders. Combativeness or assertiveness may be combined with gaining acceptance in changing others' expectations of one's interaction. A younger person may make it clear, for example, that he is not going to be "squelched" while at the same time exhibiting a willingness to profit from the experience of older people, and an older person may assert his convictions that are based on years of thought and experience, when these convictions are disregarded by younger people, while also making it evident that he is capable of trying to understand younger people's points of view. The ability to be assertive when necessary and to gain acceptance, and to combine the two, can be taken as one index of adaptability.

Modifications in One's Expectations of the Interaction of Others

Probably one of the principal ways in which modifications in one's expectations of the interaction of others comes about is through gaining more knowledge of a person. Through experience with people in similar positions one may believe that an individual in a given position will interact in the position in a particular way, but upon meeting this person, be pleasantly or unpleasantly surprised. Knowledge of others provides the data necessary to appraising their interaction and to formulating and modifying one's expectations of their interaction. In spite of opportunity to gain knowledge of others, nevertheless, expectations are not always modified realistically in the light of this knowledge. The man, spoken of previously, who did not stop the attempt to force his wife to give up her religion, until she became seriously emotionally disturbed over the conflict he precipitated, might be taken as a case in point. In spite of opportunity to gain knowledge of her, he did not modify his expectations realistically or in accordance with what was possible for her.

Many examples of unrealistic expectations of the behavior of others can be cited in interpersonal relationships involving interaction in age, sex, and hierarchy positions. One striking example is the expectation that sometimes seems to exist that children will have a higher level of muscular coördination or comprehension than it is reasonable to expect them to have in view of their limited experience and physical maturation. In the position of female in the American culture, women often unrealistically expect men to be more romantic than they are and men unrealistically expect women to forego many of the romantic desires they have acquired in this culture. In hierarchy interaction subordinates frequently forget that superiors have human desires for deriving a sense of importance from their positions—the young reporter may unrealistically expect the editor to welcome his

suggestions as to how the newspaper should be run—and superiors frequently hold unrealistic expectations to the effect that
subordinates will not consider themselves as competent as their
superiors.

From the foregoing examples, it can be seen that an explicit
consideration of how realistic one's expectations of the interaction
of others are can have adaptive value for the individual. This
step in itself does not guarantee that such expectations will be
modified. A parent who holds unrealistic expectations of a child's
coördination, comprehension, or ability to achieve may continue to push the child in unrealistic ways in spite of knowing that
this pushing is not appropriate to the child's level of experience
and physical maturation. The parent's failure to modify his expectations of the child in such an instance may stem from his own
needs which are likely to be in the nature of wanting to make sure
that the child, as his "representative," "measures up." Similarly, a
woman's needs for romantic attention may result in her continuing to expect her lover or husband to behave in a more courtly
fashion than is possible for him, even though she may know that
her expectations of him are not entirely realistic. In spite of the
fact that consideration of how realistic one's expectations of the
behavior of others are does not guarantee any adaptive modification in these expectations, it can, nevertheless, constitute a first
step in bringing about such modifications. The wife who disagrees with her husband about the handling of the family finances
may have difficulty in accepting his desire to retain complete
control over all expenditures, because of her own needs. Nevertheless, an explicit appraisal of his needs, and of the extent to
which they can be altered, puts her in a better position to determine under what conditions he can make concessions in the matter or if he can make any at all. Once having determined these
facts, she may be able more readily to adjust her expectations of
him in accordance with his actual characteristics and potentialities for change. In many marriages, it might be noted in passing,
husbands and wives apparently learn to live together more comfortably after having reappraised their expectations of their
mate's behavior. Such reappraisal seems to lead in many cases

to cessation of attempts to reform and a corresponding increase in mutual acceptance.

A further aspect of the appraising of how realistic one's expectations of the interaction of others are, is that the attempt to do so furnishes the individual with experience in analyzing the factors involved in interpersonal relationships, even though he may not always actually modify his expectations realistically simply as a result of such analysis. Expectations of the behavior of others often seem to function automatically with virtually no thought being given to their existence or the possibility of modifying them. Members of "going concerns," on the other hand, constantly engage in consideration and modification of their expectations of others' interaction. Although politicians may be tempted to take it for granted that contending factions will give up their interests easily, experienced leaders of political parties who hold the parties together do not adopt this expectation. Compromises in the party platform and in the naming of candidates are worked out, instead. Suspect as "politics" may be in the American culture, the techniques of compromise and appraisal of expectation of others' interaction, that are found in political maneuvering, are probably not too far different from such appraisal and compromise as it is found in "going" marriages, families, industrial concerns, educational organizations, etc. Evaluating expectations of others' interaction is more likely to occur when the individual is relatively comfortable in his environment in the first place. One aspect of comfortable and effective interaction is the ability to "look around," which includes a consideration of the structures of social groups and the interaction associated with various positions in such groups. If the individual is not so anxious, or not so preoccupied with his anxiety, that his "view of the world" is limited by his pressing concern with himself, he is in a better position to perceive how realistic his expectations of others are.

Modifications in Others' Expectations of Their Own Interaction

One way in which modifications in others' expectations of their own interaction occur is through the encountering of unanticipated behavior. Thus, one might expect that he will have to be quite formal in a given situation until he finds that the people in this situation actually behave quite informally and that he can relax himself. Similarly, one may expect that he will have to be guarded or aggressive when interacting in a given position until "taken off the defensive" by the behavior of the person or persons he is dealing with. In both of these examples, changes in the individual's expectations of his interaction take place by means of certain kinds of behavior being exhibited toward him. In attempting to bring about modifications in others' expectations of their own behavior, then, it is in order to ask what kind of behavior one can exhibit toward them that will alter these expectations.

The answer to the foregoing question depends upon the relationship and the individuals involved. A general guide to answering it can be found in terms of evaluating the other person's mode of interaction in the relationship. If the other person is dependent and lacking in confidence in his own judgment, the behavior exhibited toward him might take such forms as sometimes asking him what *he* thinks when he looks for guidance from others, if there is the interest in modifying his dependent expectations of his own interaction. If the other person is overly aggressive, the behavior exhibited toward him might take the form of "taking him off the defensive," as suggested by an example in the preceding paragraph, or of reciprocating with aggressive behavior oneself, if the interest exists in modifying the expectations of his behavior that are associated with his aggressiveness. Some experimentation might be necessary to determine whether to try to take the individual off the defensive, or to reciprocate with aggressive behavior, or to do both. The frequent necessity of such experimentation indicates that pat solutions to problems in interpersonal relationships cannot be furnished. The effective teacher, foreman, leader, salesman, or counselor is often unable to communicate the nature of his effectiveness. Perhaps one of the reasons is that his effectiveness stems from a considerable amount of trial and error experience in modifying others' expectations of their interaction and the acquisition of an ability to determine what behavior is called for on his part in a particular situation, rather than a tendency to try to prepare himself with pat or standard solutions in advance of meeting these situations.

Two prominent aspects of modifying others' expectations of their interaction consist of structuring and redefining expectations in a manner acceptable to the individual or individuals involved. By structuring is meant the communication in one way or another of what "goes" or does not "go" in a social relationship.[1] A psychological counselor might endeavor to communicate by what he says and does that a counselee is free to express his feelings and to talk about whatever he wants to. A teacher, depending upon his purposes, might structure a situation in such a way as to limit the topics of conversation and to rule out personal expression of feeling between himself and members of his class. Modifications in others' expectations of their interaction often depend upon skillful and patient structuring. A counselee may not feel free to talk about himself until a counselor has repeatedly shown in various ways that he will not be shocked, that silence does not have to be an occasion for embarrassment, etc. Similarly, a teacher who seeks more participation on the part of members of a class than they have been accustomed to in other classes may have to demonstrate in various ways that the class is as much their "baby" as it is his own. A story is told of one famous educator, who attempted to structure his classes in the manner described, to the effect that he opened each class by inquiring if there were any questions and then dismissing the class if there weren't any. As the story goes, the students finally "got the idea" and took responsibility themselves for actively thinking and talking about the material under consideration.

Redefining expectations in a manner acceptable to the individual or individuals involved is illustrated by such incidents as a father asking his young son who pleaded for an extra piece of dessert after leaving the table, when it was understood that meals were finished when this happened, what he would do if he were a daddy and had a little boy who made such a request. The son replied that he would give the little boy just a small piece. In

---

[1] The concept of structuring as employed here was suggested by the work of Rogers (1942).

making this reply the son showed evidence of shifting his expectation of the nature of his own interaction from assuming that there was no reason why he couldn't have a big piece to accepting the reasonableness of his not being allowed to have a big piece. In presenting the problem as he did, the father exhibited respect for the child and made it possible for the boy to redefine his expectations in a manner acceptable to him. The same principle seems to be involved when people show willingness to keep off the grass when asked to do so, but not when told to do so. The redefining of expectations in a manner acceptable to the individual is not only a matter of verbally stating what is acceptable or desirable about a certain kind of interaction but of responding to him in ways that demonstrate its desirable features. If the wife who disagrees with her husband about the handling of the family finances can in some way demonstrate that it is convenient, economical, or more practical for her to handle the household money, she can probably modify her husband's expectations of his controlling all expenditures more readily than simply by talking to him about the desirability of her taking care of some of the expenditures. In the example of the father asking his son what he would do about the extra piece of dessert, the father, in effect, demonstrated the desirability of the son's being flexible in his demands and expectations of his own interaction by showing willingness to consider the boy's judgment. He did not simply try to redefine verbally the boy's expectations by attempting to persuade him in some fashion that it would not be desirable for him to have another piece of dessert.

The process of enabling an individual to define and redefine his expectations of his own interaction through "giving him a voice" may result in his acquiring a technique for self-initiated redefinition in future experience. This procedure is illustrated by the father-son incident related in the foregoing paragraph. It is also exemplified by listening with a desire to understand what another person's feelings and attitudes are without the intervention of the listener's own convictions in the matter, even though he may possess such convictions. Thus, one might have a definite conviction to the effect that destruction of property is not a particularly desirable form of behavior. He can at the same time endeavor to listen and to understand the expression of rebellious feelings that may underlie such behavior. When this is done, the person expressing such feelings does not have to defend them, and when he does not have to defend them he can proceed voluntarily to consider alternative expectations of his own modes of behavior. In the example used, he might proceed to present himself with alternative expectations concerning rebelliousness or the expression of rebelliousness. To the degree that he no longer feels compelled to be defensive about his expectations of his own interaction, he may also be able to modify these expectations voluntarily in the future when it is adaptive to do so.

Reviewing Expectations of Interaction in Social Positions

Interpersonal relationships, as pointed out earlier in this discussion, involve four kinds of expectations: (1) the individual's expectations of his own interaction, (2) others' expectations of his interaction, (3) his expectations of others' interaction, and (4) others' expectations of their own interaction. These expectations can be reviewed for purposes of developing an over-all view of one's relationships with others and solving problems that arise in interpersonal interaction. In considering an employment offer, for example, one might check his own expectations of his occupational interaction against the expectations of a prospective employer concerning his interaction, as well as his expectations of his prospective employer's interaction against the expectations the employer holds of his own interaction. To make such checks, the individual might formulate various questions. He might ask whether he wants to travel, what salary he expects to earn, what kind of people he wants to spend large amounts of time with, what responsibilities he wants or does not want, etc., and then attempt to ascertain what his prospective employer's expectations are on these matters. Similarly, he might ask what he desires in an employer in respect to direction, recognition, formality or informality in interpersonal relationships, etc., and try to determine what his prospective employer's expectations of himself are in his relationships with employees, or in the particular relationship under consideration. Through reviewing expectations in the manner described, a man can minimize confusion in arriving at a decision concerning prospective employment—if he is in the fortunate position of having any choice in the matter. Most problems in interpersonal relationships probably do not consist so much of decisions having to do with entering into new relationships as they do with handling relationships of which the individual is already a part. Reviewing expectations having to do with existing relationships can also minimize confusion and suggest constructive resolutions of difficulties.

The discrepancies that exist between one's expectations of his own interaction and others' expectations of his interaction, as well as between his expectations of others' behavior and their own expectations of their behavior, cannot always be resolved by compromise. If an employee thinks that he should earn a certain salary and an employer has a more modest conception of what the employee should earn, the employer's expectations on this score will probably prevail. Even when compromise is not possible, one can determine through reviewing expectations what issues he wants to "fight out" and what issues may not be worth fighting about. A man may not hold the expectation, to take a simple example, that husbands should shop with their wives. His wife may, on the other hand, definitely feel that husbands should shop with their wives and have very little disposition to alter this idea. In such an instance, the disagreement might be resolved through the husband's "giving in" rather than through the husband's and wife's each "coming halfway," because the husband has concluded that the difference is not worth fighting about. On other issues he might be more insistent upon a compromise. In either case, reviewing expectations in the marriage relationship could be productive of resolutions of various differences. A series of questions devised by Ort (1950) in a study of happiness in marriage might be used to good advantage by married couples in reviewing their expectations of themselves and each other in the marriage relationship. These questions afford an example of how inventory can be taken of expectations of behavior in social positions since it is through developing such questions that one can review these expectations. Some of them are as follows:

1. Should a husband kiss his wife when he leaves for and returns from work?
2. Should a husband occasionally purchase or make small surprise gifts as tokens of affection for his wife?
3. Should a husband make it a point to talk to his wife about things he may have done that day so that she may feel more a part of his life?
4. Should a husband do little things for his wife that she can do for herself, such as straightening her dressing table, keeping her clothes in order, etc.?
5. Should a husband be willing to interrupt reading the paper for brief expressions of affection at his wife's approach?

The counterparts to the foregoing questions can be asked so far as the wife's part in the marriage relationship is concerned. Differences between the husband's and wife's answers to the questions point up sore spots in the relationship that can be considered and worked out so as to make the relationship a more harmonious one.

A marriage relationship is perhaps unique in that discrepancies in expectations of interaction in social positions can be more readily discussed and thrashed out than in other relationships, although in many marriages thrashing out techniques have not been learned. Even in relationships that do not lend themselves to discussion or to the same degree of discussion of differences in expectations as in marriage relationships, inventories relating to these expectations furnish clues to adaptive interaction in social positions. Thus, a student may learn a good deal about his relationships with others through a series of questions on expectations concerning his relationship with a teacher, a roommate, his girl friend, etc. The expectations involved in a relationship with a teacher might be reviewed by questions such as the following:

1. Should a student call a teacher by his first name?
2. Should a student "hold forth" on his own ideas in class?
3. Should a student wait until a teacher has presented a point fully before asking for clarification?

4. Should a student sleep in class?
5. Should a student take the initiative in raising questions about the subject matter of a course?

A student cannot always be sure about how an instructor might feel about the answers to some of the above questions. An interest in getting such information is a part of adaptive interaction, and differs from blindness concerning other people's attitudes. Blindness of this kind can be illustrated by a student's readily assuming that he can establish a friendly relationship with an instructor by calling him by his first name without considering what the instructor's feelings may be in the matter. A similar blindness can take the form of failure to perceive that it may be acceptable to the instructor to be called by his first name under certain circumstances but not others.

The blindness discussed above may exist in relation to a roommate's expectations on all of the following questions concerning a relationship with a roommate:

1. Should a student who shares a room with another student keep his belongings in order?
2. Should a student discuss his personal problems with his roommate?
3. Should a student seek close companionship with a roommate?
4. Should a student be quiet when his roommate is studying?
5. Should a student wear his roommate's clothes without asking permission?

In many relationships between roommates, it is taken for granted that the roommate will feel as one does himself. It might be taken for granted, for example, that just as one would not mind if his roommate wore his clothes without asking, so the roommate would not mind if one wore the roommate's clothes without asking. In reality, the roommate's feeling in the matter may be quite different.

A consideration of one's own expectations in relation to the expectations of others does not necessarily imply that one must always shift his expectations to correspond to the expectations of others, and give up his own convictions, in order to get along satisfactorily in his social environment. Since convictions can be firm without being rigid, knowledge of discrepancies between one's own expectations and others' expectations can contribute to adaptive interaction in social positions. A student might hold the conviction that students should take the initiative in raising questions about the subject matter of a course rather than simply waiting for "the word" from the instructor. If an instructor is not predisposed to show much interest in questions that students raise, however, it may not be particularly fruitful to try to bring him around to another point of view toward students' raising questions. Since some instructors are more educable on this score than others, on the other hand, it might be quite productive for a student to devote energy to bringing the instructor around in many other instances. If he is rigid about his conviction, he is less likely to appraise the difference between his own expectation and his instructors' expectation in the first place, and then to proceed from there to determine the most effective way of acting in accordance with his conviction. Similarly, if he holds the conviction that his girl friend should sometimes suggest where they will go and what they should do on a date, whereas she always expects him to "take the lead," he can probably do more to bring her around by clearly recognizing that they differ, rather than rigidly pursuing his conviction without clear recognition of her feeling in the matter, regardless of whether her feeling is "right."

The rigid evaluation of others' behavior and expectations as right or wrong frequently blocks an adaptive resolution of problems in interpersonal relationships. The student spoken of above can hold a firm conviction as to what is right and still be able to understand his girl friend's attitude. It is probably only rarely, as a matter of fact, that people refrain from making moral judgments of others or judgments of what is right and wrong. The problem in understanding other people's attitudes and behavior is perhaps not so much a matter of refraining from moral judgments, as many writers on psychological topics have suggested, as it is a difference between what we have been speaking of as firmness and rigidity in the holding of moral convictions. Psychologists themselves probably do not refrain from making moral judgments in their professional positions, but they may refrain, or try to refrain, from becoming morally indignant. Thus, a psychologist is likely, in reality, to consider the behavior and attitudes of a mental patient as in some way wrong or undesirable, but he at the same time can endeavor to understand the patient and accept him as another human being, even though he cannot accept his behavior and attitudes. In view of these considerations, it does not seem likely that moral standards or moral judgments can be dispensed with in human relationships. All kinds of practical problems are, of course, handled in terms of moral codes. "Thou shalt not murder" is a moral standard that gives direction to human affairs, even though it is not consistently followed, and even though people differ in their opinions of how absolute a standard it should be. The abandonment of this standard, or a similar standard, is difficult to imagine in any society. It is, nevertheless, possible to understand impulses to murder and the desires and capacity to murder that any human being might have, even though one does not approve of murder. Such understanding, furthermore, may contribute to murder's becoming a rare occurrence. This understanding is more likely to arise from a firm, as opposed to a rigid, moral conviction concerning murder, although the two kinds of convictions can be in agreement on the undesirability of murder.

UNIQUENESS IN INTERACTION IN SOCIAL POSITIONS

The popular expression "Everybody must lead his own life" expresses the significance of uniqueness in behavior. The conditions of everyone's life differ and modes of interacting in social positions, therefore, must be unique in certain respects. The interaction that is adaptive for any one individual is determined by his particular resources, and the feeling he has about his own resources functions to produce or eliminate defensiveness in his interpersonal relationships.

The Individual's Resources and Uniqueness in Behavior

When an individual selects the modes of behavior that are uniquely suited to his past experience and particular resources, he accepts certain possibilities in his interaction and rejects others. If engaged in an argument with a very witty individual, for example, with whose wit he cannot realistically expect to compete, he rejects the possibility of attempting this kind of competition but may accept the possibility of laughing off the "cracks" as he "holds up" his side of the argument. The adaptive acceptance and rejection of possible modes of interaction is a twofold process of recognizing limitations and at the same time exploring one's potentialities, so to speak, for purposes of functioning as effectively as one can. The bald proposal that one recognize his limitations is often interpreted as a recommendation to resign oneself to the hopeless state of his potentialities. If limitations are recognized for the purpose of determining how to make the best use of one's resources, however, the individual can then focus upon his positive potentialities without being pessimistically preoccupied with his limitations. If realistically, rather than hopelessly, resigned to one's limitations in competing with a witty antagonist, preoccupation with feelings of inferiority is not as likely to be so intense that one is completely at a loss in coping with the antagonist.

The twofold process of recognizing limitations and at the same time exploring one's potentialities, for purposes of acting as effectively as one can, functions to enlarge the individual's resources. The inexperienced housewife who accepts her limitations and throws a meal together as best she can is making use of the resources she possesses for preparing meals, and is also learning from her experience. The actual doing of the best one can is the means by which resources are enlarged. To engage in this kind of "doing," the individual must accept certain problems as challenges. The housewife would not add to her skills in preparing meals if she did not approach the necessity of doing so as a kind of challenge. Similarly, the inexperienced foreman would not add to his skills in getting along with his men unless he faced various problems in his relationships with them as challenges. The individual's definition of the challenge itself can be formulated in accordance with his particular resources. The experienced storyteller can define the relating of a long story, calling for adept timing, as a challenge, whereas the inexperienced storyteller more appropriately defines the relating of a simpler story as a challenge. The defining of the challenge in terms of one's own resources furnishes the individual with a method of furthering his own development without having to engage in a constant comparison of oneself with others. Rather than competing with others, he competes with himself, or compares his resources of a given time with the resources that he later acquires as a result of making use of the potentialities he has, and by so doing develops a higher degree of adaptability in his social interaction.

Defensiveness in Interpersonal Relationships and Uniqueness in Behavior

The twofold process of acceptance of one's limitations and exploring the resources that one does possess for functioning effectively in his environment tends, as has been said, to diminish the tendency to compare oneself with others. When the individual is relieved of this kind of competitive orientation toward others, the chances of his evoking defensiveness in others' behavior toward him are reduced. If a man is interested in clarifying his own thinking in the discussion of a problem, for example, rather than demonstrating his brilliance in comparison to others, he is less likely to arouse antagonistic feelings in the people he is talking to. He at the same time is less likely to be burdened with tensions associated with his own demands upon himself. While effort is involved in clarifying his thinking, it does not involve the discomfort that straining to be brilliant involves.

The defensivenes that is aroused in others when the individual is inclined to compare himself with others, rather than to think and act in terms of what is possible within the framework of his own particular resources, is illustrated by the behavior of the man who is said to believe that "he has all the answers." His behavior does not endear him to his friends and associates. It is to be recognized, of course, that adaptive interaction does not always permit the individual to endear himself to others. When defensiveness is aroused in others because the individual is defensive about his own resources, however, he creates problems in his interpersonal relationships. His defensiveness may take various forms. One form it can take is the one already mentioned, i.e.,

PERSONAL ADJUSTMENT IN THE AMERICAN CULTURE

striving to "have the answer" or to maintain "the upper hand," rather than acknowledging limitations in any way. In the extreme, such defensiveness is shown by inability to admit that one is wrong. It may also manifest itself by a kind of over-control in the nature of wanting always to appear poised, self-confident, possessed, or "strong." The "poise" or "strength" that is based on such overcontrol is not particularly well calculated to take others "off guard," but often arouses, instead, the feeling that the "poise" or "strength" has too unruffled a quality, as well as a vague suspicion that the "poised" person is in some way trying to "lord it over" others. Another form of defensiveness, resulting from the individual's comparing himself with others rather than exploiting his own resources as best he can, is aloofness and withdrawal. When one is concerned about "measuring up," he can put a distance between himself and others that prevents him from being faced with situations in which he might not measure up. The girl who fears that she might not compare favorably with other girls in getting men's attention can avoid men. The person who is afraid that he might not be a good conversationalist in comparison to others can avoid talking to people. The student who fears that he might not graduate *summa cum laude* can avoid studying. The social isolation that grows out of such avoidance tactics produces strains in interpersonal relationships, because people tend to assume when they are left alone that they are not liked. When the individual is comfortable with himself, he does not create such strains, and when this comfort is a twofold process of recognizing limitations and actually making use of the resources he does possess, there then exists a real distinction between such comfort and complacency.

SUMMARY OF PRINCIPLES

1. How profitable experience in various forms of social interaction is depends, among other things, upon the individual's expectations of himself as he gains the experience. Further principles concerning the gaining of experience in social interaction are:

a. Adaptability can be facilitated by awareness and planning of practice in forms of social interaction.

b. The individual can provide opportunities for himself in gaining practice in future forms of social interaction.

c. Rehearsal in interacting in social positions can be obtained through overt activities of various kinds as well as through imaginative activities.

d. Blind imitation of others' modes of interaction is frequently motivated by a high degree of anxiety which impels the individual to look for quick and easily adopted forms of behavior that will relieve the intolerable anxiety, or what is experienced as intolerable anxiety.

e. Experimental imitation of others' interaction presupposes anxiety-or frustration-tolerance.

2. Profitable experience in interaction in social positions is sometimes thwarted by perfectionistic expectations that an individual sets for himself.

a. The individual who can allow for a "margin of error" in his experiences and activities learns to function in his social environment effectively, because he can reward himself for what he does correctly and continue to profit from experience without undue discouragement when he does make mistakes.

b. Perfectionistic expectations of one's own interaction not only impose demands upon oneself that are likely to result in discouragement, but also present barriers to profiting from others' experience.

3. Problems in interpersonal relationships arise when there are discrepancies between one's expectations of his own interaction and others' expectations of his interaction or between one's expectations of the behavior of others and others' expecations of their own behavior. Principles concerning the modification of such expectations are:

a. Modifications in expectations of one's own interaction occur when the changed expectations are acceptable to the individual or when they do not threaten his self-esteem.

b. Others' expectations of one's interaction can be modified through explanation, gaining acceptance, and combativeness.

c. One of the principal ways in which modifications in one's expectation of the interaction of others comes about is through gaining more knowledge of a person.

d. Two prominent aspects of modifying others' expectations of their own behavior consist of (1) structuring and (2) redefining expectations in a manner acceptable to the individual or individuals involved.

4. The mode of interaction that is adaptive for any one individual is determined by his particular resources.

CHAPTER 12

Toward a Theory of
Personal Adjustment

Introductory Summary

It is through the development of psychological theory that man's knowledge of himself may become more comparable to his advanced knowledge of fields more remote from himself. Theory is made up of one or more generalizations that are formulated to explain particular events, and the generalization or set of inter-related generalizations which makes up theory furnishes guides to procedures having practical significance. Since a great deal of attention has been given in previous chapters to a discussion of adaptive interaction, consideration of theory in this chapter is amplified by treating adaptability as a theoretical problem. Theory is the product of creative thinking which goes beyond observed facts, and is facilitated by asking questions and freedom from too much caution in sticking to facts. A process somewhat similar to the developing of higher-order theory is the developing of interpretations by means of which people come to understand one another.

MAN'S KNOWLEDGE OF HIMSELF

It is often said that man's knowledge of himself is primitive in comparison to his knowledge of other matters. Since the development of the atomic bomb many people have observed that man knows enough to blow up the earth, or to come close to blowing it up, but does not know enough about human relationships to keep from blowing it up. A related observation is that man has "kept away from himself" in the development of knowledge. Astronomy, physics, and chemistry are remote from the study of the psychological nature of man (although the time may come when their relationship to psychology will appear less remote, just as they now are seen to be more closely interrelated than they appeared to be at one time), and have reached a high stage of development. Fields such as psychology and sociology, however, cannot claim as high a level of achievement in the prediction and control of social interaction. Progress has, nevertheless, been made in the formulation of generalizations, principles, or relationships, such as those enumerated at the end of each of the preceding chapters, in which a greater or lesser degree of confidence can be placed.

Progress has also been made in the testing of hypotheses concerning psychological phenomena. It was at one time taken for granted, and still is in many quarters, that certain subjects, such as Latin, Greek, foreign languages, and mathematics, are uniquely suited to "training the mind" or improving reasoning ability. Actual testing of this hypothesis through experimental investigation has not supported it. A more tenable hypothesis seems to be that general improvement in reasoning ability tends to occur when principles, procedures, or methods of thinking having application to a large variety of situations are learned, whether they are learned in the context of studying history, Greek, heating and ventilation, or something else. This latter hypothesis explains the facts and "covers more" than the hypothesis concerning the unique values of particular subjects for "training the mind." *Strides in knowledge are made when generalizations are developed that cover the facts, and the most significant contributions to knowledge are those that cover them most comprehensively.* To understand how such strides are made, it is necessary to consider the nature of theory. It is through the development of psychological theory that man's knowledge of himself may become more comparable to his advanced knowledge of fields more remote from himself.

THE NATURE OF THEORY

Explanation and Theory

A simple illustration of the understanding of an event is furnished by the following example: If a particular man is observed to be belligerent, we may be puzzled by his behavior until someone tells us he is a Smith and the Smiths are known to be belligerent. A similar example is found in French's observing (1944) that "if we see a man strike himself violently in the face, his behavior is likely to seem peculiar to us, but if we discover that he was killing a mosquito, we are no longer perplexed." In both of these examples our understanding of the behavior in question is a process of "seeing" that if such and such is true, then such and such must follow. If the Smiths are belligerent, it then follows that a particular man who is a Smith must be belligerent.[1] If people defend themselves against injury or potential injury, then it follows that a man who is injured or about to be injured by a mosquito on his face will strike himself in the face. In the foregoing examples, the particular behavior in question was explained by relating it to a generalization. In the first instance, a particular man's belligerence was related to the generalization that Smiths are belligerent. In the second instance, the particular behavior, striking oneself in the face, was related to the generalization, people defend themselves against injury. An explanation consists of relating particulars to one or more generalizations, and understanding an event is the process of relating particular events to generalizations.

The development of generalizations by means of which particulars are explained takes its departure from the question: What kind of assumptions or postulates would have to be made in order to account for particular events? Since a theory is made up of one or more assumptions that are formulated in order to ex-

[1] This statement is regarded as an explanation because it takes the form of an if-then proposition, although psychologists prefer higher-level explanations containing reference to antecedent conditions, which in this case would be conditions associated with the Smiths' belligerence.

plain particular events, the question could also be stated in this way: What kind of theory would be necessary to explain particular events? The development of theory can be illustrated by means of the following example: Let us say that a man notices that when he works for an hour at a time and then rests for 5 minutes, works for another hour and again rests 5 minutes and so on, he accomplishes more in the time he spends in work than when he spends an equal amount of time working without 5-minute rest intervals. If he is curious about the efficiency resulting from the 5-minute intervals, and not content with the mere observation that one method of work seems superior to another, he might ask, "What would I have to assume or postulate in order to account for the superiority of the one method over the other?" In order to answer this question he might formulate the general proposition: The introduction of rest intervals during a given amount of time spent in work makes for greater efficiency per unit of time spent working than working the same length of time without rest intervals. The assumption would account for his particular observation concerning 5-minute rest intervals, and would result from his raising the question as to what assumption he would have to make in order to explain the superiority of employing such intervals over not employing them. It also suggests a new relationship, i.e., that the length of rest intervals might be related to the degree of efficiency found with the introduction of rest intervals. Thus, we see that as theories are developed, new relationships are suggested that had not been thought of previously.

If the prediction growing out of the generalization concerning the introduction of rest intervals held up under repeated testing, the question might then be raised as to what assumptions or postulates would have to be made in order to account for the greater efficiency per unit of time resulting from the introduction of rest periods. In answer to this question, it might be assumed that work sets up a state of fatigue which diminishes when the work ceases.[2] From this generalization, it would follow that

[2] This assumption is a restatement of Hull's postulate (1943) concerning reactive inhibition.

the introduction of rest periods would make for greater efficiency per unit of time spent in work than working without rest periods, because the rest periods would provide opportunity for the fatigue to diminish. The generalization implies not only that the introduction of rest periods during a given amount of time spent in work makes for greater efficiency, but that performance following a period of rest will be superior to performance immediately following a period of work. (An example of the superiority of performance following a period of rest is that a solution to a problem is often found after a persons has slept on it whereas he was stumped on it at the end of the previous day's work.) The prediction of (1) the introduction of rest periods making for greater efficiency during a given amount of time spent working and (2) the superiority of performance following a period of rest over performance immediately following a period of work can both be derived from the generalization that work sets up a state of fatigue that diminishes when the work ceases. This latter generalization is an example of a higher-order theory, because it encompasses the lower-order generalization concerning efficiency resulting from the introduction of rest intervals and at the same time goes beyond the lower-order generalization in that it leads to predictions not suggested by the lower-order generalization; the superiority of performance following a period of rest over performance immediately following a period of work is not suggested by the lower-order generalization. The predictions growing out of theory must hold up under testing, of course, if the theory is to be considered verified. Experiments to determine the quality of performance following periods of rest and work might, for example, be performed in order to test the second prediction stated above.

In trying to answer the question as to what kind of assumptions or postulates would have to be made in order to explain particular events, one or more such postulates may be employed. In the examples used thus far, one generalization has been employed in each instance. Postulates may, nevertheless, be employed in combination. When this is done, the postulates are drawn from a set or group of postulates used in explaining a certain class of events.

Miller (1944), for example, suggests the following postulates to explain the class of events having to do with conflicts between tendencies to approach and tendencies to avoid:

1. The tendency to approach a goal is stronger the nearer the subject is to it. This will be called the *approach gradient.*
2. The tendency to go away from a place or object avoided is stronger the nearer the subject is to it. This will be called the *avoidance gradient.*
3. The strength of avoidance increases more rapidly with nearness than does that of approach. In other words, it may be said that the avoidance gradient is *steeper* than the approach gradient.
4. The strength of the tendencies to approach or avoid varies with the strength of the drive upon which they are based. Thus, an increased drive may be said to raise the *height* of the entire gradient.

Among the events that can be predicted through employing the above assumptions is that when a person is both attracted to and fearful of a goal, increasing his motivation to approach will increase his fear and avoidance reactions. Urging a man who is afraid to ask for a raise, but who wants a raise, according to this prediction, will result in an increase in fear and tendencies to avoid. Postulates 1 and 2 tell us that there will be the tendencies to approach and avoid, the strength of which will increase with nearness, in such a situation. Postulate 4 indicates that increasing motivation to approach will increase the strength of the tendency to approach. As the tendency to approach increases, or as the individual actually comes nearer to the goal, the inclinations to avoid would also be expected to become stronger according to Postulate 2. If the drive to avoid is even moderate, the individual might not be expected to reach the goal at all, since the more rapid increase in strength of avoidance with nearness than in strength of approach with nearness (Postulate 3) could still outweigh the increased motivation to approach. Thus, the man who is very fearful of asking for a raise might only experience an increase in fear when urged on to ask for the raise, but might not actually ask for it. In the light of Miller's assumptions, it would be more effective to enable him to get rid of his fears of asking for a raise than to give him "pep talks" urging him on.

The Practical Significance of Theory

The generalization or set of generalizations which makes up theory furnishes guides to procedures having practical significance. The generalization, work sets up a state of fatigue which diminishes when the work ceases, furnishes a guide to efficient work procedures. It implies, as stated earlier in the chapter, that performance following a period of rest will be superior to performance following a period of work. In the light of this implication, it follows that the procedure of sleeping on a problem when stumped may be productive, because of the greater efficiency with which work on the problem can be undertaken after a period of rest. To have practical significance, a theory must, of course, be verified. That is, the prediction or predictions stemming from the theory must hold up under testing. If we assert that it rains, or that there is a probability of rain, when there are clouds, to take a simple example, our generalization is verified when we find that the degree of rain varies with cloudiness. It is sometimes said that a generalization, when verified, is no longer "just a theory," but then becomes a law. "Laws," "hypotheses," and "just theories" all take the same form, however. They are all the opening clauses of if-then propositions, or are contained in the opening clauses of if-then propositions. If it rains when there are clouds, then it follows that rain can be expected on a cloudy day. If work sets up a state of fatigue that diminishes when the work ceases, then it follows that performance following a period of rest will be superior to performance following a period of work. "Theory," as used in this chapter, refers to the opening clause of an if-then proposition, and "laws," "hypotheses," and "just theories" are all included under the term "theory."[3] Lee (1950) expresses the point being made very nicely in the following comments:

The terms "law," "theory," "hypothesis" can all be used in a narrower or a broader sense. In the narrower usage the distinction be-

[3] There are higher and lower levels of theory, however, and a law as well as an hypothesis is often thought of as subordinate to or derived from a higher-order theory.

tween them depends on a difference in the degree to which they are based on evidence and have been confirmed by evidence. Thus we can call a generalization based on little evidence and with little confirmation a guess or speculation; with more we call it a hypothesis; with still more, a theory; and with most evidence and confirmation, we call it a law. There is nothing very precise about this contrast of terms. The usage is mostly traditional. We still talk about the law of gravitation, but about the theory of relativity. . . .

The important point is that generalizations are always intended to be explanatory of particulars. We say that if such and such a generalization holds, then this and that particular will follow. To take a concrete example: "If all policemen have big feet, then it is not surprising that Willie, the pride of the finest, wears number 12 shoes."

It would be better to cite more important generalizations. In 1919 the Royal Astronomical Society sent expeditions to Brazil and to West Africa where a total eclipse of the sun was predicted to take place. The expeditions were to observe especially the positions of stars close to the sun, because if the general theory of relativity holds, then the apparent position of stars close to the sun should be displaced outward approximately 1.7 seconds of an arc. No one had ever noticed this phenomenon, but now when it was looked for, the phenomenon did make its appearance. The stars were observed to be displaced approximately the amount predicted, subject to inaccuracy of observation and measurement. In 1922, with instruments of greater precision, the displacement was further verified. These were crucial observations in establishing the general theory of relativity.

Note that I have been careful to retain the hypothetical form of the statement of the principle. "If the systematic body of generalizations making up the theory of relativity holds, then certain events will take place." Thus on the ground of accepting the general theory, the events, when they do take place, are explained. When the events have never been observed before their prediction, the explanatory power of the hypothesis is spectacularly revealed upon their observation. Cases in point are the first observation of the planet Neptune and the case I have already described, the displacement of stars close to the sun. Nevertheless, the principle is the same when the hypothesis explains something previously observed, such as the advance of the perihelion of Mercury or the occurrence of an ordinary eclipse of the sun or moon.

Although the practical implication of verified theories are greater than of unverified theories, it is the attempt to formulate theory, even though it remains to be verified, that produces the solutions to practical problems. When the question is raised as to why people behave in certain ways, we begin to develop theories or generalizations as to how this behavior can be brought about, prevented, or changed. We might ask, for example, what generalizations could explain the deep depressions of certain emotionally disturbed patients. One explanation that has been proposed is that depression is related to guilt. In more detail, this theory holds that depression, or the particular kind of depression under consideration, is an accompaniment of the individual's guilt over his underlying conviction that he has committed an unpardonable act. A soldier might run from a battle scene, for example, and later react with strong depression and a feeling that he is responsible for the death of friends or comrades who were killed in this battle, or that he has no right to be living when they are dead. According to the explanation, his guilt over running, an unpardonable act in terms of his standards of loyalty and honor, precipitates slowing up of activity and depression. One suggestion that this formulation carries is that the guilt, and the depression accompanying it, can be relieved by punishment in much the same way that a person who feels he has done something wrong feels better, or seems to feel that he has been restored to "good standing," when he pays a penalty for his wrongdoing or "takes his medicine." The fact of the matter is that many depressed patients seem to respond well, temporarily at least, to what is known as electro-shock therapy, a form of treatment in which the patient is shocked by means of electricity. In the light of the explanation under consideration, the shock treatment can be interpreted as a form of punishment that relieves the guilt. A possible shortcoming of this treatment is that it relieves the guilt only for the time being, and that it might be more effectively relieved by enabling the individual to talk out his conflicts without fear of censure so that new perspectives can be gained. Through such talking out, for example, the soldier might come to feel that while human beings, and he in particular, have standards of loyalty and honor, they also have capacities for running when frightened, and that the running does not mean that one has deliberately been disloyal.

The practical significance of theory is particularly apparent if responsibility to the public is accepted as a standard or value by people engaged in rendering service to the public. The engineer must know the theory, i.e., the principles or generalizations, implicit in the construction of buildings that will not collapse, if it is assumed that he has a responsibility to the public. Clinical psychologists and psychiatrists, similarly, must know, or endeavor to find out, why shock therapy has given effects, if it is assumed that they also have this responsibility. Simply knowing that certain procedures "work," and that others do not, cannot be considered an adequate fulfilling of responsibility. Shock therapy might "work" with some patients, but not others, just as the construction of a building in a given way might work out under certain conditions but not others. Research produces evidence concerning what "works" and what does not "work," but it is theory that stimulates research. The arbitrary distinction that is sometimes drawn between theory and practice or "pure science" and "applied science," is, therefore, open to serious question. If social responsibility is taken seriously, the practical worker has as much obligation to engage in the development of testable theory, and to encourage research growing out of theory, as anyone else, even though he may not spend much or any of his time in the actual testing of theory through research.

THEORY OF ADAPTIVE INTERACTION

Since a considerable amount of attention has been given in previous chapters to a discussion of adaptive interaction, it is now appropriate to consider adaptability as a theoretical problem. Adaptability, it will be recalled, has been defined as the ability to preserve well-being while maintaining oneself effectively in his environment. To develop a theory of adaptability, it is necessary to ask what kinds of generalizations, postulates, or assumptions might be made to account for adaptive and nonadaptive interaction. A *partial answer* might be provided by the following postulates.[4] (Other theorists might, of course, employ different assumptions.)

1. As the individual interacts in his environment he strives to preserve a sense of well-being.

An obvious example of striving to preserve well-being is found in seeking food and avoiding hunger. A less obvious example is found in the behavior of the individual who apparently seeks punishment as in the case of a person's confessing a misdemeanor that would otherwise go undetected. Even this behavior can be understood as a matter of preserving well-being when it is comprehended as a matter of relieving a guilty conscience.

2. Emotional states become associated with stimuli that occur in situations that already arouse such states.

This principle is illustrated by a study by Watson and Watson (1921) in which a child was presented with a white rat and a loud sound which aroused the emotional state of fear. After this experience the child exhibited fear of the white rat alone; previously he had shown no such fear. Many impulses and behavior characteristics become associated with fear in a similar fashion. Thus, if disloyalty has been represented to a person as contemptible, it occurs in a context that arouses distaste, and this distaste is then apt to be evoked by any suggestion of disloyalty in the person's own behavior. Sexual desires and aggressive impulses also occur in situations in which a person is impressed with their undesirability or dangerousness and themselves become capable of arousing anxiety.

In view of our first postulate, which states that the individual strives to preserve a sense of well-being, it follows that the individual will tend to avoid perceiving or thinking about impulses or behavior characteristics that have become associated with fear or anxiety (and this association is assumed to occur in accordance with the principle stated in the second postulate), since perceiving or thinking about them takes away from the sense of well-being. Thus, if one's sexual or aggressive impulses have come to

---

[4] Postulates 2 and 3 were suggested by Mowrer's proposal (1947) of two kinds of learning.

arouse anxiety, it is to be expected in the light of the present reasoning that there will be a tendency to avoid perceiving or thinking about these impulses.

3. Behavior, as distinguished from emotional states, that leads to or is acompanied by reward is learned.

This principle can be illustrated by an experiment by Loucks (1935). He attempted to train a dog to flex its leg in response to a buzzer by stimulation of a part of the brain that elicited leg flexion when the buzzer was sounded. This procedure did not work, but when food was given to the dog each time it flexed its leg, it then learned to flex its leg in response to the buzzer alone. These results would be expected in the light of the reward principle, because the first procedure did not reward the behavior to be learned, whereas the second procedure did.

The learning of expectancies can be subsumed under the principle that behavior that leads to, or is accompanied by, reward is learned. An expectancy is a perceptual anticipation that when one thing occurs, another will also occur. Thus, when we memorize a poem we learn to perceive that one word or series of words leads to another word or series of words. The dependence of such learning upon reward can be illustrated by a study by Thorndike[5] (1931) in which a list of ten sentences was read to a group of subjects ten times. Among the sentences were the following three:

Edward Davis and his brother argued rarely.

Francis Bragg and his cousin played hard.

Lincoln Blake and his uncle listened gladly.

After these sentences had been read ten times the subjects were asked to answer questions such as the following:

What word came next after *rarely?*

What word came next after *Lincoln?*

Although *Francis* follows *rarely* just as often as *Blake* follows *Lincoln,* the average percent correct from the end of one sentence to the beginning of the next was about 3.0 while from the first to the second word in the same sentence it was 21.5. This result would follow from the reward principle in that it can be

[5] The interpretation of this study given here differs from Thorndike's interpretation.

assumed that the subjects would listen to a list of unrelated sentences with questions in mind of what was in each sentence or what led to what within each sentence, rather than from the point of view of one sentence's leading to another. As they listened, then, the question of what led to what within each sentence was answered. The answer to this question constituted a reward. Since there was not any such reward for attending to the end of one sentence in relation to the beginning of the next sentence, it would not be expected in the light of the reward principle that the subjects would learn and retain the expectancy of what followed the end of a sentence.

If a response is to be rewarded, the response must be made. If perceptions are not made, then, perceptual responses cannot be rewarded. It was pointed out above that the individual will tend to avoid perceiving or thinking about impulses or behavior characteristics that have become associated with anxiety. Many instances of nonadaptive behavior, therefore, might be accounted for, in part, as a matter of inability to develop expectancies of what one's impulses or behavior leads to, because the behavior or impulses are not perceived in the first place and because the individual cannot secure the reward involved in answering the question as to what leads to his difficulties. Thus, a husband or wife who is actually hostile toward his or her mate, but cannot admit such hostility to himself or herself, because of anxiety over such a tendency, cannot perceive the ways in which hostility is expressed toward the mate, and the question cannot be answered as to what is making for the difficulties in the marriage relationship. Stated otherwise, expectancies of the nonadaptive consequences of the ways in which hostility is expressed cannot be learned. Similarly, the person who is anxious over a behavior characteristic such as timidity, which he interprets as cowardice, cannot easily acknowledge or perceive this characteristic in himself and cannot develop expectancies of the nonadaptive consequences of this characteristic such as the increased difficulty in meeting various situations resulting from habitual timidity. These expectancies cannot be developed because the timidity cannot be perceived and because the question cannot be answered as to what is responsible for the individual's problems in meeting situations. (In such an instance the perception of the timidity and the anticipation of its consequences do not necessarily solve the problem because the timidity may not be appreciably altered in the absence of active relearning experiences. Such relearning is considerably facilitated, however, by the perception of the timidity and the anticipation of its nonadaptive consequences.)

Instances of nonadaptive behavior that do not involve perceptual avoidance of impulses or behavior characteristics because of anxiety can also be analyzed as failures in perceptual expectancies. The pseudo-integrative individual, having little or no anxiety, has learned to interpret his behavior as faultless and is not predisposed to perceive it as leading to unsatisfactory consequences. When such consequences ensue, he does not relate them to his own behavior but attributes them to the lack of understanding or "stupidity" of his social environment. Learning to relate them to his behavior involves making clear the relationship between his behavior and the consequences in such a way that more satisfactory modes of interaction are suggested or implied at the same time. The discovery of the latter provides a reward for relating the unacceptable behavior to its consequences. Thus, the student mentioned in an earlier chapter who has learned to ignore the socially unacceptable consequences of his behavior, and repeatedly engages in such things as cheering for an opposing team might profit, according to the present reasoning, from having someone point out to him that his *own* behavior produces unfavorable reactions toward him on the part of his classmates— regardless of whether the classmates are "stupid" for having such reactions or not. Pointing out this relationship between his behavior and its consequences implies, of course, modes of interaction resulting in more satisfactory interpersonal relationships, and this discovery of the possibility of more satisfactory relationships constitutes a reward for relating the unacceptable behavior to its consequences, or for learning an expectancy of the unsatisfactory consequences of his socially unacceptable behavior.

CREATIVE THINKING AND THEORY

Creative Thinking as a Process of Going Beyond Observed Facts

Creative thinking is an imaginative activity which departs from observed facts, and by means of which new relationships are discovered. Inventions are the products of creative thinking. Fulton related steam and transportation in a way that had not been observed before. Theory is also the product of creative thinking. The generalization or combination of generalizations that make up theory are statements of relationships that go beyond observed facts. Even the simple generalization "All men are mortal" is not strictly factual. An impressive number of cases have been observed in which men have been mortal. To say that *all* men are mortal, however, goes beyond the facts. The advantage of going beyond the facts, of course, is that predictions can be made that would not otherwise be possible. Thus, when we say that all men are mortal, we can predict the death of living men. Our generalization is useful as long as it is supported by observed instances, but no generalization ever attains complete certainty. The reason it never attains complete certainty is that all future instances cannot be observed. We do not actually know whether all living men of present or subsequent generations will die when we say that all men are mortal. When a generalization is supported by observed instances, nevertheless, confidence is placed in it for purposes of prediction, but prediction would not be possible unless the observed facts were "gone beyond."

Going beyond observed facts in order to develop generalizations that make possible prediction can also be illustrated in this way: If we were seeking a higher-order theory to explain the lower-order generalization to the effect that all men are mortal, we would be asking, "How could it be predicted that men or other organisms would die if their mortality had never been observed?" The answer to this question would involve employing or developing principles of biochemistry or related fields from which it would be possible to derive, or logically deduce, the mortality of organisms. (Such principles, incidentally, would lead to control, or some degree of control, of mortality by indicating how certain conditions could be manipulated to shorten or extend life. Events are more fully understood when knowledge of them permits control as well as prediction.) The relating of principles of biochemistry to mortality is not simply a process of observation, but is also a process of thinking or imagination. Such principles would not be developed in the first place if the answer to some question were not being sought, whether the question had to do with mortality of organisms or something else. It is the imaginative process involved in going beyond the facts in order to answer a question, or to explain the facts, that leads to the development of theory.

Conditions Influencing Creative Thinking

The imaginative process involved in going beyond facts in order to explain the facts presupposes a question. The first step in creative thinking, then, is the raising of questions. Theory, as stated above, is the product of creative thinking. One of the conditions affecting the development of theory, therefore, is the extent to which people are encouraged or discouraged in the raising of questions. The very fact that men are always faced with immediate practical problems tends to limit their curiosity. If a man is sick, he is immensely curious to know what will get him well, to be sure, but if he gets well, he is not as likely to have questions about why he got well. He is more interested in the fact that he did get well. In spite of examples of this kind, it does not necessarily follow that practical problems and interest in theory are by any means incompatible. The fact of the matter is that practical problems are productive of questions that can stimulate theory construction. We might ask why a man gets well, for example, when a particular treatment seems to work. Furthermore, a theory which adequately answers the question will also suggest solutions to other practical problems.

The distinction that is often drawn in the American culture between technical and "liberal" education is possibly one condition that limits the raising of questions. In some technical schools there tends to be a contempt for questions that are not immediately related, or that do not appear to be immediately related, to practical problems, and in some nontechnical schools there tends to be a contempt for concern with practical problems. The engineering student and the liberal arts student, accordingly, often engage in the pastime of ridiculing each other. Although some degree of specialization of training is probably necessary in a complex industrial society, it may not be essential for this specialization to limit curiosity. As suggested earlier in the chapter, the engineer or doctor can be curious about why the techniques he is trained to use "work" or do not "work." The curiosity of the individual who is less immediately concerned with practical problems that arise in his culture can also be stimulated by these problems.

Another condition, associated with educational practices, that may have a bearing upon creative thinking is what might be called overindoctrination in working hard. Although hard work, experience, and study seem to go into creative achievement, it is also true that great discoveries often come to the people who make them during periods of relaxation. Weisskopf (1951), accordingly, says that "educators may find it profitable to advocate a passive, inattentive attitude to their students not as a permanent condition but as a stimulating technique during specific phases of their intellectual work. As Bateson (1941b) states, '. . . the advances in scientific thought come from a *combination of loose and strict thinking,* and this combination is the most precious tool of science.' "

Needless to say, the inattentive attitude that Weisskopf speaks of above is productive only when the individual is trying to answer a question, even though he does not actively grapple with the question during the period of being inattentive. The answer to the question may not only be thwarted by "working at it too hard" all of the time, rather than letting it recede from awareness during periods of relaxation, but also by overcautiousness. As stated earlier, creative thinking goes beyond the facts, rather than cautiously confining itself to the facts. The caution may take many forms. One form it takes is posing as "scientific" by continuing simply to accumulate facts rather than ever stopping to consider what the facts mean or what generalizations could embody them. Another form of caution that blocks creative thinking is learning what everybody else has said on a given subject without venturing to have any ideas about it oneself. This kind of caution receives a considerable amount of sanction in scholarly and educational circles. One can gain a reputation as a "deep thinker" if he has read enough. While a great deal can be learned from reading, being "well read" in itself does not furnish any guarantee that a person will have any ideas of his own. He can instead become a kind of memorizer and "parrot" what he has read with little real comprehension. In such instances, it is as though the person said, "I have it right here," as he turns to a book whenever a question arises. Books, unfortunately, do not always have "the answers." Different books may also have different "answers." Such differences may be taken as occasions for thinking for oneself, but refuge may still be taken in consulting more books.

Perhaps one of the reasons that refuge is taken in reading as a means of avoiding thinking independently and creatively is that such thinking requires that one "stick his neck out," because when he thinks for himself he cannot be sure that he will agree with anybody else nor that he will be right. Creative thinking, therefore, requires anxiety-tolerance, because new ideas are always open to attack. This attack can serve a constructive purpose, but whether it does or not, creative thinking "invites trouble." Lee (1950) summarizes the matter nicely in the following comments which suggest that encouraging people to "stick their necks out" and training them to endure the anxiety associated with doing so are among the conditions that foster creative thinking:

When a new hypothesis is proposed it should be attacked and defended with vigor. Only in this way can it be thoroughly tested. Today we are apt to judge that Priestley's attack on the new combustion theory of Lavoisier was not well taken. Perhaps Priestley held to the phlogiston theory too long and against too much evidence; but perhaps his attacks on the combustion theory helped to establish it by forcing its defenders to subject it to thorough testing.

On the other hand it is good that new hypotheses should not be accepted until all conceivable attempts to overthrow them have been made. It is also good that the supporters of a new hypothesis should hold on to it and push it, so that it will not get lost in the shuffle, or even worse than that, get squelched by authority.

There should be no such thing as scientific authority, although unfortunately there is. In the 1880's C. A. McMunn made a contribution to the understanding of the way in which the transfer of oxygen from hemoglobin to the tissues takes place. After a little controversy, he was put down by the bio-chemist Hoppe-Seyler, who twenty years earlier had made the very important discovery of the role of hemoglobin in carrying oxygen from the lungs to the tissues. Hoppe-Seyler printed a note alongside McMunn's last paper saying that he considered further discussion superfluous. McMunn apparently subsided; at any rate discussion was dropped, and it was not discovered that he was correct and Hoppe-Seyler incorrect until forty years later, in the 1920's. It might have saved forty years if McMunn had been a little more tenacious of his hypothesis.

UNDERSTANDING PEOPLE BY MEANS OF THEORETICAL THINKING

The purpose of developing theory is to explain or "cover" observed facts. The thinking process involved is comparable to the problem-solving that a good detective engages in when he tries to determine who committed a crime. Given certain facts about the crime, he then tries to "tie these facts together" by means of an interpretation that will point to the responsible party. This same thinking process which is directed toward encompassing observed facts or "tying them together" is employed in understanding people. Thus, we might note that a woman is uncomfortable in her relationships with men, but is at the same time apparently envious of women who are comfortable with men and who attract men's favorable attention. When we understand that she competed for attention with a younger sister who was favored by the father when she was growing up, her behavior becomes more comprehensible. Her discomfort with men and her envy of women who attract men's favorable attention are "encompassed by" or can be seen as outcomes of the earlier constellation of family relationships. Similarly, if a man is irritable with his children, absent from work more than usual, and exhausted after an hour or two when he does work, his behavior becomes comprehensible when we learn that he has been suffering from the incipient stage of an attack of influenza.

The process of understanding an individual by working out an interpretation which encompasses various aspects of his behavior can be comprehended more fully by discussing an actual illustration in detail:

A premedical student, who had wanted to be a physician for almost as long as he could remember, was on scholastic probation and sought help from a professional tutor. His decision to go to a professional tutor, even though he could ill afford to do so, emerged after he had set up and tried to follow a schedule of study which required long hours of application. When he still found himself failing many of his courses, his only recourse was to seek regular and expert help from someone else. It was extremely difficult for him to secure this help not only because he had to work his way through school and had little money to pay for such help, but because of an emotional reluctance about getting help that went beyond his concern about money.

The behavior of our premedical student as reported thus far does not seem very puzzling. He has wanted to be a physician for a long time, and it is, accordingly, not surprising that he should seek help with his studying when he needs it so badly. He may not be able to afford the help, but his plight is desperate. The fact that he is reluctant to get the help for other than financial reasons might be expected; it is undoubtedly a disappointment to him to have to seek outside help when he must have counted pretty much on his own efforts to see him through school.

When additional information is supplied, the behavior of this student is not as clear to us. He admits that he finds himself less and less interested in his premedical subjects, and that he doesn't look forward to long hours of laboratory work in medical school. All of this might not be so bad if he planned on practicing medicine, since his schooling would be behind him then; if he could get through medical school, however difficult it might be for him, the actual practice of medicine would probably prove more congenial than the schooling necessary to such practice. This student is not interested in the practice of medicine, though. He wants to embark upon a career of medical research. There now appears to be very little rhyme or reason to his behavior. If he is having as much difficulty as he is in getting through his premedical work, has little interest in his premedical courses, and does not look forward to medical school, it would certainly seem the better part of wisdom to take up some other course of study. The argument for following another course of study is all the stronger when it is known that he is interested in a career in medical research and not in practicing medicine. If he is determined to go ahead anyway, however, it seems strange indeed that he should be as reluctant to secure outside help as he is.

In the light of information about our student's life history we can understand much better the apparent contradictions in what he is doing. His father was never in good health and his mother had to work in order to support the family. The father was never reconciled to his illness and gave frequent expression to his feeling of being "no good" because he could not support the family entirely by his own efforts. The doctors who took care of his father all said that not enough was known about the disorder from which he suffered to prescribe any treatment beyond making sure that he did not lead a strenuous life. Relatives loaned the family money and assisted in many other ways. Although their help was not given begrudgingly, it was not easy for the father to accept it. The help, itself, therefore, became a kind of symbol of the family's inferior status, even though it was not offered in a spirit of condescension. In addition to all of this, the father and mother were both determined that their children would not be unduly deprived because of their misfortune. Efforts were made accordingly to provide their children with the "advantages" that other children from more financially secure families had. The children could sense the discrepancy between their own plight and that of children from these other families, however, and reacted all the more to their "disadvantages." If they had to wear clothes after they became slightly frayed, for example, the evidence of the clothes being old was taken more seriously than would have been the case if they had not been as concerned in the first place with how their clothes compared with other children's.

Given the background information that we now have, we can see more clearly why the premedical student would be so intent upon a career in medical research in the face of all of the considerations weighing against it. It symbolized for him the possibility of discovering, perhaps, not only the true nature of his father's illness but also of protecting himself against a similar illness. Medical research could put him "in the know," as it were, about sickness and empower him to combat it. Having seen the part that sickness had played in his own family, his motivations to combat it and protect himself from it are thoroughly understandable. His thoroughgoing reluctance to seek help from a tutor can be comprehended at the same time as a determination, whether conscious or not, to avoid the necessity of help that his father had found so repugnant and which, in turn, had become repugnant to him.

The determination of the student discussed in the above account to study medicine, to engage in research, to seek help only reluctantly, and to go ahead with his questionable plans all seem to hang together when we interpret his behavior in the light of his life history and his experience with sickness in his own family. Although this interpretation cannot be offered with finality, it can be evaluated as having a greater or lesser degree of probability by determining (1) how well it fits the facts under consideration and (2) whether other facts might be predicted from it. The interpretation, as already noted, does appear to fit the facts that were presented. If it holds we might suspect—in view of the inference we make from his background about fear of being in need of help—that the student would not want to get married until he had a good income. We might anticipate on the basis of the same inference that he does not like to borrow money. These predictions might then be checked by finding out how he feels about marriage and borrowing money. If they were borne out, more confidence could be placed in the interpretation. If they were not borne out, the interpretation would have to be modified, of course.

It would probably be generally agreed, among psychologists at any rate, that an interpretive process of the kind we have been discussing must be engaged in if one is to have a genuine interest in understanding others. Such understanding often contributes to reducing strains in interpersonal relationships. When an employer understands that an employee has been suffering from the incipient stage of an attack of influenza, for example, he is more likely to try to find constructive remedies to various aspects

of the employee's recent inefficiency. Similarly, the student's desire to pursue a career of medical research might evoke less
disgust in a friend, because of its impractical features, when it
is comprehended in the light of the student's background.

A final observation to be made about interpreting people's
behavior is that preconceived frameworks to be employed in such
interpretations may be helpful if they refer to conditions that
actually have some relevance to the way people behave, but they
may also be misleading. Interpretations of behavior based upon
the constellation of heavenly bodies at birth are not helpful because there is little relationship, so far as we know, between such
constellations and behavior. Interpretations based upon what
Freud called the Oedipus complex, which refers to certain
relationships between the child and his parents, on the other
hand, are more likely to prove helpful since there is good reason
to believe that early relationships do have relevance to the way a
person behaves. Freud's conception of the Oepidus complex
might be imposed, however, so as to force facts to fit it or to
exclude consideration of other interpretations.

The boy has an Oedipus complex, according to Freud, compounded of love for the mother and jealousy for the father who
is his rival for the mother's love. In the light of this idea our
medical student might be seen as a person with what has been
called an unresolved Oedipus complex who is still competing
with his father for the mother's love. Pursuing a career in medical
research might, for example, be interpreted as a matter of trying
to be "in the know" about medicine in order to be more invulner-
able to sickness than his father was and better able to win his
mother's love. Such an interpretation might or might not have
some validity. An automatic imposing of it by immediately thinking about Freud's general outline of the Oedipus complex, and
then fitting the facts to this outline, does not involve any real
interpretive thinking, however. Such a procedure is more in the
nature of following a formula without considering how well the
formula applies.

To determine how well any formula for interpreting an individual's behavior applies, it is necessary to determine as best

one can the extent to which conditions producing given kinds of behavior were or are present in the experience of the particular individual under consideration. (We would want to consider carefully, for example, the extent to which conditions were present in the student's experience producing rivalry with the father over the mother's love if we were to employ the "Oedipus complex formula.") To answer this question adequately it is necessary to determine what evidence there is that certain conditions produce given kinds of behavior among people in general. (For example: What produces rivalry between father and son—and what forms can it take—among people in general?) When these questions are combined with the two suggested earlier in our discussion, i.e., how well does our interpretation of the individual's behavior fit the facts and how well does it enable us to predict facts that have not been considered, a rounded and scientific evaluation of the interpretation of individual behavior can be achieved.

SUMMARY OF PRINCIPLES

This book concludes with a chapter about personal adjustment and theory, because it is through the development of theory or explanation that knowledge of human relationships will grow, and also because it is believed that such a chapter is likely to be more meaningful after reading a series of chapters devoted to a discussion of man's interaction in his social or interpersonal environment. As psychological theory grows, books of this kind will become relics of a past era. Theory will in all probability continue to develop, and ideas concerning the nature of explanation or theory itself may change and be replaced by ideas that "do a better job" of making man's world and himself comprehensible. Some of the principles of theory construction and creative thinking, by means of which theory is developed, that now appear tenable are listed below. The first five are concerned with the development and function of theory, the next four with creative thinking, and the last two with interpretation of individual behavior.

1. Development of theory

a. *An event is explained by relating it to a generalization.*

b. As theories are developed, new relationships are suggested that had not been thought of previously.

c. A higher-order theory encompasses lower-order generalizations.

d. In trying to answer the question as to what kinds of assumptions or postulates would have to be made in order to explain particular events, one or more such postulates may be employed.

e. Attempts to formulate theory produce solutions to practical problems.

2. Creative thinking

a. *Creative thinking goes beyond observed facts.*

b. Creative thinking presupposes the raising of a question.

c. Creative thinking requires periods of relaxation.

d. Creative thinking tends to be blocked by overcautiousness and continuing to accumulate facts without stopping to consider what the facts mean or what generalizations could embody them.

3. Interpretation of individual behavior

a. An interpretation of an individual's behavior can be evaluated as having a greater or lesser degree of probability by determining (1) how well it fits the facts under consideration and (2) whether other facts can be predicted from it.

b. To determine how well any formula for interpreting an individual's behavior applies, it is necessary to ascertain as best one can the extent to which conditions producing given kinds of behavior were or are present in the experience of the individual under consideration.

Bibliography[1]

ALEXANDER, F. 1946. The principle of flexibility. In *Psychoanalytic therapy* by F. Alexander, T. M. French, *et al.*, The Ronald Press Company.

ASHER, E. J. 1935. The inadequacy of current intelligence tests for testing Kentucky mountain children. *J. Genetic Psychology*, 46:480-486.

BATESON, G. 1941a. The frustration-aggression hypothesis and culture. *Psychological Review*, 48:350-355. Reprinted by permission of the American Psychological Association.

BATESON, G. 1941b. Experiments in thinking about observed ethnological material. *Phil. Science*, 8:53-68.

BENEDICT, R. 1934. *Patterns of culture.* Houghton Mifflin Company.

BETTELHEIM, B. 1947. The dynamism of anti-semitism in Gentile and Jew. *J. Abnormal and Social Psychology*, 42:153-168. Reprinted by permission of the American Psychological Association.

BURGESS, E. W., and COTTRELL, L .S. 1939. *Predicting success or failure in marriage.* Prentice-Hall, Inc.

CAMERON, N. 1947. *The psychology of behavior disorders.* Houghton Mifflin Company.

COLE, L. 1936, 1948. *Psychology of adolescence.* Rinehart & Company, Inc.

DAVIS, A. 1944. Socialization and adolescent personality. *Forty-Third Yearbook of the National Society for the Study of Education*, Part I, Chap. 11, pp. 204, 209-10. Quoted by permission of the Society.

DAVIS, A., GARDNER, B. B., and GARDNER, M. R. 1941. *Deep south: A social anthropological study of caste and class.* University of Chicago Press.

DAVIS, W. A., and HAVIGHURST, R. J. 1947. *Father of the man.* Houghton Mifflin Company.

DAVIS, W. A., and HAVIGHURST, R. J. 1948. The measurement of mental systems (Can intelligence be measured?). *The Scientific Monthly*, 66:301-316.

[1] Dates of books are copyright dates.

DOLLARD, J. 1937. *Caste and class in a southern town.* Yale University Press.

DOLLARD, J. 1942. *Victory over fear.* Reynal and Hitchcock, Inc.

DOLLARD, J., DOOB, L. W., MILLER, N. E., MOWRER, O. H., and SEARS, R. R. 1939. *Frustration and aggression.* Yale University Press.

DUVALL, E. M., and HILL, R. 1945. *When you marry.* D. C. Heath and Company.

ERICSON, M. C. 1947. Social status and child-rearing practices. (From "Quantified interview data at two class levels, rather closely paralleling for whites the Davis-Dollard data for negroes," a paper read at the American Psychological Association's 1946 meeting.) In T. M. Newcomb and E. L. Hartley, eds., *Readings in Social Psychology,* Henry Holt and Company.

FISHER, V. E. 1937. *An introduction to abnormal psychology.* Reprinted by permission of The Macmillan Company.

FISHER, V. E., and HANNA, J. V. 1931. *The dissatisfied worker.* The Macmillan Company.

FREEMAN, E. 1936. *Social psychology.* Henry Holt and Company.

FRENCH, T. M. 1944. Clinical approach to the dynamics of behavior. In J. McV. Hunt, ed., *Personality and the behavior disorders,* Vol. I. The Ronald Press Company.

FREUD, S. 1938. *A general introduction to psychoanalysis.* Garden City Publishing Company.

FROMM, E. 1941. *Escape from freedom.* Rinehart & Company, Inc.

GILLIN, J. 1946. Personality formation from the comparative cultural point of view. In *Sociological foundations of the psychiatric disorders of childhood.* Child Research Clinic, The Woods Schools, Langhorne, Pa. Reprinted in C. Kluckhohn and H. A. Murray, eds., *Personality in Nature, Society, and Culture,* Alfred A. Knopf, Inc., 1948.

GORDON, W. 1923. *Mental and scholastic tests among retarded children.* London, Board of Education, Pamphlet No. 44.

GORER, G. 1948. *The American people.* W. W. Norton & Company, Inc.

GREEN, A. W. 1943. Duplicity yesterday, today, and tomorrow. *Psychiatry,* 6:411-424.

GREEN, A. W. 1948. Culture, normality, and personality conflict. *American Anthropologist,* 50:225-237.

GREENE, J. E. 1948. Motivations of a murderer. *J. Abnormal and Social Psychology,* 43:526-531.

Hollingshead, A. B. 1949. *Elmtown's youth.* John Wiley & Sons, Inc.
Horney, K. 1937. *The neurotic personality of our time.* W. W. Norton & Co., Inc.
Horney, K. 1945. *Our inner conflicts.* W. W. Norton & Co., Inc.
Hull, C. L. 1943. *Principles of behavior.* Appleton-Century-Crofts, Inc.
Hunt, J. McV. 1941. The effects of infant feeding-frustration upon adult hoarding in the albino rat. *J. Abnormal and Social Psychology,* 36:338-360.
Hurlock, E. B. 1925. An evaluation of certain incentives used in school work. *J. Educational Psychology,* 16:145-159.
Klineberg, O. 1935. *Negro intelligence and selective migration.* Columbia University Press.
Klineberg, O. 1940. *Social Psychology.* Henry Holt and Company.
Lee, H. N. 1950. Theoretic knowledge and hypothesis. *Psychological Review,* 57:31-37. Reprinted by permission of the American Psychological Association.
Levy, D. M. 1937. Primary affect hunger. *American J. Psychiatry,* 94:643-652.
Levy, D. M. 1943. *Maternal over-protection.* Columbia University Press.
Loucks, R. B. 1935. The experimental delimitation of neural structures essential for learning: The attempt to condition striped muscle responses with faradization of the sigmoid gyri. *J. Psychology,* 1:5-44.
McDougall, W. 1926. *Outline of abnormal psychology.* Charles Scribner's Sons.
McGeoch, J. A. 1932. Forgetting and the law of disuse. *Psychological Review,* 39:352-370.
McGregor, D. 1944. Conditions of effective leadership in the industrial organization. *J. Consulting Psychology,* 8:55-63. Reprinted by permission of the American Psychological Association.
Maier, N. R. F. 1933. An aspect of human reasoning. *British J. Psychology* (Gen. Sec.), 24:144-155.
Maslow, A. H. 1943. A theory of human motivation. *Psychological Review,* 50:370-396.
Maslow, A. H. 1949. The expressive component of behavior. *Psychological Review,* 56:261-272.
Maslow, A. H., and Mittelmann, B. 1951. *Principles of abnormal psychology.* Harper & Brothers.

MEAD, M. 1928. *Coming of age in Samoa.* William Morrow.

MEAD, M. 1941. Administrative contributions to democratic character formation at the adolescent level. *J. National Association of Deans of Women.*

MILLER, A. 1949. *Death of a salesman.* The Viking Press, Inc.

MILLER, N. E. 1944. Experimental studies of conflict. In J. McV. Hunt, ed., *Personality and the behavior disorders,* Vol. I. The Ronald Press Company.

MILLER, N. E., and DOLLARD, J. 1941. *Social learning and imitation.* Yale University Press.

MOWRER, O. H. 1947. On the dual nature of learning—a reinterpretation of "conditioning" and "problem-solving." *Harvard Educational Review,* 17:102-148.

Myrdal, G. 1944. *An American dilemma.* Harper & Brothers.

NEWMAN, H. H. 1940. *Multiple human births.* Doubleday and Co., Inc.

ORT, R. S. 1950. A study of role-conflicts as related to happiness in marriage. *J. Abnormal and Social Psychology,* 45:691-699.

PORTEUS, S. D. 1937. *Primitive intelligence and environment.* The Macmillan Company.

REICHENBACH, HANS. 1951. *The rise of scientific philosophy.* University of California Press.

ROGERS, C. R. 1942. *Counseling and psychotherapy.* Houghton Mifflin Company.

ROKEACH, M. 1948. Generalized mental rigidity as a factor in ethnocentrism. *J. Abnormal and Social Psychology,* 43:259-278. Reprinted by permission of the American Psychological Association.

SHAFFER, L. F. 1936. *The psychology of adjustment.* Houghton Mifflin Company.

SHAW, F. J. 1944. Two determinants of selective forgetting. *J. Abnormal and Social Psychology,* 39:434-445.

SHAW, F. J. 1946. A stimulus-response analysis of repression and insight in psychotherapy. *Psychological Review,* 53:36-43.

SHAW, F. J. 1948. Some postulates concerning psychotherapy. *J. Consulting Psychology,* 12:426-432.

SHAW, F. J. 1949. The role of reward in psychotherapy. *The American Psychologist.* Reprinted by permission of the American Psychological Association.

SHAW, F. J. 1949. A program of research on behavior changes, *Psychological Service Center Journal,* 1:99-108.

SHAW, F. J. 1950. Clinical psychology and behavior theory. *J. Abnormal and Social Psychology*, 45:388-391.

SHAW, F. J., and SPOONER, A. 1945. Selective forgetting when the subject is not "ego-involved." *J. Experimental Psychology*, 35:242-247.

SHERMAN, M., and HENRY, T. R. 1933. *The hollow folk*. Thomas Y. Crowell Co.

SPEARMAN, C. 1927. *The abilities of man*. The Macmillan Company.

STAGNER, R. 1950. Psychological aspects of industrial conflict. II. Motivation. *Personnel Psychology*, 3:1-15.

SYMONDS, P. M. 1946. *The dynamics of human adjustment*. Appleton-Century-Crofts, Inc.

TERMAN, L. M. 1916. *The measurement of intelligence*. Houghton Mifflin Company.

TERMAN, L. M., and MILES, C. C. 1936. *Sex and personality: Studies in masculinity and femininity*. McGraw-Hill Book Company, Inc.

TERMAN, L. M., and associates. 1938. *Psychological factors in marital happiness*. McGraw-Hill Book Company, Inc.

THORNDIKE, E. L. 1931. *Human learning*. Century.

WALLER, W. 1937. The rating and dating complex. *American Sociological Review*, 2:727-734.

WARNER, W. L., HAVIGHURST, R. J., and LOEB, M. B. 1944. *Who shall be educated? The challenge of unequal opportunity*. Harper & Brothers.

WARNER, W. L., and LUNT, P. S. 1941. *The social life of a modern community*. Yale University Press.

WARNER, W. L., MEEKER, M., and EELLS, K. 1949. *Social class in America*. Science Research Associates.

WATSON, G. B. 1925. *The measurement of fair mindedness*. Bureau of Publications, Teachers College.

WATSON, J. B. and WATSON, R. R. 1921. Studies in infant psychology. *Scientific Monthly*, 13:493-515.

WEISSKOPF, E. A. 1951. Some comments concerning the role of education in the "creation of creation." *J. Educational Psychology*, 42:184-189.

WEST, J. 1945. *Plainville, U.S.A.* Columbia University Press.

WICKMAN, E. K. 1928. *Children's behavior and teachers' attitudes*. Commonwealth Fund.

WOODROW, W. 1927. The effect of type of training upon transference. *J. Educational Psychology*, 18:159-172.

Index

Watson, G. B., 162
Watson, J. B., 355
Watson, R. R., 335
Weisskopf, E. A., 361
Well-being, 38, 64
  enhancement of, 143
  feelings associated with, 122
  preservation of, 142
  striving towards sense of, 40
West, J., 297
Wickman, E. K., 173
Wish-fulfillment, 198, 207
Withdrawal, 55, 76, 85, 123, 151,
  183, 205

Withdrawal—(*Continued*)
  adaptive, 77
  non-adaptive, 78
Woodrow, W., 119

Young man (autistic wish-fulfillment), case summary of, 207
Young man (submission), case summary of, 218
Young woman (ascendance), case
  summary of, 221
Young woman (motivational apathy), case summary of, 209
Youth, glorification of, 240

Zuni culture, 172